FREEDOM'S VECTOR

THE PATH TO PROSPERITY,
OPPORTUNITY AND DIGNITY

Richard C. Anderson

Bloomington, IN Milton Keynes, UK

authorHOUSE

AuthorHouse™
1663 Liberty Drive, Suite 200
Bloomington, IN 47403
www.authorhouse.com
Phone: 1-800-839-8640

AuthorHouse™ UK Ltd.
500 Avebury Boulevard
Central Milton Keynes, MK9 2BE
www.authorhouse.co.uk
Phone: 08001974150

First published by AuthorHouse 2/23/2006

ISBN: 1-4259-0329-0 (sc)

Library of Congress Control Number: 2005910757

Printed in the United States of America
Bloomington, Indiana

This book is printed on acid-free paper.

Cover Image ***The Spirit of '76*** painted by Archibald Willard

To Lorrie

For Kristin, Bruce and Susan

To be or not to be?

I think, therefore I am,
said Rene Descartes in a metaphysical act of self-creation.
The unexamined life is not worth living,
thought Socrates.

Should you think not, surely you will be not.
Thus are we free to choose.

PREFACE

My interest in the American Revolution was sparked late in life by reading a biography of George Washington. George led me to the ideas expressed in the Declaration of Independence and the U.S. Constitution. As I began to look for the source of these ideas, I discovered John Locke and our English heritage. Just about the time 9/11 took us all rudely by surprise, I had surmised that a quest for freedom was the driving force that led to the origin and eventual development of our modern democratic society.

I wanted to know what I really thought about our American democracy and freedom. The only way to find out was to write down my thoughts and read them back to myself to see if the words and ideas rang true. This work is the result.

My thanks to Dr. James and Sherri Culver, Jan Mottinger, Rev. Arthur Pickett, Gus Miller, Boake Sells, and Strobe Talbott for their reviews, to Lorrie for her patience, help, and encouragement, and to Franz Sauerland for careful editing and critical comments. Especially, I would want to thank Mary Dolan who set me on the path of self-discovery before her untimely departure.

Any errors of fact or judgment you may find, reflect only my personal shortsightedness. I hope this work presents itself as politically neutral, if that is possible.

If you love America, I think you will like this book. If you read this book, I think it may surprise or even annoy you. If it does, I will have achieved my purpose in putting these pages between two covers.

Dick Anderson
South Russell, Ohio
October 2005

TABLE OF CONTENTS

INTRODUCTION

America is a wonderful story. Its birth certificate, the Declaration of Independence, was penned by Thomas Jefferson who portrayed it as a country of free and equal people, even as its father, George Washington, attended to its bloody delivery on the battlefield, against all odds. James Madison wrote its strategic operating plan, the United States Constitution, and appended individual rights, the Bill of Rights, for each of these free and equal people. By the standards of 18th century civilized man it could have been christened American Utopia: ideally perfect; socially, politically, and morally.

Well…almost. The blacks who were counted as only three fifths of a person did not think this infant was legitimate. The native Americans thought this birth certificate was a forgery. And still do.

It took 80 years and 624,511 of us dead in the Civil War to make the black man whole, and free, and equal. Before he paid the price with his own blood, Abraham Lincoln, number 624,512, the namesake of the ancient father of Western Civilization, made this young America legitimate. His Gettysburg Address was a two minute testimonial to unity, freedom, and integrity.

In the space of 125 short years, America, with the help of its economic coach Adam Smith, had become robust beyond challenge and ready to come to the rescue of its cultural ancestors in Europe when their freedom was put in peril. Today America is the youngest successful social idea in the world and at the same time the oldest to have survived without a major political facelift. But has the old girl lost something of her youthful virtue and charm?

Is the time approaching for America to go in for a another checkup? The first checkup was in 1913-16 after which we were privileged to vote for our Senators and pay an income tax. The last checkup was in 1965 to fix a 100-year old civil rights problem, but it was clear by 1968 that some important issues had been overlooked.

Looking back at the conception of Jefferson's founding document, it is apparent that the intent he honored with his unalienable rights was that of a people who would be free and equal in opportunity in the name of human dignity. We are fortunate to have had a succession of nine wise, if imperfect, elders; Supreme Court Justices, who could refer our political miscues back to Madison's operating plan for correction, as needed. Any subsequent checkup we might undertake should assess the degree to which we Americans are free, have equal opportunity, honor human dignity, and have followed our strategic operating plan. Let's try to make that assessment in the spirit of love and respect for the better virtues of an America that has served us so well. Let's see how we might restore her original charm.

We will do this following Immanuel Kant's three great questions of life, applying them to America, its democracy, and its freedom. What do we know about it? What should we do with it? What might it aspire to (Cath. Encyc., newadvent.org)? The answers to these questions will define us as we follow this quest along the path of freedom to wherever freedom's vector might lead us.

As an applied research scientist working in GE's lighting business, I was ever mindful of Thomas Edison's admonition, "There's a better way. Find it." Applying that spirit to America's great social institutions leads to some intriguing possibilities. Surely there are better ways to collect taxes, requiring less effort and confusion, than negotiating a maze of arcane regulations riddled with loopholes and special interest provisions. There has to be a better system for conferring the essential benefits of education on the least of us, in their interest and for the good of our nation. There absolutely must be a solution to the uncertain financial state we have allowed to fester in our old-age lifeline, the Social Security system. Certainly, we can provide medical care for all citizens at a much more reasonable cost. The greatest threat to our individual freedom comes from the age-old syndicate of money and power. The corporation, the engine of our prosperity, will eventually make puppets of our government and enslave us all if we do not shut off the cash flow, masquerading as "free speech," from the corporate boardroom to Washington.

In addition to these five big domestic "opportunities," there are issues with an international flavor we can afford to ignore only at our own peril. Failure to develop a major, alternative source of energy will progressively aggravate international relations and degrade our environment. The march of Globalization will increase world prosperity, but only at the cost of labor exploitation and maybe even national sovereignty. The poor, socially primitive regions of Africa will need help if they are to avoid perennial starvation and warfare. The peoples of the Middle East need help separating Adam Smith from Allah in their quest to secure the blessings of the prosperity born of free enterprise and freedom. We stand at the threshold of developing cures for mankind's previously incurable maladies using gene therapy. With this new technique, we are preparing to improve on God's own handiwork: the redesign of our offspring to our own uncertain specifications. This open-ended enterprise will require a complete rethinking of our social relations, a recasting of our moral code, and a redefinition of what it means to be human.

Our guidelines for attacking America's insufficiencies are a handful of assumptions, to wit:

Individual freedom, equal opportunity, and human dignity are basic "goods" that we should strive to maximize.

Personal responsibility within the framework of a democratic politic is the only safeguard against tyranny.

Prosperity thrives under private management and withers under government control.

It is critically important to challenge government institutions for efficacy, that is, both for efficiency of effort and quality of result.

Foreign policy should reflect our national interests, project our social values, and embrace the use of force only as a last resort.

Our morality is the barometer of our social greatness and should reflect our best virtues.

The pursuit of knowledge is the universal quest of mankind, but does not by itself offer the hope of finding eternal truth.

Americans may have the system of government they desire. It isguaranteed in the United States Constitution which is of, by, and for us all. But we will get only the one we deserve.

Since politics is the art of the possible, politicians are limited in their ability to get to the root of America's problems. Congress has about 535 separate and divisive issues, or dogs in every show. Only the president can highlight one major area at a time for fundamental improvement, and that at the cost of expending his political capital on it. Otherwise the specter of clear and impending disaster might be the only effective catalyst for change.

The programs developed in this work are comprehensive and financially sound. But if Washington cannot or will not consider them for practical reasons, why spin our wheels in this literary endeavor? There are two reasons. One is to facilitate a point by point comparison between what is and what could be. The other is to plant in people's mind the concrete ideas of people-oriented programs that could exist if money and power did not stand in the way of freedom and democracy for all Americans. As Martin Luther King preached, you will not get your rights if you do not speak up and claim them. Don't settle for second class results.

This is a "big plan" approach to reclaiming our major social institutions, for in the words of President Dwight D. Eisenhower, "We dare not make small plans, because they have no power to move men's hearts."

PART I

DEMOCRACY

What do we know about it?

CHAPTER 1

WHAT HAPPENED?

1776. Four documents of critical importance to you, 295 million Americans, and me, made their appearance that year (Skousen). They were:

The Call: Thomas Payne published the pamphlet "Common Sense," an appeal to the 13 American colonies to strike out for independence and freedom. This ringing indictment of British rule catalyzed a bloody response leading to a new idea, a new nation, and new opportunities for all men.

The Statement: Thomas Jefferson penned The Declaration of Independence. Many people believe it to be the most important document ever published. It asserted that 2 million American colonials and their successors were independent, no longer subject to the rule of King George III and England, and free to pursue life, liberty, and happiness. The document constituted sedition.

The Discovery: Adam Smith concluded that the *Wealth of Nations* was determined by the invisible hand of the marketplace. This hand was actuated only by the freedom individuals had to negotiate their own economic agreements. He became the father of economics and the author of our prosperity.

The Warning: Edward Gibbon published the first volume of The Decline and Fall of the Roman Empire. His message was that this thousand-year-old state collapsed when its citizens lost confidence in their imperial government, a state of affairs arising from the loss of personal freedom and moral purpose. We have been forewarned.

The Wake Up Call

It was much too early to show up for the meeting. He pulled into the small parking lot of an urban apartment building about two blocks from the College Club. There he sat for some 30 minutes in his red, 1983 RX7, listening to the last tape in a series on the History of Freedom. The first tape by Rufus Fears started with the defeat of Darius' Persian army by the Athenians, badly outnumbered, on the plain at Marathon in 490 BC. Then Pheidippides ran the 26 miles to Athens to warn his fellow citizens that Darius would soon come by sea to slaughter them. Fears concluded that the fundamental threat to our precious heritage of freedom was the confusion that arises from seeing the free market economy as an end unto itself and its principles as if given by God himself. It was an act of hubris to substitute prosperity for morality, decency, and freedom. Dick wasn't quite sure he agreed with this conclusion, or even quite understood it, to be honest.

Whoosh!

Lorrie was at the Cleveland Museum of Art, listening to a tutorial lecture on the development of Islamic art, as Dick pulled into the College Club parking lot for the 10:00 a.m. ACE (Association for Continuing Education) meeting. He rather liked this group of 25 or 30 women (mostly) who were so dedicated to books and learning. They really applied their talents to overseeing the execution of an extraordinarily successful program of community book discussion groups and associated educational and cultural activities. As for Dick, he had never read a book voluntarily until that Hardy Boys job in seventh grade (or was it the Bobbsey Twins?).

Swoosh!

"Hi Edith. You look like you lost something."

The form bending over a sheath of disorganized papers on a straight chair answered, "My daughter was supposed to fly in from L.A. today, but now I don't know when she's coming."

"Oh," not knowing what else to say.

Edith, the form, now assumed an upright position, looked at Dick, and could see he didn't know. "An airplane just flew into a building in New York City this morning." Now he knew. And yet he didn't know. Not really.

Over at the museum about that time, the lecture series chairman appeared at the microphone on stage following a dissertation on the art of Islam. In a calm but firm voice she announced, "That concludes our training session for today. Please pick up your belongings, make your way to the main entrance, and exit the building." Being a group of novitiates on the Women's Council, no one spoke up to ask why a full day's schedule of lectures was being abruptly terminated. Lorrie and the others left as instructed.

Crash!

A cell phone rang during the ACE board meeting. Chelie, the book sale co-chair, moved for the exit and took her call. By then he knew from his immediate companions that a second plane had crashed into the other World Trade Center tower.

Dick drove home. All stations were broadcasting the news above with virtually no associated information. The streets of Cleveland looked the same as on any other day, and to him that seemed strange. Then came the bulletin: "One tower of the World Trade Center has collapsed!" *What? What do they mean collapsed? That building must be (have been)120 stories high*! Was it the one he and Lorrie were on 15 years ago, where Lorrie got dizzy out on the observation deck and you could see the evidence of daring-do scrawled on the inside border skirt of the topmost floor, "SPYDER MAN WAS HERE"? He remembered pressing his face against the plate glass flush with the side of the building next to the elevator shaft on the top floor, looking down at the model village far below, when that funny feeling invaded his gut and made the tip of his penis tingle. Right at the edge between something and nothing, and nothing to hold on to.

Now the voice on the radio announced a parking ban in effect for downtown Cleveland. *What is going on?*

At home. Transfixed in front of the TV. Whoosh. The first plane, American Airlines 707 Flight No. 11, disappears into the side of that building at 8:45 a.m., erupting in a ball of fire more spectacular that any he had seen produced by Hollywood's special effects teams. And here comes the second plane, United Airlines Flight No. 175, executing its rendezvous with the South tower at 9:05 a.m. Swoosh. More fire. More smoke. More debris.

Crash. The top of the North tower, 1368 feet above ground zero, disappears into the umbrella of smoke and rubble, and telescopes 65 feet below ground level to the bedrock of the island purchased from the Indians for $24 in glass beads (wampum) by one Peter Minuit in 1624 or 5 (or so legend has it). People racing in panic through the streets. Crash. The second tower imitates the first. Twin towers with a twin fate. New Yorkers–secretaries, shop owners, businessmen, young kids, a policeman–running and stumbling through a narrow canyon of glass, steel and stone megaliths. Sheer panic. A war scene.

You did not have to have any special powers of perception to know America would never be the same as it was when you got up that morning. A moderate amount of stress concentrates the mind and cements the "where was I when" elements of a surprise event therein, for the useful duration of your brain's functional life. Dick remembered that late Sunday afternoon on December 7, 1941, when he and his sister were lying on the floor listening to the radio. He knew then that things would change because war news from Europe had been an everyday affair for the past two years. Sunday, September 1, 1939. Hitler invades Poland. Dick was too young to know what that meant at the time, but he knew it was important from the solemn manner of dialogue exchanged among his adult relatives.

George Bush said this was "an attack against America." Dick thought it was an attack against freedom. Rufus Fears' lectures on freedom were much on his mind. Osama bin Laden had targeted the world center for international financial transactions, having identified this as the heart of capitalism. Dead were 2,952 people, including 658 of the 960 employees of the Kantor Fitzgerald bond trading firm handling 70 percent of daily international monetary and credit transactions. They ceased to be, the fortunate ones, in just an instant. Bin Laden, as well as Fears, perceived that material prosperity defined freedom in America. Islam was the custodian of moral character and bin Laden had the moral compass.

Taxes, Taxes, Taxes

Late at night in early July of that same year, Dick sat hunched over scattered papers on his work desk. *Two weeks to button up this IRS 1040 tax return and pay my annual respects to Uncle Sam.* He was struggling with the issue of accounting for five or six superfluous figures staring at him from the K-1 Partnership form which had arrived as a late, corrected statement, detailing one of last year's investment fiascoes. He was attempting to decipher the maze of arcane entries on the K-1 sheet:

- Partner's share of lines 3, 4, and 7, Form 1065, Schedule M-2
- Ordinary income (Sch. E, Part II, line 27, columns (i) or (k))
- Portfolio income (Sch. B, Part 1, line 1)
- Dividends (Sch. B, Part II, line 5)
- Net Long Term Capital Gain (Sch. D, Part II, line 12)
- Charitable contributions (Sch. A, line 15 or 16)
- Investment income included in lines 4a and 4b above (Form 4952, Part II, line 4a)
- Depreciation adjustment on property placed in service after 1986 (Form 6251, Part I, line 8)
- Distributions of money (cash and marketable securities) N/A

All entries were to be prorated according to state of residence. But the real problem was deeper than this. Since this had been a short sale, all these entries had to be in the negative. At this impasse, he reflected on one of Lorrie's favorite sayings, "Consider Ginger Rogers. Not only did she have to follow Fred Astair step for step, but she had to do it backwards in high heels." Doing his own taxes seemed to be analogous to Ginger's terpsichore.

Dick went to bed. He reflected on the wisdom of doing his own taxes. He reflected on the wisdom of selling a REIT (Real Estate Investment Trust) short. He had followed his initial idea many years ago to keep up with annual tax provision changes year by year. By so doing he would learn to make sound tax decisions all year and not be at the mercy of H. & R. Block and all these mystifying, esoteric tax laws. Although he didn't particularly enjoy seeing the periodic tax deductions from his pay check, he usually had a most satisfied feeling when he put his finished tax forms into the blue mail box in early April, or sometimes even in August if he had applied for an extension.

Deep down, Dick knew that to live in the United States in the last half of the 20th century was truly a privilege conferred by an accident of birth. After you discharged your annual financial obligations to the state, you could walk around knowing you were a paid-up member of America, in good standing. Dick still liked that feeling, but the obstacle course you had to master each year to arrive at the finish line was becoming more convoluted each time the pols promised you tax simplification.

How could he know that the U.S. tax code would eventually extend to 10,000 pages at latest count (and still counting). You may ask why it takes 10,000 pages of instructions for the federal government to collect enough money from the citizens to pay for its operating requirements. And what private citizen had any idea of where all the $3 trillion collected by all levels of government went? That figures out to be an average tax bite of about $10,000 for every man, woman, and child in the country. Sleep came, but it was not the peaceful rest one might have expected from Thomas Jefferson's promise of life, liberty, and the pursuit of happiness.

The following Saturday, Lorrie suggested that Dick upgrade his khaki pants and sweatshirt costume in preparation for their imminent departure to Couple's Book Club. Doris Kearns Goodwin's biography of Lyndon Baines Johnson was up for discussion. The principal lesson he learned from this tome was that you could not fight a foreign war and build The Great Society simultaneously without incurring severe economic and political consequences. On the way to this literary session, Dick dropped his completed tax documents into the blue box with the Eagle on it. Whew. Glad to have that annual chore done. For the moment he brushed aside any concern he might have had that his check for the few dollars due could be spent either for weapons or ineffectual give-away programs.

Later that evening, as the group book discussion was winding down, someone advanced his contention out of the blue that we should have a flat-rate income tax. Since this was an old saw, it didn't provoke much discussion that night. However, the idea stuck in his brain and during the 20-minute drive home, Dick reviewed the pros and cons of this issue. First, it clearly favored the high-end earners. Second, it did not address any associated tax provisions that came under the heading of non-taxable income, deductions, credits, etc. Thirdly, it was only ever proposed by guys that were on the way to higher tax brackets.

The next Tuesday, Dick was at the Case Service Center sorting books for the ACE book sale. He slipped Milton and Rose Friedman's *Free to Choose* book into the economics bin. Choose what?, he thought. He knew Friedman was a much vaunted, conservative economist who favored school vouchers. But no other details. Upon leaving the service center, he retrieved the book in question, thinking he would just borrow it for a week or so to see what choices Milton and Rose were advocating.

Bingo. There was the flat tax again (later, Dick was to find out Milton had originally proposed strictly proportional income taxation way back in 1962). And that's not all. The Friedmans were advocating a negative income tax system also. Under such a system, persons unfortunate enough to have only a very meager (or no) income in any given year would receive financial aid up to some minimum total income level. He remembered hearing Dick Nixon offer this surprise proposal for consideration in 1969. It had been hard to believe that one of America's most conservative leaders would advocate such a scheme. However, this idea was endorsed by no one and it disappeared from the political radar screen (at that time, he didn't know that Presidents Ford and Carter had made essentially the same proposal). Soon he was to think that perhaps these ideas were not so far out after all. By the time Dick had finished reading *Free to Choose* all the way to the back cover, he was snowed under with new ideas about our American economic practices and, as importantly, suggestions for changing those practices in the interest of boosting our prosperity.

He ran the bath water. Once every few years, instead of taking a quick shower, he would avail himself of the relaxing, almost dream-like, trance that could be induced by immersion in warm water. In this state of warm, wet solitude, he could think and sort through some complex ideas at a leisurely pace. Must be like revisiting the womb.

Let's see. The Friedmans proposed remedies for our school system, for the worker, for the consumer, for inflation, for our system of medical care. Each of these areas were examined and reworked with a single-minded, fundamental concept in mind. Government control creates inefficiency by placing hurdles in our path that we must jump in the interest of one or another favored group. Or expressed another way, when we are all free to choose, our individual self-interest yields the most efficacious results for each of us and the maximum wealth-creating effect for these United States. According to the Friedmans, the American economy was limping along under the onslaught of scores of special interest groups.

Enter Adam Smith. Milton Friedman is the conservative economic guru of our day and foremost disciple of the radical Scot, Adam Smith. Smith has a large following of professional economists advocating much the same set of ideas.

But how might all these sweeping changes advocated by the Friedmans be effected? They all, each and every one, tweak the nose of some congressional power broker or step hard on the toes of some vocal, subsidized group. The Friedmans' basic solution was to wrap the like particulars of each issue in one of several constitutional amendments, requiring the approval of two thirds of Congress and ratification by three fourths of the States. Fat chance. Well, Milton knows and does acknowledge the odds. On the other hand he is sure there is zero chance of effecting change if no one carries the banner and plays the tune for any and all who will look and listen. And he is not the only marcher in this parade.

Effectively, Milton and Rose Friedman are the architects of a massive restructuring plan to excise welfare-based legislation from our society and enhance freedom of choice for all. They say we should have equality of opportunity, not equality of outcome (which, of course, is communism). To Dick, such ideas held a fascinating appeal for their relation to basic conservative economic principles and for their clean simplicity. On the other hand, many of these ideas were continuously being expressed as a staple of far right Republican thinking. These guys always left him a little uncomfortable. This line of thinking always seemed to leave too many big cracks for the disadvantaged and otherwise noncompetitive members of society to fall through. The bath water was getting cold and it was time to shorten the grass and kill a few weeds before Sunday disappeared into night.

A few days and much conjecture later, Dick found himself formulating his own plan for the salvation of these United States of America. Oh yes, and for making the annual chore of preparing his tax returns much easier. In fact he had been much taken with John McCain's proposals for campaign finance reform, during the presidential campaign of 2000. Much mischief is wrought by the free flow of dollars into campaign coffers for both principal parties. What if no lobbyists with greenbacks falling out of their pockets were to show up on Capitol Hill one day? Would business suffer? Would our economy falter and stumble? Was the money put up for election campaign financing as politically corrosive as McCain and others claimed?

On the other hand, Dick seemed to remember that the Supreme Court had ruled that contributions to political campaigns constitute free speech, and as such, were protected by the First Amendment. If so, doesn't it follow that the more money you have, the more freedom of speech you have? Stated more directly, money talks and politicians have big ears. Might it ever be possible to institute a separation of industry and state? After all, it works very well for religion. The United States has better church attendance and a deeper religious commitment than other Christian countries where the institution of religion is supported by direct government subsidy.

To the uninformed mind, it was a little hard to assimilate all these ideas and practices as part and parcel of this great democratic society. It makes you wonder just what democracy is, anyway. And if you wonder, you are in good company. For democracy was the "most looked-up" word in the dictionary under "d" in 2004 (dictionary .reference.com).

These idle musings were rattling around in Dick's head before Enron took a header over the cliff, and religious-based Islamic zealots engineered the crashes that were heard around the world.

What Is Democracy, Anyway?

Whoosh!

Nine-eleven. In one instant everything changed. America fell back transfixed, attention riveted on the cathode ray tube in stunned disbelief. Suddenly nothing else mattered. All but absolutely necessary activities and transactions stopped. We all watched and tried to disbelieve our eyes, looked for some explanation, searched for context and perspective. Within days, President Bush would be *hugging* Senate Majority leader Tom Daschle on the Senate floor. Now there was only one focus for

American politics and there was only one obsessive preoccupation in a 100 million American homes. To Dick it seemed incredibly irrelevant that he could have been thinking about reforming the American system of taxation to simplify his tax preparation obligations, just yesterday.

All eyes turned east to Islam. What is Islam? Do all Muslims hate us? Do all Arabs and Persians resent our wealth? Our military might? Our culture? Our freedom? What is it about the United States of America that provoked so much anger that al-Qaeda would execute the most vicious attack on American soil in the history of our existence? Clearly it was a defiant statement and a demand for attention. The scenes of devastation that beamed out to the world in living color immediately after the event, assured that al-Qaeda would get attention and more. In addition to learning something about Islam, just maybe we should learn more about ourselves. What does it mean to live in a democracy? In fact, what really is a democracy?

That night Dick went to bed reflecting on the truly significant events he had witnessed, as they happened, in real time on television over the years. In July of 1969 he and Lorrie got all three kids out of bed to witness Neil Armstrong's "...one giant leap for mankind" onto the surface of the moon. The astronauts brought back moon rocks, but no green cheese. Jack Ruby pulls a gun and kills Lee Harvey Oswald...a lone Chinese student stands in the path of a menacing army tank in a brave plea for democracy...Boris Yeltsin standing on a tank defending his counterrevolution and urging his followers in the street to be steadfast...the Russian tanks lumber slowly around the square...they stop...the commander in the tank in the foreground rotates its turret so that the gun is pointing at the Russian White House where the Communist legislature is holed up...Bam! A shell hits the side of the building leaving a crater and a scorched blotch on the outside facade. And would you believe an American President, Richard Nixon, standing in the Rose Garden proclaiming to the world, "I am not a crook"?...Lyndon Johnson stunning the political infrastructure with his announcement just as the primary elections were getting underway, "I shall not seek, and will not accept, my party's nomination for another term in office."...President Clinton, the empathic leader who felt everybody's pain, pointing his finger at the nation and declaring, "I did not have sexual relations with that woman, Ms. Lewinsky!"...then on August 18, cornered with nowhere left to hide, admitting some imperfect behavior (but no apology). Think about it. The most dramatic and unexpected events beamed into our homes over the past thirty years were stunning surprises about power and politics.

So much for TV and all these musings about taxes and politics. Certainly it would be a simple matter to dream up proposals for an improved system of taxation or even a kinder and gentler foreign policy. Criticism comes naturally to most of us and critic is the easiest job in the world. You might look at it this way. What we are as a nation, and what we might become, springs from our national concept of democracy. In the broadest sense our interpretation of democracy determines our domestic practices and our relationship to the rest of the world.

If you watch anything but sitcoms and survival shows in the evening, you see politicians and news analysts talking about this great democracy we live in. And democracy means, if anything, participation in the actions of government, by the people, the *demos*. Abraham Lincoln said it best when he wound up his short Gettysburg address with his "of the people, by the people, and for the people" punch line. And doesn't our Constitution start out with "We the people"? Are we just standing by while our government, manned by our public servants whom we elected and pay, complicate our lives in the interest of all manner of special interest groups? If we the people in our integrated whole desire a more equitable political system dedicated to our individual wants and needs, we should be free to have it in a democracy, wouldn't you say? At the same time, there is no reason that the external manifestation of democracy should be the cause of resentment and anger for Middle Eastern Islam, or any one else around the world.

So far Dick has leaned on the word democracy. As a concept, democracy covers a lot of ground and means different things to different folks. Nazi Germany was a democracy (however tenuous) before the great war. More recently, the Iraqis were alleged to have voted 99.6 percent in favor of Saddam Hussein in his very last, single candidate election. But in America, we associate the idea of democracy with the word freedom, a state of being implying more than just bare bones voting privileges. Even the words freedom or liberty do not lend themselves to simplistic definitions. To appreciate what the words democracy, freedom, and liberty mean, you really have to understand the context within which they are used and have been used over time. If you investigate the historic context within which they have been applied, you will notice several other associated words that keep popping up, only to require additional definition and context. Words like equality, justice, property, republic, civil disobedience, and even natural law.

Dick had some phrases, really snippets of prose and lyrics, running through his brain. You have all heard and voiced them countless times. Phrases such as:

"live free or die"
"the Liberty Bell"
"let freedom ring"
"the Four Freedoms"
"the land of the free"
"the Statue of Liberty"
"sweet land of liberty"
"all men are created equal"
"with liberty and justice for all"
"give me liberty or give me death"
"to the republic for which it stands"
"to make the world safe for democracy"
"We the People of the United States of America"
"free at last, free at last, thank God almighty, we're free at last"
"that this nation, under God, shall have a new birth of freedom and that government of the people, by the people, for the people, shall not perish from the earth"

This collection of phrases is a representation of the way we would like to believe we are. As such it makes up part of a myth we subscribe to and strive to live by. Clearly the message expressed in these treasured phrases is the promise of freedom and liberty for all Americans. The word democracy appears but once on this list, as it was used by a politician elected in the last century—Woodrow Wilson. The words property and capitalism are not mentioned in this collection although they constitute important pillars of our democracy and the American myth.

So exactly what do we mean when we say democracy? What rights and freedoms does that concept convey? What can we do with it? Probably for those under age 25 it means the freedom to buy a car, party anytime, marry whom you want, and work at whatever job you can qualify for. Unfortunately for many of today's youth, their political education is finished with the last skit on Saturday Night Live (R. Lawry, pers. comm.) or the Daily Show with Jon Stewart on Comedy Central, at best. At the next stage of life it means the opportunity to choose your political representatives, be judged under law by a jury of your peers, attend the church of your choice (or none at all), and pay your taxes. After retirement it means Social Security and Medicare, or even a rest home. Democracy is often perceived to be the source of the ideas of intellectual freedom, economic justice, social welfare, tolerance, piety, moral integrity, the dignity of man, and generalized civil decency (Armington and Ellis). But is it?

The root word *demos* comes from the Greek. It means the common people. To political scientists democracy means a system of governance wherein the common people are the primary source of power that is exercised either directly or through elected representatives.

Democracy means different things to different people. Before the Common Era there was but one true, direct democracy. By the end of the eighteenth century there were just three democracies. Fifty years ago there were 20. Today there are 120 countries including 60 percent of the world's population living under some form of democracy (Koh). If we are to achieve a working understanding of democracy and its relation to freedom and liberty, we would do well to investigate what it has meant to our predecessors, how they practiced it, and how well it worked for them. Then, in the words of Immanuel Kant, we might begin to understand "what we might aspire to" under our American democracy.

The 1st: Delaware. December 7, 1787

15

CHAPTER 2

WESTERN DEMOCRACY AND FREEDOM

From the time of Abraham and before, man has been concerned with governance. More often than not the boss was exacting in his demands and not always inclined to forgive transgressions. The representative governance we practice in the West today derives from a long history of empirical trial and error. Where may we mark its beginning?

The political and cultural roots of America derive from what is now Europe, and primarily Western Europe. The Middle Eastern Islamic countries are largely omitted from our review of democracy and freedom. Nevertheless, we must acknowledge their role in picking up and significantly advancing the practices of science, industry, and culture, lost to Greece and Rome, while Western Europe languished under the exploitation of local lords and the safekeeping of the Christian Church.

In our quest to understand the meaning of democracy and its relation to freedom, it will be instructive to examine the struggle to build democratic civilization through 25 or more centuries of Western history using Will and Ariel Durant as our guide.

God's Chosen People

Almost 4,000 years ago, the shepherd Abram and his family were wandering in the desert near the land of Canaan. God spoke to him, and made with him several covenants. God said he would make him exceedingly fruitful, the ancestor of nations and kings. God said he would give Abram and his offspring the land of Canaan in perpetuity and would be its God. But it was required that all Abram's male issue be circumcised, and that he subscribe to several other covenants including the command to sacrifice his son Isaac. Henceforth, Abram would be called Abraham.

The resultant twelve tribes of Israel would fall into captivity in Egypt (ca. 1650 to 1220 BC). Eventually the day came when they would depart Egypt under the leadership of Moses, only to wander for 40 years in the wilderness before reaching Palestine, the land of milk and honey. Along the way Moses would bring them the Ten Commandments from Jehovah at Mount Sinai, as a guide to successful living. The 12 tribes lived in a loose confederation until ca. 1025 BC when Saul became their first King. This was in spite of the prophet Samuel's warnings that they would loose their freedoms under a monarch. And they did. The pre-Jewish peoples had always worshipped many Gods, a practice that gradually died out during the reign of King Solomon (974-937 BC) when Yahweh become their singular God.

In the reign of Josiah (639 BC), the King read the Book of the Covenant to his people who were chafing under the harsh admonishments of the prophets and priests. This book is thought to have been a collection of decrees, demands, and exhortations that had been imposed on God's chosen people for centuries. It was an imposed social contract. By 444 BC, after having been subjected to the rule of Babylon and Persia, Ezra brought this new written history to Jerusalem and read the Book of the Law of Moses to the Jews (substantially the first five books of the Bible, the Torah or Pentateuch). In time these two documents became the *Mosaic Code*, the fundamental cultural, spiritual, social, and political law for all Jews, wherever they might be dispersed over the ensuing 24 centuries. This adoption of the Mosaic Code marked the reintroduction of the long-forgotten Abraham to the faithful, and the formal beginning of Judaism.

During the period 800 to 1200, the scriptures were updated and reinterpreted, making scripture relevant to that day's world. In this process of *Midrash*, Abraham was eventually redefined as the founder of Judaism, or the first Jew. In time, Christians and Muslims went through a similar process of modernizing their founding myths as a means of establishing the legitimacy of their branch of Western monotheistic religious belief tracing back to Abraham (Feiler).

Subsequently, Palestine was overrun by Greeks, Persians, Romans, Egyptians, Arabs, Turks, and assorted barbarian tribes. The Jews were enslaved, persecuted, and made to leave. They enjoyed limited religious, civil, and economic freedom in other lands from time to time, but no lasting security. They were exterminated en masse during Hitler's Great War of the 1940s and finally, after four millennia, the survivors knew Jewish democracy for the first time in the new state of Israel founded in 1948. They had always had the freedom to follow or walk away from their "portable Fatherland," the Mosaic Code. Exercising this freedom of choice in the face of unrelenting pressure was a test of loyalty that developed tenacity and a deep sense of personal responsibility in the faithful. We shall see now if Judaism is able to survive democracy.

Beware Of Greeks Bearing Democracy

The Iliad and the Odyssey are thought to have been written by Homer ca. 850 to 750 BC. These legends of warrior kings and adventure contain no reference to individual freedom and certainly none to democracy.

The Greeks invented this word, democracy, describing the means by which the free people of Athens made and carried out their own laws. Solon is said to have invented the first system of democracy for the Athenians in 594 BC. This was an amazing beginning for a political system that was modified and eventually vanquished, but never completely discredited over time.

At that time the rich of Athens had accumulated virtually all the wealth and the poor had become truly desperate. Revolution appeared imminent when Solon came to power. In one bold stroke, and without bloodshed, he cancelled all debts, devalued the currency, freed political prisoners, established a graduated tax and a noneconomic honors system, abolished exemptions to the law, and established several broad "committees" open to all free citizens. Solon is remembered as the father of the Athenian constitution even though tyranny and civil strife continued until 510 BC when Cleisthenes redrew the political map of Attica paving the way for true democracy and the Golden Age of Greece (McInerney). Henceforth, justice was to be rendered in accordance with law, not just by corrupt political appointees and arbitrary decree (Wormser). This unique judicial system featured membership in a 6,000 man court and jury system, comprised of freemen drawn by lot for one year. This committee tried cases, heard appeals to magistrates, and provided jurors numbering 501 or more to judge cases nominally lasting only from sunrise to sundown.

Although most of Solon's practices were altered over time and the elected position of archon (head of state) was often usurped by a dictator, his democratic system and a strong navy made it possible for Athens to become the commercial leader of the Mediterranean. Even though it was dependent upon grain imports from Egypt, this Athenian democracy was the incubator of the cultural achievements of The Golden Age. Five hundred years later the Roman Cicero said Solon's legal system was still in evidence in Athens, despite the fact that Athens had fallen into the hands of Alexander the Great in 338 BC and subjected to Roman rule in 146 BC.

Darius confronted this political system when he brought his Persian army to the plain at Marathon in 490 BC to challenge Athens. The Athenians mustered an Army at Marathon to face the never defeated Persian Army that outnumbered them three to one. The far larger force was routed in what was a pivotal military victory in Athenian history.

This brave triumph earned Athens the respect of all other Greek city-states, and freedom for its fledgling democratic system. Ten years later, the Persians under Xerxes were repelled again and Athens built a mighty navy and proceeded to corner the shipping trade in the Eastern Mediterranean (don't we still have Greek shipping magnates?). The impending yoke of Oriental domination was slipped and Greece, with the help of Athens, was able to preserve its culture for future Western generations to build upon. If you were victorious in war, you had the right to rule. This was pretty much the meaning of natural law in those days.

The Golden Age of Greece ended in 399 BC with the trial and death of Socrates. This 100-year span is the primary reference period from which we formulate our ideas of Greek democracy. Its end was precipitated by the desire of Athens, against the advice of Pericles, to dominate the entire Greek city-state world. Athens was defeated in the Peloponnesian war (431-404 BC) by a coalition of its neighbors led by Sparta. At the outset of this war Athens lost about 25 percent of its population to a plague. By the conclusion, it was showing signs of decline. So how may we describe this Athenian democracy?

The governing body of Athens was comprised of citizens selected by lot from the free population of some 43,000. Both the legislative and judicial systems were in their hands. In fact the citizens of Athens were synonymous with the state. It was the purest form of direct democracy ever practiced on a scale larger than that of the town hall of New England. While Athens "earned" its freedom by the sword, it was not freedom for the individual, which concept was probably unknown that early in history. In his famous Funeral Oration of 430 BC, Pericles made the novel suggestion that Athenian citizens might even realize a degree of privacy and autonomy in their personal lives. By the end of this war, Socrates was sentenced to death for asking exasperating questions, by a defeated democratic nation offering no guaranteed right of free speech. Although Greek democracy was based on the idea of a cohesive cultural group engaging in active debate of all public issues (like a present-day political party), in the end it became a tyranny of the majority.

A free Athenian was defined by his status arising from his function in the state, not by his personal worth. There were no formal parties to put up political candidates because all government officials were chosen by lottery for one-year terms. The rich had more personal freedom than the poor, though all were subject to the political decisions of the free citizens who were equal under the Law in their role as the de facto state. Over time this political system did not offer a strong enough shield against the sword of Alexander nor the internal demands made upon it. During the ensuing century both Plato and Aristotle condemned the political chaos wrought by the arbitrary whims of mob rule, and democracy was never fully resuscitated.

The Golden Age population has been estimated at 315,000, by Milton Meltzer, for all of Attica, the geographic area ruled by Athens. Only 43,000 were citizens with full democratic rights and privileges. Slaves, women, and resident aliens were excluded from the franchise and any real measure of freedom. In general, women did

WESTERN DEMOCRACY AND FREEDOM

not participate in public life. As in much of history they were valued primarily for utility, genealogy, and personal services.

Slave making was one of the businesses of war. The victors had the recognized right to pillage and plunder, to kill or enslave, at their discretion. For the next 2,000 years, a soldier's wages were usually paid from the spoils of war. Slave labor, available for its minimal upkeep requirement, and the riches accumulated through silver mining, trade, and tribute from vassal states, produced a mentality that held the necessity for manual labor as an unfortunate disgrace. The Golden Age of Greece was built on the foundation of slave labor. To the citizen Greeks, if you were not one of them, you were not quite human.

Over time, the fortunes of Athens, Sparta, Syracuse, Sicily, Corinth, and other Greek city-states waxed and waned with external military pressures and internal political crises. But inexorably during the forth century BC, the aristocratic citizens of Athens lost their zeal for state power and languished in luxury. At the same time the lesser citizens acquired increasing power over the Assembly and voted themselves ever greater welfare measures. It didn't help when Pericles abolished the high court of Athens before he died in 430 BC.

By 336 BC Alexander had marched south from Macedonia and delivered a crippling blow to Athenian democracy on his way to domination of those lands to the south and east. In the process he spread Greek culture to aristocratic elements throughout both Persian and Arabian regions. Upon Alexander's death in 322 BC, Greece and Macedonia were placed under the rule of a monarch. Athenian democracy remained on life support over the ensuing 90 years until the elite intellectuals finally succeeded in burying this amazing political experiment (Woodruff). Except for the expanding Roman Empire, monarchy was the enduring political norm in the West until the great revolutions of the 18th century. In 146 BC the folks from Rome marched into town and the Greece that once was became a province of Rome. By then, Athens had long since lost its passion for democracy. Fortunately for Western posterity, much of the civilization and culture produced by Greece was soaked up and incorporated into the Roman motif. By the time of its demise, Athenian democracy and culture, comprising less than 50,000 souls and spanning only 150 years, had stamped its indelible mark on Western Civilization.

When In Rome, Do As The Romans Do

In 508 BC the Roman Senate deposed their Etruscan monarch, and an Assembly of citizen-soldiers selected two consuls, or leaders, in his stead. The local clan heads become aristocratic patricians whose descendents were to rule Rome for the next 500 years. Supreme power was vested in a Senate that had executive, legislative, and judicial responsibilities. Straight up or down voting in Assemblies decided those issues presented to it.

Voting power was correlated to wealth. The patrician and business classes, who had similar interests, could always outvote the Plebes, or working class, who were forced to resort to general strikes or attempted revolution to get even a meager piece of the pie. The patricians paid the most taxes, had strict military obligations, and guarded their position of privilege tenaciously.

Rome was a class conscious society throughout its long history, and properly labeled an aristocratic democracy. More than one sympathetic wealthy citizen was assassinated for extending an overly generous hand to the Plebes.

Rome and its provincial empire was called a republic (public property or commonwealth), at least until 49 BC when internal chaos brought dictators and emperors to power. The driving force for Roman culture and conquest was the concept of virtue or moral excellence. It was virtuous to be manly, to strive for and attain rank, ability, and power. The Roman character was shaped by the romantic philosophy of Stoicism, which valued self-discipline, sacrifice, courage, cruelty, service to the state, and respect for *logos*, the life force as determined by reason and rational thought. The young males studied military arts, as well as law, and made ideal recruits for the disciplined, near-invincible, legions of Roman Centurions.

In 451 BC, the Plebes demanded that the reluctant Senate publish written laws in the interest of obtaining justice less arbitrary and capricious. A delegation went to Athens to study Solon's work and returned to organize and codify Rome's ancient set of customs and decrees. As modified over the centuries, Roman Law became the backbone of Western jurisprudence–Rome's most important legacy.

These Romans, with some exceptions, were not very much preoccupied with philosophy, creativity, and scientific inquiry. Much of their accomplishment in these areas was borrowed from the Greeks and others. Rather they were builders of civic structures. With the help of outside engineering expertise, and slave and military labor, they built a truly amazing infrastructure of roads, bridges, aqueducts, fountains, baths, walls, and buildings. Several aqueducts and parts of the Appian Way are in use to this day.

The population of Rome was calculated at just over a million in 189 BC, with citizens, or free male adults, numbering between 200,000 and 300,000 in the preceding years. Those who could spurned work. They were little interested in trade. The Western Mediterranean was the economic playground of the ancient regime of Carthage (now Tunis). Rome depended on an agricultural economy with some wealth created by slave labor and craft industry. The limited revenues flowing from property taxes and tariffs in the first centuries were spent to develop and sustain military might.

Rome's military adventures brought all of Italy under its rule by 295 BC. It challenged Hannibal in the Punic wars for mastery of the Western Mediterranean in 264 BC, finally defeating him in 202 BC, and then Spain in 201 BC. Rome's legions engaged Macedonia in 214 BC, fought a two-front war, and by 146 BC had occupied both North Africa and Greece. The defeat of Carthage in 202 BC left Rome as the sole super power of its time.

Concomitant with these victories was the growth of luxury, cruelty, and class warfare. Cheap grain imports undermined domestic agriculture. The slave population increased and the Plebes were squeezed ever harder. Many Greek ideas influenced, if not captured, Roman culture. Robert Merry believes Rome's position of undisputed prominence led it to overextend its empire. As the empire expanded, internal stress increased. Eventually Rome had realized about all the external success it was able to manage, and Roman democracy disintegrated into civil chaos 150 years later.

In 139 BC the slaves in Sicily revolted. Many of them were once free men of conquered territories. Over time the emancipation of slaves in Rome resulted in a population wherein almost half of the citizens were descended from foreign stock and did not share Rome's Stoic ideals. Slaves remained numerous and by 71 BC Spartacus had amassed over 100,000 slaves in an unsuccessful revolt to secure their freedom (Spartacus). Still, by 30 BC, almost half the population of Rome, some 400,000, were reckoned as slaves. After severe property measures were enacted that impacted the farmer adversely, discontent led to civil war and a breakdown in social order.

The Senate and courts were corrupted by the inflow of provincial tribute and everybody was on the take. In 66 BC the government granted extraordinary powers to the military for the purpose of extracting a steady flow of tribute from its Asiatic provinces. As Rome's civil society sank into corruption and chaos, power was assumed by the military. Rome became ripe for dictatorship. As the last vestiges of democracy, freedom, and security disappeared, Rome's destiny was signaled by the death Julius Caesar in 44 BC.

Caesar was an ambitious, accomplished, and brilliant general who could be ruthless when necessary. He was fresh from the conquest of Gaul and the invasion of Britain. The Senate granted him the title of Dictator when it recognized that only strong leadership backed by force could restore confidence and save the empire. He quickly denigrated the powers of the Senate and set out to restore confidence by pushing through legislation to ease the burdens of the Plebes. The aristocracy, sensing its own demise, sent Brutus to destroy Caesar. The Ides of March in the year 44 BC were his undoing. The stage was now set for a long succession of emperors, some very, very good and some very, very bad.

Octavian, soon to be Augustus, assumed power in 30 BC and proceeded to gather all executive, legislative, and judiciary functions into the emperorship. He gave Rome a more rational set of rules to live by, but they did not prevent the Senate and Assembly from eventually withering and dying. The patrician aristocracy now shunned military service, limited childbearing, and endorsed all the sins of high living. Soon the Emperors were reduced to signing up non-Romans for legionnaire service in return for a promise of citizenship. Stoicism turned to resignation. The practical philosophy of Epicureanism surfaced and soon saw the likes of Nero as its chief practitioner. As Stoicism, the *faux* religion for 400 years, lost its hold over the populace, the old Roman Gods were resurrected.

Under the reign of a succession of emperors, military adventures were curtailed for 200 years in a period of relative peace known as the *Pax Romana*. The momentum of the influx of tribute and inexpensive imports gradually declined, although, as with an ocean liner, it would take a long time before the ship of state slowed to a stop. Slavery dwindled and the poor were put on the dole in an attempt to pacify them. Over time they quit their farms and drifted into Rome. Reversal of fortune started slowly as the edges of an overextended empire began to crumble, led by the Teutonic barbarians from the north.

By the third century, starting in 235, Rome was to have suffered 35 emperors in 37 years as the empire descended into near anarchy. In 254 the deluge commenced, led by the Goths, Scythians, Persians, and Samaritans. The barbarians had crashed the gates. Defeat discredited the notion of Roman invincibility and internal revolts broke out in many provinces of the empire.

After 284, the emperor Diocletian abandoned Rome and made his capital in Asia Minor, the better to defend his eastern Empire. From this beginning grew Byzantium and the European system of monarchial rule to last 1,500 years. By then the Empire was broke and staggering under the load of excessive welfare costs, inflation, and social decay. In 301 Diocletian resorted to comprehensive economic controls, defying the law of supply and demand, by fixing wages and prices. They were promptly modified following riots and the disappearance of goods from the marketplace. The state became a major employer and socialism was justified by fear of barbarian attack. Soon peasants were bound to their fields and workplaces, ushering in the first echo of medieval serfdom.

Enter Constantine. Constantine adopted the symbol of Christ, an X with a line drawn through it and curled around the top, as a shield mark for his troops at the battle of the Mulvian Bridge. His victory there led to his success in resolving the disputed Caesarship in the

West. By 323 he became sole emperor of Rome and legitimized Christianity as part of the Roman pantheon. Soon Christianity would subsume Rome and eventually all the known Western world.

Constantine moved his capital to Constantinople, now Istanbul, in 324-30, after which time Rome was defended only by the bishop. By 476, Rome was sacked for the last time and the Roman Empire came to an end after a 900-plus-year run. Notwithstanding all its cruelty, mistakes, and problems, we must hail Rome, but not Caesar, for its unparalleled longevity, civic contributions, and lessons bequeathed to Western Civilization, not the least of which was the comprehensive legal Code of Justinian produced in 529 (Wormser).

So what can be said for Roman democracy and freedom? The Romans themselves thought of their state as a republic, or a system of governance existing for the public. Cicero, in the first century BC, expressed the idea that government should exist by the consent of its citizens. At the same time, the people realized their identification through allegiance to the state, at least for the first 500 years. It was a democracy in the sense that citizens did have a vote in the legislative Assembly. However, the Plebes never achieved influential democratic power owing to the structure of voting privileges, and had to strike or fight for reasonable treatment or look to dictatorial power to neutralize the patrician aristocracy for them.

Rome did not make the Athenian mistake of letting the mob take over. Even the poorest citizens had treasured Roman rights under the law, but could be made into slaves for nonpayment of usurious debt. While there was economic freedom of choice, it was not easy to overcome the odds. After the demise of Julius Caesar, civil strife subsided for 200 years, but with very limited freedom for the underclass and an end to democracy. The system was stagnating and brought to power a parade of mostly unsuccessful emperors amid increasing despair and social deterioration.

The Romans did hold all men to be equal as members of the human race. This viewpoint marked the emergence in Western history of man as an individual with inherent worth, differing only in his function in society. Slavery or other social status was only a matter of the roll of the dice. Roman women were just a little better recognized than those in the Greek world. If there be lessons to be learned from the Roman experience, they may be that nothing succeeds like unselfish devotion to a cause larger than oneself, easy money begets a loss of values and driving purpose, and every system of government has flaws that may only become apparent under stress or when you neglect to nourish it.

There have been many reasons proposed to explain the decay of the Roman Empire. It started as a vibrant republic that expanded its borders using the justification of self-defense, while at the same time accumulating wealth, power, and prestige. Success resulted in a mission to bring the "benefits of civilization" to its neighbors far beyond the pale. Rome said, "we care that they fear us, not love us," whereas today we also want their love. Ultimately, easy money brought on corruption and political decay leading to dictatorship and economic chaos. A loss of confidence in leadership finally resulted in the collapse of the moral and ethical values of Roman citizens, qualities that were needed to sustain a successful civil society (Roche). *Arrivederci Roma!*

This was **The Warning** of 1776.

Forgiveness And Salvation

One day in 28 or 29 a Jew came to the river Jordan to undergo a symbolic rite of purification called baptism. John the Baptist called for the Jews to repent and prepare for the Last Judgment as he administered this rite. He was a bit of a rabble rouser. John's head was later presented to Salome as the result of his criticism of King Herod. The baptized Jew, known as Jesus in this Roman province, seemed to have had ideas in some ways similar to those held by John. He traveled through the Judean countryside telling stories or parables designed to teach his listeners how to live a better life. Those who knew him believed he performed miracles, especially of healing, and several abandoned their daily occupations to follow him.

Eventually, Jesus and these apostles went to Jerusalem during the festival of Passover and Jesus antagonized the Jewish priesthood by disrupting the money exchange services at the Temple. His claim to be the Son of God cast him in the role of the Messiah, the long awaited one spoken of by Isaiah (Isaiah 52:13-53:12), who would free the Jews from Roman oppression and establish their kingdom here on earth. However,

Jesus proclaimed that his kingdom was not of this earth, but of heaven. He had come to atone for the sins of men, offer them God's grace of forgiveness, and victory over death through the eternal life of the spirit.

The Jewish priests recognized Jesus to be a threat to business as usual, at best, and at worst, a potentially contagious heretic. Pontius Pilate, eager to preserve the Roman peace, put Jesus' case before the Jewish people who opted for his crucifixion. Jesus' teachings of love and forgiveness in a harsh age strained even the ability of his disciples to comprehend. Soon, however, belief in the news of Jesus' resurrection established his authenticity in the minds of his followers.

Of these events in the life of Jesus we know only from the writers of the four Gospels, persons who may or may not have had firsthand knowledge of his life. While these Gospels were written some decades after Jesus' execution, the Roman Jew Josephus did write of Jesus' existence at the time.

The Apostles proceeded to spread the Good News, mainly among the dispersed Jews and new converts in that part of the world. By 42 Peter had traveled as far as Rome. Saint Paul (formerly Saul of Tarsus) was a Jew who took on the task of prosecuting this new sect, but in the process had a change of heart and became its chief advocate and doctrinal proselytizer. Following Jesus' admonishment to go out and preach to all nations, he reached into the pagan communities around the Roman Empire and found a willing reception for these new ideas. Paul did not require all converts to live in accordance with Jewish dietary laws or submit to circumcision. On these issues he incurred the animosity of the hometown Jews. To them, these dispensations spelled the first step in abandoning Mosaic Law, the bedrock of Judaism.

Paul was introducing the idea of belief into the Jewish community, where practices had always been based on laws of proper conduct. Eventually the main Jewish body rejected the Christian-Jewish sect as incompatible with the longstanding Jewish interest of realizing their heaven right here on earth, and proceeded to cut it loose. As time passed into the second century, the Epistles of the by-now-martyred Saint Paul served as a unifying example for the various congregations and constituted the Pauline theology of Christianity.

Jesus Christ proposed a framework for individual behavior independent of civil obligations or authority. The stories or parables he recited as he wandered through the Palestinian countryside were morality tales emphasizing the individual's proper, responsible role in social relationships, in accordance with spiritual development. Eventually his ministry became the enduring capstone for the idea that each person had an individual free will and a responsibility to do right in the eyes of both God and man. He spoke of the opportunity to be born again and emphasized the importance of being your brother's keeper. He promised God's grace and salvation for your soul. Jesus did not speak to any secular issues of freedom but he did say to his Apostles, "You shall know the truth, and the truth shall make you free" (John 8:31,32).

As Christianity continued to spread, it underwent continuing local changes in practice and soon required a centralizing authority to promote coherence and adherence. The church in Rome had established a disputed claim to Christian authority based on Peter's early visits (Christ had said, "upon this rock I will build my church"), and by the middle of the third century had enough wealth and power to be so recognized, at least by the Western Church. It was strengthened by the Roman tradition of organization and law, and soon adopted Latin as its working language.

As Roman civic authority withered, the bishops of the Christian Church thrived, so that when Constantine left for Constantinople in 324-30, the church inherited the ship of state. With the Emperor's endorsement, the flock of new believers multiplied and spread rapidly. In 452 when Attila the Hun knocked at the gates of Rome, he was met not by the Praetorian Guard, but rather by Pope Leo I who bribed him to return home in peace ere winter defeat him in the field.

Coincident with this period, Saint Augustine (354-430) advanced the Christian idea of original sin as man's inheritance and espoused the later-day Calvinist claim that the powers of the church should take precedence over the authority of secular rulers. The man who in his early years prayed, "Give me chastity, but not yet!", took all the fun out of sex and gave it a bad name by advocating strict fidelity and an end to prostitution; this in a day when women were still valued chiefly for their utility.

The shadow of Saint Augustine put new constraints on permissible social behavior and a spiritual precondition to the achievement of God's promised grace. At the same time it strengthened the church's position in the face of state power. Over time, Christianity assumed the leadership role throughout Western Europe, subduing personal freedom and any chance for democracy. It preached personal salvation, but overlooked Christ's teaching of individuality, except perhaps for the aristocratic few in what eventually became a feudal society.

In the Christian movement, the world saw a brief glimpse of freedom but no hint of democracy as that had perished with the early Roman Empire.

The Lights Go Out In Europe

As Western Europe sank into the Dark Ages, Roman civic power in the West was replaced by the church, which reengineered Roman social institutions to meet its spiritual program. For almost 1,000 years, the Christian Church was in charge of art, literature, and education, such as they were, as well as the care of the poor and the burying of the dead (Dawson). Civic power was assumed by whichever barbarian tribe or local aristocrat had the might to prevail and was heavily influenced by the church. The spiritual power of Christ's message knew no geographic or political boundaries, and became the great unifying influence in men's affairs in the West.

Democracy and freedom went into hiding and there was no opportunity for peasants or serfs to create or generate personal material wealth in a world believed to be economically static. There were scant means of accumulating food and the staples of life. Wealth was measured in land, animals, serfs, and castles scattered across the landscape.

Lacking incentive or recognition or any franchise with which to effect personal improvement, most of the common men worked just hard enough to survive the lash of the lord of the manor. They had precious little hope for change and depended upon the good will of the local lord for their security. Where the Romans were interested in virtue or the possible perfectibility of men, the church was interested in dispensing salvation in return for spiritual, moral, and financial obedience.

It was an age when serfs and peasants did life's basic work and there was little thought that knowledge might be bent to the task of making life less arduous or more productive. The church had no charter for increasing temporal knowledge or enhancing the material aspects of life. Christianity was not part of the march of material progress; that was put on hold in the West for much of the next millennium.

In the year 610 at Mecca, the trade capital of Arabia, the Angel Gabriel appeared to Mohammed and proclaimed him to be the messenger of Allah. Repeated visions convinced Mohammed he was a Prophet of God and could offer a paradise of earthly joys to all who would heed his words. He became embittered against the Jews for rejecting his new teaching, just as the Christians before him had criticized the Jews for not listening to Christ's promise of salvation.

Nonetheless, Mohammed's new religion of Islam spread like wildfire, eventually winning many Christian lands in the process. The science, technology, culture, and philosophy developed by the ancient states and forsaken by the West, eventually found their way through the Eastern Christian Church and Syria to the Muslim world, where it flowered and enriched the lives of the privileged peoples of the Middle East for the next millennium.

Eventually the new order of Feudalism established itself in the West. Under the Feudal system, the local aristocrat provided military protection and security in the form of basic needs for his serfs. In return, the serf was bound to render military support in time of emergency, a percentage of the land's bounty, and his labor to keep roads in repair and otherwise serve the local noble's needs. Agriculture accounted for around nine tenths of all resource production. From his labors, the serf or peasant may have netted about one third of the product of his toil after all taxes, including those of the church, were remitted. Labor was plentiful and slavery dwindled as a result. In time Chivalry made its appearance as a means of keeping social order, achieving aristocratic recognition, conducting war, and realizing the spoils thereof. It was a stable system that offered security in return for agricultural labor.

The most noteworthy attempt to put together a new civilization in Western Europe was made by the German Charles after he become a king in 771, just prior to the end of Western economic decline. He conquered and assumed control over much of the European landmass, offering the inhabitants a choice they could not refuse: Christianity or oblivion. In 800, Leo III crowned him Emperor, the first since 476, and Charlemagne assumed the lost title of Roman Emperor, the first of many to assume that mantle over the next 1,000 years.

This coronation established the tradition of *investiture,* the future claim of Christianity as the authorizing agent for monarchical rule, and freed the Western Church from domination by Constantinople. Ultimately, it established the claim of the divine right of kings, a doctrine even yet to be named. Perhaps the seminal social achievement of Charlemagne's reign was the *Capitulare missorum*, a document authorizing periodic audits by the king's emissaries, of aristocratic misdeeds against the common people, and the legislation of a system of civilized controls for all facets of social interaction.

However, the system Charlemagne put in place could not withstand the pressures of the age and shortly began to crumble under the rule of his sons. His was a system of monarchical-granted liberties not to make their appearance again for many centuries. Alas, Charlemagne was something of a man before his time.

Europe Looks Eastward

It took another 300 years for the West to start digging its way out of its economic and intellectual slumber. In 1070 the Turks took Jerusalem and began making inroads into the Byzantine Empire, which eventually appealed for help from the Roman Church. Pope Urban II was sensitive to the call to save Christianity from the Islamic threat and was mindful of the opportunity of extending the control of the successful Italian trading cities throughout the Eastern Mediterranean.

It is possible the Pope even entertained the idea of the Roman papacy realizing supreme authority over all of a unified Christendom.

Urban II lobbied the Western powers for support, which he got, and assembled a hoard in excess of 30,000 assorted defenders of the faith, bribed with religious, political, and economic concessions, as well as the prospect of spoils. The first wave of holy warriors departed in 1096. After terrorizing the towns and inhabitants that stood in its path, the vanguard of this rag tag, bloody army entered the gates of Jerusalem in 1099, realizing at least partial success for their first mission.

For 200 years the mania for extending Western influence and control eastward continued, even to the extreme of sending off a Children's Crusade comprised of teens and preteens that met with utter disaster. In the end, this protracted military approach was a complete failure, except for the stimulus to trade that it produced. The much superior Muslim culture bolstered by the military genius of Saladin forced the Crusaders out of Jerusalem in 1187 after their initial success. As an unintended consequence, however, they gave Western Europe its first glimpse of the advanced products, science, technology, and intellectual freedom accessible in the Muslim world. This exposure was just the spark needed to light the slow burning fuse that ignited the Renaissance 200 years hence.

The papal interest in unifying Europe under one banner had to be postponed 700 years until the European Union came into being without the Pope's help. Ultimately, Western Europe's nations did perceive the trade and mutual security advantages to be gained by relinquishing their sovereignty, and adopted the Euro as a common currency and precursor to political unity.

In the meantime, a little noted meeting took place on the field at Runnymede in England between King John and his discontented aristocracy in 1215. Unpolitic decisions and indifference to his calling provoked King John's nobles and clergy to prepare a contract granting them a cornucopia of rights and severely limiting the king's arbitrary powers. Although it was a bill of rights for the privileged class, it set down the principles of Habeas Corpus, trial by jury, and financial control by the pre-Parliamentary body of the day. King John acquiesced to the terms of the Magna Charta, by which action the English monarchy was put under constitutional control, at least in theory.

This most prized of English documents was ignored for centuries, but never forgotten. In time it became the seminal reference point for developing the rights of man in today's Western Civilization.

Awake At Last

As the crusades had the effect of weakening Islamic culture, back home in the West, rudimentary industry was slowly developing and taking shape in the form of craft guilds including the church-supported, Freemason cathedral builders. Metal working technology was being advanced as the art of gear making was developed to make mechanical clocks, and the textile industry in Florence grew rapidly with the development of sophisticated looms. The expansion of sea trade in the Western Mediterranean brought prosperity to Italian ports and by 1300 the business community was overshadowing the aristocracy in political matters. By 1400 some 3,200 males in Florence, mainly business people, had voting privileges in this city of well over 100,000 in population.

Consequently, it was here in Florence where the Renaissance was born, even before the Black Plague took some one third of Europe's population, principally in the peak years of 1348-1350. Sponsored by church and individual wealth, industry and a burst of creative artistic activity awakened the genius of Western man, extending freedom, at least to those with sufficient funds.

Barbara Tuchman portrayed the six popes of Rome reigning from 1470 to 1530 who badly damaged the "good" name of Christianity by their secular venality, amorality, avarice, and quest for funds to pay for the renovation of St. Peters. The ad line for this campaign, "As soon as the coin in the coffer rings, another soul from purgatory springs," was contested by the Priest Martin Luther with 95 theses for debate nailed to the church door in Wittenberg in 1517. His idea that this campaign transcended the authority of the church and violated the religious rights of the common Christian was a statement of natural law, a concept that was to gain recognition as the struggle for individual freedom gained respectability over time.

Close on the heels of Luther's audacious challenge was Henry VIII in 1527 when he excommunicated the entire Catholic Church from England because Pope Leo refused his divorce petition. The Reformation began before the Renaissance had run its course. Western Europe now looked westward just in time to see the Portuguese men-of-war return home from the new world laden with silver and gold.

In 1611, the Authorized Version of the King James Bible was written by *God's Secretaries* (Nicolson). It was a labor commenced by Tyndale back in Luther's time. Translated from the Greek, this poetic masterpiece became the workaday spiritual reference source for English-speaking Christians until the middle of the 20th century. Up until 1688 England had been dealing with a succession of Catholic-leaning monarchs, to the displeasure of the English, quasi-Puritan Parliament. The availability of scripture to "everyman", bought into question the legitimacy of the divine-right-of-King's claim established over 800 years earlier when Charlemagne was crowned by Leo III.

One hundred years later, King Louis XVI still did not accept this restriction on his absolute power even as he was taken to the guillotine, to be followed nine months later by the Queen, Marie Antoinette, riding in an oxcart. In England the stage had already been set for the Glorious Revolution.

England In The Vanguard

The early 1600s ushered in the breakdown of Feudalism in England. Factory based industry sprang up and with it the need for capital to finance expansion. The bourgeoisie, or professional and business occupations, proliferated and demanded a larger voice in government. Commercial interests wanted more influence in economic matters. Industry and trade vied for importance with land and agriculture, the traditional sources of all wealth. The working class was caught in the crossfire and lost purchasing power as the gap between rich and poor widened. These rapid developments produced fundamental institutional strains and severe social tensions.

During this period many Puritan followers left for the New World as Pilgrims, dissatisfied with the residual Catholic influence and the perceived laxity of moral discipline in the Anglican Church and laity. Finally, in 1688, the succession of Stuart Monarchs came to an end when Parliament fired King James II. The job was offered under pressure to William III of Orange and Mary within the framework of a Declaration of Right, a document that rendered the monarchy subservient to Parliament forevermore. The Glorious Revolution was accomplished with a single document.

This document (later retitled a Bill of Rights) forbade the monarch from arbitrarily making or rescinding laws, conducting courts, or appropriating the funds of the realm. Two strictures that did not survive the test of time related to outlawing Catholicism and prohibiting the maintenance of a standing army. While this power shift did not automatically grant any expanded rights to the individual, the political sea change was an event that allowed John Locke to publish a set of concepts that would soon set men on the path to unheard of personal freedom.

John Locke published his two *Treatises on Government* in 1690. His purpose was to legitimize the new English political structure created by The Glorious Revolution, by providing it with a solid philosophical foundation. His genius lay in his taking a number of ideas about human rights which had been touched on by political philosophers over the years and reengineering them with his own perspective to rationalize the current political scene. A short outline of the precepts he offered is comprised of the following:

The doctrine of Divine and Absolute Right of the Monarch was contrary to both liberty of the individual and any possibility of political order.

It was man's "natural condition" to be free and equal with others in their rights.

In this condition men might execute a "social contract" to give up their claim to individual earthly rule. Sovereignty would rest with the whole people.

A duly elected representative would be duty bound to carry out the people's will. If not, he could be replaced. The authorizing power for government would reside with the people.

The primary function of government is the preservation of property, the value of which accrues as the result of applying man's labor to the land.

The powers of government should be strictly separated (in this case the executive from the legislative).

These governance guidelines were promulgated in the name of all men. They were a complement to the Bill of Rights, setting limits to the power of the new monarch. At long last the English legislature was free of dictatorial rule.

The immediate effect of all these changes, however, was increased support for business interests by a Parliament staffed by nobility in the House of Lords and industrialists and merchants in the House of Commons. The House of Commons, originally formed in 1295, purported to represent the people, but was not legitimized by a full popular franchise until the 19th century. Even at the time of the American Revolution, the Commons were elected by less than 250,000 votes out of a potential 3 million subjects (not including women), and many of these votes were purchased (Beard). Democracy and freedom for the common man were not yet ready to blossom. First the aristocracy and bourgeoisie were to be served.

The political philosophy expressed by John Locke, and its gradual application in English society, influenced the likes of men such as Voltaire who carried these ideas to France spiced with his own brand of clerical and aristocratic cynicism, and Rousseau who followed him with his romantic interpretation of the state as the embodiment of the general will. In the *Spirit of the Laws*, Barron de Montesquieu provided context for the English system by framing it in his study of government types throughout history. He noted also that government can be no more virtuous than the level of virtue practiced responsibly by its subjects. His work had a direct influence on the construction of our American system as well.

The Glorious Revolution of Merry Olde England constituted a democratic breakthrough in the history of mankind, paving the way for unheard of individual freedom sanctified and protected by the power of the state. In one hundred years, the colonists in the New World would appropriate Locke's ideas even as they rejected King George III and his quasi-democratic Parliament.

The 2nd: Pennsylvania. December 12, 1787

CHAPTER 3

LAND OF OPPORTUNITY

Birth Of A Nation

The opportunity to apply these lessons of political history was even then maturing in the New World. When the call came, it was the smile of good fortune that brought forth men who were schooled in the past, experienced in colonial politics, and possessed of the measure of courage required to carve out the future. We are in large measure the product of their efforts.

The 13 American colonies were chartered between 1606 and 1733 for the purpose of establishing territorial claims, enriching the Crown and English investors, and securing religious liberty. After a rocky start they began to thrive, impeded only by the elements and the eventual resistance of the native population, estimated to be 20 million or more (Mann). Since the Indians did not have state-of-the-art technology or immunity to European germs, and did not recognize property ownership, they were steadily dispossessed of their territorial freedoms. As in most of history, the rulers-to-be at any given time showed up without hand engraved invitations.

The economic philosophy of the time has since been labeled as Mercantilism. Simply stated, it was based on the idea that national wealth increased in proportion to the surplus of exports over imports.

Tariffs, duties, subsidies, and transportation laws were enacted for the purpose of maximizing exports and minimizing imports. Occasionally you might be rewarded with a bonus, as the Portuguese and Spanish were with New World gold and silver.

The colonists did their part by sending lumber, wood products, pig iron, milled flour, rice, and eventually, West Indies indigo to England. From the very beginning they raised and sent tobacco, which for a time was even a proxy for money in a land very short on specie. When the ships returned, they were laden with manufactured goods, new immigrants, indentured servants, prisoners, and slaves–especially slaves–whose trade made money for the English and the New England merchants, and whose labor made money for the southern colonial planters. By 1788 the slave population of the colonies was estimated to be 750,000 (90 percent of whom lived in the South) out of a total population of something over 2 million (Melzer).

Early on, the colonies all wrote constitutions spelling out the obligations and rights of colonists as well as the functions of their respective legislative bodies. They were free to formulate local law; however, the English reserved the right to make merchant law. The Navigation Acts required trade to be carried on English ships. Eventually the English proceeded to add restrictions requiring most trade to be with or go through the mother country.

The colonials considered themselves to be Englishmen due all the rights accorded to their cousins back home. Gordon Wood presents a good account of society in colonial America. Social relations were patterned after the hierarchical relation of the King to his subjects. In any household the oldest able male was in charge, with all other men and women, children, boarders, servants, and slaves assuming an appropriate position in the pecking order. The master was responsible for his extended family and the family was responsive to his will. At work, which was 90 percent agricultural, people tended to relate one step up or down, but not much further. The local gentleman was usually a man of some means who would extend credit on a book entry basis, or barter, owing to a scarcity of coin. In this way a web of community relationships was established based on outstanding obligations and favors due.

There were no guilds or associations of cobblers or blacksmiths. Only the gentry carried on intercourse outside of the community, and they were without title. But all "the meaner sort" knew who this 10 percent or so of the population were and respected them. These privileged men were engaged in community affairs, supposed to have been educated, and did not work in business, at least not openly. It was a patronage system where public service might mean committing one's assets to community improvements, but with the expectation of reciprocal enrichment. It was expected the gentry would favor local artisans with work orders designed to beautify their abode and promote their status in the community. It was expected that the locals would turn out from time to time to maintain roads, bridges, and other community infrastructure.

Eric Foner writes that individual freedom in the early Puritan era was viewed only as the right to do good, a right that flowed from God and civil authority to which all must subscribe. The Pilgrims sailed for the new world in a quest for religious liberty, but only for themselves, not for everybody.

The settlers generally were not completely prepared for life in the wilds of America and depended on the natives for help and instruction. They had to learn the primitive arts required for creating the artifacts of life, from scratch and from the land. Thus they became self-sufficient, self-reliant, and very independent. There was land for the buying or taking, a commodity which was absolutely not available back home. In time they forgot they were the freest people on earth, at least from a local political standpoint. This freedom and independence required, and promoted, a very mature sense of responsibility for these New World pioneers.

The more adventuresome pushed west, over the Alleghenies, to where the grass might be greener, and life even freer. The gentleman sponsored exploration in the west to stake out future claims for land grants or speculation, using surveyors like George Washington. The Crown did not like this because they had made occupation treaties with the Indian tribes, restricting the trespass of the white man outside of the colonies. King George III, and Parliament especially, did not like this because of their obligation to protect settlers against Indian attacks, in part instigated by the almost 10,000 French trappers and traders wandering about east of the Mississippi. The result was the seven-year French and Indian War, starting in 1756, for which the Crown had to supply troops at considerable expense.

Back home, George III, struggling with illness and mounting government indebtedness, meant to recover these costs from the colonists. Britain was in debt to the tune of 160 percent of its GDP (Gross Domestic Product) by that time (Ferguson, Empire 2004). So England (technically Britain since the Scots' inclusion in 1707) made an attempt to collect the molasses tax on shipments from the West Indies. Normally this raw material for rum fermentation had been smuggled in. Then England imposed the stamp tax in 1765, which action really riled up the colonists. This was an act of parliament, a body whose jurisdiction they did not accept. This was a tax on property. The colonists stopped ordering from England, boycotting trade. The merchants and traders, seeing their business going down the tubes, sided with the locals. Soon King and Parliament blinked, at least temporarily.

Next the Tea Act threatened to end tea smuggling by the colonists, and to monopolize this trade for the benefit of England. When the chests of tea aboard ships were scuttled in the infamous Boston Tea Party, the English merchants changed their tune. This was destruction of their private property. Until this time the colonial governors and judges had been paid directly by the colonial assemblies. But now the Crown wanted their stipends and those of the local English Tax Commissioners cycled from the colonies through the royal treasury, placing the local English officials beyond the control of the rebellious colonies.

The colonists felt betrayed by King George and saw their political and economic freedoms being confiscated along with their money. Their fears were reasonable, but at the same time they did not know what a sweet deal they had compared to their cousins back home. They had been out of touch and misinformed, living with the comfortable illusion of a grateful, beneficent monarch.

The King and Parliament treated the colonist's intransigence alternatively as an irritant, then as a serious problem. They had never closely supervised this developing piece of the Empire. Over a 150-year span, none had ever visited the place. They regarded those colonists not as cousins, but as barely civilized, second-class subjects. Parliament consisted of aristocratic administrators (without any administrative qualifications) legislating largely for their personal benefit and ego. They were arrogant. Still…they had become dependent upon this profitable transatlantic commerce.

The American response to these and other British provocations was the first Continental Congress called in 1774 to issue resolutions and express grievances. These were treasonous actions in the King's eyes.

The powder keg was ignited in 1775 when the Brits headed out of Boston for Concord to destroy a cache of arms, thought to include cannon, a strictly offensive weapon. Along the way, the Revolutionary War started in Lexington when someone fired the "shot heard 'round the world." It was not to end until the British were bottled up in Yorktown in 1781 by the joint French-American army, financed largely by the French franc and dependent on the siege experience of the French General Rochambeau.

Thomas Jefferson's Declaration of Independence adopted July 4, 1776, by the second Continental Congress, sealed the fate of the American colonies. At the same time, it boldly voiced the ideas that modern man was just beginning to realize might actually constitute the covenant under which they could be free of arbitrary rule. As such this document bears examination for content.

The statements,

"We hold these truths to be self-evident…" rests on the concept of natural law, i.e., that which is true, right, and just in the eyes of every man; the fair standard by which we would like to be judged.

"…that all men are created equal…" does not bear a literal interpretation, but rather a moral one. We construe this to mean that no man is born with a superior state of rights.

"…that they are endowed by their Creator with certain unalienable Rights…" recognizes the origin of human rights to be intrinsic, God-given, and not a boon granted by some earthly power.

"…that among these are Life, Liberty and the pursuit of Happiness," to name just a few. Your life is your own and not the state's. That you should have freedom is a condition of ersonhood. The pursuit of Happiness is not a phrase narrowly meaning "Party! Party! Party!" By Life they meant the right to live your own lifestyle, follow your chosen vocation, associate as you please, expand your capabilities, contribute as you are able, and hold property as a mark of personal identification—in other words, to be your own man.

This declaration goes on to state specifically that one purpose of government is to secure these rights for men and that its just powers derive form the consent of those governed. Further,

"...when any Form of Government becomes destructive of these ends, it is the Right of the People to alter or abolish it, and to institute new Government."

Restated simply, the second paragraph of the Declaration of Independence claims that the rights of man derive from God, and man institutes government, in part, to protect these rights. If the government fails to do so, man may reconstitute it.

This was The Statement of 1776.

Goodbye to monarchs. Goodbye to unchangeable legislatures. Goodbye to a ruling aristocracy.

Now if you flash back 86 years to John Locke's Second Treatise on Civil Government, you will see plainly that Jefferson's ideas about the freedom of man are pretty much a direct takeoff on Locke. It is interesting to note, however, that Jefferson chose to use "pursuit of Happiness" whereas Locke had used the word "property." It had been the bedrock of understanding since before the time of Solon that private property rights were the building block of all rights and freedoms for people. Government ownership of property was tantamount to control of men's lives.

The apparent distinction between Happiness and property was not real, however. In the context of the times, property meant more than mere physical assets. It meant those things that defined you in the eyes of the community: your vocation, your extended family, your reputation, and social standing—your very identity. The pursuit of Happiness must be understood to mean the opportunity to develop your property. When the founding fathers fired King George, they expropriated John Locke's philosophy of government.

In retrospect, this is not surprising since Locke (along with Sir Francis Bacon and Sir Isaac Newton) was ranked by Thomas Jefferson as one of the three greatest men who had ever lived.

The American Plan

After Yorktown in 1781, Americans went back to being Virginians, South Carolinians, Pennsylvanians, and so on, as they always had been in their hearts. In the meantime the Continental Congress had just reconstituted itself into a Confederation, to better address the necessity for a secure union among the colonies. But it soon became evident that the Articles of Confederation were too weak to bind the colonies to any common purpose. Any action proposed for the common good was dependent upon the goodwill of each of the colonial assemblies, and they were loath to agree, especially when funds were required.

The union was drifting into oblivion when an extralegal meeting of commissioners from several of the colonies met in 1786 and called for a convention for the purpose of proposing changes to the Articles of Confederation. This convention was supposed to report its recommendations back to Congress for further consideration. It never did. The historic meeting which took place between May and September of 1787 in Philadelphia has been chronicled in detail by Clinton Rossiter and Catherine Drinker Bowen. For our understanding of the contentious issues that were hammered out at this meeting, we owe our thanks to James Madison, the only delegate to take notes.

The delegates from 12 colonies (Rhode Island was a no-show) straggled in bringing their special interests and parochial, political baggage, but no plan for how to proceed. That is, except for the Virginia Plan presented by Edmond Randolph. In fact this plan was the product of a three year study in depth by James Madison of government forms and performance throughout the ages. This plan provided the framework for a new government structure, brought immediate focus to the major issues, and no doubt saved the convention from the frustration of wrangling over a host of secondary issues of local interest. Rather than just revising the Articles of Confederation, the delegates were dedicated to the creation of a wholly new political infrastructure for a wholly new nation. It was the product of centuries of governmental success and failure since the time when Solon first gave the Athenians a true democracy. It was a brand, spanking, new arrangement based on ideas for a fledgling, but brave new country based on equality and individual freedom.

During this five month period the operating rules for these United States were written. Certain major issues are worth examining here as they relate to our ideas of democracy and freedom. The delegates were educated men with political experience. They were men of means and property, each bound to represent the interests of his state-to-be. They were the American equivalent of European aristocracy in every sense save one. They had no title outside the political arena. They were not sanctioned in their life station by any higher civil authority. The cardinal concerns of these men were:

- ✓ securing fair representation of the several states in a legislative body
- ✓ defining an executive role without giving it excessive power
- ✓ providing for a check on the power which might be assumed by any of the three branches of government
- ✓ finding a resolution to the differing viewpoints on slavery
- ✓ balancing the overlapping powers of the federal and state governments
- ✓ writing a charter that would be ratified by at least nine out of the thirteen colonies

The state representation issue was solved by creating two legislative bodies, one wherein voting power was equal from state to state, the other having representation based on state populations. The representatives were to be chosen by the people of each state through their electors, whereas the senators were to be appointed by the state legislatures. Formulation of qualifications for voting in legislative elections was left to the individual states. However, two important legal protections were adopted after the British system. They were prohibitions against issuing a Bill of Attainder (punishment without a trial) and suspension of the Writ of Habeas Corpus (demand to show cause for custody of a person).

The executive (President and Vice President) were to be elected by Electors from each state.

Thus the constitutional delegates adopted a plan whose only democratic feature was a provision for the election of. representatives, and that was designed primarily for the purpose of defending the national treasury. Since the individual states were accorded the right to set voting requirements, only men of property had a vote at first. Political freedom was next to nonexistent in the beginning.

The legislature was charged with making law by majority vote. Proposed law could be vetoed by the president, in which case a two-thirds majority vote would be required to override the veto. Law made would be subject to supreme court approval upon challenge. This protection was not actually expressed or realized until 1803 in the case of *Marbury v. Madison* at which time Chief Justice Marshall wrote an opinion establishing the Supreme Court as the court of last resort in interpreting constitutional law. The Supreme Court justices were to be appointed by the executive for life, with the advice and consent of congress. By these interlocking checks and balances, Locke's power-limiting, governmental safeguards were established. So far in our 218 year history, these simple safeguards have served us well in the face of occasional attempts by government to impose tyrannical measures.

The issue of slavery did not get resolved at this time. As a practical matter it received little attention because the delegates knew it could not be settled in Philadelphia that summer. There would be no 13-state Union if it were prohibited, as Georgia and South Carolina would not sign on without slaveholding rights. The best that could be done was to disallow slave importation commencing in 1808. In retrospect, the practice of slavery had gradually died out over many hundreds of years in the Western world, largely for pragmatic reasons. Most people sensed that slave holding was morally wrong; nevertheless, economic factors trumped morality when the prospect of gain was strong enough. After all, the practice could be justified by dehumanizing the slave, claiming a sub-human nature for this black person, and strictly denying him any opportunity for education. It was at least noted that the subject was addressed and found disturbing to many. Black freedom would await another day. Nor was the native American population endowed with the white man's franchise, and it was much too early in history for women to be considered.

States rights were not explicitly spelled out in the main body of the Constitution. It was assumed states had the freedom to pursue any course not expressly prohibited in the Constitution. By default, individual freedom also was specifically not mentioned. This imprecision regarding the seat of ultimate power rendered the issue of the location of sovereign power implicit and unresolved. It is left to the Supreme Court to adjudicate the conflicting claims of federal and state governments, and the people, on a case-by-case basis.

The Constitution of the United States reflects the men and their time. They made a federal republic. It was federal in the sense that the national government was given the dominant power to govern the whole, while the unit states might govern for themselves within the national framework. It was a republic in the sense that government governed in the name of all the people through their representatives. The preamble to the Constitution, "We the people of the United States…" acknowledges the people as the authorizing power that legitimizes government. It cites the realization of Justice, domestic Tranquility, common Defense, and the Blessings of Liberty as aspirations to be fulfilled.

The Constitution did not provide for a general democracy. The founding fathers were literate men and all too familiar with the shortcomings of both Greek and Roman democracy. Control of the levers of government by direct vote of the public contributed to the chaos leading to dictatorship in both cases. The document they took to the various colonies for approval and ratification specified powers, limitations, and mechanics, not individual liberties as such.

The signers of this document decided they needed the approval of only nine states to make it binding upon all and that the assent of each state should be gained from a convention of delegates chosen by the people. In this way they finessed the various colonial governments who jealously guarded their parochial interests, just as they had finessed the mandate of the Confederate Congress that had originally authorized the convention. These actions were very much in keeping with the spirit of an independent people who had engaged in wholesale smuggling and had illegally challenged the authority of King George III and his Parliament.

The process of ratification was heatedly contested in each colony. In the end the belief that George Washington, already a living legend, would assume the first presidency was a significant factor in this successful effort. An unofficial condition of approval was the demand that a bill of rights be attached to the Constitution as the first article of business to be undertaken by the new congress. Madison and Jefferson were opposed to this request on the grounds that any statement of specific rights might be taken by default to mean all other conceivable rights were not protected. Nonetheless, in the first session of the new congress, Madison led the effort to produce a bill of rights. And it's a good thing he did, because the 10 amendments in the Bill of Rights have endured as the building blocks of American freedom ever since.

It is these first 10 amendments to the Constitution we regard even today as the earliest rationale for calling ourselves a democracy. In particular we are keenly aware of the Bill of Rights' provisions that prohibit the abridgement of freedom of speech or of the press, or the establishment of a state religion, as well as many other critically important protections. The Ninth and Tenth Amendments speak to personal and states' rights, albeit leaving the door open for liberal interpretation in favor of the federal government.

These 10 Amendments, the Bill of Rights, are in fact a broad statement of prohibitions aimed at protecting citizens from the power of the state. They comprise liberties to be guaranteed by the government. Within a few years of the Constitution's adoption, it was the recognition of these liberties that won grass roots support for the new American strategic plan. It is these liberties which we rely on every day as we "pursue our Happiness", or as some would say, the American Dream.

At this juncture it is well to make two fine, but important distinctions in term usage. Democracy, as a form of government, in the minds of 1787 vintage men, implied direct voting on statutory proposals by citizens. This form of direct democratic participation is practiced only in a few places, as in Switzerland, and through our state and local referenda. More broadly, if we are called on to define our democracy, we most likely cite the liberties granted by the Bill of Rights. But these liberties qualify as democratic rights only indirectly, only insofar as we may claim their authorship because the legitimacy of government derives from the consent of "we the people." In a technical sense these liberties should qualify only as indirect democratic rights.

The word *liberty* itself implies a right granted by some authority. It is used interchangeably with, and in many ways is synonymous with, the word *freedom*. But certainly not in all senses. For instance, you may be *free* as a state of your existence. But you may only be *at liberty*, by common usage of the term. Wherever appropriate I use the term freedom in lieu of liberty throughout this story.

Your freedom to do, to think, or to be, are as much a product of self-definition as they are of circumstance. In the extreme, all men are free, if they only but think they are, according to Rose Wilder Lane. In a coherent society, you may be free in your actions only insofar as you do not obstruct your neighbor's freedom, that is, if all members are to enjoy the same freedom. We may be the freest people on earth, but we are subject to certain restrictions. We are limited by the idea of equality of freedom for all. Further we are limited by countless government laws and regulations.

When we are granted a liberty, we need only take care to not exceed the boundaries of that liberty. If we are free to do whatever is not expressly prohibited, a new and very important consideration comes into play. Since the range of possibilities for action is broad and not expressly defined, it is absolutely imperative that we take personal responsibility for our behavior. In socialist societies where much security is provided, to that extent freedoms are also not conferred. More freedom usually means fewer security guarantees. An important part of taking responsibility is that aspect which requires you to take responsibility for your own well being.

Adam Smith had something to say about freedom and economics in his 1776 book, *The Wealth of Nations*. Basically what he said was that the way to maximize national abundance is to allow the greatest freedom of economic interaction possible between individuals. This assumes each party to a transaction will be interested in realizing the greatest personal advantage of the bargain. If that be the case, then some would say greed and avarice would be unleashed in the name of capitalist interests. A more even-handed view would be that each individual is interested in realizing the most benefit from his talents and labors. By this means, we prosper in relation to how well we serve the needs of others.

This was **The Discovery** of 1776.

The Wealth of Nations is a work that wanders down arcane avenues of economic history for almost 1,000 pages. It is likely not a book you would want to read just for the purpose of understanding Adam Smith's basic economic thesis. Smith's revelatory conclusion regarding man's economic life was couched in the phrase, "he is…led by an *invisible hand* to promote an end which was no part of his intention." when pursuing his own self-interest. The Invisible Hand is mentioned only once in this work, but has become the metaphor upon which the modern day science of economics was established.

The mercantile theory of gaining a trading advantage with other nations, as a strategy for wealth creation, was discredited by Adam Smith as a beggar-thy-neighbor strategy. However, protective tariff practices die hard in a world still evolving toward full economic diversification. Free enterprise practices are exposing a fundamental economic flaw in socialist systems, i.e., the inability to define cost and value. An individual trading for his own account knows the cost of his commitment and the value of the return he bargains for. A third party (the government) has only a general notion of how its edicts will play out in the billions of transactions undertaken almost every day in a major economy. To boot, these edicts are very often motivated by the goal of altering social behavior to the detriment of efficient economic activity, no matter how laudable the intent.

Another byproduct of mono a mono transactions is the promotion of value. Not only is the auction principle at work here (finding the highest bidder for your product). The process of adding value through authentication, increased utility, and desirability catalyzes the enhancement of value. Neither Smith nor Marx (Beck) ever fully appreciated the notion that the level of wealth is very much a product of value promotion. Price is determined by the perception of value, not by intrinsic value. This concept is being applied to the economies of second and third world countries today by Hernando de Soto, President of the Peruvian Institute for Liberty and Democracy. In the 1990s he directed a project to redescribe and legally retitle the assets of the Peruvian Telephone Company, thus rendering it a viable asset for international sale. The amazing result was that this company which had been valued at $53 million on the Lima Stock Exchange was sold three years later to Telephonic of Spain for $2 billion. The full value of a tangible asset can only be realized if its properties can be documented in an accepted, standard format, like a deed. This document serves as the item's passport.

At this point it is well to inject one crucial caveat. The application of economic principles can do no more than enhance our physical well-being. Important though that may be, "man shall not live by bread alone" (Matthew 4:4 and Deuteronomy 8:3). Before the sun finally sets, we must find some common ground for tempering the potentially destructive effect of economic practices run amuck.

When the Constitution was written, the Invisible Hand was already at work, unseen, in its influence on free economic transactions. The Constitution did not speak directly to the regulation of trade between individuals. It expressly provided for property rights, but finessed the issue of slavery for the time being. It provided for the regulation of commerce between states, with other nations and Indian tribes; and for taxation, monetary regulation, and civil suits at law. It left open the scope of allowable economic practices between individuals and business entities, pending statutory actions that were to be enacted in the future. It was the tenor of the time to rebel against excessive economic control from the top (remember the Stamp Act of 1765).

The value of individual initiative in taming a new country was much depended upon. By default, the stage was set upon which Adam Smith's idea of the Invisible Hand could be verified or disproved. While many other factors must also be taken into account, it was the closest approximation of an ideal, large-scale, economic experiment you could ever find. To date, the results must be judged most favorable even though the legislators have progressively muddied the waters of free enterprise over time, especially with the entrance of modern corporations into the mix.

The Constitution of the United States has weathered these 218 years with only 17 amendments since adoption of the Bill of Rights in 1789. It defines the oldest existing system of government for any major nation on earth. America is by far the most powerful and prosperous nation in history. It is arrogant. It is violent. It is tolerant. It is open. America is an economic beehive. It has friendly neighbors and until 60 years ago, had the option of isolating itself from turmoil in Europe or Asia. It is the freest place to live. But it is changing and gradually losing some of the freedoms that enabled its people to make it great. It has become a democracy, resurrected in a new form, which now serves as a model for the nations of the world.

Much has changed over the past 218 years. The territorial jurisdiction of the United States of America has increased tenfold. Citizenship has multiplied a hundredfold. A continental coast to coast trip took about a year and a half when Jefferson sent Lewis and Clark to explore this vast land in 1803-6. Today it can be done inexpensively, in comfort, in six hours. And you may communicate your ideas instantly at virtually no charge, thank you. Three percent of us produce the food necessary to feed the rest. Fifteen percent of us make most of the factory-made, tangible items required for our comfort and convenience. We have played a major role in the effort to map out the 30,000 or so genes in our DNA (deoxyribonucleic acid) which differentiate each of us from all other individuals. In concert with others, we are starting to tinker with these genes to change the very nature of life itself.

In constructing the Constitution, this country had a few very important advantages over other societies that attempted to forge a new pathway to nationhood. Most importantly, there were no seriously entrenched stakeholders, who might have an equity position in the structure of the old regime, to oppose new ideas. There was no powerful, centralized economic infrastructure to contest the creation of a new system. There was land in abundance to be taken from the original inhabitants when agriculture was still the overwhelmingly primary source of economic sustenance. The colonists-become-citizens did not fully realize it, but they had European germs as a deadly weapon against the locals. There was a legacy of enlightened political practice and ideas from Britain to borrow from, even though King George III himself was rejected.

And finally, America had a ready cadre of experienced colonial leaders who were educated in classical ideas and the history of political systems, and realized they had both the opportunity and urgent need to forge a new social blueprint based on the best ideas they could give written form to. Perhaps the lack of political competition freed them from the human proclivity of holding out for personal gain, and encouraged them to pledge "...to each other our Lives, our Fortunes and our sacred Honor." You shall know the measure of such men as Washington, Hamilton, Adams, Jefferson, Madison, Franklin, and others, only when they are put to the test.

That these men had a truly historic appreciation of the momentous undertaking they were engaged in is evidenced by the Great Seal designed in 1782 and imprinted on the back of every dollar bill in your pocket. The unfinished pyramid symbolizes the grand undertaking initiated in 1776. The eye of God at the top indicates the approval being cast upon this project from on high. That we still carry these symbols with us is our assurance that this structure is sound and still relevant today, but also that we have the responsibility to keep adding to it, all the while seeking an appropriate capstone for the pyramid.

With the happy advantages conferred by men of great honor, the cornerstone upon which the United States was to be built was set in place. It put into play a country constructed of ideas. Before 1787, factors such as ethnicity, religion, local geography, resources, tradition, history, and domineering personalities determined the character of nationhood. If we would quarrel with the ideas we live by, they are ours to debate and change; not hastily or arbitrarily, but after due consideration, deliberation, and acceptance.

At the time of the Revolution, the world outside of Great Britain and France took little note of the armed quarrel taking place in the new world. But in due time much of the world would look to this political experiment for inspiration in forging a new world order.

In 1789, the year after George Washington took office, the Bastille in Paris was stormed, sparking the French Revolution for "liberty, equality and fraternity." The French were not so fortunate as the

Americans. Their revolution ended with the blood of the revolutionary leaders in the streets, a shattered aristocracy, and a new dictator, Napoleon Bonaparte. The United States was more fortunate because the only fundamental issue separating the interests of the individual colonies was the question of slavery, a question that was wisely finessed pending future rectification.

If the Declaration of Independence was a statement of who we *were*, it now serves as a guide for what we *should* do. If the U.S. Constitution is a blueprint for what we *must* do, the Bill of Rights is a clear account of what the government *may not* do.

We have just started the task of defining America in the context of democracy and freedom.

America Comes Of Age

When George Washington was sworn in as the first president, the federal government consisted of George, his Secretary of the Treasury Hamilton, and his Secretary of State Jefferson. Immediately, Hamilton's idea for strong central government catering to capitalist trading and manufacturing interests clashed with Jefferson's idyllic view of an agricultural society with distributed power and equality for all men. Jefferson was not able to push his philosophy of equality until 1801 when he assumed the presidency.

By the time both Jefferson and John Adams died, exactly 50 years after the first Independence Day, on July 4, 1826, they had experienced moments of despair fearing that this new nation might be on the road to ruin. The evangelical and capitalist interests were getting their hands on the levers of government, and worst of all, the common, uneducated, and meaner sort were coming to believe they were included with equal voices under the tent of "we the people."

The founding fathers did not ever anticipate that the unwashed masses would have the interest, time, or background to engage in political life. In 1829 the new President Jackson brought the common man aboard in his administration, dirty boots, liquor-swilling, and all–right into the White House. Political patronage was brought into government, never to disappear. The ideal of equality advanced by Jefferson, and endorsed by both the Declaration of Independence and the U.S. Constitution, had come home to roost. Democracy gained another foothold. The public was getting into the game.

Since setting the qualifications for voting was left to the various states, they were differentiated state by state. But one qualification was universal at first. Property ownership was your ticket to the ballot box. As a property owner you had a stake in the political decision-making process. Ownership was evidence of personal ability. The franchise and your position in society were your property and your Happiness. By 1825, property requirements were being rescinded, uniform suffrage for white males became the norm, states began to allow for a popular vote for president, and voting participation grew rapidly.

Unknown to some even to this day, the vote is only for electors who then cast their votes for president and vice president. The populace began to exercise this democratic right to vote, and although the electors' function was to convey the results of any election to Washington in person, there was always the possibility that the Electors might vote their own convictions.

The tradition of voting for our president marked the first time in history that the demos were able to determine directly who would be their chief leader. When America entered World War II 150 years later, Franklin Delano Roosevelt was cast into the role of leader of the free world and had the power to affect the lives of virtually every soul on this planet.

In 1845 a man living in Concord, Massachusetts, refused to pay the state-levied poll tax and sought refuge from the constable at Walden Pond. Henry David Thoreau believed it was man's natural right to live according to his own fashion, free from government interference. He should not have to answer to government. Government should answer to him (the people). He laid out his position in a tract entitled Civil Disobedience that put the idea of man's freedom before government regulation, industry, and any special interest groups that might infringe on individual freedoms.

Thoreau was not a petty lawbreaker looking out for Number One. He was an eloquent, if somewhat belligerent, advocate of natural law and man's property rights as he saw them. The problem with invoking natural law as a defense for one's position is, of course, that this concept of law rests on moral precepts of right and wrong, and we may honestly and honorably disagree as to where the line of distinction might be drawn. So what court do we appeal to for justice under natural law? Only the court of public opinion can render a valid judgment in cases of civil disobedience based on the assertion of the rightness of natural law.

Since there is no body of written law to present as a defense in such cases, it is imperative to have some guideline to refer to as a check against the public passions of the moment. For any case to be worthy of a hearing, it is only common sense to draw a conclusion about the claimant's motivation. The test we intuitively use is that of integrity. Stephen Carter wrote that acting with integrity means trying to do what is right, *always*. Not what your mother, your friend, or some talk show host tells you is right, but that which the process of reflecting upon your life experiences speaks to you as true. The sticking point, however, is acting *even if the consequences of your action may put you at personal risk of loss.* This is where the cheese gets binding. If you are not successful in convincing the court of public opinion of the validity of your position, you must be ready to stand in judgment before the people in a court of law.

Although Thoreau did not have much at stake in refusing a minor tax obligation, his eloquent defense of freedom for man became a reference point which served as an inspiration for the likes of Mahatma Gandhi and Martin Luther King, Jr. It was a democratically developed claim of individual freedom from tyranny. It goes back to Sophocles' portrayal of the king's niece Antigone, in a play written in 441 BC. Antigone perpetrated an act of civil and familial disobedience when she defied her uncle's command, and buried her brother's corpse on the battlefield. She believed it was the right thing to do.

While Thoreau was still protesting his poll tax in America, two men in England were inventing a new social system destined to have repercussions around the world and become the arch foe of democracy and freedom. In 1848, Karl Marx and Friedrich Engels published their Communist Manifesto, a political view of the world predicting that revolution would bring economic equality to the proletariat, or working class. This equality of outcome would not destroy capital, but rather entrust the control of production and the distribution of its material benefits wholly to the state. It would be the ultimate expression of equality and security for mankind. But the great Soviet experiment of 1917 was soon expropriated by Joseph Stalin, a candidate for the most brutal leader in history. The apparatus of the state was used to consolidate party power while the Central Planning Committee called for too much toilet paper and not enough writing paper for schools and students (S. Antzak, pers. comm.).

Everyone had a job and everyone had some money, but there was little to buy in the people's stores. The 5 percent of land designated for private use yielded 50 percent of the food supply. Through every step of production and distribution, a percentage of the product was siphoned off for personal use. The guys issuing production orders did not know the value of the intended results or the cost of the methods in use. The 94 percent of the people who were not members of the Communist Party did not apply themselves because there was no incentive, no reward for effort.

In 1989, the system collapsed, a demise precipitated by President Regan's economic threat of Star Wars, Gorbachev's recognition of communism's failure, and *Charlie Wilson's War* (Crile), the clandestine CIA adventure in Afghanistan. The communist state had been suffering from social disillusionment and a lack of infrastructure investment, especially in its client territories. There was no true democracy. There was no freedom. But there was lots of equality and a gray, dismal life for the proletariat.

Since the United States had first been established, a power struggle between North and South had developed and intensified, especially over the issues of trade and slavery. Legal slave importation ceased after 1808, but the black population was self-sustaining without the benefit of fresh replacements, albeit sometimes with the loving, personal assistance of the master. One by one the northern states outlawed slavery even though the northern merchants were still prospering by sending the black ships from Africa to South America.

In 1816 tariff laws were passed as a means of protecting northern industries still in the incubation stage. They also had the effect of forcing the South to buy more of its manufactured goods from the North at a higher price than they might otherwise have paid for imports. The tariff wars raged on until 1857. In 1830, South Carolina asserted that the Union was merely a league of independent states, any of which might sever their ties at any time by unilateral declaration.

The fuse to this long smoldering powder keg was lit when Lincoln was elected in 1860. In spite of his assurances that he would not interfere with the institution of slavery in states where it existed (but not so in the new territories), South Carolina seceded from the Union followed by six other southern states. In his inaugural address, Lincoln reiterated his position and declared secession illegal. When the Confederacy fired on Fort Sumter off the coast of Charleston, the battle was joined, which was to cost 624,512 American lives, including that of Lincoln himself.

The institution of slavery had come to an end in the New World. The states learned they could not break the constitutional covenant. Before he died, Abraham Lincoln visited the battlefield at Gettysburg and in less than two minutes gave the address that is still repeated publicly in my town every Memorial Day. It was a new declaration of freedom for the United States, whose government was "of the people, by the people, and for the people"; a new beginning reasserting the tenets of Jefferson's Declaration of Independence, sanctified by the blood of her people.

The Thirteenth Amendment outlawing slavery was passed in 1865 in a victory for freedom.

The Fifteenth Amendment granting the franchise to blacks was passed in 1870 in a victory for democracy.

The Interstate Commerce Commission, established in 1887 to prevent abuses by our infant railroad system, was charged with the duty of regulating the economics and services of transportation. This was the first serious devolvement of power to legislate, execute, and judge within the confines of a single, powerful, unelected body. In time, agency control of business, industry, and other special interest groups became commonplace. These government agencies are stand-alone, boutique governments, exercising great power within their prescribed charters. In time many of these government agencies crept under the covers with the industries they were regulating and surrendered much of their virtue to them. Their actions in regulating commercial affairs for the benefit of us citizens, while admirable in most respects, has sometimes been wide of the mark, especially when members of congress would volunteer their friendly advice from time to time.

Prior to World War I, America was portrayed as running a *laissez faire* (let it be) economy. In fact what now passes as progress through free enterprise was made possible, in part, by a pro-business government, permitting the rise of the Standard Oil monopoly and the Americans–American Tobacco, Brake Shoe & Foundry, Can, Chicle, Fork & Hoe, Hide & Leather, Ice, Locomotive, School Furniture, Seeding Machine, Snuff, Stogie, Window Glass, and Writing Paper–each dominating 70 percent or more of the business in their respective industries.

At the same time, the federal government had undertaken huge national programs including the acquisition of all lands west of the Mississippi, the Homestead Act, the subsidy of rail development, and the building of the country's rural infrastructure by the Army Corp of Engineers. These were massive government programs with broad social application, largely, but not exclusively, dedicated to the constitutional charter of providing for the general welfare.

American politics and business practices underwent a metamorphosis on the eve of World War I. With the admission of Arizona to the Union, the continental expansion of America was complete. America's wealth was now owned by a tiny minority of its citizens. At this juncture, government stepped in to put some limits on free enterprise and strengthen the country's institutional infrastructure.

The Sixteenth Amendment authorizing a federal income tax was passed in 1913 paving the way for a major new source of income and creating a mechanism for future borrowing and social control. Prior to that time, the principal sources of government income were tariffs and excise taxes, with tobacco, liquor, and sugar leading the list. The follow-on Revenue Acts of 1916 and 1918 were made necessary to pay for the costs of mobilization for World War I. The "debate of 1916" resulted in a law whose basic structure forms the foundation for the current system of taxing the value of income, profits, and the assets that some people leave behind unprotected when they die.

The Federal Reserve Central Bank was established in 1913 to manage the nation's money supply, rendering our national banking system independent of direct political control for the first time. The Seventeenth Amendment providing for the popular election of U.S. Senators was passed in 1913, also in a victory for democracy. These crucial economic and political reforms followed a vigorous crusade by Teddy Roosevelt against the abuses of laissez faire business practices. However, it was just the first volley of many to be fired in a fusillade by which government eventually came to exercise increasingly more control over both business and the lives of its citizens.

The Social Security Act of 1935 imposed a mandatory income set-aside as a safety net for the aged and needy. In time this would turn into a grossly underfunded national liability, especially after Medicare and Medicaid were appended to the program as part of President Johnson's Great Society in 1965.

Gearing up for World War II required a massive diversion of national resources to put the nation on a wartime footing. The income tax structure was escalated such that the number of taxpayers increased from 4 to 43 million from 1939 to 1945, increasing federal revenues tenfold, to $45 billion. After the war, collections were modestly reduced, but a burgeoning demand for costly social programs soon started to burn more and more cash. Today almost half of the over $3 trillion federal and state budgetary total is financed from personal income taxes.

The Nineteenth Amendment allowing women to vote was passed in 1920 in an overdue victory for women and democracy. This was the culmination of a crusade kicked off in 1848 by 300 women at a convention in Seneca Falls, New York. This meeting, organized by Elizabeth Cady Stanton, issued a Declaration of Sentiments calling for equal rights for women. Stanton, later along with Susan B. Anthony, was in the vanguard of a movement started in Britain, which eventually influenced women's lives (and men's, too) around the world.

The United States faced a major challenge in the 1930s signaled by the stock market break on Black Thursday, October 24, 1929. It was the end of a speculation mania fueled by the excesses of the jazz Age, wherein illegal booze flowed freely, and cars, radios, washing machines, and tungsten-filament light bulbs rolled off the assembly lines into the arms of a public that was celebrating a "new era" of prosperity. Flappers were doing the

Charleston and letting the good times roll. General Motors, RCA, and General Electric were riding the crest of the Industrial Revolution, whose origins were roughly coincident with that of this country. Speculators operated to rig the equity markets and you could buy $10,000 worth of stock for $1,000, a friendly broker lending you the balance. When the knell sounded, margin positions were quickly wiped out and the selling cascaded until by 1932, American business had lost 90 percent of its value and 25 percent of American workingmen were unemployed, on the street, selling apples and scrounging for a handout with which to feed their families.

The Federal Reserve lowered interest rates through September of 1931, but then tightened the money supply in late 1931, just when the economy was starved for funds. The Securities and Exchange Commission was established in 1934 to oversee the financial markets, a great protection for capitalism and all investors. But capitalism and democracy had failed dismally and many were ready for the welfare state of socialism, if not communism. In fact, the Roosevelt administration was very receptive to many socialist ideas as it struggled to put a deathly sick economy back on its feet. It would take the production stimulus of war preparation to revive the American industrial machine, starting in 1939. It was a lesson to keep in mind. You do not know the strength of any political/cultural system until its prosperity falters and/or its positive cash flow is cut off. Yes, the dismal science of economics is important.

Since when the Civil War was fought, blacks in this country were endowed with all the rights and obligations of their fellow citizens. But the country's view of blacks, which had been engendered by slavery, survived the law. Open discrimination was a way of life in the South and a thinly disguised practice in the North. The 1954 Supreme Court decision in *Brown v. The Board of Education of Topeka* prepared the path that was taken by nine black students at Central High School in Little Rock, Arkansas, in 1957; and by James Meredith at the University of Mississippi in 1962. Already in 1955, Rosa Parks had brought antiblack sentiments to the surface when she refused to give up her seat in the front of a bus in Alabama. By 1960 Martin Luther King, Jr. was jailed for the first time for participating in a lunch room sit-in in Alabama. By 1963 he had given his stirring "I Have a Dream" speech on the steps of the Lincoln Memorial. By 1968 he had given his life at the hand of an assassin.

In just three years King managed to tap into the mortal soul of blacks and many whites alike. He told blacks they *did* have rights, but they must take the personal risk of violence that accrued from peaceful demonstration, to realize them. Many blacks came to believe for the first time that they were real, first-class citizens in the USA, and that they might prevail of their own determination. Many learned to take responsibility for their own destiny as the only way to achieve acceptance and self-respect. King was a man for his time and his people. He was an inspiration for us all. He had gone to civil disobedience school on Thoreau and Gandhi.

In 1961, President John F. Kennedy created the Committee on Equal Employment Opportunity, ordering federal contractors to "...take affirmative action, to ensure..." that there would be no discrimination "...with regard to race, creed, color, or national origin...." This attempt to outlaw discrimination was amplified in the important Civil Rights Acts of 1964, '65 and '68, which were passed to honor our constitutional promise to all U.S. citizens. Another important victory for democracy and freedom.

In time employers and educators resorted to preference-screening and hiring quotas to avoid prosecution. By 1978, quota criteria were rejected, and the idea of achieving diversity in academia was advocated by a decision in the *Regents of the University of California v. Bakke* case. Diversity has since come to be regarded as a good end in itself. Nevertheless, William McGowan has described how the crusade for diversity in the newsroom has corrupted American journalism, and Peter Wood calls it "Identity Politics," asserting that, "Our liberty and our equality demand that we hold one another to common standards and that we reject all hierarchy based on heredity...even the hierarchy that comes about when we grant present privileges to make up for past rights denied."

In Summary

The real character of America was developed as it grew and thrived. Its conceptual fathers would not recognize this young adult today. It has grown strong and has accomplished much to be proud of. But it has developed some warts and ailments along the way, especially since World War I.

A brief review of Western political history shows that democracy does not automatically bestow success or happiness upon its practitioners. In fact there is nothing democracy does for people that could not be done by a benevolent and all-knowing king or dictator, if ever there was such. On the other hand, neither was there much prosperity or happiness for very long in the complete absence of some democratic practices.

The first and purest democracy was practiced by the "free" Athenians. It lasted almost 200 years, but was done in by the sword of Alexander and the pen of Plato. It allowed for freedom, but freedom was really a group concept then, in much the same way Rousseau might have defined it as the "general will." The free citizens could vote for legal measures, but all government posts were filled by lottery. You might say that Athenian freedom died from too much democracy.

The aristocratic democracy of Rome survived for over 400 years, but succumbed in the end to being more aristocratic than democratic. Yet you have to applaud the Romans for their stoic dedication to state purposes. The patricians were much freer than the plebes. You could say that Roman freedom succumbed from too little democracy.

Did Rome clear the way for Christianity or did Christianity sound the death knell for Rome? Either way, Jesus Christ focused men's attention on the means to personal salvation, emphasizing the idea of individual will and action, and even offering the hope that your basic character might be born anew. His was a program dedicated to the freedom each individual had to do good in this world, as well as to survive it.

Without the leadership of the Roman Empire, Western Europe forgot about progress and settled for salvation instead for almost 1,000 years. The church elevated the importance of dogmatic belief over secular knowledge, assisting the local lords with the preservation of order. The advance of civilization in the West was put on hold. There was no democracy and very little freedom.

Without meaning to, Luther retrieved the idea of individual rights as separate and distinct from the power of the church, although he had no interest in civil or political freedoms. He translated the Latin Bible into German so that people might read the Bible without depending on a middleman for interpretation. That was the first opportunity for the common man to see The Word for himself—the first ray of democratic freedom to appear in a millennium.

The English snuffed out Catholic influence and put the king under the control of the English Parliament. John Locke even claimed that government was legitimized by people and should protect their property as their primary duty. Voting for Commons representatives was sanctioned, and along with increasing trade, eventually expanded people's democratic station.

The signers of the Constitution envisioned a United States of America where men would be free and the executive would have limited arbitrary power. However, the people wanted guarantees of freedom and demanded a bill of rights. Over time it was the 10 Amendments in the Bill of Rights, which became the first line of defense against tyranny and defined a political system now called a liberal or constitutional democracy.

The American colonies went from being a British experiment in empire to an independent country in the space of 160 years. Unknowingly, these Americans put Adam Smith's Invisible Hand to work, unleashing previously unheard of personal and economic freedom. Democratic practices were strengthened as the new society picked up steam and within 100 years, the British Empire was being challenged for economic supremacy by its offspring.

For the past 100 years, we have become about as democratic as you can get in a republic, but in the process, we are inexorably ceding our personal freedoms to government in exchange for security. Our democracy appears to be aging a bit. It no longer automatically confers robust freedom upon us. Or was freedom ever automatically bestowed? Daniel Yergin asserted that the United States has become a highly regulated welfare state, corporations bearing much of the regulatory liability. It is time we assess our democracy in the light of Western political history to see if there might not be a way to shore up any cracks or reinforce any wear spots.

The 3rd: New Jersey. December 18, 1787

CHAPTER 4

DEMOCRACY AND RESPONSIBILITY

We are now in a position to examine the nature of our American democracy in the context of historical political practices. Defining our democracy sets the stage for understanding its relationship to individual freedom as well as equal opportunity and human dignity, the three conditions of life we would like to honor in keeping with our founding principles. Very importantly, this leads to a discussion of the responsible role to be played by each citizen if freedom is to be preserved.

American Democracy Defined

The United States is the first and most successful constitutional, liberal democracy in the world. We are inclined to assume that our unmatched prosperity and freedom derive from this democracy and perhaps from even something special in the American character. However, in 1933 Adolph Hitler was democratically elected by an educated and industrious German people. In the space of a decade he brought anything but freedom and prosperity to his people. Today, democracy is not equal to the task of preventing dictatorial rule in Haiti or Venezuela where the democratically elected leader simply tore up the old constitution and wrote a new one to his own liking. On the other hand, several East Asian countries, especially Singapore under Lee Kuan Yew, have made excellent economic and limited social progress over the past few decades without the benefit of true democratic elections. And now we must add China to the growing list of "Asian Tigers."

It is only rational to conclude that democracy is neither sufficient nor necessary for achieving freedom and prosperity. Since we are interested in the results achieved under any political system based on the nature of the system itself, it is instructive to examine the nature of American democracy in some detail and the role it plays in our well being.

If you were to ask anybody you know, or even a random sample of strangers walking down the street, "What do you think we mean by democracy in America? What do you think democracy really is?", how would a cross section of American citizens respond? I am fairly certain that the most common response would be that we get to vote, even though fully one half of us who are eligible usually don't. Those who watch national news regularly might throw in freedom of speech. Some might even venture separation of church and state or trial by jury. A few might even append the idea that we are hardworking, kind, fair, and generous, as democratic attributes. And maybe this actually isn't a bad start considering most of us have not had occasion to sit in on a discussion of democracy since our brush with American History class, if then. By default, this may be an indication that our personal democratic rights have been well enough protected and/or taken for granted that many of us probably never thought to question if they had ever been denied. Or perhaps we just haven't noticed their gradual erosion over time.

Demos, or the common people, means you and me. It follows that democracy is about you and me. Democracy provides the entrée by which we can influence the game of power politics in government. If we are going to play the game of America well, we must get acquainted with the rules.

Most properly I would call our political system a democratic federal republic. It is federal because the national government recognizes the legal prerogatives of the states, but may claim its superior legal status in many areas. It is a republic because it governs for the people and is representational in form. It is democratic because as citizens we:

- enjoy universal suffrage for almost all adults (felons, D.C. residents, and territorial peoples excepted)
- elect congressional representatives
- elect our President and Vice President
- judge each other under the law by jury trial
- cannot be imprisoned without a public indictment (*habeas corpus*)
- cannot be punished without a trial (Bill of Attainder)
- have a host of very important rights and liberties in the areas of
  - ✓ religion
  - ✓ speech
  - ✓ publishing
  - ✓ assembly
  - ✓ grievance redress
  - ✓ arms possession
  - ✓ search and seizure
  - ✓ double jeopardy
  - ✓ self-incrimination
  - ✓ due process of law
  - ✓ property rights
  - ✓ eminent domain
  - ✓ speedy trials
  - ✓ legal charges
  - ✓ legal counsel
  - ✓ bail and fines
  - ✓ punishment
  - ✓ equal protection
  - ✓ and other rights not expressly prohibited

The infringement of these rights is proscribed to the government by the U.S. Constitution, the Bill Of Rights, and other amendments to the constitution. They are written and conceived of as express prohibitions on government action. It is these liberal democratic rights that keep government from tyrannizing people even if votes do not.

These democratic rights are guaranteed by a written, amendable Constitution that is the highest law of the land, against which the validity of all other laws and actions may be tested before the Supreme Court. This law applies to *all* citizens, without exception. The constitution further provides that the actions of the president and congress must be cross-confirmed by checks and balances and be in conformance with the Constitution. Shortly after the Constitution was adopted, it was established that the determination of the legitimacy of any government action would be the indisputable responsibility of the Supreme Court, a body whose members are not elected, but appointed for life.

The United States government is authorized by no civil or religious authority, but rather directly by the people, the demos. It is legitimate only by our consent and may be reconstituted at our pleasure. Not frivolously or in haste, but by constitutional protocol. Unless this provision is nothing more than a theoretical construct, it is the cornerstone right, the true and ultimate essence of all democratic rights in America.

Our Constitution honors a unique democratic principle expressed in the Declaration of Independence and confirmed in Lincoln's two-minute address at Gettysburg: a nation "...of, by and for the people...."

These elements transcend the classical concept of direct democracy which refers to a system wherein the demos are eligible to vote as equals, make *all* law, and decide legal liability. Our modern, Westernized version of democracy, is a "liberal democracy" that scholars refer to as "constitutional liberalism," a broad category embracing those rights not expressly concerned with elections or law making. Even so, our Westernized system of democracy does not guarantee prosperity, only specific democratic rights. Democratic systems which grant only the right to vote (as in the old Soviet regime, prewar Germany, and Iraq) are termed "illiberal democracies" and have proved to be dangerous without a supporting package of public rights.

Liberty is espoused in the U.S. Constitution. The Ninth Amendment states that, "The enumeration in the Constitution of certain rights shall not be construed to deny or disparage others retained by the people." The Tenth Amendment states that, "The powers not delegated to the United States by the Constitution, nor prohibited by it to the states, are reserved to the states respectively, or to the people." These amendments in tandem can only be construed to mean the citizens of the United States are guaranteed a generous range of individual freedom of action.

The body of the Constitution provides for government to be responsible for the general welfare of its citizens and grants three fifths of a population count for each of those inhabitants not free, toward state representation in the House of Representatives. The Thirteenth Amendment abolished slavery and the Fifteenth granted voting rights to former slaves. The Eighteenth prohibited commerce in alcoholic beverages but was repealed by the Twenty-First. The Sixteenth established the income tax. Here, it is worth noting that the income tax amendment is the only amendment still standing that in any way expressly restricts the freedom of us United States citizens. The U.S. Constitution would be ill used if minority special interests were to appropriate it for the purpose of restricting our freedom to burn the flag, marry any other unattached adult, or seek an abortion.

Knowing what American democracy is, is different, however, from knowing what it means, what it stands for, or how it bears on our lives. Some may see it as our guarantee of freedom or as our protection against government intrusion into our lives. But these things it is not. Greece and Rome once were democracies, as was the USSR. Haiti and Venezuela are, but you wouldn't know it if you went there looking for much individual freedom or a user friendly government. Where there are no guaranteed individual rights, the fruits of democracy just wither and rot without harvest, as they are doing in South America. Neither democratic voting rights nor a written constitution are strong enough by themselves to hold tyranny at bay. Something more than democracy is required to insure freedom.

Irving Kristol (1972) wrote, "For a system of liberal, representative government to work, free elections are not enough. The results of the political process and of the exercise of individual freedom–the distribution of power, privilege, and property–must also be seen as in some profound sense expressive of the values that govern the lives of individuals." Democracy is nothing more than a useful tool for securing our constitutional guarantees of individual freedom, not a guarantee of it, per se. At the end of the day, both democracy and freedom perish if not nourished by leaders with integrity and a firm sense of moral values. The very idea of justice is not rooted in law, but in the interpretation and application of these moral values. Nevertheless, if properly structured, a liberal democracy is the only political scheme by which people may legally express their interests and seek to protect themselves against bad government.

Freedom vs. special interests

While most of us place a lofty value on freedom and recognize that limits are necessary in the general interest, we may differ as to where these limits should be fixed. The interests of any subset of society may even prevail at times over those endorsed by the majority. Furthermore, many of us would like to transcend the idea of equality altogether in order to "get an edge," to become just a little more equal than everyone else. Some people would just like to avoid the consequences of their own actions. To these ends, special interest groups lobby elected officials and rule-making authorities, using everything from the promise of votes to outright bribes. When successful, someone wins and the rest of us may lose. In this manner are the freedoms of all of us degraded.

Elected and appointed officials are not lavishly compensated for their services (outside of congressional pension plans) although they can subsequently make up for this in private life, based on contacts made while in government service. Their driving interest is power. Business leaders and wealthy asset holders are interested in money, the flow of which is heavily dependent on government action. Our system of campaign financing services these interests seamlessly. For every concession gained by industry, there are millions of small losers. A dollar here, a million there, and pretty soon it all adds up.

There is no way to accurately and completely quantify the net cost to the public of the targeted legislation crafted by congress each year. There is no way to assess the degree to which our individual freedom is unnecessarily infringed upon to another's advantage. There is no way to ascertain the drag on our national prosperity resulting from government micromanagement of business operations. There is no way to reckon the loss experienced, both in terms of national strength and human capital, because we neglect to invest our social capital compassionately in the least of us. But we do have some indicators.

These losses are reflected in our $7.4 trillion national debt. By the $400 billion not paid by industry because they are pardoned from paying two thirds of their 35 percent income tax rate. By the multibillion dollar deficits incurred annually by pushing costs into the future. By the $37.2 trillion long term, unfunded, off-the-books liability for social and medical services promised, for which there is no source of funds except the future productive power of our children. Perhaps the most reasonable educated guess of the total productive waste in our economy was made by Peter Peterson who estimated this to be around one trillion dollars annually, or about 10% of our GDP. For this much inefficiency we know the proximate causes, in a general way at least, and we can partially quantify the effect in dollar terms. However, it is more difficult to reckon the social losses accruing from a declining trust in government and a flagging loss of spirit in us citizens. It is not possible to translate these numbers into an assessment of the state of individual freedom in America.

Our first inclination always is to cast a resentful eye on government for over-regulating our lives or allowing these transgressions to occur. But we must dig a little deeper to uncover and examine the root cause of unnecessary regulation of our American society. For the true culprit behind much of our frustration is the ever-present special interest group. Every piece of major legislation initiated in the interest of the general public is used as a Christmas tree upon which a host of special interest ornaments are hung.

Licensure laws passed to protect the public often become the vehicle whereby trade groups are immunized from competition. Do teacher certification and tenure practices serve this purpose?

The very openness of a democratic society, where the process of legislative planning or even agency rule-making can be monitored as it takes place, invites interested parties to dog the process of legislative development every step of the way. Inevitably their interests are reflected in the final bill or regulation because politicians must listen to the voice of energized minority interests or risk the loss of financial backing required to reach the voters. This is where the rubber meets the road, unless, of course, the legislation has in fact already been drafted by the lobbying group. The public, which is little affected by or even aware of pending new legislation, is left to deal with an endless parade of new regulations, including their cost (direct or indirect) that it meets at every turn.

Lobbying groups such as the Zionists, the Cubans-in-exile, the NRA, AARP, and PhRMA (Pharmaceutical Research and Manufacturers of America) have influence beyond their numbers because they have money to distribute, are vocal and energetic, and/ or have a following that can swing a lot of votes. Business and labor unions, too, have the money to secure favorable legislative or regulatory treatment, if not out and out subsidies. Money spent in the political arena often yields a better return than a direct business investment per se.

An important virtue of our democracy is the protection of minority views both out of respect for other opinions and as a means of preventing the emergence of tyranny in government (Madison). But the risk we face more and more is not that of snuffing out the voice of the minority. It is the tyranny of many minorities using the power of the state, each for its own narrow benefit. The end result is that our government is increasingly no longer able to effectively serve the best interests of its individual citizens collectively. Government becomes progressively less the property of its owners and more the tool of all manner of deep-pocketed, vocal, NGOs (non-government organizations), each with its own axe to grind. Government by special interest group is not the same thing as government of, by, and for the people.

There is no single focus group that might serve as a devil's advocate representing the general public interest on a case by case basis, although the ACLU (American Civil Liberties Union) attempts to fill this need within its area of interest. Outside of the ballot box, we may voice our democratic interests to the president, however; he can't hear us since we speak with so many voices simultaneously. Besides, his capacity to command change is limited to a handful of major issues and an occasional veto or a cluster of eleventh hour pardons upon leaving office. There are conceivably three avenues of approach to combating the problem of government by special interest group. One is to separate politicians from the source of money required to finance their elections. Another is to isolate special interest groups from the working process of legislative development as this is the point at which lobbyists have their most telling influence. Yet another is to do a better job educating the American public about the workings of our democratic system that they may better represent their collective interests to their elected officials. All three approaches working together would succeed best.

However, one word of caution is in order here concerning majority democratic rule and the referendum process. The Greeks proved that direct democracy was incapable of sustaining harmonious social order over the long term. Self-approved welfare programs voted in by the masses serve only to drain the resources of the state without providing for its long-term financial nourishment. The fact is, you may not expect the general citizenry to have the specialized knowledge or the spare time required to design and maintain an economic machine capable of delivering a sustaining prosperity far into the future.

Our own state of California is a case in point. Californians have crafted a political system best described as government-by-referendum. This attempt to wrest control from the state politicians has left the pols with barely 15 percent of the state budget at their disposal in the face of a huge $35 billion debt to pay off as of 2005. The referenda they have approved have been costly to craft and launch, and are clearly not always in the best interests of all citizens. Worse yet, they only approximate the original intent of the voters. They are created and staged by specialists, special interest groups in their own right, who have the opportunity to bend citizen intent to legislation of their own design, offering no compromise, only an up or down vote for passage. There were 16 such referenda on the 2004 California general election ballot.

Too much democracy?

In his book, *The Future of Freedom,* Fareed Zakaria made the case that democracy, in fact, is the vehicle by which many of our inherited freedoms have been attenuated and our culture debased. In his view, government is the problem only insofar as democracy has been the pathway by which special interest groups and the marketization of our economy and culture are undermining the American Dream and destroying our greatness. If freedom is in many ways restricted by government, it is largely because government increasingly has become the instrument of special interests.

Zakaria's thesis has opened up a debate that can only shed light on the role democracy plays in the technological age of this modern world. He also suggests that the operational control of certain of our complex government institutions should be directed by elites with appropriate background and training, and be removed one step from the direct control of elected politicians. This would free legislators from the continuous meddling of special interest groups, following the example of the autonomous operation of the Federal Reserve, the military, and the Supreme Court. This approach to isolating congress from special interest group influence would result in legislation better representative of the needs of the nation as a whole.

In fact, a loose approximation of this organizational approach is already in widespread use for many areas requiring government regulation; for agencies such as the FTC (Federal Trade Commission), the FCC (Federal Communications Commission), the FDA (Food and Drug Administration), and the FEC (Federal Elections Commission). While this agency approach is necessary in a complex society, you cannot decouple regulation from politics altogether without creating a series of autonomous mini governments. There are other ways we can promote the relative independence of regulatory control from political meddling; by moderating the incentive, for instance.

Zakaria also describes how much of American life has been democratized by market forces, by concepts of fairness, and by the misapplication of equal opportunity guidelines. Private organizations have been pushed by antidiscrimination laws to open their membership roles and shed their exclusivity. Civil rights legislation drove business and academia to affirmative action and quota systems.

Television programming needs the revenue produced by advertising to survive. Until the advent of cable TV, the national TV news was limited to a half hour per night on three networks and one public channel. Cable brings you 24/7 coverage on several different channels. While there is more time to develop the background of and explain the news, the intense competition for viewership drives programming to cater to the mass audience, necessitating a mixture of sound bite news and entertainment geared to a low common denominator, such as the sitcom or some demeaning survival show.

Our zeal for democratic rights culminated in the 1978 Supreme Court decision in the *Regents of the University of California v. Bakke*, declaring that applying the principle of diversity to school enrollment was justified; in fact it needed no justification. Thus were meritocracy and means testing set aside in favor of the indefinite standards of the time and place. This admission criterion would not even be an issue if our public schools were able to provide an equal opportunity education for all. It is always easier to paper over the symptoms than to confront a cause directly.

Over 2,000 years ago the philosopher Plato, made some negative observations about Athenian democracy. It has been suggested that were he alive today he might conclude that the weaknesses of *our* democratic system were that politicians would run on their personality, appeal to emotion, spend your money carelessly, not ask for sacrifice, and put image over substance. He might say that putting image over substance would pave the way for the "sophists" who would twist rhetoric to their own deceitful ends. Today we call these people public relations specialists, lobbyists, spin doctors, political apologists, advertising agents, and "527 group" advocates. Putting image over substance would inevitably lead to failure of any government for inattention to basic problems. Don't we see this process at work every day, often served up with murder trials and sex crimes in lieu of hard news? If these comments bear any relevance to the American condition, it would be well to consider if they are the product of democracy per se or some failing in our basic character.

Look back at the 2004 election campaign. Candidates were altering course almost daily depending on the results of the latest poll. They hastened to put popular new programs, such as for Medicare prescription drug benefits, into effect. We were hung up on the difference between one candidate's campaign ribbons and his war medals, and both candidate's service records. Even the serious issues such as jobs, taxes, war, and the cost of living were addressed only in terms of last month's statistics and yesterday's polls.

It was not until after the election that President Bush claimed he had a "mandate" and would use his "extensive" political capital in an effort to partially privatize social security and simplify the income tax code. Perhaps this scenario says as much about the level of interest of us citizens as it does about a politician's tactics. If our 21st century Plato offered some valid criticisms, he would have missed one important weakness in our contemporary democratic practice. He did not see how politicians would line up to sell our unalienable birthright to well-heeled special interests for a few pieces of silver and another term in office.

The spirit of democracy has permeated all levels of society and culture, gradually eroding the unfettered authority of government to direct the American show without undue influence from special interest groups. Democracy is not by itself a guarantee of prosperity, individual freedom, equal opportunity, or human dignity. It is only a set of political tools by which the public interest can be expressed. To function in the long term interest of all Americans, it must be tailored wisely and used responsibly by each of us if we are to honor our political heritage and earn its potential blessings throughout the 21st century. Else it can devour us in the end.

Although democratic prerogatives do not guarantee individual freedom, they are the only legally recognized standard protocol by which people can secure it. Nondemocratic societies stand in danger of the most powerful interest quashing all competing interests. In history this has usually been the case when the ruling party is sustained solely by police power, religion, economic might, or government-instigated social turmoil. Christianity sponsored only religious art and no science until the Renaissance. Communism endorsed no religious dogma or private economic power, only post office art, the Gulag, and fake five year plans. It distorted the application of science, except in space and military programs, as these were meant to glorify and enlarge state power. It revoked the Law of Supply and Demand. Politics, religion, science, commerce, and art all have critically important roles to play in a progressive, modern society. Only democracy, nourished by responsible citizens and leaders, can assimilate all of these important social functions without distortion or omission.

The full value of democracy can only be realized when its power is understood and exercised responsibly. It is a set of tools that must be kept in good working order for the purpose of protecting freedom, but alone can not guarantee freedom. Its one operating virtue is that we may remove political leaders from office periodically if they are found wanting. This democratic prerogative makes it the first line of defense against tyranny. And in America the changing of the guard has always been peaceful.

Having defined democracy in narrow, technical terms, and explained it in its liberal sense as fortified by democratic rights, we have still not fully described its power and vitality as it might be operating today in America. This can only be done by assessing the degree of open debate by the public on issues of substance, and the extent to which government conduct may be challenged under freedom of expression. Nevertheless, the full realization of our democratic potential is possible only if we exercise our freedom thoughtfully in the interest of others.

Responsibility

Democracy holds the promise that when responsibly exercised, it can enhance individual freedom and maximize personal opportunity, dignity, and prosperity. The operative word here is *responsibly*. If democracy is the first line of defense against tyranny, responsibility is the last line of defense. The essence of success for a free democratic society is the collective sum of personal responsibility exhibited by its members.

Robert Storey wrote, "Freedom and Responsibility are inseparable. Personal freedom cannot be maintained without protection. Freedom is not free. Many citizens conscientiously believe that freedom is automatic under a democracy." Medgar Evers, the courageous civil rights organizer repeated the phrase, "Freedom is not free," to his wife Myrlie in Mississippi just five days before being shot to death in 1963. Forty-one years after the fact, on June 22, 2005, Ray Killen, on trial for a second time for the murder of Evers, was convicted of manslaughter, at the age of 80 years. The wheels of justice can grind exceedingly slow.

John Lukacs pointed out that the path of freedom is not an easy one. Negotiating this path requires a knowledge of self and a sense of responsibility required to impose and observe boundaries to one's own actions. Only when we nourish our culture, our political system, and our relationships with personal responsibility can we secure the full blessings of freedom. In this manner, the very idea of voluntarily restricting our own freedom of action helps preserve democracy and the very freedoms it is designed to protect.

The enemies of freedom are ignorance, greed, fear, lust for power, and a narcissistic concern for personal individual security. These drives are anticompetitive, in opposition to equal opportunity, and serve to sap the vitality of group effort. They are no strangers to a capitalistic society where inequality of wealth and status are the norm—the differentiated result of unequal talent, training, ambition, or connections. If the promise of equality of freedom for all is to be fulfilled, these drives must be subject to some limits, the breach of which would be irresponsible. Without a high degree of responsible behavior on the part of citizens and leaders, freedom suffers as one person's special advantage translates into everyone else's general liability.

We treasure freedom because history shows that, in its absence, authoritative control can lead to neglect of the people's well-being, their servitude, and even a callus disregard for life itself. Whenever societies have existed for long under dictatorial rule, its members usually live with little or no hope of material improvement, if not in misery and squalor. An important present day exception to this rule is China, a nation in transition.

Ever since the turbulent '60s, elements of American society have been seeking special entitlements and greater protective security. In his 1961 inaugural speech John F. Kennedy electrified youthful voters when he challenged them by saying, "Ask not what your country can do for you, but what you can do for your country." Then he gave us a mission: land a man on the moon by the end of the decade. We did. Now we are once again asking what our country can do for us. The chorus of demands for targeted entitlements is met by sympathetic politicians who dare not appeal for our vote without a bag of goodies to bribe us with.

It is sad but true that people in our great country are increasingly turning to the state to protect them from the consequences of their own actions. In 2003, Marcy Noriega, a Madera, California, police officer sought to subdue a bound prisoner with her stun gun, but retrieved and fired her service sidearm instead, killing her captive. The city sued the Taser corporation for any financial award that might arise from a wrongful death suit filed by the victim's family, charging the officer was not at fault because the mistake could easily have been made by any trained officer. When Nita Byrd was rushed to the emergency room following a failed minor medical procedure in 2002, her three daughters claimed this action produced "negligent infliction of emotional distress" on *them,* and sued the doctor and the hospital The case went all the way to the California Supreme Court before it was finally dismissed. Mary Ubaudi of Madison County, Illinois, was in a car wreck and sued Mazda Motors for "in excess of $150,000," claiming it "failed to provide instructions regarding the safe and proper use of a seatbelt" (Cassingham). The Federated Church of Chagrin Falls, Ohio, is being sued for sexual abuse by two men who had only ever attended a "sister church," because the named church had provided financial assistance to their church where the alleged molestations had occurred.

It is not uncommon for a parent to blame the school because Johnny can't read, after having sent Johnny to school hungry, unprepared, unkempt, and untrained in even the most basic social skills. The precedent for this attitude was set a generation ago when the California school system was successfully sued for passing a student along through graduation, even though he was unable to read.

Such are not the actions of people who take personal responsibility. They are the attempt to invoke a claim of victimhood, using the courts to transfer personal responsibility to some other person or group. In the end we all pay to protect the irresponsible few, thereby progressively losing our margin of freedom made possible by efficient and responsible, social and economic activity.

At the bottom of many claims is the rationale of unfairness, or a sensitivity to inferred prejudice. After encouraging passengers to be seated by saying, "Eeenie, meenie, minie, moe, pick a seat, we gotta go," a Southwest Airlines flight attendant was sued by two black passengers (Jacoby). She won, but lost her job, her reputation, and $30,000. While the constitution protects free speech, the law can exact a heavy toll for its defense.

We exercise our freedom when we make choices. Exercising our freedom brings consequences. When we accept these consequences we take responsibility for them. If we expect another person to protect us from the consequences of our own freely determined actions, we are not acting responsibly, we are behaving dependently. We are exhibiting the behavior common to children who are not psychologically strong enough or morally mature enough to undertake responsible, independent action. When we expect the state to protect us from our actions, we are just shifting responsibility, anticipating the state will provide security. This outcome for some can be arranged by the state only if the freedom of others is abridged.

The little guy is now doing to business what business itself has long been doing to government. He is suing for security by shifting responsibility for performance and outcome to both government and business as well. Over the past 25 years, the passion to acknowledge the interests of specialized groups of little guys has marched under the banner of political correctness. If mainstream society has sometimes been negligent in democratizing the promise of equal protection under the law, political correctness has responded by focusing attention on the assumed "rights" of all manner of special interest groups, at times to the injury of the majority.

Government plays the pivotal role in setting standards for responsible behavior, through its legislative actions and by the example set by our elected officials. The principal threat to individual freedom arises from the actions or inactions of government. A long term interest of any stable government is that of controlling its subjects for the purpose of maintaining social tranquility and harmony. This interest may be in opposition to many of its citizens' desire for unequal advantage or protection. The government's negotiating gambit to all is the promise of security. Government will offer it in return for control. People may take this offer, but as Benjamin Franklin warned, "Any society that would give up a little liberty to gain a little security will deserve neither and lose both."

Business and industry will use any legal means available to make a profit. That is their only mission in life, and they are good at it. In the process they generate the wealth and prosperity that most of us share. In this process they may also infringe on the freedom of individuals, if permitted even indirectly by law. Protecting individual rights is, or should be, a cardinal responsibility of government. However, this responsibility has been compromised by both small and large special interest influence. Nonprofit NGOs lobby government for support of their unique interests, some with millions to attract Washington's interest. In addition to the little guys, the corporate big guys are in the game with many millions to spend, with the objective of procuring some "unfair" business advantage.

The exercise of responsible leadership in both government and industry is of critical importance. It requires a sense of responsibility even beyond that required of us followers. It would be irresponsible for an elected official to disregard the well being of his constituents or his country in the interest of personal gain. But some do. All formal leadership positions in society carry with them the implied expectation that the office will be exercised responsibly, consistent with applicable social standards at a minimum. When leaders fail this responsibility, followers may follow suit. Lack of confidence in leadership erodes the will of us, the followers, to strive and honor our social expectations. Clearly, this is where personal integrity shows, either by its presence or its absence.

You would hope the leadership positions in society would be filled by our best and brightest, but leadership's resolve to act in our best interests has been weakened by the onslaught of special interest democracy. Some CEOs of public companies find ways to enrich themselves at the expense of us, the owners, putting personal gain ahead of managerial excellence. Even directors of some tax-exempt, charitable organizations promote good deeds with one hand as the other hand is reaching into the till. The priesthood reserves to itself sexual favors practiced only by child molesters. Lawyers attack the deep pockets in class action suits with as much as a 40 percent interest in the outcome. Not all leaders game the system for personal privilege and benefit, but enough do and set a disturbing example in the process. These behaviors signify a widespread decay of moral values, a social phenomenon that portends growing problems for America.

The greater the state guarantee of security that is associated with managing outcomes, the less incentive people have to strive for improvement. In an extreme welfare state there is no incremental economic reward available for risk taking or tackling difficult tasks. Freedom under Soviet Communism was pretty much limited to relations with extended family, tending a personal garden, and a vodka or three after dinner. The system survived by illegal, but widespread, dealing on the black market, the surest sign of national unfreedom. Economic decline as experienced under Communism is the inevitable terminal condition for an extreme welfare state.

Without the economic rewards available in a free marketplace, political stability may be in jeopardy unless there is an external source of wealth, such as a positive cash flow from captive, client states. But "free" money makes for inflation and destroys incentive, as tribute did in Rome, as new world silver and gold did in Spain, and as oil revenues are doing in Saudi Arabia and Kuwait. It follows that you cannot fully realize personal freedom without economic incentive. As Adam Smith taught us, you cannot maximize the value of your labors without economic freedom. This is the great social discovery of the last 229 years. And you cannot sustain economic freedom without responsible leaders and citizens.

While the law very often reflects the moral values of society and may be necessary as a means for protecting our rights, sound moral judgment is the true basis of responsible action. Morality calls on us to see others as humans; law commands us to treat them as objects. Furthermore, developing a sense of responsibility requires mature reflection on one's personal experience. It requires good judgment and even integrity.

Less dramatically, we rely upon individual virtue and our moral sense to nourish personal responsibility in everyday living. Society ultimately breaks down if individuals and groups are granted special status and seek to shift responsibility, and its leaders do not act in conformance with high standards of morality. Morality provides the standard against which the responsibility of our actions is measured (Trueblood).

Relaxation of standards of responsibility has contributed to the excessive democratization of the culture, often accompanied by undesirable side effects. Democratization has opened the door for special interest security claims to receive a favorable hearing from permissive leadership. It has undermined the role of leaders in standing up for the interests of all citizens. It has impeded the progress of business and raised its costs. It has worked to dumb down our school textbooks and expectations for student performance. It has distracted attention from interest in ideas, events, and accomplishments of great social significance. It has worked to promote political bias in journalism in a competitive effort to gain audience share. The news has become politicized, editorialized, and made to be entertaining at the expense of informing and explaining. Irresponsible legislation has created a needlessly convoluted tax code costing billions of dollars to administer and presenting a maze of obstacles to negotiate when considering the many economic decisions to be made in life. It has eroded trust and confidence in government resulting from over regulation. It has spawned an army of litigators searching the statutes for a chink in the legal armor just wide enough to drive a lawsuit through. Negligent legislation has provided a ready excuse for many citizens to abandon the hard road of responsibility for the easy path of victimhood.

The notion of responsibility requires the acceptance of a social obligation to the group, to respect equality of opportunity even while allowing for inequality of outcome under capitalism. Do our moral values or the structure of our institutions need improvement? Or do both require attention? Is it technology, or just the act of hubris in substituting prosperity for morality, decency, and freedom, which has nudged us off the course originally laid out by our founders?

If responsible conduct is a necessary condition for the preservation of freedom, Amartya Sen pointed out that the reverse is also true; that is, there can be no exercise in personal responsibility without the freedom to make decisions in the first place. He has shown also that economic prosperity is the primary foundation of freedom and social democratic action. It follows that in a free, democratic society populated by informed citizens, the only threat that can undermine freedom and prosperity arises from irresponsible behavior on the part of its citizens; behavior that might even be endorsed by government. Under a true liberal democracy featuring free expression, if public debate is informed and criticism of government is constructive, then freedom and prosperity will not be denied.

Freedom and responsibility are symbiotic, that is to say, they are interdependent and mutually reinforcing. They are indispensable to a flourishing society. They are the key to making our handmaiden, democracy, work effectively on our behalf.

If ignorance, greed, power, and extreme security demands are the enemies of freedom, how may we cultivate responsible behavior as an antidote to their corrosive influence? Thomas Jefferson is believed to have said, "Eternal vigilance is the price of liberty," meaning you have it only insofar as you are able and willing to defend it. Following Jefferson's caution, we should also understand that it is necessary for the state to deploy sufficient force to subdue that small percentage of antisocial miscreants who stand to undermine our freedoms. This was the lesson demonstrated by the successful effort to revitalize the mixed income, East Lake, housing project in Atlanta, Georgia, known as "Little Vietnam" prior to the elimination of all felons and drug dealers from the community (Grillo). Excising the tiny minority of bad guys from that besieged community and requiring that all of its residents either have a job or be in school, proved to be the key to bringing forth the virtuous behavior residing in the vast majority of all people.

Employing personal responsibility as the last line of defense, Thoreau attacked the issue of presumed unjust state power 150 years ago, and King acted on the same principle in the 1960s when he inspired his followers to stand up, march, go to jail, and even suffer physical violence in a quest for freedom denied by unequal treatment.

To this end, it is essential we ensure that all members of society recognize the importance of responsible action in everyday life. This can only be accomplished through training in the home, reinforced by the practices of an education system geared to good citizenship throughout one's formative years. Responsible behavior must be incorporated into the moral infrastructure of society. This can be accomplished only if leadership shows the way by setting a good example.

The keys to having and holding freedom are a liberal democracy and responsible citizens. When this freedom is exercised in the marketplace, it produces prosperity. When Alexis de Tocqueville visited this still new United States in the 1830s, he asked himself this question: Why does this novel system of democracy even work? His answer was that these Americans had learned how to work together. Taking his conclusion one step further, we might speculate that already over just two generations, these new-world Europeans had found that freedom under democracy was paying off better than any system under which they had previously labored. They were putting the Golden Rule into practice.

However, this prosperity born of freedom does distribute itself unequally throughout society. The democratic promise of equal opportunity and a full measure of dignity has, so far in American history, been only imperfectly realized.

In 1994, after 27 years in prison and four more of continuous negotiation, Nelson Mandela was democratically elected as the president of a multicultural South Africa, a country reborn in freedom. Reflecting for a moment on this unparalleled achievement in political history, he said, "But I can rest for only a moment, for with freedom comes responsibilities, and I dare not linger, for my long walk [to freedom] is not yet ended."

American freedom is our heritage. It would be a tragedy to let it slip away in the pursuit of personal interest or for lack of any interest at all.

The 4th: Georgia. January 2, 1788

CHAPTER 5

OPPORTUNITY AND DIGNITY

A morally healthy society should value freedom, provide for equal opportunity, and honor everyone. While we have good reason to be proud of the benefits made possible by our free enterprise system, the social needs of as many as 10 percent (my estimate) of us go unmet in part for want of financial resources. Although many of the needy may be needy by choice, attitude, or sheer indolence, most do about the best they can in a competitive society. For society to turn its back on the least of us is to deny the role of both genetic and environmental factors in determining the human condition. Samuel Johnson wrote in the 1700s that, "A decent provision for the poor is the true test of civilization." A low score in this area by a rich society suggests that other human values may not be held in high regard either. Neglect of the poor is a moral failing exposing a selfish character, one that is bound to be found in other facets of life as well.

The U.S. Constitution was framed with the intent of establishing justice and promoting the general welfare. Nowhere do our founding documents say explicitly that we should expect the state to assume responsibility for equal opportunity or even human dignity, but certainly they were designed such that, and very strongly imply that, we might realize both. The idea of equal opportunity as one blessing of freedom was implicit, but not available to slaves, women, and the landless. Jefferson's ideal of equality was a lofty goal, not a practice of the day. For 90 percent of white American males, equal opportunity started as field work, on-the-job training, starting at age 14 or so. From there a man was free to progress socially or economically as far as talent and ambition might permit. For women it meant full time domestic service. As for slaves...well, you know that sad story.

By 1965 the franchise had been expanded to virtually all adult citizens, and we could say for the first time that we had achieved social as well as political equality. This promise, implied in the Declaration of Independence, became the explicit law of the land. We had realized the equality of access to take part in the social and economic segments of modern American life, but not always the means.

We live in a different world today. There is no equivalent of field labor for a boy of 14. That would be prohibited child labor. Anymore, you can not hope to make financial and social progress without the bare essentials of a high school education. Even entry level work today requires being equipped with the fundamentals necessary to interact with sophisticated machines and information systems. It means working interactively in highly organized group environments where your role is often well-defined and must be fulfilled on schedule. Very importantly it requires you to be willing and able to manage your personal behavior in the interest of group effectiveness. Without these attributes a young kid today has little hope of doing more than scraping along the bottom of the economic food chain, foraging for scraps of prosperity.

You are barred from most knowledge-based employment by your lack of intellectual capital. Equipping a person to become competitive and productive in today's workaday society constitutes a minimum starting point from which he may qualify with any true equal opportunity. While this point is attainable by virtually all, the public school system is unable to confer a quality learning experience in many inner city school districts. Aspiring to college or for knowledge-based work without a sound academic foundation is like going swimming without your swimming trunks. You will be noticed when the tide goes out.

The downside of a free capitalistic system is the frustration of those who cannot compete successfully. They do not want to be viewed as the recipients of handouts. They must have appropriate work that they can accomplish for the sake of self-respect (Hoffer).

Clearly, equal opportunity to learn was recognized by the individual states when they made education compulsory, with public funding, through age 16. It was recognized officially by the federal government in 1964-5 when anti-discrimination civil rights and Medicare/Medicaid legislation was passed. Human dignity was mandated when we were required to contribute to social security in 1935 and financially augmented when the federal government made welfare subsidies broadly available with the establishment of the Administration for Children and Families.

If we want to understand where America falls short of its founding promises, however, we must come to terms with the social realities of the 21st century. Our public education is good only in those prosperous school districts where parents prepare their kids for learning and insist on teacher performance. Our medical delivery system services 15 percent of our citizens only in the breech, and costs between 30 percent and 70 percent too much by any international standard. Despite growing American prosperity, giveaway welfare programs often serve largely only to institutionalize poverty.

The shortcomings of our education, medical, and welfare programs are interdependent. These systems are all directly or indirectly managed by the government without sufficient attention to efficiency or results, at least until the TANF (Temporary Aid to Needy Families) bill was passed. Otherwise these programs are or should be an embarrassment to a rich and powerful nation. They fall short of embracing a full measure of equal opportunity or human dignity. However, they can be overhauled and made to work much better. A democratic recipe is man's best social invention for achieving a healthy society. But responsible leaders and citizens are the indispensable ingredients that make the bread rise.

The major government program designed to ensure the preservation of human dignity in old age is Social Security. This safety net was designed to provide for one's minimum needs when the need for resource outstrips one's ability to generate it. While this program is very effective, it is destined to fall short of meeting its promises during your children's lifetime. For all other human needs there are well over a hundred individual, overlapping programs available at every level of government, each designed to respond to a different problem. Eligibility for any of the numerous programs, each with specific requirements and benefits, is most difficult to determine, especially by those in need. Being so numerous and scattered about, they can be somewhat inefficient with a disproportionate share of their funding going to administrative expenses.

Most local programs are funded by federal grants passed through state hands, down to county agencies. Some funds are derived from local referenda. These efforts tend to be the most effective because they can be tailored to local needs. Federally funded programs tend to be less than perfect, especially since accountability for the expenditure of federal funds is not to the community but to the government in the form of paperwork. Adequate funding at the case worker level is always tight and administrative costs can siphon off much of the money available.

President Johnson initiated his War on Poverty as one means to realizing the Great Society in the mid 1960s. Until then poverty had been spread fairly evenly across the country and had been decreasing steadily over the previous 25 years. It was officially designated at 11 percent by the early '70s and has stabilized in the vicinity of 12 percent as of 2003, with little or no apparent effect from the TANF welfare reform act of 1996 (U.S. Census Bureau, census.gov). In 1955 the government spent $621 million on AFDC (Aid to Families With Dependent Children) payments. By 1987 this amount had increased to over $16 billion. Women on AFDC had only three requirements: have babies, don't earn more than a minimal wage, and don't get married. Overall welfare spending was originally undertaken by the federal government to help the poor. The Census Bureau reports that a scant 12 percent of the $1.2 trillion annually spent for benefits goes to those families below the poverty line. There are benefits for everyone now.

At the same time that program costs were ballooning, poverty was becoming more concentrated in pockets in the South, Appalachia, and the inner cities (A. Weiss). Fathers disappeared from the family scene and illegitimate births skyrocketed. Two thirds of all black families are fatherless and 40 percent of our jail population is black (Parker). "…Daniel Patrick Moynihan told us at the outset of the War on Poverty: that no amount of government money and good intentions can make up for an absent dad, drug use, lack of education and the like" (*WSJ*, December 30, 1999). As G. Gordon Liddy was fond of saying, "What you subsidize, you get more of."

In any discussion of poverty as measured by income level, it is well to remember that a fair proportion of people assigned to this social category are there only temporarily. A temporary loss of employment and income can land you there for census purposes and many people do escape each year as others take their place. Some even own their own homes (Stein). Some people classified as poverty stricken just need a temporary hand to get started again while others need extensive reconditioning. Among those are the 93 percent of single mothers who didn't finish high school.

The 1996 TANF program did put the brakes on AFDC spending. This welfare-to-work program reduced costs to $17.6 billion (in 2004 inflated dollars), slashed the case load by 54 percent in 2002 and put 75 percent of TANF recipients to work during their first year off welfare (US Dept. HHS, firstgov.gov). These results, realized in a stubborn social sector, must be attributed in part to the robust employment levels of the late 1990s, of course. As in much of life, timing is everything. Reduced welfare costs notwithstanding, this program did not make a dent in the poverty level which still hovers around 12 percent in 2004–only in its cost.

Efforts at the federal level have had some distinctly counterproductive effects. Federal housing has been a bonanza for investors holding tax exempt bonds without risk, while the tenants are ghettoized in separate large buildings infested with drug dealers and in the process of being trashed. Chicago's infamous Cabrini Green housing project was built to the sky for economy, but only succeeded in isolating tenants from social interaction in the streets (Sennett). The welfare reform legislation of 1996 did encourage many welfare mothers to find employment at $7 or $8 per hour. But much more effort is required to teach people how to get *and* hold a job, or even just realize permanent, incremental improvements in their financial and social position.

Discussions on poverty tend to center on level of earnings, although data are available that include various welfare payments and services, including in-kind medical benefits, housing assistance, food stamps, and school lunches that come gratis. But level of income is only a part of the poverty problem. Worst of all for the chronically unemployed, welfare means you don't have to hustle or meet anyone else's schedule. It becomes a way of life. Freedom from personal responsibilities becomes a trap as recipients lose the benefits of interaction with the working world. Freedom from *having to* results in the loss of freedom arising from *not being able to.* The surest way to induce people to relinquish their freedom is to offer them financial security as an entitlement. It ends in loss of self-respect and the disdain of the tax- paying public.

In his extensive research, Sen found that, "...unemployment has many far reaching effects other than loss of income, including psychological harm, loss of work motivation, skill and self-confidence, increase in ailments and morbidity (and even mortality rates), disruption of family relations and social life, hardening of social exclusion and accentuation of racial tensions and gender asymmetries." Robert Rector found, "...prolific spending, intended to alleviate material poverty, has led to a dramatic increase in 'behavioral poverty'...a breakdown in the values and conduct that lead to the formation of healthy families, stable personalities and self-sufficiency."

In the moral interest of securing a full measure of human dignity for all citizens, I would suggest there are two cardinal principles that must be observed. First, the state must come to the immediate aid of all persons who fall into a state of despair and/or hopelessness. This would include short term financial as well as other social assistance. This is a matter of giving people hope, when hope may be the one thing they need to save them from psychological and social decay.

Second, for those unfortunates who fall below some socioeconomic index level indicating a chronic failure to thrive, an assessment of needs must be undertaken and a program worked out mutually with the clients whereby necessary assistance is supplied with the expectation of the attainment of realistic progress toward increasing self-reliance. It often must start with a simple to-do list with demonstrations (like how to brush your teeth, etc.), in order to teach method and self-discipline.

Real progress requires help with the overwhelming problems very poor people face every day in life. Effective help requires establishing a personal relationship built on trust and hands-on attention. This is a matter of inspiration and encouragement as well as material assistance. It is a question of identity, that is, striving to generate a self-image of accomplishment and progress, not relative to others, but with respect to individual development. The "comparison problem" is probably the ultimate psychological impediment to progress for those mired in poverty in a capitalistic economy. The poor are reminded of their plight every time someone waves a "We're No. 1" logo for all to see. What is needed is the Special Olympics approach to poverty where participants get a medal and recognition just for running; where they learn the value of trying their best and compare the results only with their past performance. Their efforts must be celebrated by everyone else.

A job can engender pride of accomplishment and self-worth; however, all too often, the motivation to work is not strong because the financial rewards of work may be only marginally better than welfare support, even when supplemented by an EITC (Earned Income Tax Credit) of up to $4,000 (DeParle). In chapter 7 you will see how the Wealth Tax Credit can trump this problem of marginal advantage by minimizing the current disincentives that go hand-in-hand with a loss of welfare payments.

Certainly the most impressionable welfare recipients are children, and it is to them special attention must be directed. Here, the importance of a father figure in the home can be vitally important to the psychological well being of the kids and should be strongly encouraged, except in the most adverse of cases. Real progress may depend more on providing personal guidance than on financial aid.

Realistic goals monitored by periodic accountability reviews are the only conditions under which the state should undertake a continuing program of support. A perpetual stipend promotes only dependency and loss of personal spirit. Completely unresponsive clients with no extended family support may have no recourse other than to become wards of the state. This is the case (directly or indirectly) today for 4 million Americans with developmental disabilities attributable to mental and/or physical impairment likely to continue indefinitely (US Dept. HHS, cdc.gov). Many of these unfortunates are housed not in psychiatric institutions, but in jail.

Since government is not by nature able to administer to social needs directly, dealing with biological, spiritual, emotional, and environmental needs, should be contracted out to case workers and even qualified parasocial agents who would be responsible for recommendations and results auditing. At the same time, state-provided services should in no way interfere with family or private charity efforts to nurture and encourage the needy, but rather complement them (Chatterjee).

We have had a minimum wage requirement in this country since 1938. Should we continue to have one and if so, at what level? Obviously if there were none, marginal employers would force entry level wages down to the point where the most needy could barely cover the cost of being employed. This would incur a degree of supplemental welfare cost to the state which in fact would be a subsidy to keep marginal businesses operating. On the other hand, a high minimum wage would put undue pressure on labor intensive businesses and idle the inexperienced and least capable, again incurring more need for welfare assistance. The U. S. Department of Labor estimated that a 10 percent rise in the minimum wage in 1988 would have cost between 100,000 and 200,000 jobs at the time when the minimum wage was $3.35 an hour. The answer to the minimum wage dilemma probably lies in achieving a level which would result in the lowest welfare cost. This level, by definition, would result in the least hardship for entry-level and low-wage workers. How this level might be determined would be a matter for social analysis.

For cases where gainful employment is nearly impossible to come by, there is no reason why government programs such as the depression years' WPA (Work Projects Administration) or CCC (Civilian Conservation Corp) might not be set up on a community-wide basis (Ellwood).

Human dignity can be realized through personal effort, with help and guidance from the state where needed. Public funds spent on active welfare programs to teach disadvantaged people to better care for themselves and live a life they have reason to value, would be well spent. The key is to teach people how to fish, not just to bring fish around every week. The dividends would accrue to the social vigor of the nation, the well being of our unfortunate few, and the strengthening of the bond of trust between people and their government. In the final analysis, the surest route out of poverty to human dignity is through true equal opportunity.

It is true that a significant number of Americans do not believe the state should be tasked with the responsibility of guaranteeing equal opportunity and dignity for all. Notably, Libertarians believe that the government should have no right to require that their assets be surrendered for the benefit of the poor. Meeting their needs should be left to the discretion of family and people's individual charitable inclinations. However, it is difficult to believe voluntary private support would prove to be adequate for a unified set of programs needed to attack poverty in an effective manner. The charities that attract the most funds are those identified with the most obvious needs, and the competition to pluck your heartstrings is intense. Furthermore, the nation (meaning all of us) pays the economic costs arising from loss of productivity as well as the resource required for rescue efforts for our neglected distress cases.

Capitalism and free enterprise have one very important, but narrow, objective: to accumulate wealth and put that wealth to work reproducing itself. When the top 1 percent of Americans had amassed over 55 percent of America's wealth prior to World War I, most of their fellow citizens were still humping just to make ends meet and many lived in dire poverty. However, the issue of the sanctity of private property in our free democratic society is one deserving of full and open discussion in realistic, not just theoretical, terms. This will be undertaken in the next two chapters along with several major schemes for greatly improving both our medical and education systems while maximizing our sphere of freedom.

If poverty is a sad problem in the United States, it should be noted that in 1999 the IMF (International Monetary Fund) and the World Bank announced they would work to cut the worldwide rate of poverty in half in the span of 15 years. This to be done by lending money to the 77 poorest countries (less than $1 per day income per person) at a 0.5 percent interest rate, through the Poverty Reduction and Growth Facility program (IMF, imf.org). In order to carry out this self-assumed, internationally popular mission, the IMF just erected a new $250 million office edifice in Washington DC and is calling for more resources to boost its failing program. Better quarters and more money for the poverty fighters.

Paul Wolfowitz was recently appointed president of the World Bank and will head up its international poverty reduction program. Will he be able to improve on his previous efforts to plan for peace in Iraq? Just as we were wishing lots of luck to an organization that has a track record of sociological mismanagement around the world (CorpWatch), and right after the Bank declared it was having difficulty finding funds for its poverty program, the UN announced it was taking over this task and even enlarging its objectives. A new international crusade is underway to raise funds for the IMF and World Bank in order to cover the $40 billion cost associated with a proposed debt-forgiveness program aimed at the 18 poorest countries, found mostly in Africa.

The intent of this international effort is laudable and cannot be faulted. Nevertheless, the approach of turning over big bags of money to the corrupt leadership of these failed states sounds like a feel-good exercise launched in the triumph of hope over experience. One can only hope that this program is in no way designed to atone for international inaction while genocide raged in the Congo, Darfur, and Rwanda. Extreme poverty presents a most intractable problem, especially as population and misery are increasing exponentially in the sub-Saharan regions of the African Continent.

Of course, by the measure of a dollar a day per person, the United States has virtually zero poverty. Even at 10 or 20 times that level. But poverty cannot be adequately measured or dealt with in dollar terms alone. You must appraise the social effects as well as financial circumstances, and treat them simultaneously. Poverty in America is more a state of mind than it is any lack of economic resource.

For over 200 years, hundreds of millions of Americans have had the unsurpassed good fortune to be born into or accepted by this true land of opportunity. Caring properly for and aiding the poor among us is a small price to pay for this privileged membership. The ringing answer to Cain's question, "...am I my brother's keeper?" (Genesis 4:9) is "Yes!" Full realization of equal opportunity and dignity for all Americans permits no other. We would do well, each of us, to remember, "there but for the grace of God go I."

The 5th: Connecticut. January 9, 1788

PART II

FREEDOM

What can we do with it?

CHAPTER 6

TAXATION AND SOCIAL PROGRAMS

The United States with its 300 million citizens produces almost one third of the world's goods and services, as measured by our annual GDP of $12 trillion. About 30 percent of this amount is soaked up by federal, state, and local governments for the purpose of running America's affairs. That 30 percent is our total tax bill; the portion we give back to government to protect us, defend us, and otherwise provide for our general welfare.

We all pay taxes directly or indirectly and we all know the income tax system is frustratingly complicated. Over one half of us find the process of figuring our taxes to be too taxing, so we hire a professional to do the job for us. There must be a better way–and there is.

There are three major social programs that require massive funding, eating up fully two thirds of government's tax revenues. They are health care, education, and Social Security. Our health care system is good, but far too expensive and reaches 15 percent of us only poorly through Medicaid. Our education system is spotty, ranging from excellent in affluent school districts to dysfunctional in the inner city. Our Social Security system is not financially sustainable over the long term. Any effort to improve our tax system in any basic way must take account of how these three vital institutions are managed, both in terms of social effectiveness and financial viability. In short they must be structured efficaciously to give us the most bang for the buck.

In this chapter we will consider how these three programs may be better structured and run in the public interest, and the effect any changes would have on taxation needs. Since these programs, as well as our various systems of taxation, are extremely complex, I will tell you up front where this discussion is going. In chapter 7 we will be developing a dual tax system based on a flat income tax applicable to all wage earners, and a flat wealth tax applied to virtually all assets of any value. The proceeds of the wealth tax would be available as a Wealth Tax Credit (WTC) to all citizens in the form of a debit card which may be used to augment services as they may deem appropriate in any of several social program areas.

As the first step, we will consider in this chapter how our health care, education, and Social Security systems might be improved in the interest of our country as well as each of its citizens. Along with the financial consequences, we will consider how any proposed changes might promote our freedom, opportunity, and dignity.

Education

After an exhaustive, life-long examination of world history, the Durants concluded that the most important lesson of history was that of passing along all manner of knowledge to our children. The Durants were anticipated by over two millennia by Diogenes who wrote, "The foundation of every state is the education of its youth."

The two governing factors that determine how we do civilization are belief and knowledge. Primary patterns of behavior, speech, and attitude are learned at home before much of the outside world is encountered. Social patterns and limits to free will are established most easily in developing minds that are still soaking up the nature of the world around them. Fundamental character development is well underway by age four or five, for good or for ill. Even the street smarts later acquired during "on-the-job" training prepare one for working in association with others.

Kay Hymowitz pointed out that parents must teach behavior, right and wrong, virtue and morality, before school takes over. The civilizing process has to start at home where manners, accountability, good habits, and emotional development can be nurtured in a loving (hopefully) environment. When the formal education process is superimposed on our children, their first challenge is to accommodate their home training to group learning and relations as part of that group of peers. Schools that are now tasked to develop morality and situation ethics should be working with a prepared product rather than starting from scratch or, worse yet, from a negative position. The social role of formal education should be confined mainly to reinforcing positive social behavior within the context of our best moral values.

The goal of formal, public education is to foster the acquisition of knowledge–knowledge of how the world works along with some mastery of the skills required to work with it successfully. Understanding the workings of the world, as well as mastering new technologies and skills, is in the vanguard of progress guiding us into the unknown future. Education makes possible the acquisition, dispersion, and application of new knowledge, which determines the state of our material existence. It also helps define our concept of self and the world, as well as the shape of our institutions. A proper education prepares you for successful "doing," the hands-on engagement of people and things. It also introduces you to "knowing," the discovery of the "how" and "why" of the universe.

Learning and discovering are a human passion which almost seems to be driven by some inner chemistry, sending out interconnecting axons from the billions of neurons comprising our gray matter. Given freedom of inquiry and availability of time, it was inevitable that Francis Crick and James Watson in 1953, or someone else at another time, would define the essential, structural nature of life design: DNA. A great "Ah-Ha," or "Ta-Da," in the history of science. That, like many other wonders, was and are just waiting to be discovered. Often in the past it has been impossible to forestall this process of learning and discovery, witness Copernicus, Galileo, or Columbus. For the sake of expanding our understanding of this planet as well as of the universe, they were driven to risk much. On the other hand, forcing even elementary knowledge on an unwilling mind can result in abject failure as our public school system bears witness.

Our public school system is as good in some school districts as it is miserable in others. In more affluent school districts, students through the high school level may get an education approaching the best a private school has to offer. In these neighborhoods, children arrive for their first day in class, school-ready, and get a level of instruction matching their potential. In the poor inner city, many parents have little support to offer the school, don't know what to ask for, or how to get it, frequently sending ill-prepared kids off to an exercise in futility and failure. The majority of parents want schools to train their kids well, but a critical minority of street smart youngsters can sabotage and "dis" the system that seems to have nothing to offer them. James Fallows asserts that while the one third of our youth who fail to graduate from high school on time are not prepared to function in any serious role in life, some countries realize a failure rate of only 5 percent or less.

What works best are concerned parents who prepare their infant children at home for schooling, expose them to positive role models, and show them the pathway to achievement. What works not at all is parents who pass the responsibility for discipline on to the teacher and just accept whatever program the school is able to stage. If parents had a choice, they would look for the best educational opportunity they could get for their kids. This includes the majority in poor neighborhoods, those who haven't yet given up, settled into welfare, and taken on the role of victim. A concerned parent armed with choice and financing power would get the quick attention of a school administration and teaching staff alike. It is very likely that parents and teachers would partner up to upgrade the quality of their product in a private system unencumbered by tenure rules, union interests, government requirements, and the latest fads in educational pedagogy emanating from our nation's graduate schools of education.

Failure cannot be laid at the doorstep of the schools themselves, at least not entirely. The causes are many and complex, but in the end stem from a breakdown in family relationships, personal values, parenting skills, meager resources, a broken physical infrastructure, and a sense of despair in those people swept out of the mainstream of American life. Each year both state and federal governments offer more funding support, new teaching requirements, and new criteria for the redistribution of school district taxes, busing schemes, voucher programs, and special education requirements. The teachers' unions seemingly will go along with about any new responsibility demands made on the schools as long as the funding is adequate, seniority-based pay scales advance, and the system of tenure remains intact. My own anecdotal experience is that many teachers are more concerned with the impossible responsibilities heaped upon them in the classroom than they are about level of compensation.

The ongoing tinkering with our education system seems to have little or no effect in propping up education standards. To demonstrate the interest of each new "Education President," the administration throws another billion dollars or so at the schools, then turns to more pressing matters. Now that over $50 billion in federal funding is fed into the education infrastructure each year, Washington has come to realize its stake in the process. The most recent result is "No Child Left Behind." Much of the federal money allocated to education is funneled through the states. State funding in Ohio provides 55 percent of public school costs. Consequently, the legislature and state school board in Columbus have long been deeply involved in managing Ohio's system. With the sanction of state school boards, some very counterproductive programs have been adopted.

The "math disaster" began in the 1960s with the introduction of the New Math, an approach dedicated to learning through self-discovery. Subsequently, it morphed into Whole Math, Complete Math, Chicago Math, and now the Trailblazers and other approaches. These teaching methods are based largely on the idea that a student should discover how to solve problems without any "how to" instruction, but rather by trial and error or by a detailed examination of the theoretical elements behind basic problem-solving techniques (Mathematically Correct). The ability to solve a problem successfully became subservient to the process of discovering a way to solve it, and at a premium in time spent. The age old exercise of committing the multiplication tables through 12 x 12 to rote memory was abandoned for a much lengthier and uncertain procedure. When some of these new-math-trained students eventually enrolled in calculus classes, they found it difficult simply because they were not proficient at handling numbers algebraically.

There used to be a bullet proof, if unforgiving, method for determining if a student had learned some procedure or principle in math—did he or she get the right answer? Today, you get credit for figuring out how to attack a problem by using or inventing some theoretical approach, the correct answer being of secondary importance.

Our very first learning experiences come from observing and copying. Elementary verbal English is a useful tool long before sentence diagramming and etymology are introduced. Poems may be retained for a lifetime, once memorized, and serve to convey meaning even if you never learn about iambic pentameter. For many things in life it works best to master certain truisms by rote, for they are but the basic tools that allow us to tackle and comprehend complex and sophisticated relationships.

New textbooks are introduced every few years in spite of the fact that the basics of math through the high school level haven't changed in many decades. Pythagoras found the formula equating the lengths of the sides of a right triangle about 2,500 years ago and it hasn't changed one wit since then.

The content of textbooks available to teachers in many of our public school systems is dictated by 21 state and a number of metropolitan, textbook adoption commissions. Special interest groups comprising these commissions have banned 700 specific words and a host of cultural representations from our publicly-funded textbooks. Kids would rather listen to hip-hop music than read their homework assignments because rappers use bigger and much more colorful words (Radvitch). In many new-edition textbooks you may not portray women doing kitchen work or men doing repair work on a roof. That's just the beginning of a list of politically correct no nos that have distorted the reality of life as represented in many school textbooks.

Consequently, the texts are "dumbed" down, devoid of any interesting literary character, and 50-percent graphically illustrated with pictures having little content or learning value. Books published before 1970 are hard to find in the recommended or approved literary lineup issued by many state school boards. This "administrative book burning" filters out the hard-won lessons of the past as portrayed, for example, in the stories of Antigone, Ahab, Bovary, Hamlet, Job, and Candide; or by writers such as Kafka, Tolstoy, Orwell, Dostoyevsky, Remarque, and Ellison. Rejection of this guidance from the past greatly diminishes our slate of values, making it seem as if we do not come from anywhere at all. The students in states subject to adoption-commission-control of textbook content score lowest in tests on math, reading, and other hardcore academic subjects (Wang).

This is nothing more than brain washing at the expense of education, making for an exercise in valueless learning, censored and approved by extreme moralists from both conservative and liberal camps.

Content control is a process reminiscent of Ray Bradbury's book, *Fahrenheit 451,* wherein the censorship, outlawing, and burning of books was undertaken to suppress the spread of ideas and knowledge. Several editions after it was first published, the author was infuriated to find that the publisher was now censoring *his* original work without his permission. But even if the words and meaning of real life cannot always be found in the class room, condoms are still available in the nurse's office and there is no subject or graphic representation which cannot be found in the back of many video stores or at home on the Internet. Libraries still have books with big words and politically incorrect themes. Learning and exposure to real, successful role models stirs the imagination and leads to doing and achieving. Stories of personal conflict and moral failure promote the development of a student's own sense of values. Hopefully we will yet be saved from the petty, pernicious practices of some of our state school boards, working with our own money yet. Our schools are the core institution created to disseminate knowledge and facilitate understanding. They should not be politicized. Somewhere buried in this controversy must be the First Amendment guarantee of free speech.

In 1843 Horace Mann, the father of American public education, advocated an education system loosely patterned after that existing in Prussia at the time. It was a system designed to socialize students in line with the state's interest—obedience without creative thinking (Gatto). It would seem now that the language police are interested in selling a new social program to our kids by shielding them from any controversial words or ideas. One result is that state universities and community colleges are forced to require remedial reading (and arithmetic) courses for more entering freshmen. The politically correct special interests have hijacked the principal learning tool, reading, of many of our public schools. This is a prime example of the over-democratization of American society as argued by Zakaria.

Frederick Hess assigns the problems of our public education system to a stubborn dedication to the status quo, which calls for more money, more teacher training, support for new pedagogies, and continued tenure security. He believes the system should be designed around competition and accountability. It should be graded by results, not process. There must be direct consequences, for instance, in the form of pay differentials, for teachers and school administrators, based on performance; performance that can only be measured by student testing.

It is in the mutual interest of both the individual and the state that all people develop some minimum level of competence so they may be capable of becoming productive, self-sufficient members of society. This level can be achieved by almost everyone by the time their high school studies are completed. Ensuring that everyone has the opportunity to achieve a minimum standard of competence is of such great value to our country that it is reasonable to ask all citizens to foot the bill through taxation even within the context of a privately administered education system. The price for government financing should be accountability to the public in the form of publicized, standardized test scores.

The controversial "No Child Left Behind" program mandated by Washington funnels money through the states that are charged with the responsibility of complying with its terms, including the construction and execution of standardized testing programs. While standardized testing sounds like a great way to define educational effectives, it can be misleading in the extreme. Randy Hoover of Youngstown State University conducted an extensive statistical study of the 1997 state proficiency test scores for 593 Ohio school districts. These tests covered math, science, reading, writing, and citizenship at four grade levels. Although the specific test questions bear, and have received, legitimate criticism, these test results were believed to be a fair indicator of student abilities. In addition to measuring individual ability and knowledge, we might expect these tests to have been a good indicator of school district performance. But this they were not.

This study found that internal factors such as teacher education and per pupil funding level had only a very weak effect on test scores. The best predictors of difference in cognitive levels of student achievement were such factors as community education levels, poverty rate, and resident income levels. The correlation between these socioeconomic factors and test scores was a statistically very robust 0.80, a level rarely found in social cause and effect studies. The implication of these results is clear. While you can measure the level of scholastic attainment for individuals, the group results are not indicative of the relative performance of the teaching staff, school, or administration. In fact the test scores may be relatively high or low while the system performance might be exactly the opposite. To uncover this information, you would have to normalize (the mathematical process of determining the dominant causative factors) test scores by district. Otherwise you would be comparing apples and oranges. For instance, one local school district was ranked No. 4 in the state by these 1997 test scores, but only 234 out of 593 when these scores were normalized by extracting community factors. A school system which boasted an exceptionally high performance ranking was not able to attribute its very high raw test scores solely to staff efforts.

Since the controlling socioeconomic factors can be made available quantitatively for each school district, this task would be feasible given a little added time and effort. In fact, it would be a critically important exercise to undertake should you want to rely on test result statistics as a factor influencing school choice. Although this process is not on the horizon as a part of school proficiency testing, normalized school test results will be assumed as the basis for exercising school choice throughout this discussion of a proposed education system.

Perhaps the most controversial aspect of No Child Left Behind is the straight jacket it mandates for teaching methodology and the requirement for preparing separate study assignments for LD, gifted, and other unique categories of student now being mainstreamed in the classroom. Young teachers are turning away from an education system that takes the fun out of teaching and turns off the kids.

Our school system suffers from too much external interference. Government mandates special education, imposing a high cost or the necessity for mainstreaming, a practice that can result in the impairment of group learning. Some state school boards endorse the recommendations of textbook commissions who specify what may not be taught and how the residual learning must be represented. Educators foist new methodologies and education theories on school districts, programs that may be an impediment to the actual learning process. There is no adequate yardstick by which school districts may be held accountable. There is no reward available for exceptional teaching talent and training. The community may call for nonacademic results, including solving discipline problems, teaching driver's education, or overemphasizing athletics. If it is difficult to assimilate the demands on education from interested NGOs, history shows in can be harmful, if not truly dangerous, for government to interfere with the learning process, as when it attempts to replace science with belief. Such was the case in the Soviet Union for three decades during which genetic research was discredited and comrades starved as the result of low potato yields under the misguided, unscientific teaching of Trofim Lysenko (Lysenkoism, nationmaster.com).

The California public school system has plummeted from one of the top in the nation to one of the worst in just 15 years. John Merrow reports that financial equalization, Proposition 13, and private funding through local foundations, have combined to wreck a model system once dedicated to excellence. Political interference with the curriculum and hyper-democratization have rendered the system incapable of coping with the influx of immigrants and finding adequate resources for poorer California school districts.

The basic structural questions that must be unambiguously sorted out for our public education system are: what to teach, how to teach it, how to assess effectiveness, and how to fund it. The subject matter to be mastered should be left to the determination of a cross section of successful members of the public. The choice of both the tools and techniques of education would be best left to the discretion of working professionals, the classroom teachers, with the concerned public able to judge the results based on standardized, normalized, published achievement test scores, as well as by monitoring their child's progress. Funding should come direct from the government or from clients, as appropriate. What follows is a model of a better education system.

A better system

Our national education system could be administered as a public/private partnership with two distinct missions in mind. The public mission would be dedicated to teaching that core knowledge vital to everyone's needs, so that all were prepared to achieve basic success in society or qualify one for post-secondary academic training. This system would be compulsory, require standardized testing, and be financed by government. The private mission would be to allow maximum choice of program emphasis on an optional basis. It would be administered under a certification program covering any subject approved in accordance with community standards. It would be financed on a program-by-program basis from each family's available Wealth Tax Credit (WTC), a supplement to family earnings to be discussed in chapter 7.

Our compulsory school system could be run as a private enterprise. Since making available the core aspects of both primary and secondary education is of critical importance to the nation, funding for this required part of schooling should be provided from the federal treasury.

Achievement standards could be drawn up for each grade level covering the following essential subjects:

- History and geography - American, world, and current events
- Civics - government, politics, and citizenship
- Science - physics, chemistry, and biology–theory and technology
- Mathematics - theory and application through introductory calculus
- Computer - common programs, information exchange
- Creativity - problem solving and "what if" thinking
- Effective communication - reading, writing, speaking, and standard English
- Health - hygiene, fitness, and disease control
- Basic technology - everyday mechanics and electronics
- Elementary finance - household, business, and investing
- Relationships - school, family, social, and business

Tests covering these subjects would be strictly achievement based, not IQ oriented as in the Stanford Benet or even in the SAT (Student Aptitude Test). No ambiguous or trick questions as are present in many state proficiency tests. The only requirement for schools to receive state support would be for each school to administer semiannual tests for each grade level and publish average results by grade and subject, along with a ranked, normalized score for each school district. Learning requirements could be tailored to be doable in about one half of the present normal schooling time and be scheduled for the morning hours.

The standardized tests could be made up by a national board comprised of members representing a broad cross section of accomplished Americans charged with revising and upgrading tests each year for each grade. All previous tests could be made available to students as a study guide tool. The standard objection to "teaching to the test" would be greatly diminished if test questions were geared to discovering the degree to which essential knowledge and procedure had been absorbed, and not to intellectual puzzle solving. Teachers would have the opportunity to object to questions they feel might be inappropriate, or suggest others not otherwise included.

By this means, government would be precluded from mandating both what should be taught and the results to be achieved. The decisions would be in the hands of knowledgeable consumers. The methodology would be in the hands of the classroom teachers, the experts who have been trained to present the subject matter most effectively. The public would be at liberty to choose any school for their children factoring in the published, normalized, performance levels met by each school.

The required subject matter outlined above is heavily oriented toward the traditional idea of emphasizing content, providing tools, and teaching factual knowledge. This does not rule out the more progressive modes of teaching or the stimulation of creative intelligence in our children. It does, however, require a no-nonsense approach designed to equip each student with a sound working knowledge of the world he or she will shortly inherit.

Schools otherwise would be run as private, for-profit enterprises with enrollment criteria based on the mutual assent of school and family. State support and testing programs would end after the 12th grade. This system would allow every child to receive the basic preparation for a productive life in a school of the family's choice, regardless of financial status. It would put education on a competitive basis. After the high school phase, the state would have no compelling interest in subsidizing specialized education for all students, but would rely on personal interest in achievement, social status, and/or potential financial reward to fuel the desire for further study, just as it does today.

You may be quite sure that parents would demand a useful educational experience when they choose a school where the administration and teaching staff were directly responsible to them. Can a private school system do worse than the public school system has been doing? Not if the system's command, control, and execution is left to the working experts. A competitive system would be self-correcting if normalized, standardized, test results were made available to its clients periodically.

What would be the cost of the publicly supported core program laid out? For the 2001 school year of reference the nationwide average per pupil cost (including capital costs) was about $7,800 (NCES, nces. ed.gov; ASBJ, asbj.com; and S. Osborne, pers. comm.). Assuming the core education curriculum would require one half of this amount, the bill would come to $273 billion each year for our 62 million public and 8 million private school age children (Univ. of Oregon CEPM). These costs are developed in the Appendices. Reimbursement from the government would be designed to cover this fractional cost of salaries, benefits, supplies, and capital debt obligations, all on a standardized basis.

As for the cost of public education, funding at much over the $8,100 level (2003 average) is not a primary factor in promoting quality. The Washington, DC. School District spent about $15,000 per child in 2003, twice the national average, but is said to have produced the worst educational results of any school district in the country (Thernstrom) (here it should be noted, however, that the DC system serves a very high cost of living area). Irving Kristol (1978) observed in the 1970s, "We insist that our schools fulfill impossible dreams—and so they pretend to be able to do this (given a larger budget, of course)."

The optional school curriculum segment could be managed very differently from the compulsory program. Music, fine and performing arts, language, literature, advanced placement study, special education, sports, physical, vocational, or driver's training, or a college preparation package could be available as optional programs, and paid for by each student's or family's WTC. Separating core academic achievement from other worthwhile learning experiences would allow parents to choose which of these other pursuits to include in their optional programs, at no out-of-pocket cost up to the limit of their WTC. Many of these activities, like driver's education, dilute school effectiveness as the current system tries to accommodate all manner of social demands. Certification of optional programs would be the responsibility of and at the discretion of each local school district based on their interpretation of community standards.

To be approved for certification, a private group would be required to submit a descriptive package detailing the specific character of any program being offered; including mission statement, prerequisites, attainment objectives, location and time, progress measurement, cost, reporting procedures, child safety precautions, provision for parental feedback, and be subject to on-site inspection. Within this framework, parents could choose to commit any portion, or all, of their available WTC to certified programs only. They could choose to emphasize athletics, advanced intellectual pursuits, performing arts, vocational training, or any other combination of developmental programs which might meet the talents and needs of their children.

To anticipate your objection to my omission of the humanizing half of the curriculum from the list of "essential subjects," I offer this explanation. The core curriculum administered under this public/private system is designed to help solve what I believe to be the basic problem in education, namely, to bring virtually all our youth up to minimum working speed. Those who don't reach this plateau currently are those who derive scant benefit from any esoteric programs. The parents of those children who do benefit greatly from these studies are the ones who certainly will demand and pay for the nonessential elements, if only with their WTC. The public, compulsory program is designed to yield maximum essential knowledge *and* equal opportunity for the minimum tax revenue expenditure. The private, optional program is designed to accommodate the special needs and interests of each child as its family may perceive it.

While the state supported core curriculum is tailored exclusively to the basic plan of achieving a high level of bare bones functionality, the optional portion of the curriculum is that segment which can initiate the transformation of a mere boy or girl into a human being with great promise. In accordance with local cultural interests, the optional program could be designed to emphasize whatever skill, creative, or academic theme that might be developed to advance that promise. As you will see, this seminal benefit is available to just about all through the WTC.

If we examine the quality of the product of our current, all inclusive, school curricula, we may see that far too many of us are not academically prepared to engage in life productively, even after the full public school treatment. And many do not even pass the test of minimal functionality, much less show interest in the civilizing aspects of a rounded curriculum. Across the nation, inner city 12th graders read and do math at the 7th grade level–those who have not already left school for the streets, that is (Kozol). In my city, remedial reading and arithmetic for high school graduates entering community college once started out with learning *how* to read and do simple addition (S. Lau and G. Gilooly, pers. comms.). I think they still do.

Doesn't this approach neglect the development of intellectual capital as afforded by university study? Yes. Just as it does now for advanced education, except for state-subsidized universities and the student loan program. Won't high school graduates of this program have a very narrow focus on life if they do not participate in the optional half of the K through 12 curriculum? Very possibly, and that is where the WTC kicks in, to finance this *and* higher education, in part, if not in full. An example in chapter 7 will show how the cost of the full optional program would be easily covered for almost all families.

A solid, private, K through 12 educational system would increase our national social capital, qualifying people for more-productive work or education. More people would be qualified for advanced employment opportunities beyond the range of those jobs lost to outsourcing, an issue we will continue to face in our high wage American economy. In an open border, globalized economy, there is only one fundamental way to compete against worldwide, low labor rates, and that is by building our social capital through better education for everyone (Parsons). In order to enhance our international competitiveness as well as honor the benchmark for equal opportunity, Lester Thurow advocated a comprehensive, knowledge-based, K-12 curriculum for all kids, over 20 years ago.

This approach would solve two of the three important problems inherent in today's publicly financed school system. First, it would eliminate state interference in the educational process. Next, the teachers' union mantra, which is for tenure and pay raises, but without differentiation by merit or demand, would be challenged to accommodate a more competitive professional environment.

Education reform is a necessary, but insufficient step all by itself to solve the problem of inequality of opportunity. The third, and most intractable aspect, is embedded in family attitudes and practices, and cannot be overcome without a successful attack on poverty. Accountable social support as described in chapter 5 will help make it possible for parents to raise socially well-adjusted, self-confident children. Parents who are not thriving must be helped and taught to give their children unqualified love, firm (not stern) direction, good examples, forgiveness always, time to reflect, and the experience of decent people, and constructive ideas.

According to the Federal Reserve Board Chairman, Alan Greenspan, it is the attainment of a solid education for all which in turn is the necessary prerequisite for shrinking the wealth gap between rich and poor in America. As with freedom and responsibility, the symbiotic relationship between poverty reduction and education holds the key to realizing equal opportunity. Unfortunately, even when properly undertaken, this quest may take a generation to bear fruit. Too bad we didn't start 20 years ago.

Too many youths today suffer from an egotistic attitude, a debilitating loss of spirit, and degraded moral standards according to William Damon. Of them, too little is expected and too little is generated in terms of skills and behavior in return. Better parenting skills may be the determining factor in laying the groundwork for success, so that weakened moral standards and lost virtues can be restored, lest the sins of the parents continue to be visited upon the children.

Finally, why should we believe that a private school would be able to serve the educational needs of the traditionally under performing students found in our inner city public schools? On the whole, fledgling charter schools around the country have not yet been able to meet their promise of turning out measurably superior students relative to the public school system. The answer can be found at the private Amistad Academy (Amistad, amistadacademy.org.), a New

Haven, Connecticut, charter school. Serving a random cross section of 240 city kids in grades five through eight, it has scored higher in all test scores than all other New Haven city schools after just three years in operation. It has far surpassed all state public schools in writing skills and has attained this level of performance at a per pupil operating cost below that of the New Haven public school system. The core philosophy for this school is spelled out in its REACH program, standing for Respect, Enthusiasm, Achievement, Citizenship, and Hard Work.

Another charter school, the Factory, run by Pacific Rim, has achieved remarkable results by having everyone in its first graduating class of 11 students accepted for college study. This expanding school for sixth through twelfth graders is administered in a dilapidated, abandoned factory building on an eight-hour-day schedule, eleven months a year. The secret is a dedicated teaching staff that refuses to let any student fail (Boo). Not only is there no magic here, but these performances were achieved without the help of the teachers' union, or any direct political influence, or the high costs associated with the regular private school system catering to the affluent.

While the two examples cited are exceptional cases, they clearly embody some attitudes and methodologies that are worth emulating, unlike those stuffy guidelines issued by state and federal bureaucracies.

Education is the key to achieving first class citizenship in today's competitive world. Knowledge, brought to life by the skill required to apply it, is the foundation upon which a life of value can be built. As a nation, we cannot afford to let the 30 percent of our people who don't complete public school, languish in the backwater of an uninspired, dead end existence. This educational foundation has become acutely critical in a world that has become "flat" according to Tom Friedman (2005). Information has been democratized by the Internet, even in lands that are not. The stage is set upon which the explosive IT revolution is about to unfold, leaving all who are not prepared without a ticket to the show.

While the influential German theologian Dietrich Bonhoeffer was awaiting the Nazi hangman's noose in 1945, he wrote, "The test of the morality of a society is what it does for its children." *All* of its children.

Health Care

The quality of our medical delivery system is good, but not as good as it might be. We do have the best technology, training, and research in the world. We have been able to unravel the mysteries of more diseases and develop treatments for them than anyone else. We develop and bring to market about half of all new drug medications. Medical treatment is administered when needed without long waiting periods. The mortality rates from heart disease, cancer, and HIV infection have been steadily dropping. That's the good news.

Comparatively speaking we do experience some shortcomings relative to other first world countries. The American system lacks overall organizational integrity and is wanting in certain low tech areas. Fully 15 percent of us are not covered by some major medical insurance plan, whereas many of these other countries cover virtually all of their citizens *and* visitors (with some limitations). Our prescription drug costs are approximately twice that of other countries for exactly the same preparations produced by American pharmaceutical firms. In 2000 the World Health Organization ranked the U.S. health care system 37th out of 191 (WHO, who.int).

Japanese citizens have a three year average life expectancy advantage at birth over us (81 vs. 78 years). Our infant mortality rate is higher then that of other major industrialized nations, although this may be influenced by other factors such as public health measures, lifestyle, or diet. Each year about 7 to 8 percent of the deaths occurring in this country are premature as the result of medical treatment errors (Brownlee). A significant percentage of these deaths would not occur if standardized-cause mortality statistics were kept and published by health provider institutions. We lack a vigorous, preventative-medicine, promotion program and universal access to primary care (Lamm).

"Doctors do not know, for example, whether regular mammograms for women in their forties save lives" according to Shannon Brownlee, who recommends setting up a Clinical Services Institute to define drug and medical treatment effectiveness. The evaluation practices of modern medicine are at times reminiscent of the introduction of the Halstead radical mastectomy technique for breast cancer years ago. If the patient did not return to the doctor for checkups after this barbaric assault on her body, the operation was considered a success, and so this mutilating procedure became standard surgical practice.

But most remarkable of all, our health care system costs 22 percent more per person than Germany's and 78 percent more than Britain's in 2000, based on the percentage of our Gross National Product (GDP) consumed. In 2003 we spent 14.5 percent of our GDP, or $1.6 trillion, on health care. Our total health care cost continues to increase at 10 percent a year, over three times the rate of inflation (Sourcebook for Journalists 2003, allhealth.org), compared to only 5.1 percent in 1960. Further, Medicare costs are projected to grow by more than 7 percent a year until 2012, even after adjusting for inflation. The biggest driver of cost is technological innovation (D. Peck).

Prior to World War II, medical insurance was something of a rarity. The family doctor would very often come to your home to examine the patient, and accept whatever fees you might be able to manage. Coming out of the great depression, doctors expected to have a respected place in the community, but not grow especially rich. Medical procedures have been advancing since the Civil War although specialists were not at all common prior to the spread of private medical insurance. Before the development of penicillin during World War II, a physician had virtually none of today's modern pharmaceutical preparations or diagnostic tools at his disposal.

But within the span of the last 60 years, medicine has been revolutionized by science and industry, with new knowledge, sophisticated equipment, and many hundreds of new drugs. We have mapped the genetic code of life that determines what we are at birth and distinguishes us as individuals from all other living creatures. We can peer into the body without taking it apart and we can take it apart to upgrade many of its worn parts. We have a battery of medications to deal with disease, mood, pain, and neurotransmitter deficiencies, in addition to the original "wonder drug," aspirin.

The medical insurance problem

These advances in understanding and practice did not come without a price. In order that these miracles of medicine might be made available to us, we have built a complex patchwork of insurance programs over the years, administered by both private companies and government at all levels. There is private insurance offered through private business or even directly to individuals. There is Medicare for the elderly and Medicaid for those with marginal income and assets. There is the State Children's Health Insurance Program (SCHIP). There are block grants from the federal government to the states, which in turn get reallocated to countless local programs. Then there are the uninsured who seek emergency care when necessary, but are often unable to foot the bill. They may do without, or just get minimal emergency treatment leading to greater complications and costs down the road.

To understand the economics of medicine, it is necessary to examine the workings of these various insurance programs as well as the role of government and industry in administering them. Private medical insurance coverage was encouraged and popularized by the federal government during World War II as a substitute for raising wages that were controlled in order to contain inflation. Later, coverage was extended as a benefit fought for by labor in periodic contract negotiations with industry. This benefit mushroomed as the post war economy boomed. The illusion that this work benefit was "free" accelerated demand, and the resulting spread of insurance coverage financed the creation of additional medications as well as more and improved patient care. However, the cost of care must be paid for by somebody, and this is a system underwritten by your hard work.

With advancing technology and increasing benefits, it was inevitable the price tag to business would rise and cost containment pressure be applied to the private insurance carriers. Unfortunately, when under pressure to cut costs, the insurers may turn to cost reducing strategies like excluding high risk applicants if they are allowed to, or increasing the level of co-pays or deductibles to their clients. They "select out" costly applicants by profiling, by denying coverage for pre-existing conditions, by lowering the dollar caps for expensive or repeated procedures, and by raising premiums (without advance notification) on covered clients with excessive claims. Although such practices are common for auto and life insurance, it is in the national interest that all citizens have access to affordable medical care.

In their legitimate pursuit of profit, private insurance firms resort to any scheme they can to keep costs down. They generally pay out only 70 to 80 percent of premiums collected for claims (Terhune), the balance going for internal costs and profit. By contrast, the federal government incurs only about 3 percent in administrative costs for its Medicare program. Medicare applies the same claims criteria over all 50 states and is not in the business of extracting profit dollars from the system.

Under a private insurance program, you may be covered for a bone marrow transplant, but it will be an unpleasant surprise to find out you must still come up with $10,000 to cover the cost of a search for a donor (Marcus). In an effort to contain costs, medical decisions have been more and more falling into the hands of accountants in managed care plans. The cost of any service or medication is predictably never a topic of discussion between patient and doctor. Neither has much interest in minimizing the cost/benefits ratio of any procedure undertaken, as long as it is a covered protocol.

As medical care consumers, we have virtually no direct voice in determining the cost of care. We have very little to say about what care is covered. Through HMOs (Health Maintenance Organizations) and PPOs (Preferred Provider Organizations), we are progressively realizing less, or even no choice regarding who is to be our doctor.

Private insurance obtained through an employer is not usually portable. If your employer terminates your services, you have the option of continuing your medical insurance for 18 months through the COBRA (Consolidated Omnibus Budget Reconciliation Act) program, but at a really hefty premium. After that you are on your own.

The provisions stipulated in your private medical insurance policy are heavily influenced, if not directly controlled, by government. At their whim, state governments may impose costly requirements superseding private insurance contract agreements, as they have with the domestic partners coverage requirement. By 1997, 1,000 such mandates were being issued per year and had raised the cost of health insurance to the average family by 30 percent (Martinez). Sooner or later the cost of these new service provisions comes out of your pocket.

The paperwork requirements to administer this sprawling system are onerous to the point of being overwhelming. They were estimated to siphon off some 31 percent in administrative costs compared to 16.7 percent for the Canadian, single-payer system, according to a Harvard Medical School study in 1999 by Steffie Woolhandler and David Himmelstein. Overhead in Canadian insurance plans was 1.3 percent compared to 3.6 percent for Medicare and 11.7 percent for private insurers in the U.S.

In 1965, the 1935 Social Security legislation was expanded to cover two new Great Society programs, Medicare and Medicaid. The introduction of Medicare for all seniors over 65 in 1965 afforded retirees an entrée to medical care just at the time in life when the need for care was accelerating. Since then, the cost of care has grown steadily because of the development of sophisticated machines and procedures, and increases in life expectancy of more than five years. This increasingly expensive population of old timers, many nursing chronic medical conditions, is ballooning and challenging the resources of the residual working population available to underwrite the program. It is ironic to note that lung cancer deaths due to cigarette smoking shortens life expectancy by eight years on the average and greatly *reduces* the overall medical costs associated with the chronic diseases of old age. Yet the $246 billion smoking litigation settlements to compensate states for associated medical costs were expressly justified on the basis of what were claimed to be *increased* costs.

The advent of Medicare has made the federal government the largest single purchaser of medical services, and as such, it plays the major role in establishing standards for availability, procedures, cost, and reimbursement practices in all areas of medicine. Government has a controlling effect on drug prices by virtue of the fact that it already administers 52 percent of the drug market output (Frontline, June 19, 2003). Medicare costs were $217 billion in 2001 and increasing at the rate of 7 percent per year without considering any of the additional benefits which are proposed periodically. To endorse the recent $40 billion prescription drug program proposed by the president, both Democrats and Republicans reluctantly voted it into law while keeping one eye on the 2004 election campaigns already underway. Before this program went into effect, the cost had doubled, as will be discussed in chapter 8.

The Medicaid program introduced in 1965 targeted the medical needs of the low-wage uninsured. Congress passed the buck to the states to set up and pay for over 40 percent of this federally mandated program. The program grew rapidly as it became more user friendly and in 2001 cost the federal government $129 billion in addition to state contributions, which in total account for at least 20 percent of all state budget expenditures.

In an attempt to extend medical coverage to all of its low-income citizens, the progressive ex-Governor Kitzhaber of Oregon had championed explicit medical service rationing as a means of containing Medicaid costs while broadening service availability. The Oregon Health Plan (OHP) was approved by Oregon's voters in 1994 (US Dept. HHS, cms.hhs.gov), but soon ran into funding problems with the federal government. This controversial program has had limited success, but is noteworthy mainly for its bold attempt to include everyone by laying out, with the input of its citizens, specific, uniform practices to be covered. This is the first step required to implement any insurance system where demand is virtually unlimited but resources are. The OHP is a work in progress that bears watching as a potential learning tool for broader application, if we are ever to close the 15 percent gap in national coverage.

The legal community has found we live in a time where juries can be induced to grant astronomical punitive damage awards for pain and suffering in medical malpractice or negligence suits. Malpractice claim awards zoomed from $550 million in 1999 to almost $1.4 billion in 2001 (Ed. *WSJ.* May 1, 2002). Malpractice insurance premiums may consume 25 percent of the revenues of a doctor in private practice. They commonly exceed $150,000, and have been known to top $1 million for certain high risk specialties. Is it not understandable that doctors may routinely order unnecessary tests just to "cover their butt"? Some are trading in their stethoscopes for fishing rods, prematurely. A jury of one's peers is generally not competent to understand complex medical issues or business financial statements well enough to arrive at sound punitive judgments.

When the legal profession found that the key to litigating tobacco cases was to sue producers on behalf of the states, they found the pot of gold worth over $246 billion in 1998. Since most of the claim money is going to the states, the governors had found a new best friend. Meanwhile, the millions of smokers dying or prematurely dead of lung cancer did not receive so much as a sympathy card from the cigarette makers or even a thank you note from any law firm.

In the olden days, prior to the availability of health insurance, doctors would often agree to future payment, even in the form of farm produce or a thanksgiving turkey if they had to. But today, health insurance has changed the financial terms of medical service transactions and shifted the reliance on cost/benefit analysis to insurance providers and away from any doctor-patient agreement. Why should the principals in a transaction worry about cost when the services are prepaid by a third party, your employer?

Doctors and particularly hospitals routinely charge $1,000 when the insurance carrier will cover only $500, and that only for providers who have agreed to take assignment. Please explain that pricing policy to me. The patient may be billed for 20 percent of the $1,000 "list price" instead of 20 percent of the $500 allowed fee, as is implied in the insurance contract. When the price of a standard good or service fluctuates widely depending on arbitrary factors, you do not have a free market. For medical care, both the supply and price of products and services are managed, and not for the benefit of the patient. The medical care delivery market is controlled ultimately, if indirectly, by our governments who are trying to dictate demand and support price. While the supply and unit pricing comes from privately owned firms, this is anything but the free enterprise market it started out to be.

Will we soon employ MRI (magnetic resonance imaging) scans as a diagnostic tool for all headaches that walk into the doctor's office? Certainly this multi-thousand-dollar procedure has a greater potential for contributing to revenue than a couple of aspirin. And do hospitals need a life flight helicopter or the latest expensive body scanning equipment, to remain competitive with their neighbors or even just for the prestige factor? The alarming prices attached to an overnight stay in a semi-private hospital room reflect the indirect costs of indigent care, overbuilding, expensive specialized equipment, and government regulation. If an inpatient needs an aspirin, he may get a $40 per day air purification system instead.

Big Pharma

The fastest growing segment of the medical market in terms of the rate of cost escalation is the pharmaceutical business. The drug companies claim that aggressive pricing is necessary because of the high cost of new drug development and testing, a process occasionally requiring a billion dollar investment and taking as long as 15 years. Even then the FDA (Food and Drug Administration) may disapprove a new drug candidate if safety, efficacy, or dose levels cannot be established satisfactorily.

The number of prescription medications commonly stocked at your local drug store stands at maybe 1,500 preparations, a tenfold increase in recent memory. You can purchase these very same drugs, often at half price, and sometimes at an 80 percent discount (Burton), if you shop in Canada. Since foreign countries negotiate maximum costs for imported drugs, ethical pharmaceutical companies sell their drugs generally for less than half price overseas and require Americans to make up the difference at home. Is that ethical? Now the FDA is shutting down American importers that bring drugs in from Canada for their domestic customers (Burton and Lueck), standing behind the caution that they might not be safe. Is that government in the interest of its citizens? Especially when an estimated 10 percent of drug preparations arrive at your local pharmacy through clandestine channels, anyway (Eban).

The pharmaceutical business community claims that high prices for new, patented drugs are required to underwrite the high risk and cost associated with underwriting research and gaining FDA approval. To this end they have a good argument, but just how pricey is a matter worth examining. Let us compare the financial statistics for Merck, a premier ethical drug firm, with those for General Electric, the preeminently successful manufacturing and financial conglomerate of the last two decades under Fortune's "business manager of the century"-leadership of Jack Welch. Both companies have excellent A++ financial ratings and a notably high 95 percent level of earnings predictability. Over the past five years GE's profit margin was 10.7

percent (well over the industry average) compared to Merck's 25.8 percent. The relative return on investment was 5.85 percent vs. 21.8 percent for Merck. In 2003 GE paid its investors a 2.7 percent dividend compared to 3.2 percent for Merck. These performance comparisons are valid not just for the near past. Throughout the 1980s, GE's rate of profit growth averaged 10 percent next to 13 percent for Bristol-Meyers Squibb and 16 percent for Abbott Laboratories. These are phenomenally good stats for businesses that have prospered without major changes in mission over a 25-year period.

By further comparison, GE managed its performance in a highly competitive, free enterprise environment, while the pharmaceutical business is protected, there being no cost/benefits tradeoff made by the customer at the point of distribution. Under patent protection for at least 20 years, the price of a new drug may be set based on no known relation to cost, and often without regard to relative merit. The FDA criterion for effectiveness is that a new drug work better than a sugar placebo, not its performance compared to similar drugs already on the market.

No medical insurance company nor the U.S. government does cost/benefit studies. This is one reason why your doctor may prescribe Celebrex (believed to be best for joint pain) or VIOXX for pain while ibuprofen might do the same job at 10 percent of the cost (Brownlee). Recently VIOXX was taken off the market, a full two years after it was known (allegedly) that it doubled the incidence of heart attack and stroke (Angell) and is now known to have been responsible for 28,000 deaths (Barlett and Steele). There are allegations that over 100,000 patients may have been severely impaired. The same company (Merck) that asserted vigorously over the first half of 2004 that VIOXX was safe, is one of the same companies that oppose importation of cheap U.S. drugs from Canada—on safety grounds. In August of 2005, Merck was tagged with a $253 billion punitive judgment for the death of just one of its customers. With an estimated 50,000 potential claims just waiting in the wings, the prestigious drug firm Merck may now be in a fight for its very survival.

The other reason doctors prescribe the latest expensive drug preparations is that drug companies spend twice as much on drug promotion as they do for research. They send out detail men with free samples to visit physicians and, more recently, pitch directly to the consuming public on television. Why should the doctor deny a patient his drug request (if not harmful) when he has free samples to dole out and neither he nor the patient thinks twice about the eventual cost?

Only the 11 million, or 27 percent of the population, who are on Medicare but lack supplemental health insurance, care much about prescription drug costs (Cong. Budget Office, cbo.gov/showdoc.cfm?Index=5668). And as of this year they will become more pleased with their government for Medicare's new prescription drug subsidy, overlooking the higher payroll taxes their grandchildren will have to pay. This bill passed with the provision that the government would agree not to negotiate bulk discounts on prescription drugs, and without any discussion of easing the import ban on drugs from outside the U.S. Do you suppose if we dusted for fingerprints, we might detect the presence of our very prosperous pharmaceutical firms on this legislative package? Since incumbent congressmen and their parties receive generous campaign support from drug firms and have a 98-percent-plus success rate of reelection, it is easy to see why your local senator or representative has little interest in actually reducing health care costs.

Big Pharma enjoys a favored position in the array of American businesses. Much of their basic research is done by universities funded by the National Institutes of Health, whose budget is pushing $30 billion a year. The drug companies then pick up potentially promising drug candidates by paying a royalty fee for university patent rights. Virtually all of the drug firms' new products are protected by patents making possible an extremely aggressive pricing strategy. This is true even for "look-alike" or "copy cat" drugs having only minor chemical modifications from the parent. Sometimes, the major contributions made by the drug companies are that of developing the drug production and manufacturing process, contributing financial support for the FDA certification program, and building a marketing campaign around a new brand name.

Product certification by the FDA constitutes guaranteed acceptance in the international marketplace. Marcia Angell, former Editor-in-Chief of the New England Journal of Medicine, asserts that the FDA may be partial to the pharmaceutical firms since around one half million dollars of the cost of FDA drug testing services is paid for directly by them with each test application (Budget Documentation, fda.gov). This financing arrangement, legislated to put the approval process on a fast track, is alleged to be influential in enticing the FDA to assume a sympathetic viewpoint when reviewing test results for approval.

Assuming the drug makers sell their meds at cost or above internationally, their gross profit margin for the large domestic market must be at least 100 percent (depending on relative distribution costs). Since the grant of a monopoly position in business is conferred by patent status, it should be morally, if not legally, possible to require drug companies to sell abroad at some price no lower than the domestic price. This is only a just requirement for any domestic business operating under U.S. patent protection, which monopoly, after all, is set up solely in the interest of the American public.

The pharmaceutical firms are multinationals who manufacture and sell around the world, as are the equipment and medical supply companies. They spread money around liberally for medical conferences, meals, transportation, door prizes, and doctor, nurse, and technician training. They advertise brand name medications to the exclusion of comparable over-the-counter preparations, generating a demand through on-site, doctor-education sessions, free samples, and direct-to-the-public advertising on television. They spent $91 million on lobbyists in 2003. It is apparent they have the United States Congress in their corner, if not the FDA. They are getting richer and we are getting the bills along with the pills.

Then there are always the socially difficult cases to deal with like the $28,000 per injection price tag for Zevalin, an experimental drug shown to have extended life for 25 percent of the cancer patients in a small scale test. Before adding this or somewhat less expensive drugs to an approved insurance formulary of medications, a hard-nosed cost/benefits analysis should be undertaken to head off political pressure that can be applied to approve insurance coverage based primarily on the emotional response of the news media or public (Lognado).

The cost factor

We must keep in mind that the pharma companies are in business to make money. They learned from Jonas Salk years ago that there was no money in curing disease. Polio, almost eradicated in this country, is not the source of a dime's worth of revenue. The money is in prolonging the life of the chronically ill who stay alive on chemical life support. Malaria, the biggest killer by far in countries like Africa, attracts no research funding because the afflicted have no money to buy expensive, beneficial drugs (Barlett and Steele).

In fact, to promote drug sales, pharmaceutical firms sometimes invent diseases. The common old age loss of sexual vigor in men formally known as impotence was renamed "erectile dysfunction" when Pfizer brought Viagra to market. It was covered by health insurance and became so popular that it is now advertised as a recreational drug for the under 40 crowd who want to be sure they are ready at all times, drunk or sober. Some have justified the cost of subsidizing better sex by pointing to the fact that these ED drugs are getting men to the doctors office, who might otherwise not have gone. This might be where your rising insurance deductibles and co-pays go while the truly needy are turned away from emergency room treatment by the process of "ER diversion."

Who are the principal decision makers, the agents who write the checks to the providers of medical treatment? They are the federal government for Medicare and Medicaid (along with the states), and private industry through private insurance companies. These are the agents that determine who gets what treatment within what financial limits. These are the decision makers who, in reality, *ration* health care. All other socialized medical systems around the world are cost-capped by the government and administered under explicit rationing programs. Yes, health care is rationed, albeit quite generously in this country. But there are no universal guidelines specifying who may get a hip replacement, who may be covered for a $10,000 a year drug prescription, and who will be left out. So the real question to address is not *if* health care should be rationed, but rather *how* it should be rationed. Using the British system as a model, Henry Aaron and William Schwartz of the Brookings Institute explain why serious consideration of health care rationing is inescapable, in their forthcoming book, *Can We Say No?*

In a mixed system where government and private interests intersect, the government has a compelling interest to regulate the terms of service delivery as well as the requirements for both medical decision making and financing. The private interest for profit and the political interest of government converge at the doctor's office and in the operating room. The result is a system that arguably costs 40 to 100 percent more than the amount required to render 85 percent of the nation's citizens functional and disease free (Frangos). According to Brownlee, 300,000 patients die prematurely each year due to medical errors (wrong meds, hospital infections, etc.). She further asserts that this is a marketplace with no available outcome data, one that lacks competition because we reimburse providers according to their efforts, not according to their results. There is no independent auditing of the health care system for effectiveness of treatment.

Who ultimately does pay for these services? You know who. The same people who get the medical care—all of us. In spite of our several overlapping insurance packages, we still pay about 24 percent (Goodman and Musgrave) of our medical costs out-of-pocket, through co-pays, deductibles, extra direct charges by insurers, and for non-covered services, drugs, and supplies. We pay for Medicare and Medicaid through present and future payroll taxes to the federal government, and through income taxes to 50 state governments. We pay for private insurance coverage indirectly by wage and salary reductions at work and/or higher consumer prices at the store.

This critically important area is now consuming 14.5 percent of our GDP annually. Between the late 1960s and early 1990s, costs went up at three times the rate of inflation and have outpaced GDP growth by more than 4 percent over the last five years (Beever, Burns and Karbe). Hospital occupancy rates for a semi-private room have been doubling every seven years and hospitals are now phasing them out for even more expensive private rooms (Moore). Many small business entities cannot afford to offer medical benefits, so their employees, mostly the working poor, do without.

The average cost for each of us is pushing $6,000 a year. $314 billion goes to doctors and their services, $451 billion to hospitals, and $141 billion goes for drugs (Henninger), the fastest growing category, increasing at the rate of 15 to 20 percent yearly (Frangos). These huge sums of money support the biggest single business segment in the U.S. By the 1980s, the Cleveland Clinic Foundation (CCF) had become the largest private employer in my town, surpassing General Electric, Ford Motor, and Republic Steel. CCF employs better than 2 percent of the city's total population on site now.

By the middle of 2003, unfunded government liabilities for future benefits for all currently covered people came to $11.7 trillion for Social Security, $18.0 trillion for Medicare, and $7.5 trillion for new drug benefits (Peterson 2004), amounts promised for the care of current and past payroll tax contributors. Unfunded means no money in the bank to help pay off a total liability far beyond our ability to even imagine. Is it beyond our capacity to deal with effectively also?

In his recent book, *The Brave New World of Health Care*, Richard Lamm points out that our medical system overspends on sophisticated care for individual problems. Consequently we are overstaffed with specialists and short on primary care practitioners where you get more bang for the buck. Medical ethicists advocate heroic efforts for special cases without regard for costs or the overall public welfare. In Britain, when medicine can do no more, the old folks are allowed to go home to die, instead of being forced to endure heroic, costly measures. In the U.S., hospice advises families giving terminal home care to loved ones *not* to call 911 in an emergency, because patients will fall into the clutches of the medical establishment and be subjected to procedures and costs according to its discretion.

The preoccupation with challenging individual cases, the unwillingness to embrace overt rationing, and lack of a national vision, has resulted in a system where the costs outweigh the benefits while millions remain poorly served. Four overlapping systems working through 50 states and hundreds of insurance providers makes for an expensive tangle of regulations and paperwork. Only doctors should be relied upon for medical recommendations and decisions while government should be limited to control of mission, oversight, and the public purse.

The new science of gene therapy promises cures for many of the most dreadful human maladies, such as Parkinson's disease, that have forever defied medical treatment. Virtually everybody feels we should make haste to exploit this new golden age of medicine. Who can easily overlook human suffering with the promise of a cure just over the medical horizon? The very nature of gene-therapy technology suggests these cures will be costly and beyond reach if not covered by insurance. This wonderful, new, medical miracle will be targeted to the few and paid for by the many. It is certain to compete for funds with the need to extend basic care to all Americans. It is just one more reason that a complete overhaul of our medical delivery system is so urgent.

The system is broken, not because it doesn't deliver for most of us, but because it is a black hole into which we are poring $1.6 trillion annually, some of which goes for products and services of questionable value. Each year the individual demand for health care grows, adding to the total cost, while our attention is directed toward specific tangible causes of cost escalation. Government will have to collect the monies to discharge these obligations as they come due, penny by penny, or renege on its promises. We must come to terms with the voracious appetite of this black monster before it consumes us. We must examine its structure, highlight its flaws, and find better ways to deliver good health care services to all citizens, for ourselves, our children, and for our nation.

If we wish to bring the 44 million uninsured Americans into our health care system, we must accept the idea that it will never happen in a private, pay-for-play system. The cost for care is so high that well over 15 percent of us will either forego treatment or show up in the emergency room with empty pockets. But there are good reasons to include even the least of us. If we are to achieve equal opportunity for everyone to realize a responsible and productive role in society, it is imperative that no one be disadvantaged unnecessarily by poor health. If we are to honor human dignity we must not turn our backs on those who are afflicted by illness and suffering. The downside of neglect is a requirement to support those who might have made the grade, but now need assistance for life.

The plain fact is that free enterprise does not work in the field of health care. It doesn't work because the client does not know what treatment he needs when illness strikes, or the value (or cost) of any specific treatment available. Generally, he is limited in seeking out a new physician, once stricken, and has no training which might allow him to gauge the potential effectiveness of any particular treatment available to him. These are the necessary conditions that must prevail if a free enterprise system is to work for the benefit of the buyer.

A better system

Since the state must step up to the task of organizing and providing health care for the over-65 crowd as well as those without private insurance, it is only logical for the state to do the same on a single-payer basis for us all. That is, assuming the state is able to put together a system that is fair, efficient, and equal to the task at hand. Indeed this is the format for health coverage adopted by virtually all other developed countries of the world.

Socialized medicine is a hot button phrase in this land of free enterprise. But it must be remembered that whenever we ship our money off to Washington, or even just to Columbus, Ohio, government performs a socialistic act by spending it on our behalf. Government already is the predominant manager of our medical delivery system. It controls the flow of private funds, also. As with all government-run programs, this expensive lunch is not free.

To exercise financial control over any insurance scheme, you must know what demands are being made on the check writers. Our audit trail starts in the doctor's office and ends in Washington, DC. Insurance has the effect of virtually freeing doctor and patient from factoring cost into the consideration of possible treatment protocols. Neglecting cost may offer a margin of benefit for the patient, but it can be injurious to the insurance system if not subject to some control. Therefore, the first responsibility of the underwriter is to set an overall cap on expenditures, consistent with premium collections. A single-payer system (government) presents the simplest way to finance health care for all, out of payroll taxes collected, as will be described in chapter 7. The key to making such a system work without political interference would be to charge government with the responsibility for setting the national spending cap annually, raising the tax revenues required to meet the cap, conducting oversight and audits, while making the terms of service exempt from direct or indirect control by Washington.

Factoring in and building on all these considerations allows us to generate the outline of a greatly improved medical insurance system. The outline of a better system might look like this:

- A birth to death Universal Health Insurance Plan (UHIP) system whose mission is to keep all citizens disease free and help them maintain their function in society
- A system covering doctor, hospital, drugs, and therapy for both physical and psychological needs, as well as home care, vision, dental, medical education, and long term care. Of these needs, mental, home, and long term care would have to be closely monitored for cost control
- Primary health care providers to accept any client applicant that they are set up to treat, up to their stated maximum case load
- Required client participation in drug rehabilitation therapy or family hygiene and nutrition management training, if recommended by both medical and social authorities
- A requirement that prescription drugs protected under U.S. patent law might not be sold outside of the United States below the domestic price, since patent law exists in the interest of the American public
- Total system cost to be capped by congress annually as a percentage of GDP and covered by income tax collections
- A role for government limited to oversight and setting co-pay and deductible levels
- Provision for co-existence of a private health care system to serve the needs of any who might find the public system limiting or inadequate
- All elective medical care costs to be eligible for payment through the WTC system and/or personal funds. This would include any private supplemental health insurance premiums, deductibles, and co-pays
- Provision for a Standards Committee to determine and review periodically those treatments and procedures covered, at what cost, and for eligibility requirements, based on a cost/benefits analysis where possible. Committee members to be appointed from a broad cross section of knowledgeable citizens, including government officials

and members with a professional interest who would have advisory status only

- Provision for a Medical Practices Audit Board charged with the responsibility of investigating system abuses and recommending discipline
- Provision for a Medical Practices Court system designed to be a forum for malpractice and other medical-claims resolution. This would require close government supervision and a user-pays approach to malpractice suits "...to discourage long shot cases..." and make "...use of experts [witnesses] answerable only to the courts, rather than contending experts hired by the parties" (Olson).

The UHIP system we have outlined is a single-payer rationing system. In reality all economic exchange systems are rationing systems when demand is virtually unlimited and supply is essentially restricted by cost or some other factor. Such a plan requires a cap on costs based on services and products which must be spelled out in detail. In the UHIP system we are proposing, the sole underwriter would be the U.S. government, which would not be allowed to politicize the process by participating in the determination of available services and eligibility requirements for health care items. The doctor should be the sole determiner of need, but not have control over availability. Medical services or aids not covered could be obtained in the private health care market.

The overall plan developed here must be judged from the standpoint of whether it honors the principles discussed and, of course, whether these principles are reasonable and in the public interest. In addition to the benefits explicitly outlined above, some positive features of the UHIP would be:

- unrestricted access to any available primary care doctor of choice
- a guaranteed minimum standard of care for all citizens without any portability or COBRA issues
- elimination of the plethora of costly programs such as Medicare, Medicaid, SCHIP, private insurance, and numerous state and local agency services

- lower doctor and hospital costs resulting from uniform and enlightened disposition of malpractice claims, and risk pooling across the industry
- elimination of costs to business or non-profit organizations for health insurance that would translate into lower product and service costs, or possibly better wages.
- a reduction in paperwork saving $206 billion, assuming administrative costs might be cut almost in half following the Canadian example (Appendix F), a savings potentially set at $286 billion by Woolhandler and Himmelstein (thirdworldtraveler.com)
- a reduction in cost of $39 billion by recapture of profit realized by private insurance carriers (Appendix F)
- elimination of the multi-trillion dollar unfunded liabilities lurking in our expanding Medicare and Medicaid programs
- a truly important contribution to equal opportunity and human dignity across the health care spectrum

The total specified savings of $245 billion would cut our total health care costs by 2.6 percent of GDP, to 11.9 percent total The current total expenditures of $215 billion on Medicaid would cover the total medical cost of our uncovered 15 percent of the population, under UHIP (Appendix F).

How may we be assured a system like this would deliver as neatly and efficiently as described? Stuart Butler has proposed privatizing many government programs with a view to containing spending by restricting government's operational role. His plan to limit government's role to mission definition, overall funding, oversight, and non-operational regulation, is roughly coincident with the ideas expressed in this work. However, it may be that the only way such a system could function without political interference would be if it were protected just like speech, the press, religion, or assembly are–by constitutional amendment. Clearly, politicians will go anywhere they are not constitutionally forbidden.

The final and telling argument for putting medical care on a sound financial footing was provided by Laurene Graig in 1991, in a study showing that the primary determinant of health and mortality is not clinical medicine. It is in fact such socioeconomic factors as education, nutrition, housing, sanitation, and working conditions. Our Department of Health and Human Services agrees. Only five of the last thirty years' gain in life expectancy over the past century can be attributed to clinical medicine.

Social Security

If the performance of our public education system is very uneven and the cost of our health care system is excessive, the security of our Social Security system is precarious. It will visit financial pain upon our offspring just to meet its promises, and it is unlikely that it will ever be restored to full economic, self-sustaining viability. It is likely that the social well being of each successive generation will be an increasing burden to be borne by the next.

The Social Security tax did not exist before the Great Depression of the thirties. Today, for most of the working poor, it is the major hit they take on their weekly paycheck: 7.65 percent of gross earnings in paycheck deductions plus another 7.65 percent never showing up because it was siphoned off for payment by the employer (actually, 2.8 percent of the total is taken for medical services, but this is neglected for illustration purposes).

In defense of Social Security, it must be said that this program has conferred a dignity made possible by a degree of independence for people at the end of life when they can no longer fully make their own way in the world. Also it has taken the burden of parental support from the shoulders of mature adult children who otherwise had looked forward to enjoying their "salad years." That said, it must be noted that our payroll taxes finance a gigantic Ponzi scheme, plagued by increases in our longevity, the addition of Medicare and Medicaid in 1965, increasing health care costs, and outright abuse by politicians in their zeal to give away the cookies before they are baked and placed in the cookie jar.

The Social Security Trust Fund is a trust fund in name only. Except for periods during which premiums just exceeded benefits (as at present), your premiums are not invested for your "account," but turned around and sent out directly to your retired father. It is a scheme that obligates our children to pay for our retirement home in Florida. The return on investment is currently about 1 percent because there is almost no investment. Your "account" is nothing more than an informal promise to pay you benefits in the future, a promise that finesses the hard task of finding an adequate source of funding, leaving the task to tomorrow's politicians and tomorrow's workers.

When tomorrow comes, and it is coming, the ratio of payers to payees will be extremely unfavorable, about two to one (Kotlikoff). In periods where there is an excess of "contributions," the government borrows that excess to fund its deficit spending, issuing government debt in return. The current Social Security surplus of $1.7 trillion has been spent and replaced by U.S. treasury bonds. The day of reckoning *will arrive in about 35 years*, and we will reap what we have been sowing. What will happen on June 1, 2040 when some of us folks, maybe frail and withered, open the mail box and find a greatly reduced benefit check from our Uncle Sam—along with our latest edition of Modern Maturity.

Not-for-profit organizations have a tendency to spend until the till is empty, then come begging for more. It's easy to spend other people's money. Government has the advantage of not having to beg for money; it just takes it or borrows it using our kids as collateral. It can be misleading at the very least in its accounting to the public. The $5.6 trillion, 10 year budget surplus loudly predicted in 2001 turned into a $440 billion deficit for 2003 and $413 billion more for 2004 as the result of 9-11 and the return to sanity of the ".com" securities' markets.

The young adults of Generation X are being conditioned to believe there will be no cookies left for them, only crumbs, even after years of working to fill up the jar. The years of government profligacy are even now starting to have a corrosive effect on any faith the Gen Xers might have had in government. The outrage flying just under the radar screen can be addressed in only two ways within the present system. We must raise payroll taxes yet again, decrease benefits, or do both. Period. Without any reduction in benefits, Social Security and Medicare/Medicaid will take more than one third of our offspring's income by 2050 (du Pont). The capitalistic United States of America will have further socialized 90 percent of the population and relinquished freedom, power, and money to the other wealthy 10 percent. Back to square one for democratic progress.

Experience teaches us that those folks who are the least likely to put aside money for their late years are the most likely to need it eventually. For this reason some minimal level of social security taxation should be required. Long life, as well as social concern for dignity and independence in old age, are recent phenomena in the history of mankind. A sustainable program providing social security would be a boon for the recipients, those in line to be caregivers, and so for the whole of society.

A better system

Here is one way that a mandatory social security program able to guarantee independence and dignity in old age might be structured. For the purpose of this discussion, all figures are in current dollar valuations.

- Impose a tax rate of 5 percent of gross wages up to a maximum annual contribution level of $3,000.
- Deposit all tax proceeds in a private investment pool divided into personal accounts, just as a mutual fund does.
- Make all account balances, as well as premiums and payouts, exempt from taxation.
- Provide for optional annuitization of account balances in the form of lifetime payments, any time after age 59.
- Structure the national social security fund to be a private fund regulated by the government, managed by the private sector, and limited to investment grade, public, domestic securities.
- Allow for payroll contributions to be topped off at $3,000 annually, if need be, by augmentation with the Wealth Tax Credit (WTC) and/or out-of-pocket dollars.
- Limit total contributions to $3,000 annually to head off any attempt to shelter personal investment funds from income and wealth taxes.

For an individual who exercised the option of funding his account at $1,500 (one half of the maximum of $3,000 a year) for 40 years, and retired at age 65, the annual retirement benefit would be $10,600, increasing at the rate of 3 percent a year for life. Intermediate payout levels would depend, of course, on the total amount and specific times at which contributions were made and the age at which the account was annuitized.

As shown by the supporting calculations in Appendix C, we may have a high degree of confidence that this level of payout benefit could be realized over the long term, provided account funds were invested in a mix of domestic, investment grade equities and bonds, and account funding was diligently maintained over the long term accumulation period. These results would be consistent with the continuing prosperity of this country, not dependent upon the temptations of political manipulation.

The $1,500 annual funding level would produce benefits approaching those of the present system, requiring 15.3 percent (employee + employer) of your paycheck, because it would accumulate tax free for individual investment accounts instead of being paid out immediately to your folks in Florida. That's the secret behind compounding your own tax-free investment nest egg and the reason the program should be fully funded much as required by law for commercial insurance annuities. The cost to the U.S. Treasury of this program in lost Social Security taxes will be shown at the end of chapter 7.

The rationale for restricting all funds to U.S. investment grade securities is to provide for reasonable returns with superior security for all account funds. A government-sponsored and tax-subsidized program should have bullet proof integrity based on sound fundamentals. This plan is based on the average returns available over an 80 year period, from 1920 to 2000. Any interest in personal investment or speculation could always be exercised in personal, private investment accounts. In essence, the government should be willing to guarantee that all participants in a compulsory government program would prosper on a par with the economy of the country. At present the return on your Social Security taxes is predicated on the somewhat thin assurance that your children or their children will be willing and able to deliver on behalf of political promises made for us today.

As a reminder, the benefits upon retirement would double if the full $3,000 in premiums were paid in each year. Furthermore, these benefits would accrue to every contributing individual regardless of work history. If income does not allow for taking out the full $3,000 each year, the difference could be made up from the WTC or out-of-pocket. Anyone who could manage to pay in $1,900 a year for 40 years based on their 5 percent payroll tax plus any WTC dollar input, would receive a benefit equivalent to today's full share at age 65. Even any individual not working. The total potential benefit for an elderly couple could exceed $40,000 per year, tax free (Appendix C).

As with the UHIP medical system, the government should play no role in the operation of this national fund except for oversight, audit, and determination of annual contribution maximums.

Now you may think the social security program outlined above sounds too good to be true. Is it really possible that we might be able to run a private social security program with benefits comparable to those available today at one third (on average) of the current cost? Here it might be noted that Peter Ferrara concluded that private investment accounts would have yielded about the same benefits as Social Security does now, at only one forth of the current cost, by assuming just slightly higher investment yields than assumed in this example. Would our proposed program be self-sustaining into the long term future?

The answer is yes—and no. Yes, it would work, at least to the extent America is able to nurture a vital, growing economy. No, it will not be possible until and unless we solve an $11.7 trillion problem. $11.7 trillion is the amount by which our current Social Security system is underfunded. Effectively, this is the amount by which government has over-promised benefits to current workers when they retire, while diverting payroll tax collections to our folks and to other government programs. It is the amount of our personal resource that should have been deposited into the Social Security Trust Fund, a fund that has never since its inception been anywhere near fully funded. If all of us 120 million or so wage earners tried to cover this obligation with our credit cards, we would have to charge close to $100,000 apiece—way over our credit limit.

Eating the elephant

A recent change in Social Security regulations calls for increasing the age at which full benefits are available, to age 67, for those born after 1960, effectively advancing the retirement age by almost one month each year. This is the first step in scaling down the promised benefits in order to forestall the day of reckoning still to come. Rather than dropping another shoe every few years allowing the return on Social Security premiums to grow continually skimpier, it would be more productive to tackle this obligation head on, one bite of the elephant at a time, putting in place a system offering robust investment returns instead.

If we were to institute the "5 percent-max-program" laid out above, our social security premium costs would shrink dramatically, even for equivalent benefits. To solve our huge $11.7 trillion problem, here is what could be done.

First, institute the 5-percent-max-program outlined above, immediately for all workers age 21 or less, leaving everyone else on the present Social Security program. Second, prorate the coming shortfall in benefits of the present system to the younger, 5-percent-max-program workers on a percent surcharge-to-income basis. Until about 2040 while the number of workers covered by the 5-percent-max-program is still relatively small, there will be no red ink. As the red ink from the outgoing system increases, so will the number of new-program payers, until after the 45-year conversion period, the $11.7 trillion liability will have been fully discharged. It is the 5-percent-max-workers who would benefit the most from the new program, and it is those same workers who otherwise would have been faced with the burden of meeting huge premium hikes sure to be levied in the future under the present system.

If the surcharge to cover the $11.7 trillion shortfall were levied evenly over the 45 year conversion period, the constant-rate surcharge level required would be approximately 6 percent by my rough estimate. Best of all, there would always be a positive reserve fund accumulated to meet the benefit payout required for participants in the outgoing Social Security system. Certainly the 6-percent-level income surcharge is not strictly accurate, and the assumptions behind it are necessarily imprecise. Nevertheless, the conclusions are robust enough to suggest this approach could be on the right track to eradicating an issue considered to be the "third rail of politics." In the meantime, the total payroll tax would come to 11 percent instead of the 15.3 percent current rate, paving the way for the elimination of this $11.7 trillion financial millstone.

This approach to "eating" this $11.7 trillion financial elephant one year at a time would eventually put many trillions of dollars in invested assets into the hands of the middle class. This would be very stable investment capital put to productive use funding domestic enterprises. It would compensate for the loss in tax-advantaged, corporate security funds (see chapter 7) held in custody for many wage earners by their employers who are $450 billion in arrears funding their private, defined-benefit, retirement programs as of 2005 (Belt). The capital stock held in private social security accounts would probably total somewhat more than all pension fund reserves, currently amounting to about $8 trillion, held on behalf of today's workers by employers (Fed. Res. Board, federalreserve.gov). This forced-savings social security plan would fully make up for any loss in pension fund reserves resulting in no net loss to our national capital savings.

Putting social security on anything like this 5-percent-max plan requiring 45 years to fully mature may sound unduly optimistic. Who can foretell the challenges we will face before 2050 arrives? On the other hand, Social Security is one major program that can be reclaimed without posing any threat to the vested interests of either power or money. In fact, the idea that Social Security is the third rail of politics is a myth standing in the way of developing a simple, if long term solution, to a basic, festering social problem.

Some defenders of the status quo argue that we can string out the present system indefinitely by tweaking it from time to time, by carefully extending the full-benefits retirement age and boosting the premium level gradually. Maybe you could condition the public to accept the greater pain over time, but how will you accommodate the even larger health care liability at the same time? The above analysis does not account for the effect of extending the full-benefits retirement age, or the fact that, of the present total 15.3 percent payroll tax rate, 2.8 percent goes for medical programs. There is a better way, and we should take it.

Of all major important social programs needing fixing, this one could be the easiest to restore. The new 5-percent-max program would be indefinitely self-sustaining, obviate the need for continuously hiking payroll taxes, and lower these same taxes immediately for younger workers enrolled in the new program. And yet, the administration's proposal to fix Social Security by privatization is raising a storm of protest centered on the idea that committing one's social security funds to the stock market would be an irresponsibly risky option. The Democrats say we should preserve the current system by raising the cap (again) for mandatory contributions beyond its present $87,000 salary limit. As usual, the left wants to retain a government entitlement with no thought to the wealth creation process necessary to sustain it.

President Bush wants to partially privatize Social Security and put it into the hands of the people, but has not indicated how the administration would raise the estimated $1 to $2 trillion conversion cost. This unpleasant little detail would most likely be resolved by borrowing, adding a trillion dollars or more to our national debt–a move making Bush's deficit reduction pledge look anemic by comparison. The underlying issue is that Bush would like to start the process of converting the Social Security Trust Fund to a personal savings plan. At the heart of the Democrats protest against private accounts is the fact that Social Security is their invention and is the basis for their identification with the interests of the American working man. Republicans keep out!

If Social Security is to be rescued, it will have to be tied carefully and rationally to the engine of wealth production–business. Liberals would like to deny this verity. Conservatives would like to hide the cost. There is a better way.

As we leave this issue, it is worthwhile noting that while America is delinquent in meeting its obligations to our Social Security system, the rest of the developed world is in worse shape, especially Italy and France (Peterson 1999). As these countries face up to their financial misdeeds, they will become less competitive on the world scene and experience increasing social distress. The U.K. may be one exception. In the 1980s Margaret Thatcher converted the British state pension system to one dependent on contributions, not inflation. The

British social security system was rendered solvent just as ours would be by pegging benefits to each individual's economic circumstance. However, the British system is beset by high transaction costs because individual subjects are purchasing securities from costly private brokers.

As an example of applicable low cost financial management, the Vanguard S&P 500 Index Fund operates on a no-load basis with an annual expense ratio of 0.18 percent, a level which does not materially impair gross investment returns. Unfortunately, at this writing the securities brokers are queuing up outside the Congressional Office Building to lobby for legislation cutting them in for what could be a very lucrative business handling private retail accounts. Stepping up to our own Social Security shortfall (without giving away the store) is every bit as important as any other direct investment we can make in our productive economy.

The 6th: Massachusetts. February 6, 1788

CHAPTER 7

A DUAL TAX SYSTEM*

Charge It To Labor

In 1690, John Locke zeroed in on the capitalistic concept of property rights as the paramount economic rights of private individuals. He defined property value as the product of labor applied to the land. Labor was not generally taxed directly by the state. It had always been taxed indirectly by the landlord in the form of the two-thirds or so fractional take of labor's agricultural product and by direct labor conscription as in the French *corvee*. The state, or king, took a cut on commerce in commodities such as salt and tea, but had no effective means of taxing labor. We may infer from his writings that what Locke meant was that the sovereign should not have the right to enslave people by usurping (read taxing) their labor directly.

Prior to the industrial revolution, when the great majority of people were tied to the land, much commerce was carried out by barter and/or on credit. For the working class, cash transactions were the exception to the rule. But in time, factory work brought people without personal assets to the city to work for wages, and the

---

* Financial data used for analyses are from the Bureau of Economic Analysis based on fiscal year 2001 unless otherwise noted. More recent statistics will affect exact dollar amounts, but not the conclusions in any material way. See Appendices for all detailed, supporting calculations.

proletariat was born. Still labor did not face direct income taxation by the head of state. At the same time, the working class did not prosper because a surplus of labor generally exceeded the work available.

In America, an income tax was first levied during the Civil War, but was declared unconstitutional by the Supreme Court in 1894. It took the Sixteenth Amendment in 1913 to reinstate the income tax. Interestingly enough it was the working man who agitated for our first income tax. At the time, government was supported solely by regressive tariffs, duties, excise, and use taxes, and it was thought an income tax would shift some of the tax burden to the super rich. The new income tax was at first slapped on the country's millionaires, but, as we know, was expanded to cover virtually all working Americans in time. Within two years of the passage of the Sixteenth Amendment, tax levies expanded as America geared up for World War I. Over time Washington began to realize it had tapped the American pot of gold and hastened to find national needs that only more money could satisfy.

Prior to World War I, the cost of our federal government had never exceeded about 3 percent of the GDP (Slemrod and Bakija). Since that time, the federal budget underwent several more growth spurts before reaching today's outsized proportions. The 2004 federal budget was $2.23 trillion, which resulted in a $413 billion deficit. The total outlay consumed almost 20 percent of our $11.55 trillion dollar GDP, the annual sum of all domestic economic activity. State and local governments spent another $1.26 trillion, or 54 percent of the federal budget total, bringing our total tax load to 31 percent of our GDP. In return, the government provided a plethora of programs, goods, and services that can be grasped only in the broadest of terms.

The cost of our federal government has increased dramatically since 1917 when its revenue was $809 million, an amount almost equal to the total of all prior budgets between 1791 and 1916. The First World War pushed collections to $3.6 billion in 1918. By 1941, internal revenue collections stood at $7.4 billion, then jumped to $45 billion by the end of World War II in 1945 (Slemrod and Bakija). Where the 1917 budget took only 1.4% of GDP to run the country, Uncle Sam now needs $2.34 trillion or 20 percent of the GDP to do the job (Wheelock).

From World War I until now, the federal budget has increased at the rate of about 14 percent per year while the average wage has increased only about 6 percent per year including inflation, which was 3.2 percent per year. Since 1949 the minimum wage has increased at the rate of about 4 percent per year, most of which was eaten up by the average inflation rate of 3.6 percent over that period. If we normalize this analysis of federal budget growth since 1914 by taking Social Security and Medicare/Medicaid out of the mix, we find that the comparable cost of federal government would now still be 3 1/2 times the pre-World War I level based on GDP per person. The message is that government spending has far outstripped the growth in wages. If this be the price of progress, I'm not sure how much more progress we can afford.

Following his American visit in the 1830s, Alexis de Tocqueville wrote, "This young republic will probably endure until its politicians learn that its people can be bribed with their own money." It would seem that he saw the future for America as clearly as he had seen and described this new nation in his own day. Until a tax on income was first collected, government did not carry excessive debt. Even governments cannot easily borrow money without some collateral to offer. But borrowing is simple for the U.S. government because its collateral is the virtually unlimited future taxing power authorized by the Sixteenth Amendment. Thus we are now being bribed with our children's money. To quote Richard Lamm, "Christmas is a time when kids tell Santa what they want and adults pay for it. Deficits are when adults tell the government what they want and their kids pay for it."

When Alexander Hamilton was appointed Secretary of the Treasury in this new republic, he advocated the controversial idea that the new federal government should assume all the very unequal debts that the states had each incurred to foreigners during the Revolution. While this plan sounded unfair to many, his theory was that the central government would have a better debt negotiating position than each of the states did independently. Furthermore, this move would enhance the power of the federal government to speak for American interests in world affairs. The idea was adopted and worked as planned.

The demands of the World War II military buildup that precipitated a sharp increase in taxes necessitated government borrowing also. Deficit spending became the norm as government program demands outstripped tax receipts in most years. As government spending was facilitated by increased tax revenues and borrowing, the relative power of the federal government grew faster than the economy. Programs in the public interest under the Great Society and welfare expansion grew apace. And as Jefferson pointed out over 200 years ago, the state with the power to do things *for* people has the power to do things *to* them. It was the Hamiltonian idea of power achievement through spending, revisited after 150 years or more.

In addition to expanding government power by taxation and borrowing, government became more aggressive in promising Social Security and health care benefits for the future, a process which is still alive and well. These promises are reckoned as totaling $37.2 trillion over the next 45 years. At the same time, congress has been increasing corporate welfare. Industry now pays only one third (on the average) of the net income profits tax rate prescribed by law.

The programs being cooked up in Washington are a mixed bag. Certainly Social Security has met a growing need, and medical advances have been a blessing for all of us. Surely, poverty required more attention than it was getting before World War II. On the other hand, medical care has been allowed to develop very inefficiently, Social Security was never put on a self-sustaining basis, and much of welfare has only served to institutionalize poverty. Industry and special interest groups have commanded costly concessions from Washington and the public has become burdened with a complicated tax code whose intent is to control individual behavior as well as collect taxes.

Wages have grown much more slowly than government costs for several reasons. Employers manage their costs by paying labor only what the market demands. Since World War II the workforce has gradually absorbed a larger share of America's women and more foreign labor, both as immigrants and through job outsourcing. The net result has been a plentiful supply of labor, except for very brief periods. Take-home pay has been held back also because of rapidly increasing payroll taxes withheld to meet the demands of a growing population of seniors, and to cover the rising costs of private major medical insurance. In short, wages have suffered because of a surplus of labor, health care costs, and the actions of government in providing more social services.

The other result is that when the American economy prospers as it has over the last two decades, the rich get richer faster, as indicated by the increase in wealth held by the top 1 percent of Americans–from 22 to 40 percent just over the past 25 years. In spite of our general prosperity, the richest of us recede farther and farther away into the economic distance from the poorest. It is true that our primary measure of prosperity, GDP per person, has increased fivefold over the last 100 years to almost $40,000 per person. But GDP per person is not a true indicator of our standard of living increase because of the many new cost requirements we deal with just to make progress in everyday life–transportation, education, and the need for social support late in life.

The personal income tax accounts for almost half of the federal government's revenue collections. However, it serves another important social interest, also. That is the interest of congress in micromanaging our personal life. The tax code is built around the intent of rewarding certain behaviors in line with congress' wishes and punishing others not to its liking. In fact the specifics of our complex tax code have little or nothing to do with raising revenue per se, and everything to do with behavior control. It is a monument to social engineering, largely incoherent and contradictory, but remarkably efficient at penalizing our democratic freedoms. The income tax code is Washington's primary instrument by which it controls our daily life.

A Tangled Mess

Every two years or so politicians call for a simplified 1040 tax form, then proceed to pass measures that complicate it. As of 2002 we were dealing with some 9,500 pages (2.8 million words) of tax code plus over 50,000 pages of instructions and rulings...and counting. The total cost of tax planning, filing, and collecting taxes, including IRS (Internal Revenue Service) expenses, professional help, plus business and personal time spent, is quite impressive. President Bush reckoned this cost at "6.1 billion hours, or 3 million person-years, spent on filling our tax forms, keeping records, learning tax rules and other tax-related chores" (Ed. *WSJ*, April 15, 2002). Reckoning personal time spent at $15 an hour, this cost was estimated to be about 10 percent of the total income tax collection, or some $140 billion (Slemrod and Bakija). Those of us who choose to prepare our own tax returns approach this task with apprehension, if not a gnashing of teeth. A casual perusal of the table of contents of J. K. Lasser's popular tax guide for individuals (itself over 700 pages) reveals the following mind-boggling topics:

- Tax status of employee-provided insurance plans
- Amortization of bond premiums
- Adjusted basis of property sold
- Restrictions on withdrawals from 401(k) plans
- Checklists of rental deductions
- Status of estate or trust income
- Deductible moving expenses
- Unreimbursed expenses of volunteer workers
- Investment interest limitations
- Deductions for assessments
- Assessing casualty losses
- Job expenses not subject to the 2 percent AGI floor
- Travel expenses of a spouse or dependent
- Support test for divorced or separated parents
- Long term capital gains
- Adjustments to the AMT
- Children not subject to the "Kiddie Tax"
- Qualifying tests of EIC
- Backup withholding
- Penalties for underestimating taxes
- Personal and business use of a home
- Foreclosure sales to third parties
- Custodian accounts for minors
- Taxable social security benefits
- The "wash sale" rule
- Tax-free armed forces benefits
- Third year recapture of alimony
- Education tax credits
- Unified tax rates and credits
- Write-offs for authors and artists
- Keogh plan distributions
- Depreciation
- Ordinary income recapture

- Effect of wages on self-employment tax
- Disputing audit changes…and so on, and so on, and so on

This list was not put in here for your reading pleasure, but rather to point out that it takes a tax lawyer, not a tax payer, to even translate this financial/legal nonsense into American.

Typical of many criticisms is this statement sent to the U.S. Treasury Secretary by the American Bar Association "…taxpayers have lost not only the ability to understand and comply with the law without expending considerable resources, but also respect for a tax system that increasingly makes them victims of its unintended consequences and outdated or ill-conceived policies…." This cannot help but "…undermine the public's general confidence in government" (Letters. *WSJ*, April 2001).

Presidents and many congressmen have expressed dismay with our system of taxation, and several have called for a complete overhaul. President Carter called it "a disgrace." Alan Greenspan expressed his dismay with the convolutions of the tax code in a 2003 report to Congress. Might it be more user friendly if all congressmen were required to do their own taxes?

The motives that drive Congressman to make taxpaying so onerous are easy enough to recognize. They are:

- wealth redistribution—sincere efforts to help the little guy, especially those in targeted categories
- Money—as offered by lobbyists representing Political Action Committees (PACs) seeking legislation favorable to their client
- Power—gained as the result of reelection and identification with legislation favoring some special interest in one's constituency
- social engineering—the tax code is the primary instrument Congress has for nudging and/or coercing us citizens to behave as they would like us to
- Compromise—outlandish specifications resulting from the need of opposing interests to achieve partial victory (remember the three-fifths, slave representation rule written into our Constitution?)

For these reasons the structure of the tax code has become a tattered 10,000-panel patchwork quilt with overlays, stitches, loopholes, tears, textures, colors, rips, frays, and tweaks. Amid this bewildering, complex pattern are woven many threads only faintly related to taxation. Virtually every element of the tax code affects the choices we make in our everyday life. If we buy, how we borrow, when we marry, or contribute to charity. Directly or indirectly, the tax code affects almost every aspect of our life. Should we rent or buy? Should we put our assets in trust? Should we sell stock now or later? Should we offer our services "off the books"? It encourages home ownership and saving (or spending). It influences decisions on child care, parenthood, education, retirement age, and the disposition of one's assets after death. Indirectly, our choices are affected by a host of institutional taxation measures: research and investment tax credits, charitable tax exemptions, empowerment zone designations, import tariffs, investment depreciation schedules, fair pricing laws, and direct subsidies to business. All have had an influence on what we can do or purchase, and at what price. All are designed to control our economic and social behavior or manipulate the economy.

When we add to this mix the extensive body of legislation ground out each year targeting business practices and all other social issues, we can just start to comprehend how much our lives are increasingly regulated. The relative power of the federal government grows apace with the increasing flow of money to Washington. This process takes place year by year, about the same way you would cook a frog. You can't throw a frog into a pot of boiling water like a lobster because his reflexes are so quick that he will instantly jump out. But if you start cold and heat the water slowly, by the time the frog realizes he is being cooked, it is too late (Williams). It is by this gradual process our freedoms are being eroded little by little over time. This frog has been cooking now for 90 years and is in very warm water. Furthermore, the size of our national debt and the projected cost of our promised health and Social Security programs ensure that the water temperature will continue to rise.

Society and government function

The reality is that we have become a "managed economy," managed by the heavy hand of our Uncle Sam. If the personal income tax code weighs heavily on each of us, the corporate tax code along with other comprehensive legislation is a primary determinant of the profitability, or lack thereof, of private business.

The proper role of federal government can be examined bearing in mind the legitimate, constitutional interests of both business and the American people. Actually the "to do" list for government is quite short. Nevertheless, the tasks are both extremely critical and extraordinarily complex. We may expect government to be responsible for:

- ✓ Protecting us citizens and our system of government from external interference
- ✓ Protecting us citizens from abuse of our freedom of person, beliefs, property rights, or legally contracted agreements
- ✓ Protecting us citizens from the results of any significant "market failure" transaction consequences to third parties, e.g., environmental damage
- ✓ Providing for the general welfare of us citizens by (1) overseeing the function of civil institutions, (2) undertaking national improvement projects that have broad-based benefits, but are beyond the scope of private enterprise, and (3) ensuring every citizen has access to equal opportunity and a full measure of personal dignity

This is the mission that our public servants were "hired" to fulfill. Clearly these are important responsibilities requiring talented individuals and substantial resources to discharge them effectively. To this end we endow government exclusively with the legal right to use force in order to ensure compliance with law. Conspicuous by their absence are any references to managing business or spinning a complex income tax code. Unfortunately, government intervention in economic affairs has far exceeded that which is necessary for it to accomplish its mission.

Our tax system can be designed such that it is no longer an instrument of social control. It can be made relatively simple, enforceable, economically constructive, and fair. Since fair (or just) is a personal judgment influenced by our position in society, we cannot ever expect to achieve complete unity of agreement on what constitutes fairness. Still it is imperative that a tax system appear to be reasonable to the great majority of us. Properly constructed, a tax system can provide for control of the wealth differential between the haves and the wanna-haves. And it can have very important, far-reaching benefits, as will become apparent in the unique tax plan laid out and described below.

A Dual System Of Taxation

There are many ways to tax people and organizations, and most all are in use today. Tax may be levied against income, wealth, land, tangible assets, consumption, transactions, people, use, imports, for occupational licenses, or as penalties. Our federal tax system is based on both business and personal income. Our states tax both income and consumption (sales taxes) for both people and business. Local taxes are primarily wealth-based (personal property and business assets). It is interesting to note that most European countries have adopted a "hidden" consumption tax, the VAT or Value Added Tax imposed on business, as a primary source of revenue.

In the broadest sense it makes little difference where the funds are extracted from the private economy as long as they are spent productively for the public good and all citizens receive reasonable compensation consistent with personal freedom, equal opportunity, and human dignity. However, it is important that reasonable compensation be considered fair by the great majority of the recipients; meaning, in relation to social contribution.

Income tax systems tend to be progressive (higher rates of taxation for higher income people) because some wealth redistribution is generally perceived to be fair. They tend to be complex for many reasons The high rollers lobby for loopholes, tax shelters, special privileges, and trust arrangements. As a result they actually pay something less than the top tax bracket rate (currently 35 percent) suggests. At the low end (where the votes are), congress is eager to arrange for relief for the working poor in the form of exemptions and credits. In the end there are special tax privileges for everyone and a multitude of exceptions that render fully one half of all income nontaxable.

Consumption taxes also have some disadvantages. A sales tax over about 10 percent is an invitation to evasion as retailers would just stop reporting sales. Wealth tax proposals face several objections that cannot be overlooked:

1) The value of wealth residing in assets such as a private business, personal residence, or artwork may be difficult to quantify.
2) A tax on wealth would diminish the stock of investment capital.
3) A tax on wealth could drive capital offshore or into hiding.
4) You will be taxing inflation unless you adjust for it.
5) Article I of the constitution expressly forbids a direct tax upon the people.

There is a rational response to each objection. Answering these objections in the same order:

1) If you allow the asset holder to submit an appraised evaluation of his artwork or his home, consistent with inflation, for example, any underestimating can be corrected for at the time of sale, from the sale proceeds. Private business assets can be valued by continuing the requirement for filing a tax return, as is done now.
2) In our present system there are taxes levied on dividends, capital gains, estates, business, and shelter. Except where such proceeds are used for living expenses, these taxes decrease the value of the capital stock from which they are derived.
3) True, *if* the wealth tax rate is excessive. Money will always seek the highest return consistent with risk. Money leaving

this country will have to negotiate higher risk, in general, or be subject to the higher cost of social programs abroad.

4) Asset inflation means wealth increases accordingly and will capture greater overall investment returns or proceeds from a sale.

5) The income tax already is a direct tax upon the people, as authorized by the Sixteenth Amendment. Furthermore, the practice of taxing income and capital gains arising from property holdings is well established and accepted. Taxing the profits derived from wealth is just an indirect way of taxing wealth itself.

A simple, dual tax system could be structured to meet the criteria of simplicity, enforceability, fairness, and economic progressiveness. A clean, flat tax on both individual income and wealth could provide the funds required to finance government and promote our legitimate sociopolitical goals at the same time. A flat tax is one where all income or wealth would be taxed at the same rate. A clean tax system means that deductions, exemptions and credits are kept to an absolute minimum. What follows is the skeleton of a model dual tax system that might best honor our need to fund government while promoting our dedication to national prosperity, opportunity, and freedom.

Caution! We are about to take a leap of faith that is based on changes in tax practice that you may feel are not feasible in that the following provisions do not make a distinction between federal, state, and local taxing entities. While this may not be technically realistic in the context of entrenched political interests or even claims of states rights, this approach lends itself to the objective of analyzing and optimizing our political and tax practices, and developing the true potential advantages of a better tax system.

Individual income tax

Tax all individual income at a fixed rate except:

• inheritances or winnings from pure games of chance (lottery)
• any amount contributed to religious or 501(c) organizations (charities and foundations)

- the first $10,000 of earned income (zero tax bracket)
- that amount contributed to social security accounts, up to some specified limit
- social security income received from annuitized accounts
- capital gain
- interest
- dividends

All labor tax to be withheld and paid *for* the employee *by* the income provider.

Individual wealth tax

- tax all net wealth (property, tangible, and financial assets) at a fixed rate
- all wealth tax to be paid *for* investors *by* business organizations based on audited fair market value or market capitalization if ownership is public
- tax on personal tangible items above some threshold value to be paid directly by individuals

Business tax

- no tax on profits
- pay environmental taxes and/or penalties as appropriate
- withhold and remit tax on wages and salaries on behalf of recipients
- remit wealth tax on behalf of equity owners

Other taxes

- tax on Trusts - same as individuals
- no sales tax (consumption)
- no excise taxes (use)
- no estate tax at death (wealth)
- no others

In order to understand how this simple, dual tax system might work out, we have already looked at our three major social programs in chapter 6 and tailored them to meet our broad sociopolitical and financial goals. Now we will have to develop the detailed cost parameters and taxation metrics to illustrate how the entire system fits together. In the following text, we shall highlight only the major aspects or this plan. The statistical facts and detailed calculations supporting these findings are developed in the several appendices.

Income Taxation Simplified

The proposed new income tax system is radically different from the one we labor under now. It has very few tax deductible expenses and a radically different approach to specifying exceptions from taxable income. Very importantly, however, it would have certain far-reaching effects not immediately obvious.

Income currently directed into IRAs (Individual Retirement Accounts) would no longer be exempt from taxation. Private (or public) pension plans such as 401(k)s would no longer enjoy tax privileges. Company pension and profit sharing plans would be available only as company financed benefits, if at all.

Property taxes would no longer be tax deductible, although taxes would be levied on property as part of the wealth tax code. Mortgage interest would no longer be tax deductible. Supplemental, industry-sponsored health care insurance, if any, would no longer receive a business tax deduction because business would no longer pay an income tax.

On the other hand, contributions to social security accounts would be tax deductible and required, up to some maximum income level as discussed in some detail in chapter 6.

Tax credits and most all exemptions to taxable income would no longer apply, except for a zero bracket exemption arbitrarily set at $10,000. Currently such credits and exemptions go a long way toward reducing the tax burden on individuals only marginally employed. There would be no EITC.

At the same time, there would be no tax on interest, dividends, or capital gains, realized or not. These taxes are levied against the investment value of wealth and as such are indirect taxes on wealth. Nor would there be any estate tax or AMT (Alternative Minimum Tax).

There would be no sales or excise taxes, which in practice are indirect taxes on labor.

With no income tax for business, one primary rationale for partnership organizations would disappear. The partnership business format fits the working practices of lawyers, accountants, and certain business agencies whose partners bring in their own clients and operate with a large degree of independence, generally with the guidance of a managing partner. Also, it fits the format for raising capital for defined projects with a finite lifetime, as for a Real Estate Investment Trust.

One significant advantage of doing business as a partnership organization is the ability to pass though all partnership profits, untaxed, to the partners. This allows the partners to sidestep the double taxation of dividend distributions they would experience if working within a corporate framework and having an ownership stake. In return for this business tax forgiveness, the partners are subject to some form of joint business liability. The risks of this arrangement came home to roost in the case of the prestigious auditing firm of Arthur Andersen, which was put out of business overnight for the questionable actions of a few partners in the Enron debacle. Without this relative tax privilege, many business organizations would not assume the liability risks attending a long term partnership arrangement.

The trust agreement is a primary instrument for protecting assets, avoiding estate taxes, enhancing income, and controlling the disposition of one's assets even after death. As a legal instrument, the trust originated during medieval times in England, where kings had assumed the prerogative of confiscating the property of any aristocrat who might be convicted of a felony. In defense, the aristocrats developed the idea of giving legal title of their land to the church (which was exempt from the king's predatory practice) while reserving equity or use rights to themselves.

This "trust" became embedded in the law as a method of protecting capital assets for personal use (beneficial ownership) by relinquishing actual ownership (legal title). This practice in its numerous modified forms is used today as a legal means for protecting assets and income against taxation by the state. Although trusts can serve many purposes, they are often designed with tax avoidance in mind.

Trusts would be subject to the same tax treatment as individuals. The wish to preserve family assets for one's heirs has made the trust agreement a primary vehicle for postponing or even bypassing the estate tax that until recently could take as much as 55 percent of the assets from large estates. This tax, on occasion, has forced the sale of a family business to raise the necessary tribute for the state. The popularity and effectiveness of trust agreements is attested to by the fact that $94 billion was tied up in split interest trusts in 2000. Irving Blackman wrote a book which "...teaches you how to use the system and its 22 strategies to pass your entire wealth (or even increase the amount of wealth) to your family without any reduction for taxes or other costs."

The estate tax is a "porous tax"* that most wealthy people find a way to minimize or even avoid altogether by forming trust agreements or establishing private foundations, sometimes to great family advantage. While this tax is scheduled to expire gradually over time, its ultimate demise is by no means a done deal. Under the dual income and wealth tax plan proposed here, there would be no tax advantage to executing trust agreements since trusts would not be tax-preferred instruments and all wealth in trust would be subject to taxation. This tax avoidance device would largely disappear. The exceptions here would be to protect one's personal assets from damage claims, as with a professional worker, to bypass probate court, to specify powers under joint ownership arrangements, or to honor some post-mortem, taxable distribution caveats laid out by a trust grantor reaching out from the grave to control his heirs.

Presently, capital gain taxes on appreciated assets can be sidestepped by donating such assets to foundations and/or charitable organizations, or by just passing such assets on to one's heirs at death instead of selling

---

* As a crude estimate, deaths among the top wealthiest 1 percent (3 million people) owning 40 percent of the $53 trillion national wealth would produce $250 billion in taxable estates annually given an 80 year life expectancy. Using 2001 criteria, a 55 percent tax rate and a $675,000 exclusion would yield tax revenues of about $120 billion annually. The actual estate tax collected was $28 billion in 2001. The uncollected difference of approximately $90 billion can be attributed to legal, tax-preferred, asset transfers to foundations, trusts, and charities, and to clandestine events such as extralegal transfers to family members and offshore accounts. (Note: this rough projection does not include missed revenue for the many less-than-1-percent wealthiest individual millionaires who die, nor does it account for the offsetting ~$11,000 annual tax-free gifting provision).

them and realizing a taxable capital gain. If passed along, the tax liability normally incurred by selling and realizing gain does not attach to the inheritor. The new asset value for tax purposes (the tax basis) becomes the value at death. The wealthy employ many other legal means, such as tax shelters, for creating net income by minimizing their tax bill. Many of these involve limited partnerships dedicated to low income rental housing, natural resource ventures, or even phony leaseback arrangements which are especially attractive when the top tax bracket is set very high or a large capital gain otherwise carries a big tax liability.

Thus far we have set forth the elements of a system of taxation that is very simple and would be easy to live under. It would eliminate some 10,000 pages of income tax provisions, many of which are politically motivated, and the associated restrictions on our personal freedoms. It would eliminate about $100 billion in tax preparation-related expense and illuminate the true cost of government. It would help to restore efficient, free market operation and promote the feeling that we and government were on the same team.

To gauge this proposed plan, we must look at its cost and the sources of funds that we would require to finance it. First, we must determine the new taxable income base against which we can levy personal income taxes. We will do this using financial figures based on the 2001 tax year. Appendix B details the results of this calculation: $5.484 trillion in taxable income.

Next, we must calculate a new 2001-equivalent expense budget. Tables 1, 2, and 3 in Appendix A show the old and new budget expenses based on the taxation changes proposed above. These tables also reflect the assumption of all medical and education expenses into the federal budget, and the absence of social security expenses, as they will be handled directly by the private sector (Appendices C and E). Table 3 indicates we will need to raise the 2001-equivalent of $2.703 trillion in tax revenues under this proposed tax plan, $2.265 trillion for the federal budget and $438 billion for state/local expenses.

This will require a flat income tax rate of 49.3 percent; 41.3 percent for federal and 8.0 percent for state/local use. The federal tax rate reflects the assumption of all health care (Appendix F) and one half of all education expenses (Appendix A) by the federal government. While this rate may seem exorbitant, you will see that the total overall cost to the public will have been reduced and the service options expanded.

This proposed income tax plan has certain practical advantages worth mentioning. Individuals would no longer have to contend with 1040 forms, as all income tax due would be provider-paid at the single applicable rate. The provider would also remit all tax-exempt, social security deductions to the individual's personal account (see chapter 6). As a second bonus, this system would eliminate the need to search for tax avoidance schemes that take time to develop and may distort investment and other economic transactions.

Admittedly, this is a grossly oversimplified model and would require many refinements to cope with the unintended consequences that inevitably arise when sweeping changes are made. On the other hand, you may have seen other major tax system overhaul proposals advocated with virtually no discussion of even the obvious secondary effects that might ensue. There are several major reasons why it would be difficult to adopt these suggestions, and we shall discuss these in chapters 8 and 9. Nevertheless, this model would have a host of very great advantages for America and all Americans, compared to our present practice.

While the flat income tax with a minimum of tax preference deductions has many virtues, it would be like a man with only one leg to stand on, without compensating provisions to prevent destabilization of society arising from the inevitable, great wealth differentials that would arise. Clearly the most ambitious of us would find a way to accumulate almost all the national wealth. This would drive the rest of us into penury, as the alpha males (and females) erected an oligarchy for family and close friends. The robber barons and corporate monopolists were on their way to achieving this financial coup throughout the "Gilded Age" leading into the 20th century.

However, we have not yet developed fully half of our tax story. This is where the wealth tax comes in as a second leg to stand on.

Wealth Tax

What is included in this broad category of assets referred to as wealth? It may be defined as the net sum of the nation's tangible assets held by individuals, such as real estate, as well as financial assets, like savings, equities, pension fund reserves, and equity in nonpublic business. The fourth quarter, 2004 Flow of Funds report issued by the Federal Reserve Board put our national net worth at $56.8 trillion for 2003 (Fed. Res. Board, federalreserve.gov), or $193,000 for each and every one of us 295 million Americans. Think of it. It makes you wonder where *your* family's share is, doesn't it?

Many people, especially those at the very top where most of the wealth is concentrated, will find the idea of taxing wealth a violation of their property rights, if not a pernicious flirtation with socialism. But in fact we do tax wealth even now. The 55 percent estate or death tax was a tax on wealth. The 35 percent tax rate on corporate profits is an indirect tax on wealth, although the actual tax burden has been whittled down to just 11 percent, courtesy of various credits and tax shelter schemes (Frontline, February 19, 2004). So are the income taxes levied on capital gains, interest, and dividends (which are taxed twice). Local property taxes are paid by everyone of the two thirds of us who live in our own home, and by the other third, disguised as rent. The AMT on excessive income stands guard to ensure that you do not become entitled to an excessive level of legal deductions. This AMT surcharge to the income tax captures excess income that was headed for wealth accumulation, but is increasingly ensnaring more middle class tax payers each year as inflation boosts apparent earnings.

As previously outlined in this chapter, almost all of these taxes would go away, replaced by a direct tax on wealth. As of 2001, the top 1 percent of the population who owned 40 percent of all private wealth, paid 34 percent of the total federal tax collected, but would have paid only 18 percent of the total under a flat income tax system (Tax Foundation Publications, taxfoundation.org).

Why would anyone be inclined to think that a tax on wealth might be considered wise? Especially when the constitution forbids a direct tax on people? When John Locke pointed out that a property tax is the first step along the path of depriving property owners of their freedom? When wealth is the source of investment that drives our economy? When it might drive capital away?

As already mentioned, the constitutional prohibition of any direct tax on the people was breeched by the Sixteenth Amendment in order to institute the income tax, now the major source of government revenue. It is very important, however, that any plan for taxing wealth must accommodate some economically realistic limits so as to preserve its availability for investment.

Levying a tax on wealth while at the same time exempting wealth-derived income from taxation can render the tax consequences a wash, or drive the balance either way depending on relative income and wealth tax rates. Appendix E shows that the net return after inflation on investment grade corporate securities for the wealthiest investors would yield a return within 0.25 percent, if we set the wealth tax rate at 2%, whether it was invested under the present system or the proposed system. Wealth is no more economically sacred than labor and should not be amassed at the expense of labor. Wealth and labor only develop their full potential in terms of their symbiotic relationship. You can't have one without the other and still prosper. Fairness would depend on establishing a reasonable balance between the two tax rates.

There is another very important goal, which can be realized using the proceeds of a wealth tax. It can be used to honor the implied promise of equal opportunity for all in areas of critical importance to both the nation and its citizens. With careful planning and execution, a Wealth Tax Credit (WTC) could be put to use by individuals according to their particular needs without the interfering command and control of the federal government.

It is important to each of us and in the collective interest of society that every one be able to maintain a sound body and mind, prepare to live a productive life that he or she values, be afforded equal protection under the law, and live in independent dignity when time starts to take its toll. Education, medical care, legal representation, charity, child care, and social security are critical needs not ordinarily met for everyone in a capitalistic society. We have considered the three major areas in chapter 6 and now will develop the financial means for sustaining each need. The advantages and economic viability of this proposed wealth tax system will be discussed at the end of this chapter.

We will not all accomplish the same ends no matter how hard we try, but we should have the same opportunity to take a shot at them. Let us now consider how this wealth tax might be put to work.

FREEDOM'S VECTOR

Citizen Allocation Of The Wealth Tax

Skipping right to the bottom line, the dual income and wealth tax system to be developed will call for a clean, flat income tax rate of 49.3 percent (Appendix B) and a clean, flat wealth tax of 2 percent if all the changes and assumptions inherent in the proposed program modifications were adopted. The 2 percent tax on net taxable wealth would yield $3,035 per person annually, to be available as the WTC (Appendix D). In the scenario developed here, all health care and the core half of the education program would be covered by the income tax. The optional half of the school funding would be covered by the WTC along with the other discretionary uses highlighted below. Social security would be handled directly through the private sector.

Before you close the book, you should know also that this system certainly should make it possible to *decrease* the cost of running America, *increase* its productivity, and promote superior prosperity for all. Before dismissing these tax proposals out of hand, follow the program development and analyses with an open, if skeptical, mind. You will see that what at first glance appear to be draconian tax rate proposals can serve to enhance our personal prosperity and democratic freedoms, improve the vitality of our nation, and go a long way toward restoring confidence in government.

The purpose of the income tax would be to provide for essential government services. The purpose of the wealth tax would be twofold. First it would serve the need to stabilize the wealth gap between rich and poor in the interest of civil harmony, a function now performed clumsily by our complex income tax system. The second purpose would be to supplement our basic education, health care, and social security systems, with a discretionary credit available to all citizens.

In this process the wealthy would see a relief from taxes on all investment proceeds, such as interest, dividends, and capital gains, elimination of the estate tax, and a reduced need for tax planning. We would all see a relief from property, sales, payroll, and excise taxes. We would see lower consumer prices and perhaps higher wages. The least of us would see improved education and health care opportunities without any destruction of incentive to strive for improved personal circumstances.

The proceeds from the wealth tax would be designated as a WTC, available to every man, woman, and child. In addition to the education, medical, and social security programs covered in chapter 6, the following important, if lesser, areas would be eligible for coverage by the WTC.

Room and board

There will always be individuals who find it beyond their ability to secure a satisfactory economic position in society for any of a number of reasons. As noted in chapter 5, our social standards of dignity make it imperative that we provide emergency help and even accountable, ongoing assistance. Where necessary, otherwise uncommitted WTCs would be available as the first line of defense to defray food and shelter costs when personal resources have been exhausted. Such humanitarian use of the WTC would require authorization by a case worker and trigger a tracking process, if applicable.

Legal

The WTC would be available to pay for legal representation, if needed. We are constitutionally and morally obligated to guarantee every citizen equal protection under the constitution. The right to legal representation can better be served if the WTC is available for this purpose.

Child care

The WTC would be available for child care for working parents. Preschool children require constant supervision. This requirement can make it nearly impossible and/or too expensive for some parents to pursue a livelihood and attend to the necessities of raising a family.

Public interest

The WTC would be available for the creation and support of tax exempt 501 organizations. Charitable giving and public interest program support, mentioned in the last chapter, would be deductible from taxable income and/or eligible for WTC support.

The Tax Program In Action

- Every citizen would be issued a National Identification Debit Card (NIDC) annually with a charge limit equal to the wealth tax credit (WTC).
- Use of this NIDC would be limited to medical, education, legal, child care, charity, social security, and emergency food and shelter purposes as described above.
- Every card holder would have the option of supplementing any government provided service in these areas with his WTC or private funds at his discretion.
- Credits would be transferable for use among all adult members of a legally-defined, nuclear family, except for minors whose credits could not be transferred away.
- The NIDC would carry a photo of the owner and require a PIN (personal identification number) for use. A biometric identifier, such as a fingerprint, could be used if necessary for safeguarding WTC entitlements.
- Upon expiration annually, the unused balance remaining on the NIDC would roll over and add to the card holder's new annual supplement.

A simple example can serve to show how the proposed tax scheme featuring the WTC and a $10,000, zero tax bracket tax exemption might be put to work for a family of four with two school age children. The earned income of $18,200 a year is set to coincide with the official poverty level for this family in 2001. This example assumes an annual WTC of $3,035 per person (Appendix D), and an average school system cost of $7,810 per pupil (Appendix A), the core half of which would be government-financed, and the optional half to be paid for from the WTC.. It is based on an 11 percent social security premium and a $4,000 pass through credit (see footnote **).

Item	Present Program	Proposed Program
Income	$18,200	$18,200
WTC	0	$12,140
Income Tax	0	$ (4,043)
Payroll Tax	$ (1,392)	$ (2,002)
School*	0	(7,810)
Benefits**	free school	$ 4,000
Net Apparent Income	$16,808	$ 20,485

The income tax shown above is calculated using the $10,000 zero bracket exemption.

The proposed program leaves our family almost $4,000 better off, even after the optional half of the school program is paid for, for both children. However, some of this net position is made up of the WTC and the $4,000 pass through credit. The pass through credit is really the expectation of retail price reductions anticipated as explained in the footnote below.

For the 10 or so years that the two children might both be in school, it would be very difficult under the present program for our family to manage on $16,808 cash a year, depending upon geographical location, of course. Total family needs would be somewhat better met under the proposed system with the $3,677 added margin. To meet family needs in extreme circumstances, part or all of the $12,140 WTC could be converted to cash and the optional half of the school program even cut back or curtailed completely, if necessary, leaving the family with $27,000 in cash to cover emergency expenses. Under the present system, these objectionable options do not even exist. Upon completing high school, the $7,810 school expenditure would be freed up to meet other needs.

---

* The optional school costs would be determined by the student's family and could range anywhere from zero to the limit of their unused WTC.

** Retail purchasing benefits accruing from the elimination of $206 billion in profits tax, $477 billion in private health insurance costs, $309 billion of sales taxes, and $358 billion in employer-paid payroll taxes, would be reflected in the retail price of consumer goods and services. Since the average per capita benefit of $4,750 (Appendix G) would not apply uniformly depending on spending patterns, a benefit credit of only $1,000 is arbitrarily assigned for each of the four marginal-earning-family members.

Virtually every family with income above the poverty level would be able to have their children participate in the optional half of the curriculum at a school of their choice with this level of WTC benefit, and no individual would be without the $3,035 basic provision made possible by the WTC.

You may be quite certain that virtually all of the $1350 billion pass through cost reductions for business and other organizations would flow through the economy and result in lower retail prices, because that is the standard process in a free marketplace as competitors struggle to maintain market share.

Meanwhile, our family would be paying no sales, excise, or property taxes. It would have complete, standard health care services and the basic half of education covered. Any family of four would achieve some net benefit unless their earned income exceeded $25,000 a year.

In effect, the wealth tax system would strongly direct each person's $3,035 WTC to be dedicated to expenses they might normally incur anyway, if they had the money. This accelerated level of support for a family with only very limited resources would be a real boon. These are the families in most critical need of assistance and these are the areas most important to the whole nation.

Even at a 49.3 percent flat tax rate, this dual tax system would be progressive and still not destroy incentive to strive for earnings above the $10,000 zero bracket level, because higher earnings would not jeopardize the WTC entitlement. Although the exact relative benefit of the proposed dual tax plan can not be pinned down with any real precision, it is clear that the highest earners would pay higher income taxes and that the excess dollars collected would be heavily applied for the benefit of the lowest earners, that is, those below the poverty level. The structure of the income tax program would tend to slow the accumulation of riches at the top even though the direct wealth tax at 2 percent would not by itself result in any significant redistribution of wealth.

A direct flat tax on wealth would replace all the indirect taxes that attach themselves unequally to wealth. The wealth tax is a companion to the income tax that would allow "we the people" to have a direct stake in determining our education level, our health, and our dignity.

Integrity Of The Dual Tax System

The integrity of any system is defined by its reliability in achieving the purpose for which it was designed. The overall goals we set out to achieve by overhauling and redesigning our old tax system are several. They are to:

- raise the revenue required to execute the necessary functions of government
- fund and provide for the efficient delivery of education, health, and social security services
- facilitate freedom of choice according to individual need.
- ensure opportunity for all citizens
- enhance the rate at which productivity and national wealth expand
- provide for a reasonable redistribution of wealth in the name of social stability and dignity

Would our dual tax system be consistent with these major objectives? The soundness of this new design must first be tested for economic viability. This will require examining where the money comes from and what it is spent for. So, first let's run the money. Only the major financial conclusions of this exercise are presented in this section. All assumptions and calculations supporting these conclusions can be found in the Appendices.

The major assumptions used in this exercise are that total health care costs would be set at 11.9 percent of the GDP and the mandatory social security tax rate would be set at 5 percent of labor income and limited to $3,000 per year. Meeting the funding requirements of federal and state/local governments would require income tax rates of 41.3 and 8.0 percent, respectively (Appendix B), while a 2 percent tax on private wealth would produce a WTC of $3,035 for every man, woman, and child (Appendix D).

So how does our proposed dual tax system work vis-à-vis the goals set out above?

- It raises the income tax revenue required to run federal, state, and local government, including the cost of universal health care at roughly the same level of service, and the core half of the public school education program of critical importance.
- It makes possible an annual reduction of $245 billion in health care costs alone.
- It puts K through 12 education in private hands with an obligation for public, uniform, achievement reporting.
- It provides for comparable social security benefits at about one third of the present cost by providing for private accounts invested in the quality end of the private securities markets.
- It makes it possible to discharge the $11.7 trillion unfunded overhang that would have had to have been made up by increases in payroll taxes, reduced benefits, or even government borrowing.
- It provides for a progressive income tax that serves to slow the accumulation of wealth at the top along with a neutral wealth tax.
- It provides for a WTC affording everyone generous freedom of choice among health care, education, social security, food and shelter, and other items of equal importance to both our people and the nation.
- It allows individuals to augment these essential medical, educational, and social services in the private market in accordance with individual need.
- It makes possible an accelerated rate of economic growth resulting from:
  a) a basic education ensuring that almost all graduates are ready for productive employment instead of many just hanging out on street corners and learning the art of mischief making,
  b) the elimination of the need for costly, sophisticated financial planning and nonproductive uses of capital in the interest of tax avoidance, and
  c) an improved standard of health for all citizens.
- It lowers the cost of business, making it more competitive in the world marketplace while enhancing purchasing power at home.

- It gives the great middle class a more direct stake in American economic success by eventually channeling as much as $10 trillion of social security assets into the private economic market over time.
- It eliminates the tax advantages of profit-sharing or matching pension plans, rendering them a potential benefit that might be made available by business solely for the purpose of attracting good employees.
- It enhances individual freedom by eliminating the social engineering embedded in our tax code, equal opportunity by putting basic education in private hands, and dignity by securing a social security system built on assets, not just promises.
- It eliminates the $25.5 trillion unfunded liability building behind our Medicare/Medicaid system.
- Most importantly, it is designed to be a depoliticized system, transparent and easy to understand. It would be a system that would help foster faith in America and its government leaders.

If you haven't read the assumptions behind this dual tax plan very carefully or read over the low-income-family example, you may have been ready to close the book after seeing a total income tax rate proposed of 49.3 percent for all earners. In fact, this total rate is mainly determined by health care costs, without which the rate would be 27.8 percent, or 22.8 percent if you include education.

If you have a seven-figure bank account, you might look at the 2 percent wealth tax proposal and say, "No way!" But where will you put your money to work where there are no interest, dividend, capital gain, or estate taxes, and find greater safety for your return? Appendix E shows the differential net returns you might expect on secure investments, between current investment expectations and the suggested dual tax plan. Inflation-adjusted rates of return are based on 80-year averages for secure, investment grade stocks and bonds only. The comparison is very favorable.

The total financial impact of adopting the dual tax system based on overhauling education, health care, and social security is an impressive $245 billion national savings, (Appendix G). Eventually, when the unfunded Social Security deficit is liquidated in 2050, an annual financial bonus of $407 billion would accrue to all taxpayers who had been paying 6 percent of their salaries against this $11.7 trillion liability. Also, we might hope for a school system in tune with the desperate needs of our inner city youth, only 50 percent of whom graduate from high school in the Cleveland, Ohio, school district. The nation would gain immeasurably in terms of productivity and social harmony.

Were we to fund all present government expenses and our total health care bill from a tax on labor alone, it would consume about 54 percent of our total income. And if we did not cap the present level of total spending for health care and Social Security, this burden would swell to around 60 percent of our total personal effort.

Why should we think the individual states would give up their right to levy and collect income, sales, and property taxes? Under the proposed system, all taxpayers would be paying 41.3 percent of their taxable income to the federal government. There is no basic legal doctrine preventing the federal government from offering each state the right to piggy back on federal government tax collections to the level of any percentage approved by the taxpayers of that state, thereby raising their total tax load by that amount for each state. The federal government does not need the court's permission to pass through tax revenues to the states. It does so now with its block grant programs which totaled $309 billion in 2001.

The total potential savings cited of $245 billion does not take into account the huge loss in productivity experienced because labor and capital are misdirected by legislative fiat. Nor does it take note of the enormous annual cost avoidance realizable by holding the line on medical costs and Social Security premiums. The trillion dollars of our GDP estimated by Peterson (2004) to be dissipated by inefficiency and subsidy waste is a measure of the cost of supporting the status quo and the unproductive effort it spawns in the interest of America's power brokers and financially privileged members. We should now look more closely at the role played by our system of financing and conducting elections.

The 7th: Maryland. April 28, 1788

CHAPTER 8

THE POLITICAL PROCESS

The cry for help had been growing louder for several years as the prices for prescription drugs advanced relentlessly. Eleven million seniors on Medicare, who did not have private supplemental health care coverage, were being squeezed because the cost of drugs came directly out of their own pockets. America's pharmaceutical firms apologized, citing the sky high cost of the research and testing required to bring new lifesaving drugs to market. The president responded with a drug benefit program to cover these expenses, pledging the cost to be only $400 billion over the next decade.

Congress took note, bought the president's program, and came to the rescue of our growing army of seniors, some struggling with a cost for pills exceeding $4,000 a year. At $40 billion per year, this new program would provide $4,000 annually for each uninsured senior, an amount more than adequate to cover their collective drug needs. In fact it should be enough to buy private, supplemental health insurance for each of them.

The action was swift and the timing was propitious, in that the Medicare Prescription Drug Improvement and Modernization Act was passed a scant 11 months before the 2004 elections. While this program seemed to be a bit pricey, how do you put a price on good health?

In 2004, not long after the ink from the president's signature had dried on this bill, the White House said "Oops–the real cost would be $534 billion." Last March, Richard S. Foster, Medicare's chief actuary for nearly a decade, said administration officials threatened to fire him if he had disclosed his belief in 2003 that the drug package would cost $500 to $600 billion. In February of 2005 it was announced that the total cost would be $1.2 trillion, but not to worry, because $190 billion would be offset by Medicaid transfers and, along with other economies, the bottom line would be only $720 billion (Ceci Connolly and Mike Allen, washingtonpost.com). How nice. This means the typical family of four would only have to ante up $1,000 each year to cover the cost. Surely, the benefits must somehow be extensive.

For those Medicare seniors without private supplemental medical insurance coverage, who have incomes above 150 percent of the poverty level, the net drug prescription benefit will be skimpy or nonexistent unless their drug costs exceed about $6,000 a year. For those on Medicaid with incomes below 135 percent of the poverty level, the drug coverage *will* be extensive—almost complete. On balance, this new prescription drug benefit will greatly encourage the use of expensive drugs like the rheumatoid arthritis preparation Enbrel, costing about $11,000 a year. The Wyeth pharmaceutical company should see their revenues for Enbrel surge as this medication for arthritic old-timers becomes available for the first time to seniors of only marginal means.

If our unfortunate seniors without supplemental health care insurance will benefit generously from this bill, it will not be at the expense of the drug firms. They should be adding about 20 percent to their estimated 2006, $320 billion in domestic sales (Angell), and with their lucrative 15 percent return on sales, should be pocketing an additional $10 billion from the bottom line. So it's true. The benefits flowing from this Medicare prescription bill are *indeed* extensive.

In the meantime, your congressman has made 11 million voting friends for his caring response and, indirectly, assured another 30 million seniors that they will not be forgotten. If this be so, why do I feel like a frog in warm water? Is it because this 1100 page costly patch to our health care program is added to my tax bill or maybe just put on Uncle Sam's credit card, a card having no apparent spending limit? Or is it because our rich pharmaceutical friends just got another payoff in recognition of their political loyalty?

If our poor seniors badly needed this medical first aid, the drug firms were pleased to help out, as were our congressmen. Big Pharma contributed $14 million directly to political campaigns in 2002, following an industry lobbying price tag of over $90 million in 2001 alone. Between 1997 and 2003, "…the drug industry has spent nearly $650 million on political influence…," all told. The "Top 10 Drug Companies Made $36 Billion Last Year [2002]– More Than Half of All Profits Netted by Fortune 500 Companies" (Public Citizen, citizen.org).

This completes our look at one legislative package undertaken in the interest of advancing our general welfare. To mix metaphors, the scene of this slow frog cooking is Bismark's sausage factory. Otto von Bismark, Germany's late-19th-century chancellor, once said, "There are two things you don't want to see being made…sausage and legislation."

The meeting between money and politics takes place in Bismark's factory. It is here the various engines of prosperity and other interests caucus with our elected representatives. The legislators draft legislation under the close and watchful eye of the lobbyists. Sometimes, when the legislators need help, the lobbyists even prepare a draft for new bills. Sometimes you need only change one word in a proposal to make a hundred million dollar difference in the outcome. Representation at these meetings might cost you maybe $25,000 if you hope to have a voice, although no checks are written at the time. Nor do our representatives make any promises, for that would constitute an illegal *quid pro quo* arrangement. Money and power have an unspoken understanding. If you don't have the price of admission, you have to send an e-mail. Adam Smith definitely would not approve.

When the various political interests have had a chance to massage the bill to the liking of a majority, they emerge from the factory to vote in full view of us frogs who are busy watching Seinfeld reruns. In this manner, the rights allocated to citizens by the Ninth and Tenth Amendments are being cooked away gradually just as is the frog's life.

Politics And Money

If the accumulation of money is addictive, the exercise of power can be intoxicating. Money and power have a way of finding each other no matter how many obstacles are put in their path. As a U.S.

Senator, John McCain campaigned to stem the flow of soft money to political parties in the 2000 political primary campaign, spending millions in a vain attempt to capture the Republican presidential nomination. Senator, war hero of the first magnitude, undisputed patriot, descendant from a line of U.S. Navy Admirals, and tireless campaigner; he couldn't quite sell his message. The public was only lukewarm to his warnings about the pernicious influence of the "iron triangle" of money, lobbyists, and legislators, in American affairs.

After the political dust settled in 2001, McCain continued the crusade for campaign finance reform, dismaying politicians of all stripes. They all agreed reform was a good idea, just like mom's apple pie, while ducking the issue when the cameras were safely switched off. The wish without the act is a sure sign of a system sliding into decadence. Congress finally granted him the real thing in the form of the McCain-Feingold Bill, after assuring itself it could cover the loss of soft money with hard money donations and private ad sponsorship. They were right. At the same time it is encouraging to note that an occasional leader is willing to risk his political capital in the interest of us frogs.

Politicians need money to feed the cash hungry TV monster, the primary means by which they communicate their message and project their persona to the voting public. In 1960, the estimated cost of campaigns at all levels of government was $175 million, or 0.0003 percent of the GNP (Thayer). Today's politicians are a tad more expensive. The bill for the 2004 election ran close to $4 billion, or about 0.04 percent of GDP for the federal election of two executive and 470 congressional slots. In real terms, that's more than a hundredfold increase in the dollars required to get all the seats filled in Washington.

Gone are the days before World War II when you could "scatter a handful of coins on the Capitol [of California] rotunda..." and speculate "...that two bucks might start a riot," was a comment attributed by Thayer to the state lobbyist Arthur Samish. While today's sums seem quite large, they have great leverage in terms of results. The path to big business success is greased by political campaign contributions. Actually, it is a little surprising that our elected representatives can be "bought" so cheaply considering the value of their services.

As a caution, we should not denigrate the necessary and vital role that congress plays in affording us the legal protections required to advance the interests of a free society. By the same token, we should pause before branding all politicians as cleverly deceptive and innately duplicitous. The fact is that almost no politician has the level of public popularity that would be required to escape the grip of McCain's Iron Triangle.

To this end, the average congressman spends half or more of his or her working hours trolling for funds. He or she must attract several thousand dollars each and every day on the job to buy public exposure time. Imagine coming to work each day to greet a line of silver tongued lobbyists with checkbooks in hand, lining the halls outside your office door. What politician wouldn't be immensely relieved to minimize this never-ending fund raising task, and the time and finesse it takes to hear out the stream of favor seekers competing for his or her ear? As politicians, our lawmakers must balance very adroitly the latest public opinion poll against the interests of their financial backers and lobbyists, numbering about 50 for every congressman.

While politicians may just love the idea of cutting back on the time required for fundraising, in fact, few would voluntarily opt out. The simple reason is that financial support is the primary source of his or her power. Fund raising is the time consuming but necessary activity by which politicians forge their financial support base, nourish issue-based relationships, and establish peer influence in congress.

If you don't think this is important, consider the case of Robert Torricelli, the New Jersey democratic senator who "elected" not to run for reelection in 2002. He was highly favored for his renown as a big money magnate, bringing in truckloads of "soft money" for discretionary party use. When the flow of soft money was curtailed by the McCain-Feingold bill and he was accused by a convicted Chinese national of accepting illegal foreign funding in return for advocating legislation favorable to the donor, he was sufficiently tainted in the public mind that party principals called for his scalp. They convinced (allegedly) the New Jersey State Supreme Court to legitimize Torricelli's eleventh hour withdrawal from the Senate race and ran a distinguished, but 88-year-old "used-to-be" in his stead. Fundraising ability is a prime prerequisite for political success, as is public image.

The major contributors to political campaigns are industry, labor unions, special interest groups, a number of wealthy individuals, and now, an increasing army of small online donors. What is the motivation for big contributors to part so eagerly with their hard won cash? Surely there might be an element of patriotism or general attraction to either liberal or conservative ideals that induce some to support political parties and/or candidates.

However, the major contributors are not writing checks out of the goodness of their hearts or out of some altruistic impulse to support our precious democratic system, no matter how much they may value it. Most big contributors want favorable legislation or agency rulings to enhance their competitive position, an unfair business advantage, or even a quasi-monopoly as the preferred result. They are seeking competitor prohibitions, subsidies, tax credits, tariffs, loan guarantees, price controls, government contracts, and relaxed workplace and audit standards. You name it. The list is long. Some large donors will fund both political parties or opposing candidates just to cover any eventuality.

Special interest groups want to protect or broaden the rights of their constituents. They all have money and sometimes endorsements to offer. Since quid pro quo agreements are strictly illegal, contributions buy only access, principally through PACs or lobbyists provided by Washington law firms specializing in educating or just schmoozing the pols. If you can't buy access, try the Internet.

The issue of monetary influence in national politics first came to a head in 1913 when appointment to the U.S. Senate could be purchased, at least in some states. Some senators became single issue advocates. There was a "copper senator," an "oil senator," a "steel senator", and so on. The upshot of this extreme political influence peddling was the Seventeenth Amendment providing for the popular election of U.S. senators. This concession to democracy constituted a reversal of the intention of the 1787 Constitutional Convention signers who wanted no part of democracy as they understood it.

The most egregious plundering of public assets took place during the 50 years starting during the Civil War. Congress granted spectacular land concessions to the railroad builders to construct the first transcontinental railroad, a rush undertaking designed to ensure California and the West did not pursue plans to form a separate union. This historic undertaking, carried out mainly by imported

Chinese labor, netted men named Stanford, Vanderbilt, Crocker, Durant and others a fabulous prize–21 million acres, almost 1 percent of the entire landmass of the United States of America. This effort led to the expansion of the steel and associated mining and shipping industries. Over time, the people's government was bought up by the so-called robber barons who branched into all manner of business on a national scale, securing monopoly status with the aid or tacit approval of the political establishment. The Gilded Age was born when two locomotives met face to face at Promontory Point, Utah, in 1869, just 7 years before Custer lost his life attempting to finish off the last of the defiant Indian tribes.

The Horatio Alger morality shared by much of the public and supported by the strong religious convictions of the time gave rise to the Populist movement. It, in turn, led to the Progressive political movement right after the turn of the century. The Social Darwinism attitude of the time, which was offered as justification for over 55 percent of the nation's wealth winding up in the deepest 1 percent of American pockets, was finally challenged and restrained following the adoption of the constitutional amendments of 1913 to 1916.

The Gilded Age of the 1880s through the turn of the century had ushered in a spectacular rise in big business, as epitomized by John D. Rockefeller's Standard Oil Co. and its hardnosed monopolistic practices. By 1900 Rockefeller had captured 90 percent of the U.S. oil refinery capacity. He achieved this position by gaining financial control of the rail transport of oil from the Titusville, Pennsylvania, oil fields. This move was followed by under-pricing competitors in the retail market, then buying them out on the cheap as they faced financial oblivion.

This was the tail end of laissez faire economics that had prevailed for over a century, since the beginning of the Industrial Revolution. The accumulation of truly large individual fortunes by a handful of Gilded Age tycoons threatened the economic freedom of rival businesses as well as the consuming public. Monopolistic corporations were brought to heel only gradually as the government learned how to apply the still new Clayton Antitrust statutes. Since then it has become necessary to approach Washington bearing an ever-larger measure of largesse to receive a hearing.

5

You may have seen or heard a congressman declare, when quizzed, that campaign contributions have no influence on legislative decisions. And there certainly are some very strong, independent politicians in government, men and women of great integrity, like the recently deceased Daniel Patrick Moynihan. On the other hand, more than one businessman has confided that well-placed political contributions are the best investment they could make for their business.

Keep in mind that the goal and very soul of business activity is profit. Money is invested with the expectation of a return that exceeds the outlay. Elections are usually won by the candidate with the best organization and the most public exposure–the incumbents. The businessman cannot survive and make his material contribution to society without profit. The politician cannot achieve the opportunity to make the rules we live by without cash. Thus has it ever been, just as Dorothy found it to be in Emerald City. The trick for Dorothy was to sweep aside the green curtain, exposing the Wizard.

The supplicant who converges on Washington for an audience or hearing in which he can educate an elected or appointed official, buys his ticket up front with cash, the most desirable and useful commodity. But he may have more to offer. He may be able to sponsor supporting ads and endorsements to strengthen a candidate's position. And if a corporate leader can put more people on his payroll as the result of some forthcoming business boon, a politician can claim to have helped "create jobs," a truly magic phrase in the political lexicon. And who knows? Some job created might just go to someone close to either the contributor's or the recipient's heart.

The cost of creating jobs generally renders the process a negative economic strategy. The communists created jobs for everyone simply by going to the local factory and saying, "Hire these five men." It didn't work out well at all. In America, government *pays* industry to put people to work making things or providing services that we otherwise would not want to cover the full cost of. Greg LeRoy writes that the continuous roll out of state Economic Develop Programs costs us around $50 billion a year to create jobs, many of which do not even materialize. The price tag may come to $100,000 or more per job. So we have more people working and making things we really don't want very much, people who could be employed making things we really do want.

If we have excessive unemployment during stable economic times, it may be because the unemployed are not trained and organized to do what the buying public is willing to pay for. As in Alice in Wonderland, we have no way of knowing which jobs are important if government, with our money, just creates them. Wonderland economics crowds out Adam Smith, preventing us from maximizing the fruits of our labors. The objective of economic activity is to fill needs and in the process create wealth. It is not to create work.

Government legislation and regulation has the most far reaching effect of any single factor affecting the profitability, or lack thereof, of business. Every law or regulatory edict creates financial winners and losers. Robert Leone has detailed how pricing policies for natural gas have pitted producers against consumers and other producers on an international basis, how efforts to promote increases in the endangered sea otter population have determined the relative fortunes of abalone fishermen and farmers, and how banning the use of fluorocarbon propellants has affected the fortunes of container manufacturers and the cosmetics industry.

Virtually all business ventures of any appreciable size learn quickly the necessity of protecting their turf, and many become proactive in lobbying for their exclusive economic advantage. Each new edict increases the power of government in appealing to the winners and placating the losers. In this process the public has no champion save government itself, which is under great pressure to take the side of business. The public is rarely aware of the issues being contested or the economic consequences, and generally accepts them without protest.

The Sixteenth Amendment was passed to require the rich to shoulder a larger portion of the country's financial obligations. However, the income tax became the means by which government grew larger, based on our labor, and more controlling using our own money. The Seventeenth, providing for democratic election of Senators, was designed to mitigate the influence of money on politics; however, it left only a very porous barrier in place between them.

Daniel Fusfeld wrote that one of the three great challenges we face "is posed by large-scale corporations and modern technology. If democratic values are to prevail, means must be found to preserve people's rights and individuality...while retaining the ability of large corporations to operate effectively." If anything, this observation has taken on even more urgency today than when it was issued nearly 40 years ago.

The Cost Of Subsidy

Examples of legislative handiwork on behalf of some special interest are not hard to find. They abound in every administration. The now-infamous and defunct Enron Corporation spread a good deal of money around through the '90s, culminating in $2.4 million for the 2000 federal election alone (S.Weiss). A key piece of legislation, the Comprehensive National Energy Policy Act, enabling states to deregulate their utility companies, had become law in 1992. California took the bait in December of 2000 and deregulated its electrical energy production and transmission systems, but not its consumer rate structure. Enron's revenues skyrocketed from $12 billion in the last quarter of 2000 to $48 billion for the first quarter of 2001. Enron's good fortune brought California rolling blackouts as Enron and others manipulated the flow of power over the national electrical gird (Giombetti). We do not know why the Republican-appointed FERC (Federal Energy Regulatory Commission) Director failed to intervene when electric rates soared and power was shut off in California. Did Enron's several one-on-one secret meetings with top administration people play any role in this fiasco? We only know that the Enron debacle was facilitated by the accounting schemes set up under its CFO (Chief Financial Officer) and blindly endorsed by a financial community that refused to see that the emperor had no clothes (Eichenwald).

Through questionable and/or illegal accounting and business practices the investing community and Enron's own employees were deceived into bidding up the price of Enron stock, elevating its market capitalization to seventh highest in the nation. In the process they had lots of help from outside auditors, investment banks, and analysts. When the green curtain was finally pulled aside, there was no "there," there. Investors and employees all went down the tubes clutching their near-worthless stock certificates. Californians are now facing up to the elevated tax levels required to cover the cost of government ineptness and corporate greed The new governor of California, a politician known for his Mr. Universe titles, is now managing a budget shortfall and payments against a $28 billion debt for the richest state in the union.

The fallout from the Enronomics method of doing business spread to the accounting industry, the only private business segment operating with a direct, fiduciary responsibility to the public. In 1994 the SEC (Securities and Exchange Commission) proposed revised accounting standards to be implemented by FASB (Financial Accounting Standards Board), The accounting industry retaliated, on behalf of its industrial clients, with $6 million for congressional campaign support. The Senate nuked the SEC proposal and threatened to do the same to its chairman, Arthur Levitt, when he next advocated the prohibition of mixing auditing and accounting functions from being practiced under the same roof. Within six months of the 2001 Enron bankruptcy, the Arthur Andersen Limited Partnership, once the industry flagship, was put out of business, a development cheered on by the same cheerleaders in congress who had previously voted for the status quo of inadequate accounting standards.

American industry issued 200 restatements of earnings for 1999, a statistic averaging out at around only 20 in the 1980s (Wessel). This was a serious housecleaning, the need for which can be traced, in part, to internal congressional interests. What is perceived of as an American business failure, was facilitated by an American political failure. The business failure was a leadership failure on the part of a number of talented business leaders who lost their moral bearings and succumbed to greed in the face of huge financial opportunity, following the country's relaxed standards of sorting out right from wrong. The political failure allowing freedom to turn into "greedom" was precipitated by politicians at first catering to business interests, then later lining up on the side of righteous indignation.

You may be curious as to why one Alfonso Fanjul, a sugar cane producer, threw a million dollar presidential fundraising bash at his Louisiana estate in 1999. Could it have had anything to do with the high U.S. tariff on sugar imports, allowing domestic sugar prices to hover far above the world market price, to the delight of Mr. Fanjul's accountant? Is this practice in violation of NAFTA (North American Free Trade Agreement), which specifies that all sugar tariffs and duties would gradually decline to zero by 2008 (O'Grady, December 20, 2002)? It is hardly surprising that the sugar growers mounted the principal opposition to the newly adopted CAFTA (Central American Free Trade Agreement) trade agreement.

Why in 2002 did congress slide through a bonanza, 10-year subsidy of $190 billion (A. Murray, Mittal) for agriculture, the maximum permissible under the World Trade Organization (WTO) guidelines? This was a return to the Depression era supports scrapped in 1996, for farmers, few of whom were hard pressed at the time. It was not likely to "save the family farm," since two thirds of all farmers, mostly small ones, would not see any material relief. No explanation was ever even proffered to justify this additional dollop of welfare for the affluent in agribusiness. By my estimate, the cost to us nonfarmers certainly exceeded $1,000 per year per vote for the mostly red state incumbents.

In May 2004, the senate almost passed an energy bill including a provision for a boost in ethanol production, in spite of the allegation that ethanol production facilities pollute about as much as the gasoline being displaced and may take more energy to manufacture than it produces (Fialka, Aug. 23, 2002). The National Corn Growers Association and Archer Daniels Midland lobbied hard for a several-billion-gallon increase in ethanol production at both ADM and farmer-owned production facilities. Previously, Senator Tom Daschle from South Dakota had stated that significant increases in the use of an ethanol additive to gasoline should add 50 cents to the price of a bushel of corn. It didn't work for the corn farmers or Tom, the Senate majority leader, one of the few who lost his seat in the 2004 election. Now that experience has confirmed that ethanol production can require as much as $1 a gallon subsidy to be competitive, congress has raised the subsidy and simultaneously doubled the allowable ethanol production in the $14 billion, July 2005, Energy Policy Act. Nice work for the $100,000 "investment" made by ADM in the 2004 election campaign. The subsidies are so lucrative that Fanjul and the sugar growers want a piece of the "biomass" market, too, based on the conversion of sugarcane.

Micah Sifry and Nancy Watzman place the cost of corporate welfare at $1,600 per person, just short of $480 billion total for industry that pays less than $200 billion in profits taxes. The money sent to Washington to grease the skids of corporate welfare can have important secondary effects also. Corporate welfare raises the cost of all products containing sugar. It allows for the chronic evasion of meat inspection standards. It weakens attempts to lower the level of pesticides allowable in baby foods. It has made it possible for cable TV vendors to increase premiums threefold since 1989. It has blunted efforts to increase the mileage efficiency standards for SUVs. It is believed to be responsible, at least in part, for the epidemic increase in the use of asthma inhalers, up by a factor of two in five years (R. Kennedy), while the air-polluting electric utilities industry is sending $86 million a year to its favorite candidates. In the past four years, environmental laws have been reversed and/or ignored, while campaign contributions from polluters have piled up (R. Kennedy).

In short, the special provisions, exemptions, and privileges arranged for those who bring money to Washington accrues to our progressive loss of personal freedom, may jeopardize our health and environmental quality, blunts the competitiveness of business, and raises the price of conducting our personal affairs. This is how the frog gets cooked. This recipe does not honor the government's constitutional duty to provide for the general welfare of its citizens. Quite the opposite.

Profit is not the only motive driving lobbyists to Washington, DC. The National Rifle Association put up $17 million in support of congressional elections alone in 2000, representing the interests of almost 4 million NRA (National Rifle Association) members, just over 1 percent of the US population. Originally, the NRA was concerned with handgun safety, but has morphed into a Second Amendment defender of the right to bear arms, any and all arms. In 1994 there were 38,000 firearm-related deaths in the U.S., competing for top honors with a comparable number of auto traffic deaths. There are now approximately 200 million firearms in cabinets and drawers in this country, or one for every adult on the average.

It is one of Washington's best open secrets that most congressman avoid even discussing handgun registration openly. In addition to outright dollar donations, the NRA spends big bucks (allegedly north of $10 million) on TV ads and calling campaigns, to block virtually any restrictions on registration and/or possession of anything that shoots bullets, including AK 47s (Moscoso). Even the democrats lost their enthusiasm for renewing prohibition legislation on automatic weapons in 2004, allowing those statutes to lapse without a murmur.

There are yet more direct, time-honored methods Washington incumbents have for getting votes. For instance, "buying" Ohio and Pennsylvania votes from the steel workers by imposing a 25 percent tariff on certain imported steel products just before the 2002 congressional elections, in direct opposition to the president's and the WTO's stated positions on international trade. Now some may question the economic wisdom of this move, but then politics is not an intellectual sport.

These are but a few highlights of the mischief that took place in the sausage factory in the past several years. We, the public, buy and eat the sausage not knowing what is in it.

The total campaign expenditures for the 2004 federal election year of almost $4 billion should be put into perspective. This may sound like a goodly sum spent just to "educate" the voting public about the 900 or so congressional and executive candidates who ran for office. But it is less than 1 percent of the total subsidy made possible by a congenial congress each year. These several hundred billion dollars of subsidies are unnoticed because they come mostly in the form of tax-avoidance legislation for industry. There is no way to assign the numerous business subsidies to specific campaign contributions, but no one over the age of 18 is so naive as to believe the actions and the results to be coincidental.

It is certainly possible that the value of government subsidy to industry constitutes as much as a tenfold return on investment for industry. Furthermore, there is a disguised cost to many of these subsidies. They tend to prop up failing or marginal business concerns and penalize healthy ones, diverting capital investment from its most productive uses. Worse yet, these subsidies often result in environmental damage, whose effects must be rectified by throwing good money after bad (Roodman) to reverse the injury to mother nature.

The disguised-subsidy legislation continuously ground out in Washington's sausage factory is a drag on the free market economy that does not show up in federal budget outlays. It may be counted only by the loss in tax revenue that must be made up by your and my income tax contributions. There is no way to quantify the extent to which our rate of productivity growth is slowed by this political mischief. Arguably, our annual 1.5 percent growth rate of real GDP per capita over the last 140 years (Heilbroner and Thurow) might have been measurably higher if government was not in the business of specifying for business not only what must be done, but also how to do it. Like the fiasco brought on by cutting auto emissions by using methyl tertiary butyl ether (MTBE) or ethanol, or the requirement that 10 percent of the cars registered in California be electric-powered by 2004, for instance. These electric autos have yet to be sighted.

The process of making legislation by politicians and lobbyists has prompted some to observe that by comparison, sausage making is by far the cleaner and more orderly process.

The role of government has no place in domestic business except as its actions are in the interest of a majority of us citizens. Government has no incentive to legislate efficient business practices nor the expertise to supervise for-profit operations. When the FCC (Federal Communications Commission) decried that AT&T had to lease its transmission lines out to budding Internet companies at a price below its own cost, it hastened the downfall of one of America's most respected and revered business firms. Today, most of those start-up companies, hastily formed to capitalize on AT&T's misfortune, are out of business because they couldn't weather the competition brought on by that action. And AT&T is a mere shadow of its former self.

One way to look at a fraction of the cost of business subsidy to the taxpaying public is to examine business taxation statistics. Corporations paid $189 billion in profits taxes in 2004, escaping about $400 billion in taxes because of government sanctioned deductions and credits, shifting the liability to you and me. We must also pay for the direct subsidy of $19 billion each year to agriculture and for various expensive jobs programs around the country. Targeted tax breaks for business are the price it negotiates in return for campaign finance support.

Business tax breaks, outright subsidy, and all manner of legislative measures are also the politician's tools for recognizing the billions in campaign funding support received this last election year. It's an interesting process. People pay, directly or indirectly, the full ongoing cost of government operations: $2.3 trillion a year including $160 billion for interest on the national debt. In response to the public's democratic demands for better benefits, government spends each year more of the public's money to pacify it. When the elected politicians go back to work in Washington, they craft legislation in both the public's interest and the special interests who paid their campaign bills, putting a much larger bill on our tab. Government can usually kill both birds with one stone, as it has with the Medicare Prescription Drug Improvement and Modernization Act. If we the public paid the election campaign bills directly from the public treasury (about $2 billion a year), might not we get the full attention of our elected officials?

The traditional process by which Washington looks after us voters takes place under the cover of the annual Omnibus Appropriations Bill. This is every Congressman's opportunity to bring home the bacon for his constituents by "earmarking" pet projects for his district. The 2005, $388 billion bill featured 11,000 such projects costing some $16 billion. Projects such as the $100,000 Punxsutawney Weather Museum grant (to feed the groundhog?) and $325,000 for the National Wild Turkey Federation in South Carolina. The six year, $286 billion Highway Transportation bill just signed into law features such projects as a $232 million bridge for Alaska. This "bridge to nowhere" will take you from an 8,000 population fishing village to a small island with 50 residents. $950 million of the $25 billion pork package in this bill went to Alaska under the guidance of Alaskan Congressmen Don Young, the chairman of the House Transportation and Infrastructure Committee, and Senator Ted Stevens on the Senate Appropriations Committee.

Interference in private business affairs was a practice of the failed 18th century trade practice of Mercantilism in Europe. Government should let business exercise its unique talent to generate wealth and apply only those prohibitions necessary to protect citizens and other organizations from corporate abuse. Targeted legislation or subsidy for one failing business results in the misallocation of capital investment, economic inefficiency, and the production of goods and services the public would not otherwise find worthwhile to purchase. All in the interest of getting some congressman elected and enriching his political friends.

The conduct of our national affairs is determined by the dynamic balance between government, special interests, and us voters. The advantage in the system is weighed too heavily in favor of industrial money, upon which politicians depend. The result is government legislation too complex for the voting public to comprehend and damage to both the economy and our personal freedoms.

Political Campaigns

From time immemorial governments have found ways to commandeer the fruits of individual labor and put them to uses of its own choosing. From the beginning they have sought to gain control over the day-to-day behavior of their subjects, the better to maintain social stability and discourage potential challengers. It was Thomas Jefferson who warned, "The natural progress of things is for government to gain ground and for liberty to yield." The U.S. Congress is not immune from this progression.

Until the inception of the American experiment, however, no government ever had any insight into the theory of wealth creation through free market economics, as laid out by Adam Smith in 1776. America practiced Smith's ideas, although by default, under the policy of laissez faire economics. Under this hands-off economic system that prevailed during the industrial revolution, America prospered for about 150 years as its citizens were free to cut their own deals with a maximum of Yankee ingenuity and a minimum of government interference. However, it is quite clear that the American government has been watering down Smith's basic idea for large corporations. Laissez faire economics was often short-circuited by big business and politicians, for instance, in the case of building the country's rail system. The economic philosophy of keeping government's hands off business did not prevent Washington from lending a helping hand now and then.

So if private money has a major distorting effect on the political process, why not just cut the Gordian Knot and fund political campaigns from the public treasury? The esteemed 34-year veteran of congressional politics, Lee Hamilton, sees it as the only viable solution to government influence peddling. If this suggestion sounds unlikely, just consider what Madison and Jefferson were able to accomplish after nine years of wrangling in the Virginia House of Burgesses. They won passage for a bill separating church and state, an idea so far out, it had not ever been applied in Western history, Henry the VIII excepted. But by 1787 it became the constitutional standard of, if not the immediate modus operandi for, a whole new country. And this separation has worked extremely well. A wider separation between government and business could have a very positive effect on wealth creation, as well as on the practice of democracy and freedom in America, if effected properly.

Before we take a meat cleaver to the present system, however, we must consider certain of the practical problems and implications facing us. Remember. To be a businessman you *must* make a profit. Otherwise you will soon work for some other businessman. Likewise, to be a politician you *must* get elected. Otherwise you are just another citizen with voting rights. Yes, and to be elected you *must* have money. The simple and elementary explanation for the destructive power of John McCain's iron triangle of money, lobbyists, and public policy, is the need to tap major sources of dollars and entertain the implicit suggestion of influence in return.

Industry does not squander its hard-earned profits on rank speculation, and politicians are not just hanging around and waiting for a free lunch. So who might you suppose gets *by far* the lion's share of campaign contributions? The House Appropriations Committee, of course; the boys who cut all the government checks (Coburn). For instance, in 1985 the House Ways and Means Committee and the Senate Finance Committee, comprising only 10 percent of congressional membership, received fully 25 percent of all the PAC money going to congress (Slemrod and Bakija).

In the case of the incestuous relationship between American government and business, there are some formidable practical problems to consider. The first problem shows up in the 1976 Supreme Court ruling in the case of *Buckley v. Valeo,* wherein money to support political candidates was equated with free speech. Which is to say, you may not arbitrarily restrict the flow of private funds for political campaigns, because these funds carry with them the expression of free speech guaranteed by the First Amendment. The McCain-Feingold act of 2002 was passed to curtail soft money contributions, so now the money comes in through the hard money door and through the back door in the form of 527 TV ads.

Extrapolating the Supreme Court finding in the case of *Buckley v. Valeo* leads to the somewhat disturbing conclusion that legally, some of us have greater powers of freedom (at least of speech) than others. Apparently, money *does* speak loud words, if not louder than words. It strikes me that this finding is in direct opposition to the Declaration of Independence claim that all men are created equal. Either that, or we become more than equal politically, commensurate with our bank account balance.

All political campaigns should be funded from the public treasury and candidates for public office, including incumbents, should be barred from accepting any thing of value from a private source. Since well over half of government funding is provided directly by the public, compliments of the income tax, the people certainly should have a major input as to how political campaigns are funded. We just haven't figured out how to wean congress from its dependence upon private money to dependence upon the public purse. The 1998 Arizona Clean Elections Act (Jones) might serve as a model for designing a national system. Over the last three election cycles, the Arizona statutes required that any candidate for office must garner a sufficient number of certified petition signers (each signer paying a five dollar endorsement fee) to be in line for public financing at the state level. Maine, Vermont, New Mexico, and New Jersey have felt the need to adopt similar programs.

The almost $4 billion spent to restock the executive and congressional branches of our federal government during the 2004 election campaign may sound like very big bucks; however, you have to consider that this sum amounts to less than two pennies for every ten dollars of the budgeted monies the victors would be spending each year on our behalf. If this approach would completely eliminate the influence of money on the legislative process, it would be a fabulous investment. But of course it won't.

To think that private money would not somehow find its way into the system would be like believing that water doesn't run downhill.

Certainly, 527 ads indirectly supporting candidates or their positions would proliferate and would have influence. The best you might do is to require sources of indirect support to be explicitly revealed. Prohibiting direct, private donations to candidates would not be a panacea. Nevertheless, the direct spending of candidates would be equalized and they would realize equivalent self-representation on a level playing field. Call that equal opportunity for political candidates.

Clearly, money and power can not be separated in the same way as church and state. The quest for wealth and power are symbiotic pursuits that can not be completely isolated one from the other. Still, an imperfect solution is to be much preferred to capitulation. Better to allow business and special interests to support a political candidate through advertising than to buy him outright.

A cautionary note is in order here. Should we ever be successful in limiting the corrosive impact of campaign contributions on congressional action, we must anticipate that the relative power of the electorate would grow. In order to circumvent the Greek experience of too much democracy in the hands of voters with only popular interests, it would be necessary to equip all citizens with a better understanding of the democratic process and a working appreciation of what constitutes constructive legislation.

Government needs the social equivalent of the profit motive that drives private business so successfully. That motive could be the increased ease of removal of incumbents from office for poor performance, facilitated by funding political campaigns from the public treasury. However, once elected, politicians have another very potent tool for hanging on to public office—gerrymandering.

In every state the majority party calls for redistricting congressional voting districts, sometimes even between census years. The object of this periodic exercise is to carve out areas based on past voting patterns in such a way that as many majority party seats are made safe for the incumbents as possible. Since incumbents achieve name recognition and the lion's share of campaign contributions, this process is the glue cementing incumbents to their seats. It is so effective that all 50 California congressional incumbents were returned to office in the 2002 election (Cal. Sec. Of State, vote2002. ss.ca.gov). This was so in spite of the fact that California had already been experiencing rolling blackouts and soaring electricity prices. In the 2004 general election, 98 percent of the incumbents who ran for congress retained their seats. The incumbents were working with a three-to-one advantage in campaign funds.

So desperate were the Texas democratic legislators to avoid a quorum call to vote on a Republican redistricting plan in 2003, that they fled to Oklahoma, pursued by the Texas Rangers. They ran but they couldn't hide. Led by the efforts of the House majority leader Tom (the Hammer) Delay, redistricting proceeded and the Democrats lost three seats in the 2004 general election while almost all other congressional seats remained secure. Tom has now been indicted for his role in the mishandling of campaign funds. Through the power of money and voting-district control, our 535-seat congress has become an entrenched old-boys (and girls) club based on an overwhelming rate of reelection, more interested in perpetuating its political power base than in doing the nation's business in the interest of we the people. Clearly, the question of redistricting should be resolved by computer-based, objective criteria under the auspices of a nonpartisan commission, since party politics operate in opposition to our national interest in this area.

In his 40-year study of democracies both ancient and modern, Paul Woodruff concluded that money and gerrymandering were the principal destabilizing factors undermining representative government. Since incumbents running in safe districts do not have to meet their opposition anywhere near halfway during a campaign, they are free to present a radical posture. The absence of any serious challenge to their positions contributes to the acute polarization we now experience in partisan politics. Wayne Baker conducted a study purporting to show that, contrary to popular belief, the general public is not polarized in its values and practices—only the politicians and the press.

The singular exception to the political control of congressional voting districts is the state of Iowa. But if Governor Schwarzenegger has his way, California will be the second state so exempt.

Democracy is the first line of defense for freedom, because it allows us to remove public officials from office who are not working in the public interest. Unfortunately this line of defense has been breeched by incumbents who are favored by a three-to-one margin with campaign funds and run in gerrymandered districts, rendering their seats safe from attack by a weaker opposition. Until this system is fixed, political freedom will depend largely on our last line of defense–responsible public action based on political knowledge and skepticism, fortified by personal virtue and high moral standards.

The programs developed here would require that a new job description be written for elected officials. They would have less power to micromanage tax policies, medicine, education, and Social Security, and they would have more time to do it. They would have less incentive to micromanage business and less leverage with which to do it. If the fledgling Arizona Clean Elections process is any indication, public funding could attract candidates for office who are less proficient at "selling themselves" and more interested in tailoring their programs to promote freedom and prosperity.

The new job descriptions would have to provide for adequate salaries so that personal financial concerns would play no more than a minimal role in decision-making. Importantly, there would have to be a provision for our public servants to receive high-profile recognition for their still-important responsibilities, because the most accomplished politicians have high testosterone levels and big egos that must be fed. Clearly this job description would attract men and women more concerned with serving the public interest than cutting deals for the purpose of securing another term in office.

Barring elected officials from tinkering with the details of our major social and tax systems while limiting them to an advisory and oversight role would be no mean accomplishment. Clean elections funded from the national treasury along with fairly drawn election districts would be the key to unlocking this door. Disturbing the power base of politicians could bring the power of the state to bear upon those who might choose to modify the status quo. On the other hand we will find that by simply accepting the current financing arrangements, the resulting inability of politicians to do the right thing will just continue to promote America, Inc. at the expense of America the Beautiful. Shutting off the flow of money from corporations to Washington, DC is the most important single reform required if we are to recapture government in the interest of we the people.

The 8th: South Carolina. May 23, 1788

CHAPTER 9

UTOPIA OR AMERICAN CRISIS?

The Prize

In our search for a better way to run America in the interest of freedom, opportunity, and dignity, we have introduced some radical revisions for certain of our major institutions and national programs. We have developed a dual tax system featuring clean, flat income and wealth taxes to the exclusion of all other taxes. We have designed a universal, private health care system, a core, knowledge-based, public/private school system, and a true social security savings and investment program. We have specified that the proceeds of the wealth tax be available to all people, regardless of age or employment status. This supplement for the above three programs and others may be used at the discretion of each of us. Finally, we have proposed public funding for all political campaigns.

Importantly, we have shown that these revised structures are not only financially doable, but would yield substantial savings and add to our national prosperity. The prize is exceptional. The general list of projected advantages is extensive:

- a comprehensive dual tax system, extremely simple to administer and follow
- individual tax filing required only to declare worth of private business or personal objects with some tangible value
- freedom for people and business to conduct their affairs without dodging restrictions imposed by complex tax regulations
- savings valued at tens of billions of dollars in time and money currently devoted to tax planning and preparation
- better public understanding of the cost of government
- no work disincentive for low-wage earners as there would be with a negative income tax
- elimination of the need for many partnership business arrangements and tax-avoidance trust agreements
- less micromanagement of business by politicians
- significantly lower costs for business, making it more competitive internationally
- less preferential treatment of business at the expense of the public and national prosperity
- curtailment of direct money flow from special interests to politicians
- freedom for politicians from the need for fundraising and the resultant pressures for preferential consideration
- greater freedom for elected officials to respond to public needs and act in the public interest
- improved allocation of capital resources
- a $1350 billion reduction in the price of retail goods and services owing to elimination of business expenses
- unrestricted choice of school based on staff performance and optional curriculum emphasis
- social security participation available to everyone regardless of age or employment status
- lower social security payroll taxes (11 vs. 15.3 percent) without pending escalation owing to future shortfalls
- a self-sustaining social security system eliminating the $11.7 trillion overhang in unfunded Social Security commitments
- universal health care
- unrestricted choice of primary care physician

- elimination of the $25.5 trillion overhang in unfounded health care commitments
- $245 billion of national savings annually from health care administrative costs and profits
- health care, education, and social security programs exempt from government micromanagement
- a flexible WTC benefit of $3,035 per person, offering choice in areas of vital interest to each of us and the nation
- equal opportunity for challengers seeking office
- restoration of faith and confidence in government

It remains only to be shown how these proposed programs can be implemented. They have passed the first major financial test of doability. They are not only economically viable, but would confer an annual windfall of significant proportions. Of course, successful implementation would require extensive reworking and would encounter many obstacles in the process.

Are they politically feasible or just Utopian?

Can It Be Done?

The changes put forward for consideration in this work are not all completely novel in their conception. They have been developed here in some economic and social detail for the purpose of highlighting their potential utility in furthering America's greatness by building on its founding principles. They have been examined collectively to show the enormous benefits that might be realized through synergistic interaction. The very magnitude of the prize is an indication of the difficulty you might expect to encounter in trying to capture it. The comments below are not meant to dismiss casually the awesome difficulty of realizing true progress, but only to acknowledge where some of the pitfalls lie.

The major immediate savings would come from nationalizing our health care program. When the Clintons tackled the issue of overhauling this system in the early 1990s, it imploded before the ink was dry on the draft proposal, with serious damage to the administration. The practices of our largest single business sector, as well as the livelihood of about 15 percent of our working population, are rooted in the very profitable status quo. Consider, however, that we have the only nonuniversal health care system in the developed world and by far the most expensive one. This economic drag will become more burdensome year after year as the use-now, pay-later bill from Washington comes due.

Eventually, we will have to do major surgery on this patient, or the economic disease wrought by an inefficient health care program will strangle us. All that stands in the way is $200-billion-plus of vested interest blocking our access to better and cheaper health care. The pressure for action will grow more intense as congress searches for more sources of money to feed its profligacy. No solution short of single payer, universal health care will unlock the billions in wasted effort and put this vital system efficiently in the service of the nation. This change will not take place until everyone concerned comes to realize there is no real effective alternative.

Promoting equal opportunity through education reform will be difficult also. The institution of tenure stands in the way. We will need many more demonstrations of success like the Amistad Academy, at reasonably priced, private schools, before the public takes much notice. The real key to full equal opportunity in education, however, is a concerted, well planned and executed attack on poverty accompanied by choice in a public/private school system.

Social Security reform with private accounts is a no brainer, relatively speaking. Nobody makes money from this system and no politician will get extra credits for raising the payroll tax rate again. The switch can be made if we are willing to commit to a long term, sustainable program. It would start paying dividends immediately. The great debate over Social Security has started, and the liberal faction has taken its position that funds committed to the stock market would be too risky, and besides, Social Security is their baby dating back to FDR. The fundamental truth is that, public or private, social security taxes can return handsome benefits only if America thrives economically and the contributions are tied to private investment grade securities. Any surplus funds on deposit with the government have always been spent and replaced with treasury security IOUs.

A complete overhaul of our tax system would require a difficult transition. Competitive businesses would like it. Probably the general public would like it. The rich would probably object because they would lose the opportunity to craft special privileges behind the scenes, a skill they have perfected over time. Politicians would definitely not like it because their power to control the populace and confer special favors for targeted groups would be greatly diminished. Furthermore, extensive reform of our tax system would require concomitant changes in our other social programs. The federal government could force a switch to the dual tax system that the states would have to honor, or risk citizen disaffection. Wherever money and power would be affected, the opposition to massive change would be overwhelming.

Funding campaigns from the public treasury would probably rankle only those sectors of the business community that survive on government handouts and tax exemptions. However, there is a different kind of obstacle to face here, namely the Supreme Court's money-equals-speech equation. Nevertheless, the format for clean elections is being established by several states and the movement is picking up steam. Arizona reports seeing an increase in candidates who are adverse to soliciting private sources for contributions and then having to take care of the donors.

My guess is that the Supreme Court may well revisit this issue some day and find that unequal campaign contributions equate to inequality of freedom for all, especially if the public gets behind this position. The prize is immense in this area alone, where politicians make sausage and the frog gets sautéed in its own warm fat. Public financing combined with a public commission charged with redrawing rational election districts could only bring us more-independent politicians and political competition for the entrenched old guard in congress. Clearly they would not like it.

Adopting all or even part of these program changes offers truly great economic advantages. It offers an opportunity to fortify our democratic freedoms and build a partnership between the public and government that is critical to the nourishment of America's historic greatness. As our greatest hope, we must never forget that American government serves at the pleasure of the American people. Should we forget this cardinal democratic principle, the hope for a better tomorrow for America may not be bright.

To make progress in any or all of these areas would require nothing short of a national commitment sustained by the understanding that we and our offspring would all greatly benefit personally through these changes. It would require a public that would have some grasp of the goals and some faith that our political leadership was dedicated to achieving the same objectives. As we become more deeply mired in our present day socialist drift, experience growing personal and economic pressure, and see our democratic freedoms slip further away, the search for solutions will intensify. As our influence in world affairs wanes under the onslaught of China, India, the EU, or even the WTO, we will have to adjust and improve our way of doing business or answer to our grandchildren when they ask us, "Why are we paying so much for your upkeep and where have the good old days gone that you're always telling us about?"

If we cannot run a more efficient universal health care system as other developed countries do, if we cannot effectively fund and invest our social security system as the Brits and the Chileans are trying to do, if we cannot make education work for the least of us as it does in Asia and parts of Europe, it is tantamount to an admission that American capitalism as we practice it cannot be brought fully into the service of the people for whom this country was created. Inability to seriously reform or overhaul our principal social programs is the measure by which power and money have expropriated the American Dream and our heritage of freedom.

In America we have wrought and undergone many changes over our short 218 year tenure. Our founding principles have been challenged but not yet irrevocably damaged. When social change does come, it may arrive suddenly. Many of the profound changes affecting our political system over time were not anticipated long before they actually took shape. Revolution was not even a consideration in colonial America a mere 10 years before it was a fact. The one third of the country acquired in the 1803 Louisiana Purchase from Napoleon for $15 million was the result of a spur of the moment offer. The Civil War overtook Lincoln after economic and slavery issues were neglected for four years under a noncommittal President Buchanan. Bank failures, corporate monopolies, and World War I converged to precipitate legislation authorizing an income tax, popular senatorial elections, strengthened antitrust statutes, the Federal Trade Commission, and a new Federal Reserve System, all in the space of three short years. A market crash on Black Thursday in 1929, naive economic policies, and the ensuing decade-long depression that threatened to bring down capitalism, spawned the New Deal, the Securities and Exchange Commission in 1934, and the Social Security system in 1935.

The attack on Pearl Harbor thrust America into by far the largest war effort in history, a war which changed the map of the world at a tragic cost in human life. The Vietnam War split American society asunder and its companion, The Great Society, wounded it financially. The devastating event of September 11, 2001 cast America into two wars in two years and will change the look of geopolitics far into the future. From the assassination of President Kennedy on a peaceful November day in 1963 until the social upheaval of 1968, America experienced a peaceful prosperity turned ugly and sour in just half a decade. Now the new rallying cry for foreign policy has suddenly become Unilateralism and Preemptive warfare as a proxy for diplomacy; a doctrine that aims at replacing tyranny with democracy and freedom in every last sovereign nation on earth.

Whenever such events occur in a nation's history, there is no accounting for the fallout. Clearly a time of national stress empowers critics and inclines people and their leaders to entertain ideas not well thought out. We only know for sure that there will be more such events in the future, and they will be the harbingers of major change. Short of waiting for some unknown future event to trigger a climate favorable for tax and campaign finance reform, what options might be available to us now?

The means by which our government can be induced to incorporate change are limited. One is by formally invoking the constitutional amending process, as specified in Article V of the U.S. Constitution. This is cumbersome by intent and not a means by which politicians are inclined to proceed, especially if the objective is curtailment of their own power. However, this may be the only way to limit government to oversight and prevent it from interfering with the operating details of our principal social programs. Nevertheless, here in America, we still do respect our Constitution.

The other means is through piece by piece statutory legislation. Our major social programs, as well as taxation and business subsidy, are authorized by statutory enactment and can be undone by the same process. This reversal of legislative action could require a significant turnover in congressional office holders through citizen action at the ballot box, however.

The development of any social proposition based on the intellectual application of logic and factual knowledge is a sterile, even if interesting, exercise when it comes to moving men to action. Facts and logical argument may win a debate but will not capture the heart and soul. However, when frustration or fear grip society, the consequences can be unpredictable unless a charismatic leader with sound ideas steps up to the challenge. That is what Washington, Jefferson, and Madison each did to forge our American identity. This is what Hitler did for Germany in the 1930s; tragically, with an extreme, antisocial, nationalistic program.

The explosive rejection of the Clinton health care plan a decade ago was an object lesson indicating how easy it is to get burned when you threaten the status quo without preparing the social landscape. Certainly, it would be short sighted to expect that any politician would or could initiate any major program overhaul just because it would be of enormous benefit to citizen and country. However, a sea change in the nation's economic/political affairs would cause many in congress and the white house to rethink their priorities very quickly.

Just such a sea change was predicted by Paul Volcker, the former Federal Reserve Chairman. who engineered our emergence from the quagmire of "stagflation" at the end of the 1970s. He is quoted as saying recently that "we face a 75 percent chance of a [financial] crisis within five years." (Peterson 2004). When political panic develops and extreme solutions are proposed in haste, the results can be counter productive, or worse. It is precisely at such times that a set of plans for fundamental system improvement is needed. Such plans can only be put forth for consideration if they already have been taking shape in the mind of leadership and the American public. Sweeping changes always appear to be inconceivable just prior to their occurrence. They are usually precipitated by external events or the realization that some approach has reached a dead end in the face of a call for action. We might remember the old adage—success is when preparedness meets opportunity, whose appearance is seldom anticipated.

Follow the money

In order to appreciate the tenuous financial condition the United States has drifted into, we can do what Woodward and Bernstein did in the early '70s when they were investigating the Watergate break-in under the guidance of Mark W. Feldt, Deputy Director of the FBI (known famously as Deep Throat for 30 years), Follow the money!

If the United States were a for-profit corporation, it would borrow money only with the expectation of putting it to work to generate a return greater than the interest due and payments against the principal. When this strategy fails, the corporation must meet its repayment schedule by selling off its assets. When it reaches the point at which its liabilities exceed its assets, it is bankrupt and at the mercy of its creditors, who usually call for a new management team.

The United States is a nonprofit organization with no profits to cover a repayment schedule for its borrowings, only its tax revenues. It follows that the only legitimate reason for government to borrow money is to meet some unexpected national emergency, like severe recession or war. Currently our national debt is over $7 trillion. This represents money already spent, for which we must raise enough taxes to pay the $160 billion required each year just to service this debt. This is a fair piece of change, even for a country where the federal expenditures run $2.3 trillion (plus off-budget amounts) and the entire value of its goods and services produced, the GDP, is $12 trillion.

In addition to the $160 billion interest payment, the $7.4 trillion debt must be repaid some day. The country is also responsible for eventually meeting the $37.2 trillion shortfall in Social Security benefits and medical services promised to its working and retired citizens. Based on our present methods of doing business, our children will have to ante up much more in taxes or undergo a much reduced level of benefits and services. The credit basis on which the United States can borrow money is its future taxing power. That is why we say our children are being used as collateral.

Any money the United States spends on products or services from for-profit business creates revenues and profits for the private sector. Armaments and services for the military may produce anywhere from 5 to 10 percent net profit for the private sector and be expended without producing any true national wealth. Money spent for prescription drugs may produce a 15 percent or more net profit for the private sector. These profits go to increase the wealth of our most prosperous citizens, who are on track to capture over half of our national wealth again. Thus every additional dollar the government borrows will have to be repaid by our children and adds to the wealth in private hands, wealth that can be recycled through the system again.

Of our $7 trillion-plus national debt, about $3 trillion is owed to foreign powers, countries from whom we are importing goods and services at the net rate of close to $700 billion per year. The dollars we send overseas pile up and eventually come back to buy American corporation stocks and bonds, entire business properties, and U.S. government debt, thereby completing the dollar cycle. Since interest rates have been historically low for some years now, foreigners balk at buying U.S. debt because the return is noncompetitive. So they increase their rate of return by driving down exchange rates (the value of the dollar). As our total national debt becomes large relative to our productive power, foreign countries drive our foreign exchange rates down even lower to cover the elevated risk of holding U.S. securities.

The end point in this process comes when the public begins to find ways to evade increasing tax burdens and/or protests loudly because benefits and services are being cut. Then when government attempts to roll over its debt as it must do periodically, its creditors, foreign and domestic alike, will reassess the risk and balk at repurchasing it. The psychology leading to everyone protecting his own wallet develops extremely quickly, and business grinds to a halt, precluding any belated measures to restore liquidity. Paul Volcker's predicted crisis has then come to pass. The early clues are high debt, a falling dollar, and rising gold prices; all of which we have been experiencing. The final step is a sharp stock market sell off and the flight of American dollars, unseen and unheard, probably to Asia, compliments of the Internet.

At this point it becomes critically important what the Federal Reserve Board does with the nation's money supply and, after that, what constraints government imposes on employers, agriculture, and maybe imports. Should this scenario come to pass and be handled badly, as it was in the great depression, we will then be concerned about the future of both freedom and democracy. One thing is certain, however. Government will grow larger. It always has as the result of every crisis America has suffered. It is against this background that the present administration has prosecuted a war costing several hundred billion dollars, approved an agricultural subsidy of $19 billion, a $72 billion Medicare drug prescription program, and two large tax cuts. The tax cuts may have been an appropriate weapon employed to help defeat the recession in progress, but not the spending increases.

As we strive to earn the new program benefits bestowed on us by paying more taxes of all kinds, government grows larger and oversees a greater piece of our lives. In this manner most of us slip further into an American version of European Socialism, the political model that capitalists are so wary of; the form of government that restricts freedom, features double-digit unemployment, and slows the advance of prosperity. Meanwhile a fortunate few percent of us care little because they have secured their personal freedom from the wealth of our great nation and are living off the interest payments.

There is a name for the process by which you invest your money on the assurance that you will earn huge returns, even though there is no possible means by which these returns can be generated. In January 1920, Charles Ponzi collected $1800 based on his word that the investor would earn a premium of 50 percent in just 45 days. One day in July of that same year, Ponzi glanced at a story in the Boston Post that was to be his downfall. But not before he had taken in a cool $15 million.

The U.S. government is doing Ponzi a step better. It has promised a payout over time of $37.2 trillion in cash, goods, and services, for which only our children are obligated as the future source of funds. And as with all classic Ponzi schemes, the investors are the first to protest when someone suggests there may be something amiss. They will protest later when payments and services are cut and it is too late for damage control.

To believe major programs and institutions cannot be fixed because the powers that be will not tolerate any change in their status is to accept the progressive drift toward socialism, economic inefficiency, and loss of individual freedom without so much as a murmur.

Crisis and Damage Control

Anyone who writes a book warning about pending disaster can usually be labeled a crackpot or one who presents a flawed economic argument couched in a doomsday psychology. National economies have a great deal of productive momentum that can absorb and overcome any number of adverse events and undercurrents. After the fact, we shake our heads at the dire predictions of writers such as Paul Erdman and Harry Figgie, and take on the next doomsday prediction with a knowing smile and several grains of salt. The problem is, we can never know which adverse economic event might constitute the straw that breaks the camel's back. There is always someone out there crying "Wolf!" But where were these Nervous Nellies on the eve of the stock market crash of '29? There was but one lone voice in the euphoric financial wilderness, and he didn't write a book.

Burton Malkiel quoted the financier Roger Babson as saying, "I repeat what I said at this time last year and the year before, that sooner or later a crash is coming." This was said on September 5, 1929, two days after the stock market had reached its peak, followed by what became known as the "Babson Break." When Roger arose early on Thursday morning, October 24th, 1929, some stock market speculators were still sleeping off the affects of bathtub gin from the night before. He, and certainly not they, didn't know that by sundown on Black Thursday the U.S. economy would have started an irreversible slide into a deep depression that featured a 90 percent loss in national value. It would be 25 years before the market reversed its losses and 10 years before a prostrate nation recovered from the economic shock heard around the world. Are the economic storm clouds forming on the horizon dark enough to merit our serious concern? Or will these, like many others, blow over in the powerful wind of our economic productivity?

Today we understand the complexities of our credit-based, capitalistic economy much better than we did in 1929. A few men with the most impressive economic credentials are sounding the financial alarm for an America fast drifting into treacherous economic waters. Laurence Kotlikoff analyzed the economic implications of our changing demographics and concluded that we are "abusing our children fiscally" and are technically bankrupt already. Peter Peterson (2004) asserts that we are *Running on Empty* economically. The impending financial disaster predicted by Volcker would certainly be the agent to produce action, even if action came after the fact in reaction to a collapsing economy. After looking at the size of our national debt and factoring in our off-the-books, unfunded liabilities, you would not want to bet against these pros. They are looking at real numbers, not just reading tea leaves.

The core economic problem facing the Western, developed, first-world countries, is our graying populations and falling birth rates. America faces the economic repercussions of very unfavorable demographic shifts, while the Middle East, Africa, and South America do not foresee this problem anytime soon. The European democratic socialist states, along with China and Japan, will experience economic hardship before we do. Birthrates in the EU have been falling longer, and it depends much more heavily on state benefits than on private pension payments for its seniors' security. Italy, France, and Germany are headed for trouble soon, probably in that order. We old timers are fast becoming an expensive luxury with no economic return.

The bottom line is that before 2040, the working population that pays taxes and raises families will have to shoulder the full burden of supporting our graying population—one old timer for every two workers. Add to this the cost of our pricey health care system, and you will see payroll taxes increase from 15 to 30 percent of total personal income. That's before we raise the income tax rate to pay off our mounting, multi-trillion dollar national debt, which *must* be paid some day.

It ought to be painfully obvious that we must adopt a single payer health care system to capture the billions worth of futile effort and steer it to productive purposes. Financial arithmetic makes it clear we must harness Social Security to secure, productive economic activity. Our neglected welfare class must be called to productive participation in our national life through the medium of education. We must undo the straight jacket of a disgraceful tax system and take down the For Sale sign hanging over the entrance to the Congressional Office Building.

In the absence of decisive action, we will either hit the wall economically or drift into socialism as the cost of government rises from 30 percent at present to 40 percent of our GDP. With either scenario, both our democracy and freedom will be put at risk and a great nation tarnished by internal neglect.

Nevertheless, this piece is not a primer for *how* to bring about improvements in a fundamentally great system. Rather, it is a call to recognize how far we have gone in losing our basic freedoms during the 20th century, as well as a set of preliminary ideas outlining what a better system might look like.

These ideas might be classified as Utopian, because their realization seems to be so far beyond our immediate grasp. But they are not Utopian, at least in a classical sense. They do not comprise a scheme for an imaginary Camelot where everyone is blissfully happy; or for a perfectly tranquil society, as in Edward Belamy's classic, *Looking Backward*; or even Plato's *Republic* ruled by philosopher kings. Perhaps the greatest experiment in Utopian society was proposed by Karl Marx—a faceless government providing for a worker's paradise where there was a place for everyone, with everyone in their place. All persons have different abilities, environments, and ambitions. Individual freedom, exercised responsibly in a liberal democracy, can accommodate these differences by allowing for each person's unique inputs and rewarding contribution according to its value. It can thrive on differences of opinion, debate, and challenges to government. This process is indispensable, since there will always be old problems to solve and new opportunities to chase.

The realization of these ideas reflects the true spirit of democracy and is ultimately possible because the founding fathers created a system not to honor kings, but rather to serve people. The possibility of achieving any truly significant improvement of the American way of doing business may seem limited in view of the obstacles presented by the interests of money, power, and plain old inertia; however, the possibility is absolutely nonexistent if not imagined and presented in rational, concrete terms. The degree of difficulty that might be encountered in forging social change in the interest of American freedom is only a measure of the prize to be gained. Great prizes require courageous efforts.

When we understand clearly that which might be, and before America's light starts to dim, we should pause to remember some of the American crusades that led to the significant enrichment of our democratic freedoms we now take for granted. Elizabeth Cady Stanton and Susan B. Anthony pioneered the 87-year-long movement to secure legal voting rights for all women. We must remind ourselves of the moral rightness of freedom for all men and women, as the Reverend King did when he led his people to the steps of the Lincoln Memorial to claim freedom for all citizens consigned to a second class station in American life.

The working men and women of America have over many generations earned the blessings proclaimed by the Declaration of Independence, by virtue of their service to and respect for a nation dedicated to freedom and equality before the law. But a blessing, like a right, is no better than one's willingness to secure it. The American ship of state is leaking. The passengers do not know it and the captain is steaming full speed ahead. Below decks the crew is bailing faster now and putting on more damage control patches. Just as surely as steel corrodes in contact with salt water, these leaks will grow in size. Our ship has run aground twice before since being commissioned in 1787; once precipitating the Civil War and again signaling the onset of the Great Depression. If we do not put into port for some major repairs soon, it is just a matter of time before we will all have to don life jackets.

This was **The Call** of 1776.

A call for citizen action in our America does not mean revolution against government. It means reform of government institutions in the interest of its citizens. We must not assign the cause of all our problems to politicians as individuals. Like the rest of us, they operate within a system and do what they must do to survive. If we eradicate the need for private monetary support of political candidates, we will attract people more interested in *our* welfare than that of powerful special interests, as is reported to be happening in Arizona. If we can realize a cleaner election process, fixing health care, education, and Social Security will be a much less formidable undertaking.

Dare we hope to capture the prize outlined above or even any part of it? After all, no new system or method of doing business will work well without the support of leadership and the understanding and respect of the people who are part of it. No system or law can afford us protection against human failure of integrity or disdain for moral values. At the end of the day, if we are indeed a free people, government cannot resist a universal call for change without canceling that very freedom.

I do not harbor the illusion that the proposals developed in this book are likely to be adopted in whole, or even in part, as they are conceived here. But perhaps they will serve as a standard against which we can measure any forthcoming changes. With a little luck, they may even help plant the seed of possibility and serve to cultivate public opinion in a constructive manner. New thinking is needed if we are to solve old problems. If you keep doing what you're doing, you'll keep getting what you're getting.

We cannot avoid the future, but we can change it if we act in time. Sometime by 2013 at the latest, 535 congressman will sit down in Washington to craft legislation cutting benefits while significantly raising income and payroll taxes. The chairman of the Federal Reserve, the U.S. Secretary of the Treasury, and the president's Council of Economic Advisors will sit down in the oval office to advise the president. Their advice? Mr. President, you will have to go on television and tell the American people they must meet the challenge of higher taxes or we will have to cut Social Security benefits, medical care services, education funding, and other welfare programs. Translation? The most powerful nation on earth, the nation that has led the world to freedom through democracy...is courting bankruptcy and can no longer meet its promises and discharge its debts.

The alternatives? They are all ugly and counterproductive. Print money to inflate away the debt. Devalue the currency against the Euro. Institute wage and price controls. Legislate new controls on farmers and employers. By then there will be nowhere to go to borrow more money, except at prohibitively high interest rates. Before these messages are broadcast over the public airwaves, the stock market will have started a free fall. The big money will have been cashing in, and in several seconds (as fast as radio waves can circumnavigate the globe), the proceeds will be tucked away in banks in Zurich, London, Bangkok, Beijing, Shanghai, Hong Kong, Jakarta, New Delhi, and Calcutta. As it did in the Great Depression, when the value of American business dropped 90 percent in three years, the

American social scene will then experience major changes–changes that will make the suggestions developed in this work look almost anemic by comparison. It will not be possible to raise revenues to pay our debts if 25 percent of the working population is unemployed, as it was in 1932.

Beyond our families, the most precious possession we have is our American Republic. To keep it, we must understand its problems, imagine better ways to run it, and demand accountable action from our representatives. With the blessings of a just, productive system, attention to business, and the integrity born of virtuous standards, we may restore that "City on a Hill" image envisioned by John Winthrop in 1630 on his way to the New World. Winthrop foresaw this image, taken from Mathew 5:14, as America's destiny: to be a beacon of light to the rest of the world–and until now it has been.

And the future?

The 9th: New Hampshire. June 21, 1788

PART III

AMERICA

What can it aspire to?

CHAPTER 10

MAJOR SOCIAL ISSUES

Leaving the issues of domestic reform and what role politicians might play, we would do well to examine several other important matters impacting America and the world. If it were to come to pass that we might realize a new tax code allowing for unfettered economic progress and greater personal freedom, it does not mean that our problems would just melt away and we would find ourselves without important social concerns. We do, in fact, have several very important, long term situations to address, each of which we share in some way with every one else on the planet.

Energy And Environment

America has made great strides in cleaning up its environment since the creation of the Environmental Protection Agency in 1970. Lakes and rivers like Lake Erie and the Cuyahoga River (which, as everyone knows, once caught fire) are on the way to becoming swimmable and fishable again, after recovering from a near death experience 30 years ago. Thoughtless dumping into rivers and streams has been greatly reduced. Airborne emissions have been reduced significantly, even if not yet to a fully satisfactory level. A number of major pollution sources are still far from under control, however, such as ground water contamination from the Anaconda copper mine in Butte, Montana, or the agricultural runoff from farms along the Mississippi, which has killed off virtually all aquatic life for miles around its mouth off New Orleans. Or mercury or PCB contamination that contaminates fresh water fish caught in some waterways.

We owe a debt of gratitude to our children of the late '60s who insisted we stop and look around at what was happening to our water, land, and air, to our plant and animal life, as well as to our own health, instead of just pursuing business as usual.

But some environmental issues are very obstinate. The safe, long term containment of radioactive waste is a major issue. The most potent forms of it, such as plutonium and the fission product isotopes in spent reactor fuel rods, do not ever go away once created. Not ever. Never, unless you count millions of years as less than infinity. The salt mines at Yucca Mountain in Nevada may prove to be a satisfactory long term storage site for these materials, but what about the nuclear weapons processing facilities at Rocky Flats, Colorado, the Savannah River Plant in Georgia, or the Hanford site in Washington? Without some massive intervention program, radioactive ground water seepage will surely reach and start contaminating the Columbia River one day. When the oceans become contaminated, who will cleanse them and how?

About 85 percent of our energy, our industrial lifeblood, is derived from fossil fuels: hydrocarbons such as coal, oil, and natural gas. These fuels contain sulfur and mercury, a particularly insidious element which accumulates in human bodies causing physical and mental debilitation. When these fuels are burned with air, nitrogen and sulfur oxides are formed and carried many hundreds of miles downwind, to descend as acid rain, nitric and sulfuric acids, that poison ponds and kill off vegetation at high altitudes. Fully one third of our mercury emissions come from coal fired power plants (Fialka 2003) that are believed to be responsible for the alarming increase in asthma (R. Kennedy). Unburned hydrocarbons from vehicular traffic combine with ozone to create smog to the point where visibility can be limited to a hundred feet.

The most ubiquitous of all pollutants is carbon dioxide (CO_2), the product of combustion of all hydrocarbon fuels. It is believed to be the most important in terms of its potential for causing global warming.

Atmospheric CO_2 levels have risen about 30% over the relatively short span of the Industrial Revolution. Carbon dioxide traps heat around the surface of the planet because it reflects back the long wavelength radiation that normally escapes from the earth as heat. If the earth warms just a matter of a few degrees, we know the polar ice caps will start to melt and the seas will rise. We know that virtually all local ecologies will undergo radical alteration as climate change transforms agricultural conditions and modifies weather patterns throughout the world.

That's about all we know for sure. The rest is guesswork. Scientists are paying serious attention to predicting the warming trend that might occur as CO_2 is released, based on assumptions about worldwide fossil fuel use. These predictions generally show the earth's temperature to be rising anywhere from 1/2 to 10 degrees Fahrenheit by 2100. Predictions for sea level change range from 4 to 40 inches. Not all scientists agree, however. Some think sea level increase will amount to 3 or 4 inches in this century, as it did in the last.

These predictions are cast assuming no temperature changes due to external factors, those universal forces that prevailed even when there was no one around to make fires. We know from studies of polar ice cores, from fossil records, even from the corings of 3,000 year old trees, that the earth's temperature has changed erratically over time, even without our help. The majority scientific opinion is that temperatures are bound to rise measurably over the next 100 years if we do not institute some preventative measures. Still this is not a unanimous opinion. Since the data measure only one cause of warming and are not statistically robust, no one can be sure beyond all doubt.

So why not just eliminate or cut back on CO_2 emissions? Easier said than done. Much *can* be scrubbed out of combustion stack gases, but at a very high cost. The cost is so great that the present administration trashed the international Kyoto agreement that called for only minor CO_2 reductions. No one knows for sure if the game is worth the candle. Unfortunately, the present administration appears to have turned its back on virtually all proposed efforts to combat environmental pollution.

Fossil fuels are used to convert heat into electricity at a maximum efficiency of about 35 percent. This limitation arises from the thermodynamics of the Carnot Cycle inherent in all "heat machines" like the large steam turbine generators in our multimegawatt central power stations. The problems, real or projected, arising from our heavy dependence on fossil fuels, are forcing us to give serious consideration to alternative sources of energy.

Since nuclear power development has been on hold in this country since the accident at Three Mile Island over 25 years ago, and fusion experiments show so little promise, the scientific community has been dusting off some old sci fi ideas for getting "free" power from the sun, wind, tides, and ocean temperature gradients. Assuming the capital costs of building a power capture-and-conversion system would be low enough, there are still the problems of energy storage and transport to resolve.

Harnessing sun and wind power are the most promising, thanks in part to the space program. Direct radiant heating and solar cells are in limited use today, but they are basically confined to local applications where sunshine is abundant. The capital cost of silicon, the sun-to-electricity conversion agent, is still much too high to finance a national, silicon-based power infrastructure. Wind, on the other hand, is a more ubiquitous if variable commodity and, taking a page from the Dutch practice, can be converted to electricity by wind driven generators at a near-reasonable cost.

The front running proposal at this time is to inject wind-generated electricity into the national electrical grid, a scheme that could become economical in a decade or two. GE's CEO, Jeff Immelt, is convinced electric power can be produced from wind power for 4 cents a kilowatt-hour, whereas coal-derived electricity is delivered now for 6 cents (Reiss). Projections for the cost of solar power range from 7 to 16 cents per kilowatt-hour looking out two decades (*Wired*, January 2004).

In theory, our electrical power needs could be generated from the wind blowing across only five Midwestern states; however, there are some practical as well as environmental problems to be solved before large scale wind farms can be developed. No truly significant unintended consequences have been predicted for this approach as yet, but migratory birds can be shredded by faulty placement of windmill units, and the constant drone can be unsettling to many people. Wind-generated, electrical energy sites also leave a big footprint on the landscape. In Europe some terrestrial units are being dismantled and installed offshore, while in this country General Electric is building 130 units to be placed in Nantucket Sound. One primary cost limitation of wind power arises from the fact that generating units must be placed reasonably close to power lines on the national grid because of transmission losses over the low voltage feeder lines leading from each unit.

Eventually you would want to use the wind-generated power on site to electrolyze water to produce hydrogen and pipe this gas around to fueling stations for use in mobile fuel cell units. Feeding hydrogen gas into a fuel cell to generate electricity for electric powered autos would greatly alleviate the CO_2 pollution problem, since fuel cells produce nothing but pure water as a combustion product.

Fuel cells have been under active investigation for the past 50 years and have proved to be workable and reliable in the space program. Commercial prototypes are being field tested now in several dozen test vehicles around the world. Fuel cells generate electrical power at up to 80 percent efficiency, a figure far surpassing that of any combustion-powered device. Hydrogen produced locally may be stored in only limited quantities for local use or transported by pipe anywhere you wish with virtually no transmission losses. The oxygen required for hydrogen "combustion" in a fuel cell is available everywhere in the air. It has been estimated that about 50 percent of our power might be generated in this fashion by 2050.

So why will it take so many years before fuel cell energy becomes widely available? The paramount reason is cost. Fuel cells made for space travel forty years ago were very expensive power sources. The platinum required to catalyze the breakdown of hydrogen molecules into protons which then diffuse through a polymer membrane, then cost about $50,000 for a unit large enough to produce one kilowatt of electrical power. By improving the materials technology and construction techniques over the years, this cost has been brought down to the $2,000 per kilowatt range for the most efficient, small, experimental, stationary units. This is a very significant cost improvement, but the cost will have to come down to the $200 per kilowatt range before it becomes interesting for personal vehicle use, a level probably fifteen years out at least. Then there is the major problem of funding a national infrastructure of hydrogen stations for refueling cars and trucks, and a pipeline to deliver the hydrogen. At present we have about $250 billion in capital tied up in 180,000 gas stations across the country, just to give you some idea of the scale of investment we are talking about (Ball).

While hydrogen gas does not occur in nature, it can be made in unlimited quantities by electrolyzing virtually any source of water. Should CO_2 emission prove to be a really potent factor in global warming, fuel cell energy may have to be commercialized even at some premium in cost. Over the long term, this may be our best bet for circumventing the many problems associated with fossil fuels. In 20 years or so we may just start to see small stationary fuel cells powered by hydrogen, "reformed" from natural gas (methane, CH_4), put into service. However, that does nothing to solve the CO_2 problem, since natural gas reformers also produce unwanted CO_2. A fuel-cell-based solution to the greenhouse gas problem would require an extensive conversion to a hydrogen economy.

Probably the biggest technical hurdle to jump is finding a way to pack enough hydrogen onto a mobile unit to give it an acceptable range. The tiny country of Iceland has dedicated itself to showing the world how an entire country can run on a hydrogen economy, and to this end is working on some unique approaches to storing hydrogen as part of a solid state compound in land vehicles. But history teaches us to expect unwanted by-products and side effects, somewhere down the line, from virtually all new technologies. In the best cases, new technologies ultimately become victims of their own success.

While the electrolysis of water by wind power to produce hydrogen can take place at an efficiency level as high as 80 percent, the wind does not blow with anything like a constant velocity. Storage of large volumes of hydrogen produced under peak conditions is not feasible at the present time. Pumping excess power produced into the national electrical grid means the production source must be reasonably close to the power lines. Power produced must be converted to direct current for electrolysis or transformed to a high voltage level for injection into the power grid. The conversion and transformation of power produced under variable wind conditions is feasible, but costly.

It is interesting to note that the Chinese have embarked upon a new nuclear energy program using pebble-bed reactors claimed to be immune from meltdown or any accidental release of radiation. If such units prove to be reliable, they could become a very substantial source of hydrogen, produced thermally at efficiencies as high as 60 percent (*Wired*, September 2004).

It is bad enough that modern agricultural and industrial practices stress the environment, sometimes even beyond the point of reclamation. Exacerbating the problem is the fact that we spend money to subsidize many of these activities. David Roodman has detailed and quantified subsidies in support of mineral production, logging, fishing, agriculture, energy use, and transportation. To counteract the increased load on the environment produced by these subsidies, the polluters or government are then required to expend additional resources to partially contain or clean up the consequences, resulting in additional cost to the public. The cost of government subsidies for these polluting activities has been estimated at over $500 billion in the mid 1990s.

The price of relying heavily on oil to power our transportation system is becoming onerous if not unacceptable. In an effort to secure a steady flow of oil from the Middle East at reasonable prices, the U.S. has agreed to defend Saudi Arabia against attack. This agreement seems to have been strained by the $60 per barrel price currently in effect for oil pumped at a local production cost of $5 (Huber and Mills). Over time our reliance on imported oil has increased to 59 percent of our total U.S. consumption in 2002 (Fialka, November 26, 2002). Our most significant national response to this loss of energy independence has been war in Iraq. We are making every effort to ensure a steady flow of oil from the Middle East, but armed conflict generally makes for international political instability.

Our unwritten national policy to deal with this problem is based on deploying the force required to secure and control important sources around the world, wherever they may be. To this end we are dispatching the excess troops stationed in Europe to such places as North Africa and the Caucasus region near the Caspian Sea (Jaffe), from which places we are building gas pipelines to the West. To ensure quick access for rapid deployment, the Pentagon will staff bases in places like Kyrgyzstan, the Philippines, Singapore, the Horn of Africa, and Eastern Europe.

These moves are taking place against the background of our recently stated national strategy of extending "the 'benefits of freedom' to 'every corner of the world'" even if it requires pre-emptive military action (Ferguson, June 6, 2003). We have no national plan or strategy to decrease our dependence on foreign oil, other than the use of ethanol as an oxygenating additive in gasoline. However, it is possible the expensive, new hybrid vehicles just coming to market may temporarily delay the annual increases in oil consumption.

Oil production, distribution, and consumption is as much a political process as it is technological and economic. The oil trade promises to be a cause of continuing international instability, as petroleum is the workhorse of transportation the world over.

Globalization

What is meant by the term Globalization? According to Linda Lim of the University of Michigan Business School, it is "...the increasing integration of the world's peoples and nations brought about by expanded international flows of trade, investment, labor, capital, knowledge and information." Its driving force is the specialization of business activity, leading to inexpensive products and services for all to share. Its obvious drawback is that high wage labor is made redundant in one region in favor of low wage labor in some other part of the world. When coupled with the power of the Internet, the result for America is increased outsourcing of services as well as offshore manufacturing. A software project initiated by Microsoft can be picked up by programmers in Bangalore, India, then sent on to Ireland for more development, and back to Seattle for review and testing by morning.

International trade is fueled by two factors. One is the desire for a good or service not locally available. The other is differential cost, the accessibility of a given item or talent available remotely at a better price. This is a case of business specialization on the international scene. These two factors alone are sufficient to drive trade among nations unless some adverse external factors come into play.

Over the past quarter of a century, the value of international trade has increased for several reasons. First is the continuing decrease in the cost of transportation. Second is the increase in speed of negotiation, as well as information and money transfer, made possible since 1995 by the development of the Internet. Third is the standardization and arbitration authority granted to the WTO. Fourth is the falling level of tariff barriers and other restrictions consented to under WTO regulations, NAFTA, and other bilateral trade agreements.

This process of globalization delights the capitalist traders, scares the white and blue collar proletariat, and irritates the liberal intelligentsia. There can be no doubt that globalization will continue to make more stuff and services available, often at lower prices. The economic advantages are too compelling to resist, short of war. In the process, those forces that are rendering trade ever more international in character denigrate the sovereign powers of nations and governments to which labor has always looked for protection. But certainly there is no turning back this onrushing tide. It is too powerful and too important to the enhancement of world prosperity. Most people in this world live in a state of scarcity, if not penury, and will welcome any prospect of increased prosperity. Some, however, only want it a la carte; without Paris Hilton, American hip-hop, and a stiff dose of someone else's morality.

An important facet of globalization is the ease with which capital can flow to regions of the world where it can find its highest use (read best return). The game is to put together the necessary ingredients of commerce at a location on the world map most conducive to production and service activities at the lowest possible cost, including taxes. For this you need capital, technology, low-cost qualified labor, management skills, and a politically stable country eager for investment and employment opportunities. A little consideration for the local boys in charge may not hurt either. The deciding factor in most instances is low cost, qualified labor. For service needs only, the Internet brings the benefits of inexpensive labor instantaneously to your computer screen at well over a 50 percent discount from American wages.

The United States, with high labor costs, transferable technology, borders open to trade, and easy money flow, is a prime candidate for outsourcing. There is no easy, direct fix for this problem. Over time the best, indeed the mandatory, response to this job loss through the disappearance of manufacturing jobs and outsourcing is education–the broad vesting of intellectual capital in all of our people. In time we will see progressively the automation of more and more low paying service jobs in the retail and food service sectors of our economy. "Globalization has made it easier for multinational corporations to follow the lowest labor costs and tax rates around the world..." (MacGuinias).

The character of international trade is changing rapidly and starting to encroach upon national sovereignty. Will international economics and other planet-wide issues ever supersede parochial national power and foreign policy? Certainly sovereign interests are coming under increasing pressure to yield to the terms of international trade as they become more uniform the world over.

In 1900, Great Britain, the United States, and Australia were the most productive countries as measured by GDP per person. Britain had reached the peak of its powers and was about to start losing its Empire upon which the sun never set. America was just achieving a commanding position on the world scene. In Europe, the French and others were much concerned about us "Americanizing" the world, even then (Taylor). Globalization was in full swing, at least in the limited terms of transatlantic trade. After World War I, trade languished in the social turmoil existing until World War II. Trade has now taken on a much expanded significance in just the past decade.

In 2003 we exported 10 percent of our GDP and imported at a better than 15 percent clip, leaving us an ongoing $656 billion annual negative trade balance. We import about 25 percent of our consumer goods, up from 14 percent in 1987. Wal Mart is said to be responsible for importing 10 percent of China's total export volume, or $150 billion worth, all by itself. We are a nation of consumers. The world, from its top political leaders right down to the ranks of its working proletariat, became acutely aware of and even alarmed by the word globalization during the 1990s.

The WTO was formed in 1995 under the auspices of nations interested in standardizing trade regulations and establishing a court for settling trade disputes. Prior to that, trade agreements were bilaterally negotiated with only nonbinding guidance from the ad hoc General Agreement on Tariffs and Trade (GATT) association. Countries are admitted to the WTO by consensus agreement, upon certifying their willingness to honor its regulations as ratified by their parliaments. Ninety-five percent of world trade in banking, insurance, securities, and financial information is covered by WTO regulations.

The WTO regulations that deal with trade-dispute provisions have some disturbing aspects, at least in principle. Greatly simplified, they provide for resolving some disputes behind closed doors with no direct representation by the disputants. So governments have signed on to blanket, one-size-fits-all provisions that may put certain of its laws and private firms at risk without any direct government say in the matter.

NAFTA also has some interesting trade provisions. For instance, the 1990 Clean Air Act Amendment incorporated provisions on what kind of gasoline additives had to be used in certain areas of the country, not just the result to be achieved. As a result, a California firm contracted with a Canadian company to supply MTBE as a gasoline additive. It was later determined that this water soluble chemical was leaking into the ground water, so MTBE was later banned by the state. The supply contract with the Canadians was broken, so they sued for $970 million in damages.

The interesting result was that the American firm was not liable for damages, nor was the state of California, the entity causing the trade problem. Under Chapter 11 of NAFTA, claims for damages arising from trade contract disputes become the liability of the federal government. The result was that the Canadians were happy, the American contracting firm was happy, the state of California was happy, and at this level of liability it was no big deal in Washington. The risk inherent in private trade was assumed by the government on your and my behalf. Under such agreements, government becomes one step further removed from any objections to loss of job security that might be voiced by the working man.

Annual WTO conferences as well as G-8 meetings have drawn semi-organized protesters, some of them violent, to the meeting sites. The protesters are mostly working people and/or intellectual activists. What they are protesting is not something that can be adequately described in a few succinct sentences. But what they feel and are worried about relates to loss of power and jobs. Antiglobalization is largely a collection of anticorporate views. By and large, the working man looks to and relies upon government to protect his economic interests. He is told that globalization will enhance our national prosperity. While this may be true, it does not square with the inevitable loss of some jobs here at home stemming from outsourcing and product price competition. The intellectual activist often feels eclipsed by the commercial world and has learned to use protest as well as the court system to further any number of social interests.

To the extent workers and thinkers have issues they want redressed, they feel that any loss of power by their government increasingly restricts their opportunity to get attention for their own grievances, as well as possible corrective action. They don't get to vote for WTO officials or question their dictatorial positions. In America, "of the people, by the people and for the people" is taken seriously, as are jobs.

The WTO has been beset by vigorous protests overseas from its very inception. In India, in the late 1990s, the importation of agricultural commodities put local farmers out of business because they could not compete on cost. This was the very same issue India faced after World War II when Britain dumped machine made cloth on the Indian markets, below local production costs. It gave Gandhi just the issue he needed to force national independence. Gandhi convinced everyone to spin cotton for cloth at home and boycott English imports.

In early 19th century Britain, the Luddites rioted when it became evident that the new technologies of the Industrial Revolution were appropriating their jobs. The disparate collection of protesters that show up at G-8 and other international economic conferences might be thought of as neoluddites, who are concerned with not only job appropriation, but also sovereignty loss owing to corporate internationalism.

The WTO and international financial power brokers are creating a new commercial and financial world order. In this scenario, sovereign nations gradually agree to yield some of their unilateral power in the greater interest of commercial uniformity and equitable trade practices, and not just on issues of trade. The WTO has one-size-fits-all regulations on the administration of patents, currency, schools, hospitals, wildlife, and the environment; all without regard for local issues (Wallach and Sforza). In this role the WTO is in league with two other international players, the International Monetary Fund (IMF) and the International Bank for Reconstruction and Development (World Bank).

The WTO has required Guatemala to import baby formula for use even in areas having only contaminated water, endangering infants in the bargain. They have required Great Britain to pay a $150 million penalty to the United States, simply because it cannot show acceptable cause why the British choose not to import hormone-laced beef. Ninety-five percent of all formal trade sanction protests lodged with the WTO have been overruled by these self-appointed lawyers, behind closed doors (Wallach and Sforza).

Just as Europe was in 1900, much of the world is anxious about the loss of cultural identity, especially to British music and American movies and values. Television sets all over the world have been tuned in to Dallas, Baywatch, and the Sopranos, featuring affluence, sex, and the extra-legal lifestyle. Thomas Friedman characterized the opposing influences that may clash, in the rush to globalization, in his popular book *The Lexus and the Olive Tree*; the Lexus being symbolic of the drive for prosperity and the Olive Tree being the need for cultural identity. The catalyst accelerating the rate of cultural change to near-speed-of-light levels is the Internet, which came into its own only one short decade ago. The Middle Eastern nations are particularly sensitive to seductive Western cultural influences, which are perceived as a threat to Islamic religious teaching in a male-dominated world.

With the push of a button, Moody's bond rating service can signal the world that some nation is experiencing difficulty in meeting its debt repayment schedule, and with another button some George Soros archetype can start the process of destroying or building up a nation's financial infrastructure by selling or buying its debt. Shifting really big sums of money and credit around the world can be done anonymously. When the hedge funds and day trading speculators follow suit, financial collapse can strike like lightning, as it did in Indonesia and other Asian countries in 1997. As this happens, no one knows who in the faceless electronic crowd is responsible or with whom they might negotiate.

A 13 year old girl sits in a cyber café in a remote Chinese town and chats with a cyber friend in Italy about American hip-hop music. Cool, considering she has never been more than 10 miles from home, but is casually trading ideas and current cultural fashions with anyone else the world over who logs on to the chat room or blog. The mullahs in Teheran do not approve of downloading Brittany Spears' latest MTV or perusing eBAY for alien product offerings.

Information, billions of pages of it, are at your fingertips. Information has become democratized. It penetrates political borders and undermines local customs that have been relied upon for generations, if not centuries, as the social glue regulating behavior and order in any regional culture. Young people are getting alien new ideas all over the world. Officials in Myanmar, in France, in Syria, or Iran, do not like this one bit.

All the developing countries and their wannabes know they desperately need an inflow of capital investment and technology to develop trade and build the infrastructure required for prosperity. But these countries may be high risk ventures. Did your grandfather or his country ever recoup their investment in Russian bonds? Today the WTO sets the standards for international trade, indirectly affecting a nation's eligibility for international financing. You must use modern accounting methods, have a well-regulated banking system, a functioning legal system, a stable government, and a system of public security to play in this game.

Globalization favors the consumer because more products are available in more places at lower costs. It favors large multinational corporations because they have the technology and marketing clout to produce and sell anywhere. It makes jobs for some people previously unemployed, but holds down wages in developed countries, because labor is the one commodity perpetually in oversupply.

As more foreign products appear in regional marketplaces, more retail commercial decisions are made by the Joe Sixpacks around the world. Gradually, local ruling authorities lose their control over the local rules of commerce. Power is diffused into the world wide public realm of standards that no nation decrees and that you can't influence by voting. Only the WTO stands to regulate trade among nations.

Nations appear to be fast approaching a stage where the concept of national sovereignty is being overtaken by nationhood defined in terms of the market economy. In a sovereign nation, government trades with its people the obligation of protection in return for power. This political arrangement is progressively breaking down as international events and processes more and more bypass any nation's ability to protect and sustain its people. Neither the WTO nor communicable disease nor drug trafficking respect political boundaries. The Internet does not ask anyone's permission to whiz alien ideas around the world. The WTO offers entrée to the only trade game on the planet, and they make the rules you must play by. The WTO becomes more powerful in a world where no nation feels it can be left out of the trade game. As international economics assumes an even greater importance in the viability of nations, might not the WTO morph into the role of an international governing body? Each year our Supreme Court hears more cases wherein international law is an issue—nine out of eighty such in their last session. It may be only a matter of time before our high court and the WTO find that they are at odds on some issue for which they each claim jurisdiction.

The United Nations has several serious weaknesses that show when it is called upon to oversee international programs or act as if it were a de facto world government. This weakness was evident in the Security Council debates over whether it would authorize the use of force to disarm Iraq. It is the same weakness that was exhibited by the colonial Continental Congress in 1787. It has no teeth, no attack dog, to enforce its resolutions. It does not regulate the terms of international trade. It is a voluntary organization that members support and abide by when it suits their purposes. The WTO is a voluntary organization also. However, it offers access to trade and capital along with strong, economic inducements to a country to conform to its edicts.

Because we engage in the most international trade, globalization *is* Americanization, at least for now. Its logo is "www," the world wide web. It can magnify the basketball player with the greatest talent and charisma. Two years ago, when my son and his wife were in Bangkok, they bought the local newspaper and saw a picture of the then new Cleveland Cavaliers basketball sensation, LeBron James, in slam-dunk action, smiling at them in full color from the front page.

The Internet offers unprecedented opportunity for a company with an attractive new product to penetrate markets the world over. It drives international business, with governments trolling in its wake for capital and technology, no longer the controlling agent for local information dissemination. T. Friedman (1999) quotes former NBC News president Lawrence Grossman as saying, "Printing made us all readers. Xeroxing made us all publishers. Television made us all viewers. Digitization makes us all broadcasters." The pace of globalization has been accelerated by the democratization of information.

T. Friedman (2005) quotes Carly Fiorina, the ex-CEO of HP, as saying we are entering "…an era in which technology will literally transform every aspect of business, every aspect of life, every aspect of society." The impact of the new power of globalization will increasingly dictate our foreign policy strategy, influence our international trading patterns, and even modify how we conduct our domestic affairs.

Biotechnology

As of 2002 the UN (United Nations, un.org) was predicting a world population rise from 6.3 billion to 8.9 billion by 2050, at which time it should be leveling off. Of course this means there will be that many more mouths to feed in an undernourished world whose environment is already stressed by modern farming practices.

Richard Manning (*Harper's*, Feb. 2004) tells us we humans claim fully 40 percent of the planet's "budget for life," the total food yield available based on our share of the sun's energy. Farming has driven uncounted animal species to extinction as their habitat was appropriated for growing our three major crops: wheat, corn, and rice. The planet ran out of prime land available for additional cultivation about 1960. Crop yields have continued to increase based on advances in mechanization and chemistry. At the same time, herbicides, pesticides, and fertilizers are killing the ecosystem; for instance; creating a dead zone the size of New Jersey at the mouth of the Mississippi, resulting from agricultural runoff from America's breadbasket. Rich nations, eating high on the food chain, over-consume protein which, unmetabolized, turns to fat with its attendant health problems.

The ancient agricultural basis for society got a boost as the result of the selective breeding of plants (and animals) to cultivate the most nourishing, the most useful, and the most vigorous strains possible (Diamond). After World War II, the development of fertilizers, herbicides, and pesticides greatly increased crop yields. This was followed by hybridization, the artificial cross-pollination of different varieties of the same species of plant, such as corn. This Green Revolution triumphed over the dire predictions of Thomas Malthus, but at the expense of ecological degradation. Were we to continue on this course, it is doubtful if the efficiency gains required to feed us all in 50 years could be met without serious degradation of the environment, including plant and animal life.

Now genetic engineering has come to the agricultural world with the micro-technique known as gene splicing. Changing the chemical sequence of the DNA of any species can be accomplished by snipping a piece of DNA from one separate plant or animal cell and splicing it to that of another piece of DNA from a different species. By this process a uniquely new plant or animal may be propagated with its own characteristics and identity. In the plant world this has led to disease resistant crops as well as improved appearance and handling properties for produce. It has paved the way for "Round-Up-Ready," no-till agriculture, requiring no plowing and allowing for a reduction in runoff and fertilizer use (Rauch). This so called "Frankenfood" carries with it the promise of unique advances in both the quality and quantity of the world's food supply, but not without the risk that these transgenic creations might spread from farm field to the general environment, cross-pollinating with other plants, and producing biological havoc.

A much better answer according to Richard Manning (*Wired*, May 2004) is "Smart breeding," a genetic selection process which does not rely on transgenic gene splicing. This approach was first made possible by the decoding of the 40,000 gene map spread across the rice genome, by Susan McCouch in 1988. This work made it possible to scan the rice gene bank consisting of some 84,000 seed types from wild ancestors with differing properties. Within this collection are varieties representing just about any combination of properties expressible by the rice genome. Smart breeding is done by selecting one plant variety exhibiting a high yield and another with a specific disease resistance, cross-breeding them by a relatively simple gene marking procedure, and testing the result.

Unlike many hybrid crops, the seeds of the new variety reproduce with characteristics identical to those of the new plant. Consequently, these crops do not require a commercial source of seeds for sowing each year. The genes of interest are all there within the species. The interesting ones just need to be tagged and spliced to be expressed in the same reproducible plant. This process is much quicker than transgenic gene splicing, where trial and error development gives results that may be very unpredictable.

Since Mendel published his Laws of Heredity in 1866 based on extensive work with peas, it has been established that artificial cross-pollination between different varieties of the same plant and the cross-breeding of variant lower animals of the same species, endowed the offspring with genetic characteristics partially contributed by each parent.

In 1953, I was sitting in a lecture on X-ray crystallography. The professor, Dr. Clarke, announced that Crick and Watson in England had just worked out the basic crystal structure of DNA, the genetic code of life, with the help of X-ray crystallographic analysis. Biologists became molecular biologists almost overnight.

Forty-nine years later, it was announced that the entire sequence of the four amino acids, adenine, guanine, thiamine, and cytosine, had been unraveled for the human genome, under the worldwide direction of James Watson. It took some 2 billion steps and included around 30,000 individual genes, instructions on how long to grow your nose or whether you might be susceptible to developing schizophrenia. And virtually everything else about you as a unique individual among the 70 or 80 billion modern humans to have ever lived on this planet.

While molecular biologists were just starting to come to terms with the implications of the DNA structure in the 1960s, Scientific American published an article describing how you could take the cells of the skin of a carrot, immerse them in coconut endosperm, expose them to ultraviolet light, agitate them, and grow a whole new carrot, roots, body, skin, greens, and all, in about three weeks. The implications were immediately obvious. It would be only a matter of time before the sci fi story of cloning humans would be brought to life, so to speak.

Then on July 25, 1978, Louise Brown was born, the first human conceived *in vitro*, in a petri dish instead of in bed, as God had intended. This really killed the old joke about "the last time this happened, the Romans were taking a census in Bethlehem." Today over 200,000 test tube children attest to the obsolescence of the sexual necessity.

In 1996, Dolly was parented without the help of any male sheep sperm, making the public aware of the possibilities of animal cloning. Before Dolly died at the age of six, several laboratories had announced their intention to do the same with one of us. Would you like to be the first human to be reproduced not just figuratively, but literally? You could give the world another truly superior human being exactly like yourself. You might be able to replace a lost child or have one without relying on the old fashioned method requiring two sets of equipment. Do you need genetically compatible spare parts for an unfortunate family member, or maybe you see a business opportunity here? Perhaps you would just like to have a servant around the house whose temperament matched your own.

Science is at the doorstep of producing a human clone, if indeed it has not already been done. In October of 2003, Lanza and Chung "grew" a sixteen cell human clone embryo, the stage at which it was theoretically ready for implantation in a female uterus (Rohm). They stopped short of this last step only because they were interested in producing stem cells for research, not a human clone.

Certainly the responsible medical research community is interested in stem cells only as a source of material to study disease causation factors. Doug Melton of Harvard has cultivated 17 new lines of stem cells using private funding (Harvard, news.harvard. edu). They will be put to use to study the onset of disease on a cell by cell basis employing a process known as nuclear transfer. This unique procedure offers the hope of isolating the primary genetic origin of many of today's most debilitating maladies.

Nevertheless, these potential regeneration options raise some disturbing issues. Probably the most important question that must be addressed is the *why* of a clone. Would a human replica be valued for who it is? Or would it have worth only for what it might do for its progenitor? The answer marks the difference between intrinsic value and value-in-use. Does the human replicate have human dignity or only a price on its head? As with Ira Levin's *Boys From Brazil*, intent drives the decision and can make for a social class of human look-alikes.

Even before the completion of the Human Genome Project, it was possible to use DNA for such diverse purposes as absolute identification of each of us 6 billion human inhabitants, tracing genetic ancestry, identifying certain genetic defects, and now, choosing the sex of your baby. This can be done at the very first stages of embryonic cell division, or by microsorting, the process of selecting out the X from the Y chromosome sperm. Parents can use *in vivo* genetic information to abort fetuses with unwanted characteristics. Health and life insurers would want to use this information to create a differentiated-premium rate structure or even select out high risk applicants altogether. If a "defective" fetus were not physically selected out in the womb, the insurance carriers might do it for you after the fact. So far we have not discussed the alteration of genetic material, a procedure becoming more common in the world of agriculture.

Gene therapy, a technique that depends on gene splicing, is a procedure by which a selected section of foreign genetic material is introduced into the body with the intent of overcoming some inherent genetic defect, curing some disease, accelerating the healing of some injury, or conferring some enhanced ability not intrinsic to a particular body. This process works on *somatic* or body cells, and its effects are confined to the body in question, not its offspring. We might all agree that the development of genetic medicine could be a boon of such importance that it would dwarf the efficacy of today's most effective drugs. Indeed, that is the way gene therapy is justified and promoted by research, commerce, and the public at large. However, the difficulties inherent in such a sophisticated biological procedure are yet to be appreciated.

Human property enhancement will soon be achieved by the same techniques as those used for therapeutic purposes. Muscle tissue in mice has been strengthened by injecting into it a synthetic gene, and mouse memory has been improved by inserting a gene spliced from fruit flies (Sandel). Very importantly the same gene used to cure one person might conceivably be used to augment the otherwise nature-limited ability of another. Such enhancement of a person's innate capabilities would require much rethinking about the meaning of excellence, for instance, even as steroids or blood-doping do now, to a lesser extent, in athletic competition.

Certainly some parents would genetically prep their children from infancy for a life of distinction, even as they now rely on human growth hormone to promote tallness at an early age. Is the top performer to be lauded for honing his natural abilities to a fine peak, or will man-made genetic enhancement be required for all who choose to compete, even in intellectual or commercial pursuits? Will the value of a brilliant performance attach itself to a Michael Jordan or Tiger Woods and inhere in their intrinsic personhood? Or will the star be the pharmacist supplying just the right drug or the doctor with the best gene therapy techniques? What in the end will be the value or even the meaning of testing your ability to excel when the means can be found in a vial or at the right out-patient clinic? Where will value reside when performance can be manufactured rather than developed? As Cher Bono once said regarding her stage persona, "If it came in a bottle, everyone would have it."

But there is another whole dimension to the science of gene splicing,,which arises when you mix DNA from unrelated *reproductive* cells. You may now mate plants and certain lower animals to other plants and animals even of a different species, bridging a gap never crossed in nature. By this method new plants and animals have been created with transgenic characteristics never before observed. And these man-created, genetically modified organisms (GMOs) may be capable of reproduction. Since we share about 98.5 percent of our genetic code with apes, it is not difficult to imagine any number of surprises that might eventually be hatched in the laboratory working with higher mammals and humans.

There is no general theory of outcomes to guide genetic scientists in these experiments. All but the most intrepid are alarmed at the prospect of having to deal with the handiwork of a Dr. Frankenstein, newly sprung from the pages of Mary Shelly's 1818 imagination, into the realm of reality. Would this genetic menagerie escape our control and spread new genetic diseases or disabilities far and wide? While gene-spliced bacteria are now an inexpensive source of life-saving insulin for diabetics, experiments at the Mayo Clinic have shown that by injecting human stem cells into pig embryos, animal viruses could jump the species barrier to humans (*Harpers*, March, 2004).

The new transgenic game kits available on the Internet allow kids to electronically cross-breed all manner of human archetypes with assorted members of the animal kingdom so as to render your girl friend a pussy cat or your kid brother a rat. The new generation will be prepared for new animals and new transgenic proto-humans, but will they be prepared to adapt to the cultural changes sure to follow? We will have to rethink what it means to be human, revising our moral, legal, social, and religious concepts to accommodate a new social paradigm imagined only in sci fi until now.

Leon Kass (2002), the chairman of the President's Council on Bioethics, feels the pursuit of cloning and stem cell research can lead to changes in our nature so drastic that we will no longer be human, but rather post-human. He proffers that "…our awareness of need, limitation, and mortality to craft a way of being that has engagement, depth, beauty, virtue, and meaning…" are giving way to an "…objectified state of dehumanization."

It could be an unparalleled tragedy to trip over some being of indefinite humanity, with an errant gene and no pedigree, in our rush to find new cures for ancient maladies. The promise of revolutionary advances in medical science carries with it open-ended risks to humanity, both tangible and moral. Our brave new world will have to deal with the problems arising from population growth amid this new technology. Men are certain to explore the uncertain future because that's what men do. We must pause to consider if we are anxious to go down in history as members of "the last generation of natural human beings."

Rich And Poor

On September 10, 2001, Americans were in a state of peace even though we were aware there was concern about rogue states with nuclear weapons programs and a series of pesky terrorist attacks on several U.S. facilities over the years. On September 12 we were asking, "Why do they hate us so much?"

That very question was the tip off that we American citizens had no idea of the intensity of Arab grievances toward the U.S., and certainly no clue as to why al-Qaeda had delivered its message with aviation fuel and blood on 9-11 by a deed so horrendous it could no longer be ignored. Just like Pearl Harbor in 1941, this attack set in motion a response from America that is destined to alter international relations irrevocably. We immediately scanned the Islamic landscape, looking for someone to put in the American crosshairs. As we boned up on Mohammed's Koran and his successors' Sharia law, the American president and his chief advisors put into action a plan to eliminate Saddam Hussein, a plan that they had had on the books since Inauguration Day (Suskind).

One wonders if any in the government stopped to ask *why* we were so brutally attacked. Or if any cared. The die was cast. "Why" made no difference. What we knew at the time was that the Arab and Persian nations of the Middle East were struggling in the backwater of international commerce, where the only significant revenue producer was oil, and that these nations were forever squabbling amongst themselves, united only by Islam and a hatred of Jews. And now us.

Strangely enough, Islam was the inheritor of the science, technology, and the ancient commercial success of the Saracens. This civilization, in turn, got its start with the demise of Rome when Rome's developing store of secular Western knowledge made its way into the Middle East via Damascus. Without the benefit of church, state, or written law, this wide desert area blossomed with new knowledge and goods undreamed of by Europe throughout the Dark Ages.

Islam was conceived and born in a rich oasis in the desert–Mecca, the ancient crossroads of east-west trade. As such, Islam has something of a materialistic leaning wherein the next life will be all that material life here on earth isn't. Mohammed created a belief system based on jihad, man's inner struggle to improve himself and defend the faith and all its territories from infidels. It made no distinction between religious activities and civic affairs, a distinction of little consequence until modern times.

The Middle East, as well as Spain, flourished with silks and soft goods, porcelain, glass, brass, and steel from Damascus. They adopted "Arabic" numerals from the Hindus and invented the concept of zero, a calendar based on months, and calculated the value of π. From its learning centers, especially in Spain, came the development of astronomy, arithmetic, algebra, quadratics, plane and spherical geometry, the sextant, the magnetic compass, a concept of inertia, and planetary motion. They practiced advanced medicine, using cocaine as an anesthetic, table manners, and personal cleanliness, when Europe still ate with dirty hands and wiped them on their breeches (Lane, Teresi).

From its inception in 622, Islam spread rapidly throughout the hot sandy desert of the Middle East, claiming North Africa and other regions from Christianity, and eventually proliferating throughout India and Malaysia. The Muslims of the Middle East prospered until the 15th century, when the Ottoman Turks took over Constantinople in 1454 and overran the rest of the Middle East. The last Arabs left Spain just as Columbus sighted land in the new world in 1492. They came back in 2004 to blow up four trains in Madrid, killing 191 people.

Islam reached its material and territorial zenith in the 16th century under the Ottoman Empire, but did not finally lose its cultural influence until after World War II. The protracted breakdown of the Ottoman Empire and Middle Eastern Islam with it started in 1683, when it was defeated at the second siege of Vienna. This marked the farthest penetration west, of the Ottoman Empire, and was the first great setback to what had been a preeminently successful, if decentralized, Islamic Empire. When Napoleon marched unopposed through Egypt in 1798, the star on the flag had long since deserted the fertile crescent, and the Middle East slid into 150 years of stagnation, only to be partially revived by the discovery of oil and the Western demand for this black liquid gold.

The third great shock was the creation of Israel in a land expropriated from Palestine by the West in 1948. Possession of God's long-promised land was followed immediately by war and in time by a lightning defeat of the Arabs in the six day war of 1967. Although Islam respected the old testament Jewish prophets and historically had tolerated Jews, there was no real love lost between these Semitic peoples since the inception of Islam in 622. The Jews had turned up their nose at Mohammed's new religion, just as they had done to St. Paul some 600 years earlier. The two recent American wars in Iraq, with massive troop incursions, might well be the final great shock to Middle Eastern Islam—or the catalyst for an Islamic revival, with repercussions yet to be realized.

Since Mohammed and his successors did not differentiate between civic and religious leadership, the nations of the Middle East are now, after some 1,400 years, struggling to resolve this dichotomy, especially since the land was carved up into nation-states by the British and French in 1921 under the terms of the Treaty of Versailles. Where clerics rule, as in Iran, the Muslim population chafes at their bit. Where the rule is secular, as in Egypt, much of the Muslim population feels Allah is dishonored.

The relationship of Middle Eastern Islam with the developed countries of the world has been determined by oil for most of this past century. They have it and we need it. The discovery of oil in present day Iraq in 1897 was one motivation for carving up the Middle East following World War I. This action made it possible for Britain to secure a source of energy in Iran at giveaway prices. Not until American interests located the ocean of oil under the sands of Saudi Arabia in 1938 did the Brits have any local competition. Since the Arab and Persian nations have come to depend heavily upon petrol dollars, we are locked in a tight embrace with them, held fast by a love-hate bond.

As oil demand soared over time, the bonanza of easy money was unevenly divided throughout the Middle East by the fortunes of geology. The riches that flowed in from around the world, as the oil flowed out, financed new schools, hospitals, and roads with Mercedes Benzs, complete with chauffeurs, for the princesses of the 30,000 members of the Saudi royal family, who were not allowed to drive. Much of the money was seen skiing the slopes at St Moritz and watching the roulette wheel go round in Liechtenstein. However, little of this easy money found its way into factories or profitable business at home. Such investments meant work, and the youth, just two generations off the backs of camels, were disinclined to such mean occupations. The easy availability of unearned money led to power without responsibility. Thirty percent of the adult male population remains unemployed. Most manual work and technical responsibility is handled by non-Arabs.

Owing to a very high birth rate, the 30,000 members of the House of Saud will swell to some 60,000 in a generation. Meanwhile the per capita income of Saudi Arabia dropped from $29,000 to $7,000 over just the past generation (Baer). The bill for waging war in Afghanistan and for Gulf I in 1991 drove the Saudis into a debtor position, with the national debt approaching the level of $200 billion (Turkish Press). They have recovered smartly based on high-profit-margin revenues from $60 a barrel oil, but their future financial position remains in doubt pending possible supply increases over time. Indeed the non-petroleum exports from all Arab lands came to less than that of the small country of Finland in the past. The royal family may yet be in for another cut in their allowance soon. It is a time honored lesson that a free ride is seldom appreciated. Worse yet, it is a disincentive to even learning how to walk.

Oil played a decisive role in the collapse of the Ottoman Empire during World War I. It was during this war that the Arab tribes were promised full custody of their ancient desert lands if they helped defeat the Turks. They did, but the British and French reneged after Lawrence of Arabia had played a leadership role in spurring the Arabs on to an important victory in Acaba, supporting the British troops. To boot, a slice of Palestine along the coast was promised to the Jews by the British Balfour Resolution, even while the fighting raged. When the new Middle East map was laid out with a straight edge, Great Britain was finally in a position to assume control of what has become Iraq and its rich oil fields. The Brits managed to maintain a stake in cheap Middle Eastern oil until 1953, by setting up the vast Iranian oil fields, paying the locals just 16 percent of the profits.

Meanwhile the Americans formed the Arabian American Oil Company (ARAMCO) in 1935 and eventually became a major player in the Middle East. When Iran moved to nationalize its oil fields in 1953, Eisenhower supported the CIA's successful effort to overthrow the newly elected Mosedegh, and installed the puppet Shah (Kinzer). He was to remain in power illegally for 25 years with the full support of the United States, even though the Persians did not exactly appreciate him.

The supreme insult to Middle Eastern Islam came when the UN and Harry Truman endorsed the creation of the Jewish state of Israel in 1948 in what were locally regarded as Arab lands. What was worse was the immediate success the Jews had in making the desert bloom, building an industrial infrastructure, a university system, and a formidable military, where the Arabs had failed over the centuries. When the Jews, who had never been pampered by easy money, reversed the centuries-old Diaspora, they brought with them social survival skills, a tenacity born of persecution, and a Western vision of progress. The devastating defeat of Arab forces in the 1967, six-day war was the final humiliating event in a 300-year series of insults to Islam in the Middle East.

Then the unexpected happened. In 1988 the mujahideen sealed the fate of the Soviet Empire by expelling the Russian troops from Afghanistan with the help of clandestine CIA and Saudi money (Crile). Unnoticed by us, the extremist Muslim element saw this Afghan jihad as a holy war victory signaling a new day for Islam and incubating the reemergence of Arab power after centuries of decay and humiliation (Stern). Osama bin Laden, a radical Wahhabi, seized this opportunity (and the weapons) to set up an extensive terror operation to strike back at the West, particularly the United States. And that's why he attacks–to drive all Westerners from holy Arab lands in the name of Allah. The Muslims of the Middle East like their oil-financed Lexus', but are clinging for dear life to their Olive Tree.

Why did the Arab and Persian nations miss the Industrial Revolution of the 19th century? The voice of Mohammed did not stop at the Arabian national boundaries in the Middle East, just as the story of Jesus had echoed persistently throughout the economically stagnant regions of Europe for 1,000 years. In a harsh land without strong secular leadership, the idea of progress through free enterprise did not take hold, except in the region which is now Turkey, and then not until after World War II. The idea of modernity was and still is an anathema to the mullahs and radical Muslims, who regard women as inferior and Western ideas as the work of the infidel. That's us.

The basic internal conflict in Middle Eastern Islam centers around the question of how to find the way back to a lost prosperity while preserving Muslim religious values and culture. But history travels only forward with stops, starts, pauses, and detours. Never backward. The Arabs and Persians have energy and intelligence, but they need to resolve the issue of who will be in charge of civic affairs, Mohammed or Adam Smith. Law is interpreted for all Muslims by mullahs issuing *Fatwas*, or quasi-legal religious opinions, as they feel moved to do so, without reference to any unambiguous secular statutes or a central religious leader.

If the distribution of wealth between the rich and the poor is an important internal issue for democratic capitalist societies, it has become a critical international issue in our time, since information (and misinformation) travels at warp speed around the globe. Regions of the world that have always been poor are really just now starting to compare their meager existence with the material luxury available in the richer nations.

For the once proud Middle Eastern Islamic states, it has been psychologically very painful to come to terms with their second or third world status. They find it onerous to even consider adopting Western capitalistic methods, knowing that it means unrelenting exposure to the cultural baggage of teen age sex goddesses, hip-hop music, and the arrogance that comes with it. The Arabs and Persians are dissatisfied with their governments, both religious and secular, and above all, they do not want any foreign troops on their soil and certainly not Jewish neighbors in their backyard.

In the West, the under 14 population is on the order of 20 percent of the total. In the Middle East this number is about 40 percent. Muslims have been flowing into Western Europe, not to conquer as in medieval times, but for jobs. This pressure will only increase, at least until productive enterprise takes root at home. We can expect civic volatility in the Middle East to grow only more extreme in the future because of an increasing numbers of youth and a dearth of productive opportunities.

One of the strongest sociological correlations across world populations is that between birth rate and poverty. Both are soaring in Africa, a vast continent producing a bare 2 percent of the world output. The peoples of sub-Saharan Africa do not even realize there is prosperity anywhere on the planet, as they starve and die under the baking sun. This tragedy is the legacy of the European colonialists who made nations out of disparate tribes when they rode into Central Africa on the new iron horses of the 1830s. World population will challenge the biological and environmental carrying capacity of the whole planet unless human propagation is limited by force or prosperity. The preferred approach is obvious.

The U.S. response to 9-11 was to execute the neocon's plan to get Saddam Hussein. This has now morphed into a mission to install a model democracy among warring tribes in a land where Hussein got 99.6 percent of the vote and the no-voters were never heard from again. It is an undertaking of truly grand proportion in an area of the world where we are unquestionably unwelcome. Can an administration that failed to plan for imposing law and order in Baghdad following a stunning 21 day military victory, step up to the task of nation building under these adverse, chaotic circumstances? Does the imposition of an American political infrastructure upon an unprepared Muslim nation risk widening the international quarrel to one of Islam vs. America? Will radical Islam derail U.S. progress, or be the scene of our greatest political triumph in democratic nation building? The verdict is probably a decade away. Middle Eastern Islam needs our help, not our direction. America is at the top of its game at this point in world history. But where will it be in 2050 or 2100?

A foremost Middle East expert, Bernard Lewis, believes the underlying cause of Islamic poverty and backwardness may be a simple lack of freedom. The Islamic nations of the Middle East became utterly dependent upon the West for oil revenue and are now starting to serve the growing needs of China. This dependence coupled with an acute sense of economic impotence and past humiliations at the hands of the West, aggravates Islamic extremists to the point of paranoia. In frustration they lash out at the symbols of Western culture and the power that so easily violates their sacred territories.

Robert Pape has done a detailed study of suicide bombing around the world, the incidence of which is doubling yearly in Iraq. He has found that the underlying cause is not Islamic fundamentalism, but rather the extreme resentment Muslims have for foreign troops on sacred Islamic soil.

Herein lies the answer to the question, "Why do they hate us so much?".

Now, since our unilateral invasion of Iraq in 2003, 1.3 billion Muslims around the world are sensitized to the idea that America might be universally anti-Islam, an impression that has greatly accelerated the recruiting success of Osama bin Laden (Anonymous). A recent Zogby survey in the Middle East shows that the Arabs see us as materialistic, nonreligious, power-driven, and anti-Palestinian. A most interesting finding, however, is that now virtually all Arabs are adversely sensitized to American intentions, even those without strong Islamic beliefs.

America's Choice

We must somehow, at sometime, deal with these issues. We will have to respond to them sooner or later just as we are belatedly responding to terrorism today. The historical test for American democracy will be whether we can develop and execute a plan to engage these issues before they overwhelm us. Or might we just ignore them until they threaten to drive us into survival mode?

Clearly, what is required is leadership at the highest level, untainted by special interest influence, capable of communicating the importance of nonviolent action to 300 million Americans. We need the outline of a plan of attack, and we will need international cooperation. Yes, and money too. Were we able to overhaul our taxation system, our campaign financing system, our social security, medical, and educational institutions, we would be in a much better position to address these issues.

Now who would be so naive that they might believe that all these ideas could be addressed successfully, even given unlimited time and money? On the other hand, who would be so blind and ignorant that they might believe we can just go fishing and forget the whole program? For his children there may be no money to go fishing, no freedom to fish, and no fish to catch.

Right now we seem to be proving Plato's 2,300 year old observation that democracy would direct political action toward superficial issues of the demos' self-interest. Or as Zakaria pointed out, the influence of money and votes on politicians can be democracy's own undoing.

Now that America has no economic or political rivals in the world, will it choose constructive avenues to continued greatness? Or will the absence of any significant competition on the world scene set the stage for America to dictate terms to all as it sees fit? What will be the legacy of our American Empire? What can America aspire to?

The 10th: Virginia. June 25, 1788

CHAPTER 11

AMERICAN EMPIRE

"The American hegemony today is militarily supreme, culturally pervasive, technologically dominant, and economically dynamic. Its allies and enemies alike fear being swallowed up in it; it is the basic fact of international life." So says Walter Russell Mead in his historical review of American foreign policy.

We Americans are privileged to live in a country that has defined and brought to life a set of ideas embracing individual freedom in a system of governance more humane than any developed in the Western world over the past 2,000 years. We owe our English forbears a debt of gratitude for planting the seeds of liberty. We owe the Scot, Adam Smith, one also for his revolutionary idea of free market enterprise that set us on the path to unparalleled prosperity.

In the process, we have assumed the leadership position in significantly improving people's health and extending their lifespan. We have played an important role in expanding human knowledge and putting it to use in the service of mankind. During the past 125 years, America has pioneered the development of electric light, communications, flight, television, space, agriculture, and information and nuclear technology. In the process we have challenged our environment rather severely.

These accomplishments have proceeded apace with unlocking a latent store of human creativity, drawing the world's peoples closer together, offering a humane system of social practices, and advancing our understanding of the world we all inhabit. And as President Reagan said when considering our shinning city upon the hill, "The best is yet to come."

Nevertheless, tyranny, war, starvation, and disease are still our dreaded international companions. We fought a war of independence to establish our identity and pursue our own path to nationhood. We fought a war of union to determine if we were of one mind or two. We joined the fray in World War I in a senseless European conflict, drawn in by our ancestral heritage. We came to the defense of freedom in the great war while putting down a Japan bent on establishing a vast Asian Empire. We led the West in standing our ground against the red menace of Moscow, after having frustrated its advances in Asia. For these undertakings, America was respected and sometimes applauded. We also prosecuted numerous small wars around the world and major ones in Vietnam and Iraq. For these we must bear the psychological price of much bloodshed as well as the enmity of our fellow man.

What we are as a nation is reflected in our dealings with other nations. We are strong and can force our will on others. Alternatively, history shows that others will adopt and adapt our successful ideas when they come to understand them and the time is ripe. As the world shrinks, we will have to deal with its nations and their problems on a more or less continuous basis. The American story is gradually becoming the world's story by virtue of Globalization and our leadership role. We can contribute to international progress through dialogue, or we can promote fear and suspicion by imposing our ideas on the world without prior consent. Let's examine the playing field, that we may attempt to formulate a good game plan.

The Balance of International Power

The economic power, or productive capacity, of the United States can best be illustrated by comparing it to that of other sovereign nations, using GDP statistics (Shane). In the year 2000, the total world product output was about $31 trillion, of which almost one third was attributable to the United States. Those countries attaining at least 5 percent of the world total were:

The US	32 percent
China	16 percent
Japan	11 percent
India	8 percent
Germany	7 percent
France	5 percent
The UK	5 percent

These countries accounted for 84 percent of the total, the residual being divided among the 185 remaining nations. The remainder included large regions such as:

Latin America	6 percent
Middle East	4 percent
Africa	2 percent

Such unchallenged power as America possesses has been seen in the Western world only by the British Empire, since the first Roman Emperors acceded to imperial rule in the first years of the common era. The wealth basis of Roman power was derived largely through its empire of client states and provincial territories. The British Empire straddled the agricultural and industrial eras. The American Empire is leading the world into the information era.

In a world made smaller by communication satellites and the Internet, the nations and peoples of the world look to Washington, DC, and our president in order to discern the future, at least insofar as American intent, policy, influence, and actions might affect their well being. The projection of American power and leadership is the stuff of our foreign policy, the integrity of which is fortified or diluted by the conduct of our internal affairs. This is especially so today in an age of instant communications and a very transparent window on American society.

What do the peoples of the world see when they look in through the American window? They see a moralizing, but socially violent culture, busily occupied with the pursuit of material comfort and amusements.

Recently they see a segment of American society they might classify as whiners, preaching victimhood, seeking entitlements and special attention. They do not see the millions upon millions of hardworking, law-abiding, family-loving citizens. What do the others hear from us? They hear that our democracy, freedom, and free enterprise are the near-sacred shrines upon which prosperity is built. They hear us trumpet that we are in possession of universal social and economic truth. And how do they experience us? They feel the heavy hand of U.S. economic influence on international relationships. They see dictator, puppet regimes installed and supported by us. They see wars large and small prosecuted by us. They see American GIs wherever they look.

Is this a valid picture of America today or just a superficial caricature? In appraising our own portrait, we must keep in mind the warning of Lord Acton, who pointed out that "Power tends to corrupt, and absolute power corrupts absolutely," no less for nations than for kings.

The competition

Although America enjoys the dominant place in world affairs, our hold on that position can be lost sooner than one might appreciate. We have long believed that China with its 1.3 billion souls would someday get its economics right and become an international player of the first magnitude. That day is now dawning along with the new century.

Under the ruthless reign of Mao Tse Tung, China stumbled repeatedly, starting with the Great Leap Forward in the 1950s, followed by the Red Guard, young people's movement into the '70s. Then Mao's successors slaughtered hundreds of students while a worldwide television audience was focused on the bloody confrontation in Tiananmen Square in 1989. It was not yet time for personal freedom in China.

Nevertheless, free market practices had already been set in motion. China had dissolved its People's Farm Communes in 1985 and began growing at the astounding rate of 9 percent plus through the 1990s. In 1998 it began the process of switching from a planned to a market economy by embarking on a program of devolving control of many of its industries to local governments and plant managers. It is just now entering the second phase of this process of extending free market practices. The key to success was withdrawing subsidy support from industry. The demand for turning a profit put many superfluous workers out on the street, a byproduct of capitalist economics. But as Adam Smith promised, the wealth of China did increase, and sharply.

Because of its phenomenal economic growth, China's GDP has reached a level one half of ours and is still charging ahead rapidly. Without any change in economic trajectories, we could be in a dead heat with China as soon as 2020. Barring any serious political missteps, the Chinese economy could grow by a factor five or more in this century, just as ours did in the last century.

At this writing China is, and has been, racing along at an unsustainable rate of 9 to 10 percent growth annually over the last two decades. Now since 2004, lagging capacity in the energy sector may start to impair economic progress. The new rich (remember, Rich is Glorious?) are trading in their bicycles for autos that are choking already crowded streets. And do you think the Chinese are worried about a little pollution after centuries of living in dirt and squalor? China's growth rate is unsustainable not only because power generation and distribution development is difficult and costly, but also because of the social stresses brought on by rapid economic change. Just this year they have started reforming their artificially pegged exchange rate, a signal they may have started the process of reining in their intense drive for prosperity.

In 1999 China was accepted into the WTO, thereby achieving some measure of international respect as well as expanded trade opportunity. China will have a difficult time meeting all the regulatory requirements of the WTO, because of its prisoner/child labor practices and disregard for intellectual property rights. But increasing economic freedom will pave the way for more social freedoms in a dictatorial country where communism is now just a forgotten concept.

Many tens of millions of Chinese have started to taste the fruits of limited economic freedom and will soon become huge energy consumers. The sheer volume of environmentally unfriendly industrial activities will force technological change and generate international conflict centered on issues of pollution control as well as expanding trade. The Chinese expansion has driven up the price of raw materials like steel, aluminum, copper, nickel, and oil, on the world market; while companies like Wal-Mart, the world's largest retailer, doing $260 billion in sales, is recycling dollars back to China to pay for its imported stock. Internally, China will have to release its tight grip on government run financial institutions, overhaul its legal system, cut loose its currency controls, cease jamming the Voice of America and censoring e-mail, and make room for increasing personal freedoms. It's hard to imagine China adopting a democratic system at the top without a fight, but there may be no turning back.

With over four times the population of the United States, China will certainly be an imposing player upon the world stage if it even realizes a standard of living only half the level of ours. It is trying to squeeze 150 years of industrial-revolution-infrastructure buildup into one or two generations, flaunting international intellectual property rights and exploiting the environment in the process. At the same time China has its sights set on becoming the information technology capital of the world, assisted by American firms such as Intel, which committed $1.5 billion for new plant and equipment in China last year. China's first manned space flight in October of 2003 is symbolic of its intention to become a serious world player. If history is any guide, however, China will surely stumble, just as Japan did, because of the overextension of its closed banking system, a system managed not to generate profit, but to further social goals. But not soon. The spirit of growing prosperity and opportunity have generated a momentum sustained by a national, economic adrenalin rush.

China and India still have a huge reservoir of cheap labor, but now that labor is being educated. India turns out almost a million more college graduates than we do and China produces six times as many engineers as American schools do (T. Friedman, 2005). These are hardworking, well-educated Asian Tigers who want American's jobs. America's leadership position in turning out large numbers of knowledge workers is now a thing of the past, while a full third of our youngsters do not cut the academic mustard even in our public school system. Losing the education race is surely the precursor to losing the economic race and widening the gap between the haves and have-nots in America,where equal opportunity to learn is not properly nourished.

India is another Asian country making great economic strides. While China has been emphasizing progress in manufacturing, India, only a slightly smaller nation, is capitalizing on its excellent, if limited, education system by picking up computer programming and financial services work via the Internet. It is making the transition from a "string-and-two-Dixie-cup's" system to Internet cell phones faster than you can say Alexander Graham Bell. Thanks to the "zippies," the under 25 Indians who are leading India into modernity by virtue of their ambition, confidence, destination-driven attitude, and desire for the good life (T. Friedman, 2005).

The "Miracle of Japan," however, has faltered after a 40-year run, blocked by a national banking system subsidizing the wrong industries, an inefficient service sector and distribution system, and a reluctance to write off bank loans in default. The security of lifetime employment has crumbled, and the system has been stuck for 15 years. If Japan cannot reform its financial infrastructure and blunt the economic power of the *keiretsu*, which controls the purchasing and distribution decisions of many industries, it will have lost its position as America's showpiece for democracy in Asia. While China has already established its position as undisputed economic leader of Asia, with India just now starting to play catch up, it must be acknowledged that very recently, Japan appears to be making progress in reforming its banking practices.

Following World War II, the battered and bloodied nations of Europe were near desperate to have a big brother that could help them preserve light in the penumbra of the long shadow cast westward by the sinister figure of Joseph Stalin. The big brother was the North Atlantic Treaty Organization (NATO). This protective shield weathered a four decade nuclear standoff ending only with the 1989 collapse of a rotten industrial infrastructure costing more to run than the value of its output. During this period, Europe neglected to rebuild its defensive capability, relying upon the burgeoning stockpile of a mighty U.S. arsenal. At the time the EU got off the ground, the armies of Europe were more jobs programs than fighting units, the UK being the exception owing to the foresight of Margaret Thatcher in the 1980s.

The European Union was born on the still-warm, smoldering ashes of the Soviet Union. The long-time combatants of Western Europe took the world by surprise when the parties to the 1992

Maastricht Treaty actually adopted the Euro as a common currency in 2002. The successful adoption of the Euro was an uncommon event of the first magnitude among sovereign nations. Few nations in history have voluntarily given up the right to mint their own coin and determine their own monetary policy. Nations give up their sovereignty only for some very compelling reasons. The colonies of America came together for mutual protection, because they realized they were individually defenseless against arbitrary foreign interference. The 15 EU nations joined hands because they foresaw very significant political as well as economic advantages, both internally and externally. Very importantly, it was a union urged by Winston Churchill in 1946, designed to tame the internecine culture of war that had devastated Europe many times over.

This action defined the EU as something more than a mere regional confederation or discussion group. Its initial success was evidenced by 10 more eastern European nations who were eager to surrender their economic and political sovereignty in 2004 for the benefits of membership in this major, new, international power block. The current 25 nations of the EU are a match for the economic might of the United States. The EU has deliberately chosen to neglect building up its military forces, putting its resources into welfare measures and industrial subsidy instead. Nevertheless, this union has many thorny internal issues to contend with, not the least of which is paring down its heavy agricultural subsidies (for example, about $2.40 per cow per day in France, a sum greater then the daily income of 75 percent of the peoples of sub-Saharan Africa (Bildt)). The EU must also contend with the influx of a burgeoning population of Muslims from the east who are taking the place of those unborn native citizens missing because of a very low birth rate.

This rapidly emerging counterbalance to U.S. superpower status is already taking on a more independent posture in world affairs, witness the opposition to the recent Iraq war in UN deliberations by both France and Germany. But will they all ever sing off the same page on international issues? As of Gulf II, the EU members are still singing their own tunes.

The recent rejection of the proposed, 448-Article, EU constitution (compare to 7 Articles for the U.S. Constitution) by the French and Dutch citizens was a repudiation of their respective governments. They want more security from governments they do not trust, governments that understand the value of and want to follow the EU thrust from Brussels toward free market economics. This event shows not only the seductive influence of socialist security within the framework of a weak democratic economy, but also the national reluctance to endorse competition, that arises when people have lost confidence in their leaders. In the UK, the Brits were also prepared to vote down the proposed constitution, but for a different reason—because it does not more forcefully advocate free market economics. While many of the EU countries had adopted highly liberal democratic constitutions since World War II, the new proposed EU Constitution reads more like a set of guidelines wherein the voluntary act of ratification can be rescinded for any reason at any time.

The true power of the EU in international affairs is yet to be determined, although it is certain it will try to write its own common music. Very importantly, the EU promises to play the role of devil's advocate to U.S. designs for international adventures in their backyard in the future.

In contrast to the competitive, forward-looking regions of the world, whose peoples are benefiting so handsomely from mostly-free markets, we have South America in our own backyard. Rich in natural resources, populated by Europeans at the same time as North America, this large land mass accounts for just 20 percent of the U.S. total wealth production. Except for Chile, one half of its people are mired in poverty, functioning in a 15-percent black market economy, skirting "a million" laws that cannot be understood or complied with, just to survive. Alvaro Vargas Llosa writes that these "democratic" countries are plagued by dictatorial governments that make law to favor whom they please, extracting a pretty share of the wealth in return. In Peru, 2 percent of the companies create 60 percent of the wealth, and 700 people own all of the land. This is the same story that has been repeated endlessly throughout history; a story still playing out behind the scenes even of liberal democratic countries, driven by the magnetic attraction of money and power.

South America is the home of 34 democratic states. Almost without exception these states are repressive. They feature few individual democratic rights. They function on the basis of special privileges for those who buy them. They have not adopted Adam Smith. They apply law as they please because there is way too much law. They are the proof that illiberal democracies are no defense against tyranny.

Foreign Policy

The words American and empire have only recently been joined together in the popular American lexicon. We may ask, as Mead has, "What is the point of our 'empire'–to make us rich, to make us safe, or to build a better world?" The conduct of an empire can only be assessed by examining the prosecution of its foreign policy, those actions based on commercial, territorial, political, and social ambitions.

Commerce is concerned almost exclusively with filling needs and seeking economic advantage through trade. Territorial concerns center on the issue of who has jurisdictional control of what land, water, and regions of air or space. Political interest involves the extent to which one sovereign nation may have influence over or even project the threat of control over another. Social concerns cover international aid, treaties, or other agreements and discussions on issues of multinational concern.

The United States was born at a time when some colonial peoples had already been seeking greater opportunity by moving westward beyond the original colony boundaries. This aggressive practice of territorial acquisition became the de facto foreign policy of this new country, a policy which was sustained in America until Arizona was admitted into the union in 1912. Throughout the 19th century, westward expansion *was* our foreign policy even though we modern Americans have never thought of it in these terms. This expansion was undertaken at the expense of the French, the Spanish, and the indigenous American natives. It was first facilitated by the 1803 Louisiana purchase for $15 million from Napoleon, followed by the territory of Alaska for $7.2 million from Russia in 1867. Over time the United States did pick up small strategic territories around the world, but none so vast as its continental acquisitions.

In 1823 the Monroe Doctrine was proclaimed, advising European countries to cease spreading their political influence throughout the whole of the Western Hemisphere. By default, this action seemed to place these two huge landmasses in the position of being our economic playground. In 1846-8 God was enlisted as a powerful agent as early America followed its "Manifest Destiny" westward to the shores of the Pacific Ocean. The Mexican-American War pried loose the northern half of Mexico as our prize—lands that were to become California, Arizona, New Mexico, Nevada, and Utah. The Mexicans are now returning to share these lands with us.

Not until the Truman Doctrine was set forth in 1947 did the United States declare a peacetime interest in European affairs by organizing a collective perimeter of nations around the USSR to contain its territorial ambitions. This action was followed in 1948 by the $13 billion Marshall Plan to catalyze post-war-European economic recovery. The ensuing 40-year Cold War gave rise to the necessity and/or opportunity for the United States to deploy military advisers, troops, equipment, and bases in many parts of the world. This process, carried out under the auspices of NATO, marked the beginning of American Empire on a worldwide basis.

The fear of communism and the threat of nuclear holocaust drove American foreign policy until the collapse of the USSR in 1989. It led Eisenhower to approve the overthrow of the democratically elected leader of Iran in 1953 in favor of the puppet Shah (Kinzer). This was followed by the *coup d'etat* of Arbenz in Guatemala the following year. Cold War paranoia precipitated the Vietnam war and was the rationale for CIA interference in the political affairs of a number of sovereign nations. The election of the communist Allende in 1973 was subverted (O'Grady, April 25, 2003), and the dictator Pinochet took power in Chile. The tyrant Marcos was supported in the Philippines, all the while plundering the nation until deposed in 1986. We tried, but could not eradicate Castro in Cuba. American foreign policy was obsessed with this world power struggle and moved to deny the very freedoms we cherished at home, to others in the world. These highly questionable actions rendered American foreign policy a morals-free zone where fear trumped integrity in the quest to crush communism, a bankrupt system that ultimately fell (after being nudged) of its own dead weight.

Teddy Roosevelt first projected the political power of the United States when he sent the Great White Fleet comprising 12 battleships on world tour in 1907. Woodrow Wilson followed up with a 14 point plan to export American democracy and values following World War I at the 1919 Versailles Peace Conference.

He was promptly dismissed as a naïve academic who did not understand the Real Politic tradition of Western Europe–a tradition likened to scorpions fighting it out in a bottle.

Projecting the empire

Empire has always meant occupying or at least establishing on site, executive rule over some foreign territory. Today, with few exceptions, the historic empires have been largely dismantled. Political and economic influence is established now through the medium of "guest armies" and aircraft carriers (Bacevich 2002). In 1983 we had 18 percent, or 250,000, of our military personnel based overseas.

Our forces are scattered throughout 120 nations the world over, concentrated mostly in Europe, East Asia and the Persian Gulf, but having large scale deployments in 25 of these countries (Johnson 2003). We are there mostly by invitation in democratically troubled countries. We have had 37,000 troops stationed along the demilitarized zone dividing the two Koreas for fully half a century, "defending" a prosperous South Korea and reminding Asia of American interests in the Orient. We have kept over 100,000 troops in Europe, even 16 years after the collapse of Communism.

Our newest military strategy is to station smaller contingents of U.S. troops at carefully chosen seaport locations around the world, the better to secure access points for rapid deployment forces and their equipment, if needed. Our troops are manning the 725 American overseas military stations (not counting the secret ones) and 969 domestic bases we staff and pay for (Johnson 2003).

The proposed 2006 federal budget includes $419 billion for the military, a sum totaling more than the entire military expenditures of all other nations on earth (Bacevich 2005). It does not include the cost of operations in Iraq that will run as much as $100 billion this year alone. You can never be too safe, so just to be sure we still have 32,000 nuclear weapons on hand, held over from the Cold War. That's 100 times the number required to effectively destroy the world. In addition, it is believed there is enough enriched uranium stockpiled around the world to make many more thousands of nuclear weapons. Jane Fonda believes the runaway psychology fueling conflict too often follows from the macho "mine is bigger than yours" mind-set. The ever-present danger in maintaining a too-large military is illustrated by the question posed to Colin Powell by Madeleine Albright during the Bosnian War. "What's the point in having a strong military if you don't use it?" (Bacevich 2005).

International commerce

The issue of trade was of critical interest to America even before there was a United States of America. There could have been only limited commercial and agricultural development without a continuous resupply of manufactured goods and slave labor, in particular. After parting ways with the British, it became very important that we develop a source of available capital so that we could finance the new government, trade, shipbuilding, and the rude beginnings of industry. It was Alexander Hamilton, Washington's first Secretary of the Treasury, who, immediately upon taking office, set about to develop a financial system to service these needs. The answer was the Bank of the United States chartered in 1791.

The thrust for western nations to seek trade in the Orient had already been underway for some 150 years when in 1854 "Commodore Perry's orders directed him to shell Japan if the Mikado refused his request for trade and diplomatic relations" (Mead). By 1869 to 1893, foreign trade had swollen to 13.4 percent of our GDP as the result of America's success in producing agricultural products and factory goods during the Industrial Revolution. It was assumed from the get-go that a priority government task was to promote business in general and exports in particular—and so it did, providing a boost for laissez faire economics. The first effective control on industry was enacted in 1914 with the Clayton Anti-Trust Act, when the robber barons had amassed over half of the nation's wealth, and exports had fallen to 7 percent of GDP.

It was not until the 1970s that government regulations and taxes actually started to take a significant toll on business profits. Exports had been falling, which drove our current trade account balance negative in 1982 (foreigners buying America with dollars earned from net exports to America), and by 1988 we became a debtor nation for the first time in the modern era. Since America is virtually self-sufficient (except for oil), owing to its abundant natural resources and advanced technology, we are not net importers of *scarce* goods. We are importing *price* in the form of goods and services produced more cheaply offshore. The result is that we are exporting jobs, and the money we are spending on imports is coming back to purchase U.S. assets; fixed assets, stocks, and U.S. Treasury securities. Almost half of our national debt is owned by foreign powers. Our trade deficit was $656 billion in 2004. By my estimate, this dollar outflow was enough to have supported well over 5 million jobs here at home.

Within just the past decade, the character of international trade has changed radically. Globalization kicked into high gear starting in 1995, when the Internet blossomed into a rapid fire, unregulated medium for commercial use; and the World Trade Organization was established.

International Organizations

There was a time when the pursuit of economic improvement through international trade agreements was carried out between nations exclusively according to their bilateral agreement. However, since 1995 the WTO has taken on the role of referee for international trade disputes. In addition to the WTO, the IMF and the World Bank also have a direct effect on international commerce where its client states are involved.

The IMF and World Bank have been around since World War II. They are the strongest financial institutions in the world. They were created to stabilize the international monetary system by lending big bucks to countries experiencing financial distress and those in need of funds for infrastructure and social development. They often work together and even have a degree of interlocking directorates. As you might expect, the U.S. has a large stake in each institution by virtue of its position as the major financial backer.

Since 1994 the IMF has participated in financial disasters around the world from Mexico to Indonesia, Korea, Russia, Turkey, Argentina, Bolivia, and Brazil. Thirty-five billion dollars in funding for Turkey so far has produced only a need for additional funding. Pumping money into broken economies ensures that foreign private lenders will be repaid, which in turn guarantees they will continue to underwrite bad credit risks around the world, because the IMF will cover their bets.

Paul Blustein (2002) has documented the numerous costly, but errant, financial "rescues" that have littered the international economic landscape since 1994. On its own, the "World Bank has a 65 to 70 percent failure rate of its projects in the poorest countries," according to CorpWatch. Joseph Stiglitz feels the root-canal-economics of the IMF, demanding balanced budgets at all costs, have generally exacerbated the problems of its clients. The fact is that the IMF actually *contributes* to global financial instability by bailing out countries and taking the apparent risk out of private international loan deals, rather than reducing actual risk, as it was originally chartered to do at Bretton Woods in 1944 (O'Grady, May 9, 2003). When the IMF finally does pull the plug on a profligate government, as they did in Argentina in 2001, the result is financial collapse and unhappy private bondholders, who in the end were forced to settle for 32 cents on the dollar (Blustein 2005).

One caveat to borrowing from the IMF or World Bank is that you must play by the WTO's rules. This body intercedes in unresolved trade dispute matters and may impose trade penalties on any country judged to be in violation of its findings. The 146 countries signed on with the WTO have compromised their sovereignty by agreeing to allow WTO rulings to take precedence over national law in matters of international trade. They either comply with the findings of an unelected international court, whose deliberations take place *in camera,* or face penalties. The laws of a sovereign nation are not respected, even those put on the books to protect labor, health, or the environment.

Paul Kennedy believes we have entered a new international economic era, where critical issues are bleeding across sovereign borders and threatening the viability of the traditional nation-state, because of the many difficulties all nations jointly face. Among problems that can be successfully addressed only by mutual attention are SARS, AIDS, influenza, global warming, acid rain, over-fishing, rain forest disappearance, missile-born nuclear weapons, satellite communications, terrorism, and drugs. Add to this list the issues arising from the acceleration of Globalization: the WTO itself, tariff-reducing trade pacts, and 24/7 securities trading, all of which weaken national control of internal economic policies. Will a new world order evolve, based chiefly upon some form of economic governance?

Lori Wallach and Michelle Sforza believe the mounting confrontation between international corporate power and national sovereignty will be the defining conflict of the Gen X generation, the fallout of which will be a growing threat to individual freedom.

In our own interest, Mead asks, "Just how far should the United States go in pooling sovereignty with other countries for the sake of various economic or political objectives? How much of a world criminal court do we need [none, according to the present administration]? How much power should the WTO have over acts of congress and state legislatures?" Ditto for NAFTA and the upcoming Free Trade Area of the Americas (FTAA) covering South America, and CAFTA for Central America.

Trade will go on. In the U.S. we hear much about the EU's unwillingness to import American hormone-laced beef in spite of a WTO ruling overriding health-based objections. But you do not hear much about the five or six adverse rulings against the U.S. (such as our cotton subsidy level) that we have been ignoring, at least until the WTO shot down Bush's 2002 steel tariffs (Sanger). In real life, the major players don't always get overly concerned about adhering to those rules they find inconvenient. But for those of the 146 less wealthy members of the WTO who want to be blessed with IMF/ World Bank capital or general trade protection, noncompliance is a luxury they can't afford.

The steady increase in global trade favors America and the EU because we do the most trading, can negotiate the best terms, and have in place the prerequisite institutions necessary for doing international business. In addition, America has enough economic muscle to make sure our voice in matters of trade will be heard. According to William Finnegan, our international trade practice goes well beyond the promotion of free enterprise. It "...is not an ideology of freedom or democracy. It is a system of control. It is an economics of empire."

But if some political economists are correct, we increasingly will be called upon to yield more of our sovereign prerogatives in the interest of participating in a free, world-wide trading economy. Should the economics of free trade be placed on a high enough pedestal of international priorities, the WTO may well overshadow a weak UN that has no means for enforcing its accumulation of 1,600 often hollow resolutions. This would leave the UN as an international grievance center in charge of peacekeeping missions and emergency food distribution around the world, and the conduct of international social studies; while the WTO would have the power to penalize without appeal and be bound by few responsibilities to its clients.

So how do these powerful international organizations affect America's leadership role in the affairs of the community of nations? The U.S., as the major sponsor of the IMF and World Bank, and major subject of WTO deliberations, has the greatest potential influence on how these independent organizations view their responsibilities, should it choose to exercise it. A good case can be made that all three interlocking bodies, on balance, favor positions advanced by the most powerful members. At the same time, America will be restricted in exploiting weaker trading partners solely because of its superior economic or military position.

For their part, the IMF and World bank serve as catalysts in the process of Globalization by helping developing nations put their cheap or unemployed labor to work. The end result of economic self-interest on the part of the rich and powerful in world affairs is both to employ the cheap labor of the world and at the same time exploit it. But is it always exploitation when dirt poor people can earn money today, when yesterday no work was available? In this endeavor the capitalists are aided by the leaders of third world countries. These have-not countries are hungry for capital for two reasons. Capital is required to put people to work and otherwise organize and control them socially. Borrowed capital is also the means by which the principal players in any country can enhance their power and finance their private interests. A poor, working labor force can be an asset to the leaders of a backward country. It can be the bait for attracting capital. The money that arrives in big bags can be put to many nefarious uses (Bauer) or just deposited in a Swiss bank, as the Palestinian leadership did under Yasser Arafat (Samuels).

A leading world class country has not only financial muscle of its own, but indirect help as well, in securing trade on favorable terms. If the country in question "stabilizes" political regions of the world by means of preemptive war, by buying cooperation through foreign aid, or just by covertly influencing key elections around the world from time to time, it can realize significant advantages in international trade even if the WTO is not always completely understanding.

The richest international corporations of the world, in cooperation with the U.S. government, have practiced another approach for "helping" poor and strategically placed nations in distress, according to John Perkins, a self-confessed economic hit man. By negotiating loans for these countries from the World Bank or IMF, corporations such as Halliburton and Bechtel acquire the opportunity of going in and building physical infrastructure, leaving the country with a repayment schedule it might not be able to meet. Countries such as Ecuador, for instance, would be coached to raise cooking gas prices, causing riots; or to sell national assets, such as Argentina did with its social security system–all to repay IMF debts. If no means could be found to meet repayment schedules, the CIA might step in and negotiate an agreement for strategically placed military bases or cheap oil.

Perkins' claim is that the World Bank has been a chief vehicle by which America has been able to build the world's first international empire and enrich corporate treasuries at the same time, all with taxpayer money, while the most uncooperative players in this scheme just disappear. The mutual interests of government and industry have been reinforced by the revolving door between them for such players as Dick Cheney, Robert McNamara, and George Schultz. Now we see Paul Wolfowitz, the chief architect of U.S. power projection, at the helm of the World Bank.

So who is most interested in foreign trade? Private industry, of course. And who writes most of the checks for almost $4 billion to support biennial election campaigns? You need only connect the dots to understand to game. Whenever we embark on a new project, injecting ourselves into the affairs of other sovereign countries, the banner emblazoned with Woodrow Wilson's justifying motto "to make the world safe for democracy," is unfurled. But since democracy is never explicitly defined beyond suffrage for the oppressed, it's not always clear what other intentions and which parties are being served in the process.

Preemption And Democracy

I remember well sitting in a 5th grade classroom and hearing the teacher say that the next big war would be about oil. That's all I remember from Social Studies class. Ever since 1942, I had from time to time wondered about that prediction. Flash ahead five decades.

Since the fateful morning of September 11, 2001, American foreign policy has taken a sharp right turn. The precursor for this transformation was Desert Storm in 1991, itself a conflict which may have been triggered by a miscommunication between Washington and Baghdad. This war was stopped by a unilateral cease fire, leaving a shaken but improvident Saddam Hussein in power, albeit under strict sanctions. It was all about oil.

Nine-eleven was immediately interpreted in the context of an attack on both American territory and freedom—both virgin domains in the American experience. The shock prepared the American public to respond to the clarion call to arms that was promptly issued. Running the Taliban and al-Qaeda out of Afghanistan was a necessary first step. A silent war on terror was the necessary second step.

For step three, the current administration started leaning far to the right in June of 2002, when Hussein's foul deeds and presumed intentions were spotlighted for close public inspection. The abrupt right turn in American policy was launched with shock and awe in March of 2003, after a nine month public gestation period. Today our foreign policy is defined by the 2003 invasion of Iraq.

It is a war being fought with a military significantly reduced in troop strength from the 1980s levels when we were standing firm against a still militant Soviet Union. Forty percent of the present deployment of some 140,000 G.I.s in and around Iraq are drawn from the Reserves and National Guard, an action not taken since World War II (Falconer). This radical foreign policy followed a decade of having conducted 86 military operations, Iraqi Freedom being just one, using our military bases scattered to the far corners of the globe (Kaplan). The international search for al-Qaeda members planted secretly in cells around the world seems to have been superseded, at least temporarily, by a hot war against a well-financed, vicious army of Muslim extremists right under our nose and in our face in Iraq proper—a contest featuring well over a hundred suicide bombers so far. Very abruptly, we have entered a new period of foreign policy protocol that would do old Teddy Roosevelt and his Rough Riders proud.

The American foreign policy of Unilateralism and Preemption was articulated soon after 9/11 as our new National Security Strategy. The groundwork for this strategy was laid in 1992 in a set of classified policy guidelines called the Defense Planning Guidance (Frontline, Feb. 20,2003). This proposed policy for how the U.S. should deal with Saddam Hussein was rejected at the time under "Bush 41," and the ideas were not openly entertained again until "Bush 43" took office. This Bush National Security Strategy bore a strong resemblance to the dormant Defense Planning Guidance prepared by staff members nine years earlier, who were once again part of government or very influential on it.

This confederation of like minds assembled in Washington has come to be called neoconservative. They have, ever since Gulf I, wanted more than war against terrorists in hiding. They wanted Saddam Hussein, the man, ever since the abrupt end of Gulf I; and 9/11 was just the right event to convince the president to become the torch bearer for this jingoistic tide that overran the Washington policy makers. The neoconservative agenda for America promotes four principles: (1) the projection of power, (2) the use of labels like good or evil, (3) concentration on the Middle East, and (4) preemption and unilateralism (Halper and Clarke). American foreign policy has been expropriated by this neoconservative wing of the Republican party disdaining all traditional interest in fiscal responsibility. It is the international projection of American power it is interested in.

Once started, the deed was done with precision in three weeks. The invasion of Iraq opened a chapter in American involvement in the Middle East, which leads we know not where. The president has declared that Iraq is just a stalking horse, its liberation being only the first step in a process to make the Middle Eastern Islamic stronghold safe for democracy. But the plan for building peace and democracy in Iraq appears not to have been as well crafted as was the plan to subdue Saddam Hussein and his assumed weapons of mass destruction (WMD). If, as has happened, WMD and al-Qaeda support do not appear to have been adequate reasons for all out war, then certainly a compassionate concern for the oppressed peoples of Iraq is a legitimate rationale. If so, one might expect some show of concern for the estimated 50 to 100,000 Iraqi lives lost in this conflict, since most were not our enemy, but just innocent bystanders we came to rescue from tyranny.

It is strange how such compassionate concern for people, legitimate as it may be, is lost in the political din until such time as it surfaces as a rallying cry for an action taken in self-interest. But that's the way is has always been done when the pursuit of interest requires a moral chaperone.

It is against this background that President Bush has proclaimed a sweeping extension to the policy of Preemption and Unilateralism—a policy of actively promoting democracy and freedom in all regions of the world. This new Bush Doctrine is so astonishing that it challenges the imagination to even conceive of how it might be executed or the consequences that pursuing it might bring. The articulation of this policy might be construed to be an audacious expression of American intent to impose our mode of governance upon half the peoples and countries on earth.

What is quite clear is that we were greeted with a mixed reception in the land of Mohammed. Nice to see the local tyrant deposed. Now please rebuild our infrastructure quickly, accept our thanks, and go home. Or we may have your head.

Will democracy work in Iraq? In defense of his position, President Bush has cited the blossoming of democracies around the world. According to Adrain Karatnycky of Freedom House, 44 percent of the world's population lives in the 88 free, or mostly free, countries, out of 192 total. In pressing for democracy in the Middle East, the president failed to mention that not one of these 88 democracies blossomed at the unilateral, preemptive command of America or any other nation. Germany and Japan had been reduced to ashes before adopting a liberal democratic posture. In fact many of the world's democracies blossomed while America was installing or supporting the dictator governments of the Shah of Iran and Pinochet in Chile. With sufficient force you can subdue an adversary and bend it to your will, but short of that, indigenous peoples will resist any foreign occupation or coercion vigorously. There is no instance in history of democracy and freedom having been successfully imposed on a sovereign people by force. Short of utter defeat, annihilation, and/or decades of boots-on-the-ground-occupation, it is probably not possible to forcibly superimpose one culture upon another. The vanquished do not understand or find meaning in your morals and myths. They are confused by your traditions and customs. They may surrender their lives as suicidal martyrs but are psychologically incapable of surrendering their cultural identity to aliens.

Resistance to occupation is an oft-repeated lesson, brought home, for instance, by the annexation of the Philippines in 1898. This political takeover was followed by over a decade of strife and a loss of some 750,000 lives. The unprovoked invasion of Mexico in 1913 during a Mexican civil war was met with united opposition from both the government *and* the rebel Pancho Villa (Judis). It is always that way. The most powerful unifying influence in the Middle East is the American presence. This is especially so since we have announced our intention to change the way all Arabs and Persians do business. It is clear why the worldwide Muslim population no longer trusts American intentions.

Unlike Iraqi Freedom, the motivation for entering World War II was to save freedom. It was rescued and America won great admiration, influence, and many friends for democratic government in the free world. Many of our troops stayed in Europe after the war, by invitation. The motivation to invade Iraq was clearly different, and we will not be invited to stay once the suicidal murder subsides, if it subsides. "It is exactly by not abusing its power that America attained its current position" according to George Soros, and gained its positive influence in the world prior to Gulf II.

Drawing on the experience of the British Empire, Niall Ferguson (*Empire* 2004) points out that American Empire is based on military power. Once exercised, we find it difficult to stay the course when military action is concluded. The American people have little patience for the decade or more required for nation building. George Bush acknowledged this could be a lengthy engagement during the 2004 election campaign, while liberal candidates were calling for an early exit strategy in Iraq, even as the job of nation-building had just begun. Great Britain, the last occupiers of Iraq, kept troops there until 1955 after originally having "given" that country to King Faisal in 1921 (Ferguson, Colossus 2004).

This adventure places America and its lone partner in the shadow of the mosque, the ubiquitous religious, political, and social network of Islam. Most recently it has positioned President Bush in the crosshairs of an incensed opposition led by Congressman John Conyers based on Bush's alleged lies to Congress justifying the Iraqi invasion. The President's response has been the already failed attempt to link 9/11 to terrorism in Iraq–a somewhat threadbare linkup.

On the civilian front, Cindy Sheehan, a gold star mother, has become the war protest focus for a gathering number of antiwar activists by keeping a month long vigil just outside the President's ranch in Crawford, Texas.

Thus was the Cold War policy of defensive containment abandoned and the policy of offensive coercion adopted. The cost, $280 billion through 2005, compares unfavorably to the $7 billion tab picked up by the U.S., of the $61 billion cost for Gulf I, a war underwritten by our coalition partners (Civil War Ctr.). The cost in American lives is fast approaching 2,000 with many thousands more consigned to a life they have little hope of valuing. It has lost us the respect and willing international cooperation of all the peoples and all the nations of the world save one. It is by no means clear that the benefits of this adventure will be worth the price.

While this adventure in Iraq will ultimately be judged by its success, the outcome will neither explain nor justify the intent. At its economic heart is the drive to secure our vital source of oil. Surely it would be a major tragedy if Islam were to replace mortally wounded Communism as our 21st century adversary as the result.

We have enlisted only one partner in this war. We have lost the respect of the world and are losing the war of ideas. It is imperative we embark on a long term diplomatic process of showing our better virtues to the peoples of the Middle East. "The major hope for peace lies not in armaments, however important they are, but rather in ideas" (Trueblood).

American Opportunity

As Meade asked, "What is the point of our 'empire'–to make us rich, or to make us safe, or to build a better world. The reality today is that our national security and prosperity depend on the health of the world system–and the health of that system depends on the wisdom, strength, and foresight of American foreign policy—and on the willingness of the American people to back up their government's policies." Certainly we are prosperous, although we fall short of realizing the full potential of our labors in either tangible resources or spiritual development. We are about as safe as a nation can be without forging more-humane international agreements. As for a better world, perhaps the most common expression of what the principal aim of our foreign policy should be, is the promotion of democracy, economic growth, and free markets around the world. This is an aspiration many, and maybe most, peace loving Americans would endorse.

Shunting aside the present militarized version of our international strategy for a moment, we might ask how some small fraction of our great riches, that no longer augment our happiness index, might be put in the service of mankind? How might the successful American experience be made to count for something more than just our own power and wealth? We would do well to keep looking for Thomas Edison's "better way" to light the path to prosperity, personal freedom, opportunity, and dignity for all of God's children.

To be sure, there are some fine outreach programs underwritten by the American people through our government. The Peace Corps program, started under JFK, is still active, sending over 6,000 volunteers to 69 countries at a total budgeted cost of $300 million. The Voice of America (VOA) beams out 1,000 hours of programming weekly, reaching 90 million people via radio, TV, and the Internet (Heil). The 2004 budget for VOA was $563.5 million to broadcast news, educational, and cultural programs in 53 different languages.

In total, America anted up $15.8 billion in foreign aid yearly with three quarters going to Israel, Egypt, and peacekeeping activities in 2003, while private contributions to foreign countries amounted to $34 billion, about half of which came from individual donors. However, our federal level of foreign aid placed us dead last at 0.14 percent of GDP among the top 22 wealthiest developed nations in the Organization for Economic Co-operation and Development (OECD) (Shah, Am. Ass'n. Fundraising Council).

It would be difficult to claim the United States is overly generous, especially since approximately 80 percent of our official aid goes directly to cover expenses of domestic companies working overseas. Since that money never leaves our shores, we may be sure that foreign hanky panky is minimized and that the president and congressmen are not overlooking their friends at home. At home Americans give $241 billion each year for charitable purposes. Of this amount, 75 percent comes from individuals, and 35 percent of the total goes to religious institutions.

Israel receives aid, at least in part, because it is our "project" in democracy on the edge of the Middle Eastern Islamic stronghold. Egypt got help originally because we wanted to counterbalance the effect of Soviet influence as builders of the Aswan Dam, and also as an incentive to "make nice" with Israel. It is not unique to the U.S. that foreign aid is more a tool serving the donor's interests than purely altruistic aims. Foreign aid is a tool of foreign policy. There really is no free lunch. The neediest nations are generally the ones under the worst management. Outright gifts without some degree of accountability buy you only temporary loyalty and not much tangible progress. Worse yet, it may buy you only a dependent client.

As Peter Bauer has found, much money sent to alleviate hunger and suffering around the world just doesn't trickle down to the sick and malnourished. Consider Saddam Hussein who is claimed to have siphoned off $21 billion from the "oil-for-food" program under the "watchful" eye of the United Nations (Sen. Collins), whose friends allegedly took a cut for their services. We get to talk with the Egyptians and Israelis, but not much more. One time emergency aid is an undertaking that absolutely must be rendered when needed. One time "bribes" are also common as a quid pro quo inducement to foreign cooperation. It's called diplomacy. But a perpetual stipend is rarely appreciated once secured.

The bitter reparation terms of the World War I Versailles Treaty set the stage for World War II two decades later. The $13 billion Marshall Plan to catalyze the reconstruction of a broken Europe after World War II laid the foundation for a lasting peace and respect for American virtue. Lincoln's generous terms of unqualified forgiveness for a beaten Confederacy laid out in his second Inaugural Address to "...secure a just and lasting peace with ourselves..." made possible a peaceful ending to our bloody civil differences. And peace there has been, even though the South still refers to "The War of Northern Aggression." Are such altruistic ideas, requiring so little of our $12 trillion per year GDP, somehow considered to be beyond the sphere of our national interest? Is some measure of compassion a sign of weakness, or is it perhaps just psychologically incompatible with the demands of a competitive society? Even the victor in a tough negotiation takes some pity on his subdued opponent, as Lincoln did, if the contest was fair and honorably conducted.

Some Better Ideas

The conduct of our foreign affairs does not have to be exclusively a game of hardball. If you have been following the development of freedom's vector through 10 chapters, you have been exposed to my view of what is unique and good about America: a set of ideas that come alive when you use them and cost you nothing to share. These ideas are the ones expressed in the Declaration of Independence, executed in the U.S. Constitution, and confirmed in the Gettysburg Address. Of course, if you force your version of these ideas on an unreceptive beneficiary, you may have to do it at the point of a gun to get its attention. Since Americans enjoy the greatest individual freedom ever known, it wouldn't hurt to invite others to see how these ideas work in everyday practice, if they are interested. But how best might you go about communicating the importance of these ideas and the ways in which they are put to use in everyday practice?

Just as we are myopic when it comes to understanding the other guy's problems and cultural imperatives, he usually has only a two dimensional take on the America scene. If you have not experienced much freedom in your life, you don't understand that it requires a sense of personal and social responsibility just to hold onto it. If you haven't had to compete in the free marketplace for your daily bread, the prospect is intimidating to one accustomed to welfare or even a hard scrabble agricultural existence. Many Soviet defectors during the old regime came to these shores, looked around for Easy Street and, not finding it, booked passage back to mother Russia after a short stay. Some newcomers find the street violence frightening. What is familiar and obvious to us doesn't even exist in the minds of over half of the 6 billion inhabitants of this planet.

The call issued by President Bush to bring democracy and freedom to all corners of the world is breathtaking in its scope, especially since it is a 180 degree reversal of our 210-year, pre-Bush foreign policy. On one hand it is arguably an end to which almost all free, democratic peoples would subscribe in the interest of creating a better world. It certainly could be *the* mission worthy of engaging the American psyche, our energy, and our passion, in the interest of universal freedom and equality. Tragically, this aspiration is at odds with our support of the undemocratic regimes of Egypt or Saudi Arabia, for example. Might Bush's call for worldwide democracy and freedom be realized by somehow just offering it to the oppressed peoples of the world? Or must it be accomplished by force? The state of Iraq in 2010 will shed light on this ambitious undertaking.

Fareed Zakaria claims that democracy can only succeed when some minimum average income allows for a modicum of freedom of action for most citizens, and that there exist stabilizing civil institutions such as a free enterprise economy and a free press. His claim reflects the conventional wisdom as expressed in academia (Fukuyama) and endorsed by some members of the influential Council on Foreign Relations. Mark Palmer believes otherwise and has a wealth of personal experience to support his ideas. He believes the march to democracy around the world can be accelerated by deposing the world's remaining 45 dictators, *peacefully*. He would do this by convincing all democratic countries to show a continuing, uniform disapproval of tyranny through their local ambassadors, investing in communications media for local dissidents, and supporting all their nonviolent demonstration and opposition activities. The expectation that these affected countries would benefit from popular leadership, regardless of present internal conditions, is supported by statistical studies (Halperin, Siegle, and Weinstein) and could receive official support based on legislation just recently introduced in Congress.

A different approach, based on the integration of the world's communities, has been proposed by Richard Haass, President of the

Council on Foreign Relations. His policy "...would aim to create a cooperative relationship among the world's major powers–a twenty-first-century concert–built on a common commitment to promoting certain principles and outcomes." As one supporting feature of such a policy, the following education-based program is offered here.

People who have never experienced democracy and freedom, or a free market, cannot even imagine how these institutions work. They wouldn't know the American Dream from any other nocturnal disturbance. Clearly the remedy for this problem is education. Ideally you would like to be able to work with a volunteer group of foreign individuals who were old enough to grasp the meaning of the social and political foundations of American democracy, yet young enough to approach the subject with an open mind and good prospects for playing a responsible role in the life of their home country. These would be university level students. Interested students the world over could be invited to spend five years in this country studying for a degree for four years and working for a fifth under the sponsorship of a plan we might call the Foreign Students Studies Program (FSSP). Without national preference or prejudice, hopefully, applicants from all countries could be selected in the ratio of two per million population each year for a five year study and work program with acceptance contingent upon the discretion of the U.S. college or university of choice. The math says there could be some 50,000 foreign students studying here at any time with a 10,000 student throughput rate annually. Ross Terrill has estimated that 30 to 40,000 foreign students are already studying in the U.S. at any given time.

The requirements for such a program would be minimal. For instance, accepting-schools would be responsible for a first year cultural preparation program and a yearly course in American history. Participating schools also would be responsible for arranging for a one year private family placement, a one year work position, and subsidizing all tuition and academic costs over the prescribed maximum to be picked up by Uncle Sam. In turn, the student would be responsible for achieving a passing performance, all out-of-country travel expenses, an agreement not to domicile in the U.S. for 10 years, a 2,000 word critique of his or her American experience, and have summers free for work, study, or travel.

If the FSSP picked up all academic expenses up to $10,000 and provided another $10,000 for living expenses, each foreign student would cost the U.S. Treasury up to $20,000 a year for four years, or $80,000 total. The total annual bill might come to as much as $800 million per year. We may presume the elite schools with high tuitions would be willing to subsidize their excessive tuition charges for the right students, since American universities are thought to support foreign students to the tune of $1.5 billion anyway.

If we can benefit from sending out American-educated foreign students, armed with a five year exposure to our American ideas, to the far corners of the earth, we should be able to benefit from a reciprocal program. As a complement to sponsoring 50,000 foreign students domestically, we could do a mirror image program and send about half that number of American kids abroad under essentially the same terms.

The French have a saying that. "the Americans go to war to learn geography." We could learn geography and a lot more for less money by sending 25,000 of our young folks throughout the world to bring home a better understanding of how the other 95 percent of the world's people live. The only restriction would be that they would have to scatter according to foreign national population distributions. It would not work out well if a thousand American youngsters applied to the Sorbonne in Paris every year. The fifth year could be devoted to foreign work, the Peace Corp, or a year's service touring public school districts, presenting stories of personal experiences in foreign cultures. This would bring the total FSSP cost to a maximum of $1.2 billion plus administrative costs. That's about 0.05 percent of our Federal budget, or just a small fraction of the cost of a three week war in Iraq.

An FSSP program would not, all by itself, result in peoples around the world adopting democracy and embracing freedom. It could, however, make this transition easier when the time is ripe. Had we the intellectual and experiential support for democracy embedded in even a small fraction of the Iraqi hearts and minds, we might have fewer dollars going to Baghdad and fewer flag-draped coffins coming home. Maybe not, but it certainly would have been worth a try, for starters.

Along the same lines, it would be constructive if government would offer and encourage attendance at two-week class sessions on American democracy for all interested citizens. This could be offered free to all comers using public school facilities at night. The most appropriate time to offer these sessions would be during the two weeks in September ending on the 17th, Constitution Day, so named by congress this year. A little coaching on the use of our "Owners Manual" and our democratic freedoms and rights would serve to focus more attention on the importance of government and our responsibility to keep it running smoothly.

After a lifetime of gathering and codifying the history of civilization, Will and Ariel Durant concluded, "If a man is fortunate, he will before he dies, gather up as much as he can of his civilized heritage and transmit it to his children." In the same way, we can pull together the very good, very successful, and very unique ideas that define America, and share them with our brothers, many of whom labor under ancient and failed ideologies. The FSSP program represents how much can be done for as little as 15 percent of our foreign aid outlay.

More generally, we know that foreign policy is a tool of self-interest. It can lead to constructive trade agreements. It can lead to war. It always seems to do both. The war path is easy—just create the specter of a threatening enemy. People will fight for their country, if not always for their government. But people want peace. They have known since time immemorial that the Golden Rule operates in their individual self-interest. In the free United States, the outpouring of private charitable contributions and volunteer labor in support of good causes is truly magnanimous. Would not a broad program directed at enhancing opportunity and dignity on an international basis receive widespread support, as long as no direct commercial or political interests were involved? As one example, the Peace Corp has had and still is having a very positive impact on the American psyche after 40 years in operation, and at very little cost.

To the extent America wins wars of conquest or builds a great virtual Empire, it will be remembered by many, admired by some, and honored by none. To the extent it lights the way for all peoples to prosper in freedom, it will be remembered, admired, and honored by all for many generations to come. Maybe some descendant of yours with a piece of your DNA will locate you on his or her family tree and think that *you* were part of the greatest American generation.

Leadership based on coercion requires money, toughness, resolve, and blood. Leadership dedicated to contribution and improvement requires personal integrity, moral responsibility, less money, no blood, and a transcendent compassion. That is what the founding fathers brought to the party and hoped the American character might rise to.

If some of these observations sound unduly critical and the suggestions a little pollyannaish, it is well to keep in mind there is no hint or suggestion that we should abandon the competitive race for prosperity *or* a quest for happiness. These pursuits can be prosecuted with energy to spare for good deeds. It is only the strongest nations that are strong enough to work for a better world without succumbing to external pressures. It requires a sense of the possible, an understanding of purpose, and a dedication to mission. The payoff for making a contribution is the realization of something you have worked and hoped for, or even just the feeling one gets from doing a good deed. Happiness comes not from what you have, but from what you do. Joy comes from what you do for others.

Position Not Assured

America has a legitimate claim to having shown the way to achieving a generous degree of individual freedom by relying on a carefully crafted liberal democratic plan. However, our tenure as the dominant world power is by no means assured throughout the 21st century. Empires fall by the wayside, leaving only death, taxes, and newer empires to prevail. Our international leadership position is worth preserving at least until a better system is invented. What now, other than our own arrogance, can frustrate continued progress?

The past century has been witness to the demise of three great empires as well as two would-be empire candidates, Germany and Japan. The long-declining Ottoman Empire ruled as far west as the Eastern Mediterranean until the British, French, and Arabs claimed the Middle

East at the end of World War I. The famed but financially distressed British Empire was dealt a fatal blow in 1947 when Gandhi engineered a peaceful movement to reclaim India, the jewel of the empire, for Indians. The Russian Empire collapsed abruptly in 1989 after a 70-year run following the immoral, gross mismanagement of a bankrupt economy. The future of our American Empire depends not only on how we prosecute our foreign affairs, but also on how successfully we are able to cultivate two major aspects of our domestic life. First is the requirement of maintaining a positive economic experience based on our talent, efforts, and motivation. Second is the requirement of conducting our lives with compassion and respect for others.

The first requirement must be fulfilled taking due notice of the potential seriousness of our financial condition as discussed briefly in chapter 9. The direction taken over time is no more encouraging. Our GDP advanced by 16 percent between 2001 and 2004 while our national debt shot up 27 percent. We are adding to our debt at the rate of about $400 billion a year at present. We (the government) have no assets with which we might offset these debts. We only have us, the taxpayers, with our individual checkbooks. At present we pay about 30 percent of our GDP in taxes to support our national, state, and local programs. If we raised that tax rate to 40 percent, matching the socialist European states, and balanced the budget each year, it would take us about seven years to pay down our national debt. Even if we don't try to liquidate this debt, our taxes will increase just to pay for the massive future benefits that have been promised for health care and Social Security over the next 45 years. If we borrow more to cover these ballooning costs and/or finance a conversion to private social security accounts, we will soon be triggering Paul Volker's predicted financial crisis. Our financial condition is steadily deteriorating.

Over the past 20 years America has been experiencing some disturbing economic trends. Our international trade has been running a chronic deficit because, increasingly, goods produced overseas can be shipped in at prices below the costs of our domestic producers. Since the demand and the money for these goods are here in America, the physics of economics dictates that goods will flow in and dollars will flow out, with the Wal-Marts of America serving as the conduit. At the same time we are continuing to experience a loss in mid-pay-range jobs while service jobs, many low-paying, are slow to take up the slack. The labor force in manufacturing is down from 19.5 million jobs at its peak in 1979 to 14.3 million in 2004 (Cong. Budget Office, cbo.gov/showdoc. cfm?index=5078), although, much of this attrition is due to productivity gains. Japan, Taiwan, South Korea, and now China have all primed their economic pump by production and export to the West.

The American industrial labor force is going the way of the farmer, now numbered at less than 3 percent of the nation's workforce. Alan Greenspan stated that it is not so important where our manufactured goods come from as long as they are economically accessible. It is important only that economies create value. Greenspan's observation appears to be economically sound in the sense that taking advantage of international productive diversity results in more stuff for everyone. Of course, this process burdens our government with the problem of dealing with a shrinking demand for skilled and semi-skilled workers. It neglects to take into account the potentially destabilizing effect that arises when our working class falls ever farther behind our investing class in relative purchasing and political power.

At the same time, we may be setting the stage once again for domestic civil instability based on the economic distance between the champions of capitalism and the underprivileged losers. The top 1 percent ownership of American assets is now within hailing distance of the 56.4 percent level reached prior to WW I (Gates and Collins) that resulted in sweeping political changes in the short span of three years. From 1977 through 1990 the real income of the top 1 percent of families grew at 74 percent while for the lowest 20 percent it decreased by 13 percent (Slemrod and Bakija). Although the long term advance in prosperity has moved much of the population into improved circumstances, those unfortunates left floundering in poverty are far from content with their lot in life.

Our economy rests more and more on overseas investment returns and less and less on creating the staples of life at home. This financialization of the economy follows a pattern similar to that of the Dutch and British trading economies of the 1600s and 1800s, respectively. This trend favors the haves and squeezes the have-nots. Ultimately this process widens the wealth gap and leads to growing dissatisfaction, impoverishment, and unrest. International financial investment lacks the stability of domestic manufacturing investment, which is not subject to the vagaries of foreign political interests.

If our ability to create prosperity while preserving individual freedom is deteriorating, it is not due to any external causes. It is because of the way we are managing our own domestic affairs. We are propping up inefficient industries and erecting legal roadblocks to the exercise of free enterprise. We are trading away our individual freedom for security and a plethora of special entitlements. We are neglecting the development of our underclass. We are spending our productive resources on warfare and an inefficient health care system. We are allowing elected officials to place themselves beyond challenge at the ballot box and any need for accountability. We are pledging our economic future for social services beyond any hope of delivery. We have tangled ourselves in a taxation system that is frustrating to comply with and a source of estrangement from our government. Our management of domestic affairs not only impedes prosperity, but also prevents the creation of new jobs just as surely as unnecessary licensure and protective certification requirements do. Behind this socialistic drift is a government that protects its power base, its campaign resources, and pisses away the fruits of our labor.

The second element of success for maintaining American leadership into the future is moral and can be illustrated very simply by the story of Jim Green, a World War II employee of the Cleveland Twist Drill Company. One day Jim walked into the office of Jacob Cox, a company executive, just to volunteer that since joining the company, his personal life and domestic harmony had blossomed to the point of totally changing his life. For the first time in his life he looked forward to coming to work each day. Mr. Cox was surprised and more than a little touched by this spontaneous declaration.

It turned out that the absentee rate at Cleveland Twist Drill was running 1 percent compared to the industry average of 6 percent at that time. The key was that the company dealt with their employees as partners in a moral enterprise dedicated to saving the world from tyranny–not just as units of labor managed to enrich the owners.

When government comes to think of us 300 million workers and dependents as partners in a great enterprise, and not as producing, consuming, taxpaying, and voting units, I think more of us units will be happy to report for work at company USA every day.

As will be shown in the following chapter, a healthy skepticism toward government has been replaced by either cynicism or lack of interest altogether. We are working for a paycheck riddled with deductions and not in partnership with a government that holds out the promise of some achievement of great purpose.

Should we lose our economic momentum for any reason, we may "...find it difficult to accept altered circumstances: that there are now different ways of organizing industry, educating the young, distributing resources, and making policy decisions—and that these new ways are more successful. To respond to change might mean altering one's own social priorities, educational system, patterns of consumption and saving, even basic beliefs about the relationship between the individual and society," as pointed out by Paul Kennedy.

We must maintain our psychological equilibrium and not let the hubris born of unparalleled world power cloud our judgment and warp our purposes. This was the scenario that played out in Rome 2,000 years ago; a process that led to a vacuum of civil leadership in the West lasting for a millennium.

In a more optimistic sense, however, the domestic stresses and strains we are experiencing in America need not overwhelm us because they can all be successfully addressed if we act with knowledge, responsibility, and determination. Unlike the EU, or empires held together by coercion, America is unified in its basic political and economic principles. Only the policies pursued by government can divide us and detract from our progress going into the new century.

Empire, as well as national prosperity, depends on faith in government and the moral values it demonstrates in its domestic and foreign policies. We are now pondering the proposition that bringing freedom and democracy to all regions of the world is the great purpose to which we are called. If so, it will take better planning and greater compassionate understanding than did Iraqi Freedom. Continued success for America is less a matter of things and more a matter of state-of-mind.

The 11th: New York. July 26, 1788

CHAPTER 12

THE SOCIAL PARADE

The civility of our civilization depends on how successfully we carry out our social relationships. If the success of our democratic system rests on high standards of personal responsibility, what principles of conduct can we consult to judge the sufficiency of our behavior? To assess the character of our social interactions we must look to our moral values. This collection of values is referred to as our moral code, rules of acceptable behavior embedded in the group consciousness of our culture. The conventions observed in everyday social relations are very much shaped by both the myths and morality upon which our culture rests. These myths and the social behavior patterns we exhibit have changed radically, especially since the Civil War. An assessment of our social behavior patterns is germane to our story, reveals our progress, and may well be a weathervane foretelling where freedom's vector is heading.

Myth

Every culture is sustained by some belief pattern that arises by general agreement of its members. This pattern of belief is a construct of ideas that give meaning to the culture, a construct most properly labeled myth.

A myth often takes the form of a story, for instance, a classical narrative depicting the antics of gods or other mystical characters. Contemporary working myths are often descriptive in nature. A myth is to reality as fiction is to nonfiction. It sets the boundaries for a culture, the limits beyond which society does not trespass by general agreement (Campbell 1991). Trespassing these limits is considered taboo. The content and meaning of myths may be subject to the influence of changing folk traditions, customs, profound national emergencies, or charismatic leadership. For instance it was once believed you would encounter deep sea monsters and/or fall off the edge of the earth if you sailed too far west, or the king was king by Divine Right, or Aryans were a master race.

While the myth itself may be fiction, its hold over our sense of who we are and what we believe has a pervasive influence over how we act and behave in the real world. However, a myth does not actually inform us of that which is good or evil, right or wrong, in real life (Cassirer). A myth is like a novel in the sense that its meaning is not explicitly stated, but rather a verity to be inferred from the story. A factual representation of some event or situation may be an accurate portrayal of reality, but convey no deeper meaning.

There are many kinds and levels of myth. In everyday life, a myth may be a popular deception as would be a fairy tale, for instance. Many cultures have a Hero Myth (Campbell 1973). The composite, ubiquitous Hero Myth is one of adventure and transformation, wherein a young person leaves home, encounters many strange attractions and threatening situations, eventually faces his certain demise, but is inexplicably rescued by some mystical power, returns home changed as an adult, and may become a teacher or a sage. This Hero Myth is a metaphor for our exploration of and journey through life wherein we face good and evil, but somehow survive, and in the process discover who we are. That is how we establish our identity and unique powers. That is what Dorothy did when she faced down the Wicked Witch of the North and discovered the power she had always had in her red shoes. Just click your heels together three times.

Most cultures have a Founding Myth (Raphael). Primitive peoples, whose culture remains static, generally have a founding myth conjured up as an authorizing event placed in the far distant past, as do the New Zealand Maori. These ancient people believe their ancestors came ashore in canoes, except for one Whale Rider who fell overboard and was carried ashore on the back of a whale. Such myths can operate as the psychological stabilizing power in one's life, the very foundation of which may be challenged only by some significant emotional experience; for instance, by the Post Traumatic Stress Syndrome suffered by some battle-weary war veterans. Such was the case for Tayo, the half-breed Laguna Indian portrayed by Leslie Marmon Silko, whose disabling confusion following World War II was overcome only by reestablishing his identity through ceremonial ritual embracing the "stories" of his people.

Consider also the Adam and Eve myth of creation, Moses returning from Mount Sinai with the complete Torah, the first five books of the Bible in hand, the ancient origin of the sacred Kaaba rock in Mecca, or the virgin birth and resurrection after death, of Jesus Christ. Our Founding Myth, the American Revolution, is, on the other hand, quite factual in terms of events, if not always in interpretation, e.g., that the United States was created as a democracy. Nonetheless, the story of the American founding is too recent in written history to have slipped its moorings. It is our rock and refuge in a constantly changing social environment. While a myth may be based on matters of fact, the controlling or motivating spirit of any myth is not to be found in its quasi-factual substance. It resides in the meaning.

The most common representation of the 20th century American myth is the American Dream, a phrase coined in 1931 by James Adams, marking a crisis in national identity at the depth of the Great Depression. This was the working American Myth, now passé, but still found in the popular lexicon as conventional wisdom. The principal myths of dynamic societies undergo change with changing circumstances, as have our working myths.

The origin of our American Myth took shape between 1620, when the first trickle of people came to these shores from the old world and landed at Plymouth Rock, and the death of Abraham Lincoln in 1865. The colonist's experience in this country gave rise to the idea of personal opportunity as it had existed nowhere else in the history of civilization. Their individual efforts as personified by the legendary achievements of one Benjamin Franklin, the quintessential, self-made, American Renaissance Man, were many times over a success story.

85+te

It was within the power of each individual colonist or citizen to pursue his happiness to a successful end and bequeath that heritage, so created, to his children, or perhaps just to his first born son according to the practice of primogeniture. It was a heritage of freedom nurtured by a free marketplace, heralded by the liberties first espoused in the Declaration of Independence, then spelled out in the Bill of Rights.

George Washington and Abraham Lincoln, legendary figures from real life, extended the idea of personal achievement and integrity to the pinnacle of public leadership in times of historic national crisis. Washington laid the groundwork for establishing the union, and Lincoln "saved the union and freed the slaves" and told us we were all first class citizens. In less than two minutes at Gettysburg he reestablished the 90-year-old founding assertion that government was of, by, and for us all. Honest Abe fit squarely into and became a staple piece of our national myth. But it took Martin Luther King, Jr., to translate founding theory into street practice for all minorities who labored under a de facto second class citizenship.

The myth was further honed and refined by Horatio Alger in 1867 by his portrayal of such stoic and self-reliant characters as that "diamond in the rough," *Ragged Dick*. His was a final representation of The Protestant Ethic featuring virtues such as diligence, trustworthiness, frugality, sobriety, reliability, and honesty. Alger's books were immensely successful—they captured a fierce desire to capitalize on American opportunity through self-improvement. Although the Great Depression changed this bootstraps mentality, if you would know the American Dream of 1943, watch Frank Capra's classic movie, *It's a Wonderful Life*. The first indication heralding a change in the American character came with the 1937 publication of Dale Carnegie's *How to Win Friends and Influence People,* a how-to book teaching success through "reading" other people. By 1950 this "other-directed," personality-based approach to success had been recognized in scholarly works like the classic, *The Lonely Crowd*.

By the conclusion of World War II, we knew we stood at the apex of world power and had unleashed it in the interest of world peace.

Having emerged as the world's only great power, we so informed the world, much as Teddy Roosevelt did in 1907 when he sent the Great White Fleet of new battleships on world tour. Eventually, we were reminding each other of our exalted position at baseball and football games, waving big, bright, "We're No. 1," sponge rubber mitts. Jimmy Stewart as the small town Savings and Loan proprietor would be aghast at this hubris. Today, instead, we have "The Donald."

Gradually, through the 1970s, our right to freedom and personal achievement became diluted with the expectation that government would assume complete responsibility for running the economy and guaranteeing our domestic security. Government was eager to take on this role. Added responsibility meant more control. Providing security meant increased dependence of citizens on government. There would be more taxes and more power. At the same time the suppressed arrogance of Teddy Roosevelt resurfaced in Vietnam and is again today a hallmark of American foreign policy.

The simple, frugal theme of Horatio Alger had turned into the expectation that we all soon would have a good job with health insurance, a home in the suburbs with 2.4 children, a dog, and two cars. Our dream was in the process of turning into an entitlement myth. For some, the vision of the heroic individual as the essential force in mythological achievement was yielding to increased reliance on the state as a source of security. Today the residue of the American Dream resides mainly in the hearts of 8 million illegal Mexican aliens who have come north to do America's domestic and agricultural manual labor.

If the prewar depression-era adults were concerned about getting or holding down a job, their post-war children became preoccupied with carving out a professional career with visions of advancement, a tax exempt 401(k) plan, an SUV, a second spouse (or live in), and the good life at every turn. While the everyday working guy was and still is very much family oriented, his white collar counterpart, the knowledge worker, is increasingly pursuing that siren, the bitch goddess success. Success as defined by money and stuff—all kinds of stuff. We are now squarely ensconced in a money culture where for many of us, our address and country club affiliation increasingly define our value as a person.

We are a democratic nation, having become so progressively over time. However, when a politician proclaims America to be a great democracy, he would like you to accept the idea that America was conceived as a classic democracy from the start. He would like you to believe that we are free as the result of this democracy, your hard work, and legitimate democratic influence on government. He would like you to believe that he is one of us and we should listen to and endorse his ideas.

When a politician dredges up The American Dream, he is appealing to your sense of entitlement. It is the "you deserve a break today" marketing appeal. It is the approach used when he wants the vote of the common man. It is a poor substitute for a good program or position statement.

The contemporary "working" myth for any people is not easy to package in any coherent way. In fact it is a collection of generalizations, descriptions, and beliefs that serve to reconcile many separate and disparate generalized notions held by sub-sets of the culture. This collective mythos serves the purpose of explaining the local culture in quasi-rational terms and giving some guidance for acceptable behavior by creating the illusion of understanding (Robertson).

Some mythical beliefs of the '50s and earlier that are *out*, are:

- Gangsters can be celebrity heroes.
- Addictive practices can be eliminated by legal means alone.
- A woman's place is in the home.
- Women are fragile.
- Women do not like sex.
- Black people are inferior.
- Illegitimacy is a sinful condition.
- Hard work and frugality pave the road to success.

Other beliefs *on the way out* are:

- America is a melting pot (becoming a reality, slowly).
- The American Dream.
- Homosexuality is a choice.

Those *alive and well* are:

- Individual heroes acting alone can achieve happiness through wealth.
- Happiness is an entitlement.
- We are victims of society and in all fairness need special protections.
- Public school systems can assume parental responsibilities.
- More jails are necessary to effectively reduce crime.
- Voting privileges are sufficient to sustain democratic freedoms.
- Money and the police can solve all social problems.
- All females can realize freedom from domesticity.
- You can be Wonder Woman and have it all.
- You can have relationships without commitment.
- Success is the result of personal excellence (Social Darwinism).
- The American medical system is the best ever, with only minor flaws.
- Life, liberty, and the pursuit of happiness are unalienable rights.
- Politicians are devious by their very nature.
- Might makes right and success justifies any action.
- Government may spend without limit.
- Social Security is the third rail of politics.
- Property values will always go up.
- Money is security.
- Doing well is doing good.
- He who dies with the most toys, wins.
- Consumerism is happiness and is intrinsically good.

Each of these myths incorporate or exaggerate some questionable premise, but may be widely subscribed to in our time. While the myth itself may be fiction, its hold over our sense of who we are and what we might become has a pervasive influence on how we act and behave in the real world. Without myth to give life meaning, we each would be left to seek our own existential interpretation of the why of our being. If you would understand a people, you must know its myths. However, myth does not differentiate between good and bad or right and wrong. Acceptable norms for behavior are the subject of our Moral Code.

Morality, Virtue, And Behavior

Role of morality

Our collection of working myths characterizes our belief system, while morality is the collection of unwritten instructions by which we and others judge our actions. Morality is only roughly consistent with our working myths. Thomas Friedman (1989) has suggested that the original code of Western morals and ethics was delivered to Moses at Mount Sinai. These Ten Commandments formed the basis of what became known as Judeo-Christian morality, a prescription for right behavior that still echoes in our hearts and in the halls of American justice after more than 3,000 years.

The presentment of the Ten Commandments codified several cardinal elements that are required to secure a cohesive cultural group. They identified a single source of leadership authorizing the ground rules for proper behavior of individuals in the group. They put that leader, God, beyond the pale of human questioning based on anyone's earthly experience. They sought to cement the authority of this leadership through the requirement of praising only God. They stated, simply and unambiguously, the civil elements that must be adhered to in order to realize harmony and social order. These 10 instructions collectively constitute the basis of three monotheistic religions which have spiritually guided and nourished billions of people throughout the world.

That which we refer to as morality today is a modern outgrowth of the concept of virtue espoused in the ancient Greco-Roman societies (Annas). But whereas virtue refers to praiseworthy traits of character such as honesty, loyalty, fairness, discipline, and courage, morality is a set of unwritten rules which act as a guide for making right choices in life. While virtues are internalized wellsprings of behavior, morality is a group consciousness against which the suitability of your actions can be measured.

Perhaps the clearest and most concise moral aphorism ever expressed is the Golden Rule. "Do unto others as you would have them do unto you" is a principle for the conduct of life incorporated into all the world's religions. The origin of this common sense adage is lost in antiquity and presumed to have been rediscovered many times over as the basis for harmonious social interaction, a principle in opposition to the self-serving Machiavellian doctrine. The Golden Rule was recast in 1781 by Immanuel Kant as his Categorical Imperative: "Act so that the maxim of your act could be made the principle of a universal law." The Golden Rule assumes equal treatment to be the essence of justice and is strongly implied in the "all men are created equal" clause of the Declaration of Independence.

Two decades ago, Alasdair MacIntyre reintroduced the ancient concept of virtue as an answer to today's social ills brought on by the modern emphasis on the individual to the exclusion of identity through community participation. It would seem that this great moral philosopher did not realize that these virtues had been endorsed by Horatio Alger and the Boy Scout Manual all along. Since then, this ancient concept has been popularized by William Bennett in his *Book of Virtues,* for example.

The "virtue of virtue" is that it provides context for the problem of deciding how to live one's life–either in the pursuit of excellence in some chosen area, or for the purpose of material rewards, fame, or celebrity.

In the real, tangible world, your knowledge and observance of the laws of nature determine your physical fate. The social rules for our moral conduct apply to social interaction and are much squishier. In the social sphere, interactive behavior is governed by social consequences. For instance, you learn by tutoring and/or repeated experience that you may not injure other folks and expect to suffer no unpleasant consequences.

Morality is a group attribute encompassing the ideas of rightness and wrongness, goodness and badness, in its rules for good conduct and proper action. It is based on a set of common values. The old saying, "She has the morals of an alley cat" captures the idea that one's personal actions may fall outside the generally accepted limits of morality. An individual may have a personal code of moral behavior and still be immoral in the eyes of his cultural group.

The group moral code is held in custody collectively by religious institutions, family, friends, school, workplace, and law. It becomes embedded in your conscience before adulthood. In fact your conscience *is* your interpretation of morality as well as the personal expression of any virtues you may have internalized over time. While morality in the broad sense is not defined in writing, most institutions, including some families, have a set of written guidelines for internal use. These parochial, behavioral guidelines are an abbreviated, tailored, moral code known as a code of ethics.

The most interesting ethical code I ever ran across is The Gentleman's Rule for Wabash College, a small, men's, liberal arts school in Indiana: "A Wabash man will conduct himself at all times, both on and off campus, as a gentleman and a responsible citizen." Period.

Religion comes with many written rules regarding right civil behavior as well as those embracing acts of faith. It speaks to good and evil as conditions inherent in men and organizations. Morality, applying to believers and nonbelievers alike, is a social or group model which does not always coincide with Western religious teaching, e.g., on issues such as abortion and homosexuality. It is more properly concerned with right and wrong as secular, behavioral qualities. In the West over the past four centuries, morality has been increasingly perceived in a secular context. This long term trend may be interrupted, but not denied, by the three-decade rise in evangelical Christian fundamentalism.

The rules of morality allow for some degree of flexibility, some interpretation, and they tend to change gradually over time with social conditions, customs, and traditions.

Moral concepts may be institutionalized by the state, particularly those ideas embracing protection of persons and their property. A body of law specifies the limitations placed on individual actions and the boundaries of tolerable behavior, complete with penalties specified for violations. That part of the law reflects the morality of a society. However, law can be in conflict with a person's sense of morality, a dilemma calling for the exercise of personal integrity, as it did for Henry David Thoreau when he rejected his poll tax.

When both law and morality are ignored in the interest of personal gain, integrity is forsaken. If so, violating the dictates of one's own conscience may severely degrade one's spirit, as shown by Fyodor Dostoyevsky in his story of *Crime and Punishment*. To the extent human behavior is specified by law, to that extent any sense of personal responsibility may be weakened. If the law is felt to be unduly burdensome, integrity may yield to clandestine, illegal action against other individuals or the state. The thriving black market under Soviet Communism is a case in point. In the end, the entire empire built on the communist myth collapsed, its comrades having no spirit left to sustain it.

We have very high standards of morality when we apply them to others. For our politicians we have the most strict conflict of interest laws and, along with the United Kingdom, are the most likely to expose scandal in government, especially since the Watergate break-in (Garment). High "moral standards" combined with a low tolerance for deviant behavior has filled up our prisons with minor drug offenders. We have about 2 million people in jail, over 0.6 percent of the population. Over half of these inmates are there on drug convictions. Worse yet, it appears likely that 7 percent of our black population will be behind bars sometime in their lifetime (Morone). Other democratic countries with comparable crime rates incarcerate far fewer citizens. Unfortunately, the gap between high standards and actual behavior arouses many idealists who go searching for simplistic solutions to what may be complex, but sub critical problems.

Our jails have also become home for the mentally ill who are no longer since the 1960s accommodated in psychiatric institutions. Many of the one half million who are behind bars are seriously ill and without effective professional help (Frontline, May 10, 2005).

The profusion of government rules would not be so extensive if our moral code were strong enough to effectively set social limits on our actions, as it is in Japan. While we may feel that a strong legal code is indispensable for a large technological society, it is interesting to note that we have fully 25 times as many lawyers per capita as does Japan, which has a much lower incidence of crime. Many new laws or agency rulings make life more complex, unduly restrict our freedom, are a drag on the economy, and loosen the bonds of trust between us and our government. Each new complex law invites lawyers to find new loopholes by legal stealth. It is not the laws, rules, and regulations which in the end guarantee the integrity of our government, our institutions, our industries, or even our local organizations. It is the integrity of the leadership tasked with making and enforcing them. It is their understanding of and willingness to set high standards for the moral code of the culture. Along with competence and vision, this is the true and ultimate test of good leadership.

If our adventure in Vietnam generated distrust of government, Watergate confirmed it (Garment). Today, Americans go to the new World War II Memorial to remember, but they go to the Vietnam Memorial to weep. Both Nixon and Clinton, much as they accomplished, failed seriously in their leadership duty, exposing the moral shortcomings of men in the highest national positions of trust. At least you would expect our ex President, a Rhodes scholar, to know what "is," is. Loss of faith in government erodes personal values and goes hand in hand with the abandonment of personal responsibility. This mocks the "work and succeed" ethic once inherent in our obsolescent national myth, the American Dream.

Holden Caulfield, the *Catcher in the Rye* (Salinger), reflected the disillusionment experienced by many of our youth, that erupted on the streets in Haight-Asbury in the "Summer of Love" in 1967. Hippie flower children came by the tens of thousands and invented the "sex, drugs, and rock and roll" counterculture. The young do not excuse the adult world when they see morality fall victim to hypocrisy.

With good intentions and no experience of the "Hero," America's children proposed Love as the solution. But love alone was not equal to the task of amending our social ills. Still for many young folks today, the metaphysical spiritually embraced by New Age is just that–love with a touch of social license and mysticism, untethered to any mature perception of morality. As Bill Clinton reminded us in his recent book, however, the youth of that time protested not because they were filled with hate or ill will, but rather because they loved their country at heart, just as we all do.

Morality and politics

Morality plays a major determining role in where we line up politically. On the far right of the Republican Party are conservatives; capitalists who bow to Adam Smith and favor capitalism, stoic behavior, and personal responsibility, tempered by God's Word. They do not often champion equal opportunity or human dignity because most poverty is considered to be the result of people's undisciplined shortcomings.

On the far left are the Democratic liberals, socialists who bow to Karl Marx and emphasize equality, security, individual freedom, and human values. They do not often consider the means by which our prosperity may be preserved, but only that it should be dedicated to equal outcomes for all. Rounding out these oversimplified portraits are numerous other -isms.

For instance, the political philosophy of Libertarianism (libertarianism.com/) subscribes to the classical liberal principle that no man's personal freedom should be abridged unless it is used to dispossess another of his property rights or visit physical harm upon him, even if that man's behavior is self-destructive. In essence this is an endorsement of John Stuart Mill's individual freedom thesis.

Libertarianism was popularized in the 1940s in response to the socialist movements of the 1920s and '30s. It was an echo of laissez faire Social Darwinism from the late 19th century Gilded Age, which now finds its center in the CATO Institute founded in 1977. Libertarians believe individuals should have a personal right to practice the lifestyle represented by "sex, drugs, and rock and roll" or any other genre, without restriction, as they may choose. In general they do not feel they should be held legally responsible for the welfare of others, and may respect only their own personal version of a moral code. They advocate an absolute minimum of government and place a premium on individual responsibility.

An offshoot of libertarianism, Objectivism, was developed by Ayn Rand in the 1950s. She advocated success through personal achievement without reference to or dependence on any external authority, community moral code, or religious belief.

These extreme freedom movements place very heavy reliance on an individual's ability to find his way through the maze of life, which harbors success and failure, elation and despair, and fortune both good and bad. Following the French critic and champion of reason, Voltaire, they maintain that reason, logic, and personal aspirations are your only reliable psychological tools in the game of life. There is no requirement for weighing your ideas against a standard of social morality. But when everything is open to question, right and wrong, good and bad, are whatever you say they are. There is no beaten path to follow along life's way, only the pathway of personal interest. No external standard stands taller than one's own personal monument.

Just as freedom to act on blind faith in a singular idea, unchallenged by doubt, can lead one to tragic error (as with genocide), a lack of any faith or belief at all can lead to self-interest trumping integrity. Such alleged influential frauds as perpetrated in self-interest by Margaret Mead, Alfred Kinsey, Ward Churchill, and others are detailed in the controversial book, *Hoodwinked,* by Jack Cashill. Which is why there are certain moral teachings binding the generations in a culture, lest freedom be interpreted as license (Adler).

There are some long recognized limitations to individual freedom in addition to those fundamental rights protecting persons and property, which are necessary for the realization of equality of freedom for all. You may not avail yourself of free speech or use of the free press if your action presents a clear and present danger to others, defames another, is publicly obscene, or threatens government with violence. You may not traffic in drugs or refuse to pay your lawful taxes. You may not completely prevent the government from invading your property for the purpose of wealth redistribution. Moreover, a large measure of freedom lost is the result of indirect actions taken by government–legislation that directly subsidizes business or confers a favored status to any one body that results in a hidden cost to all taxpayers.

The overall cost of special benefits for some of us represents a huge financial penalty for the rest of us. Peterson (2004) roughly estimates that about 10 percent of our $11 trillion GDP is lost to counterproductive subsidy. We pay an estimated 15 percent extra in income tax to make up for tax avoidance schemes perpetrated by business corporations, the largest part of which ($100 to $200 billion) is the result of tax shelters employed with no economic purpose (Frontline, Feb. 19, 2004). The degree to which American citizens are deprived of their individual freedoms is related to the tax burden imposed by government, which is roughly 30 percent of our GDP. It is important to determine what portion of this 30 percent is necessary for government to discharge its obligations in the public interest, and what portion is not.

It is necessary to challenge government to show that its appropriations are dedicated to our welfare, defense, and the furthering of our unalienable rights under the Declaration of Independence and the protection of our freedoms under the Bill of Rights. However, instead of challenging government, we Americans have become firmly dedicated to petitioning it for special protections and security, the very actions that empower and enlarge government.

When everyone has a special privilege to protect, we are all pitted against each other and tenaciously committed to the status quo. Then it is almost impossible to mobilize public interest in the service of improving everyone's lot uniformly. The public has no voice when all voices have a different message. To make everyone believe he is just a little more than equal amounts to a divide and conquer strategy.

Behavior

Most Americans, like most people around the world, still put in a good day's work and live with the Golden Rule in mind. However, it is plainly evident that more and more individuals in positions of fiscal responsibility have exploited financial opportunities in such a way that would have been labeled outrageous 40 years ago, but are now met with only a shrug. Claims of entitlement that may have drawn only laughter at one time are now the basis for determined social demands, if not court litigation. To some extent, greed has always been with us, but victimhood has become a new and near-sacred social cause. It marches to the tune of political correctness, sometimes under the banner of diversity, a noun which underwent a metamorphosis in 1978 and became a legal concept owing to the decision of California Chief Justice Powell in the Bakke case (Wood).

For most of the 20th century, character and personal responsibility were held in high moral regard. But consider a few incidents that have recently taken place that signal the social change that has occurred over the past few decades. The Santa Cruz city council passed an ordinance declaring it illegal to taunt fat people. A girl's high school basketball coach told her she had to lose 10 pounds to compete. She developed an eating disorder, sued, was awarded $1.5 million, but then refused to seek help for her problem.

Charles Sykes cited a number of incidents where the defense of victimhood was used. An FBI agent embezzled $2,000, lost it gambling, but avoided prosecution on the basis of his claim that gambling with other people's money is a "handicap." A habitually late school employee pleaded that he was a victim of "chronic lateness syndrome." A man was killed in an accident while driving a car stolen from a parking lot, and his family sued the proprietor for failing to adequately prevent car thefts. A city park attendant with a record of 30 convictions for flashing was fired, but reinstated after a finding that he was a victim of illegal job discrimination—because he had never exposed himself in a park. To take advantage of set-asides for minorities, a 640-pound contractor demanded recognition as a minority-group bidder even though he was unable to visit job sites.

Is no one responsible for his own actions? Are we all entitled to the equivalent of a "Twinkies Defense," the one asserted by Dan White (based on the effects of sugar) in his trial for the murder of San Francisco's mayor and one of its supervisors? Self-discipline has given way to obesity. Personal responsibility has been arrested by social police wearing the uniform of political correctness. When lapses in personal responsibility become widespread, moral standards suffer accordingly.

Nor are institutions immune from these demands. In the 1990s, speech codes became popular on college campuses as a device for ensuring that minority students of any stripe would not be made to feel uncomfortable. The problem is that these codes, which foster a victimhood mentality and serve as the frontrunner for diversity politics, are being found to be in violation of First Amendment freedom of speech rights. To boot, they are in conflict with numerous college-subsidized student activity groups on campus that are organized to promote special interests and are exclusionary by their very nature (M. Adams).

The excessive emphasis on the "method" approach to teaching, combined with the word-police who remove all but flat, innocuous words from multicultural textbooks, does not inspire a love of learning (Radvitch). Content and image projection fall victim to political correctness. Long gone or fading fast is the interest in literature portraying the spectrum of the human condition.

After filming Hawthorne's story of *The Scarlet Letter*, retrofitted with a happy ending, Demi Moore was alleged to have remarked, "What's the difference? No one reads that story anymore, anyway." It seems that the great ideas that once played a role in tempering our behavior have been crowded out by the din of omnipresent cellular communications, ipods, and the popular video game, *Grand Theft Auto*. This playstation game features such powerful and violent imagery that Devon Moore offered its influence as his defense against the charge of killing three police officers. It didn't work.

Lawyers prosecute class action suits covering victims that in 90 percent of claims may present no proof of harm, but are putting over 100 firms into bankruptcy and costing over 100,000 jobs in the case of asbestos claims. Seventy billion dollars in claims were paid out through 2003 in suits naming 8,400 companies and 730,000 claimants (Cornwell). Pending some government intervention, those claims could total $280 billion. It is true that many of these firms were in possession of information pointing to the potential dangers of inhaling asbestos fibers. On the other hand, many of these claims arise from negligence merely alleged to have taken place decades ago and for which there is no proof of harm.

All manner of special interest groups use the law, i.e., the state, to inflict their demands upon the rest of us. Many prevail upon nongovernmental authorities to endorse and enforce their claims of political correctness on the rest of us. The issues at question arise from beliefs, the intensity of which may lead to the violation of our freedoms, especially of speech. They tend to promote social equality and the mentality of victim hood. To the extent they may emphasize equality of outcome, they lead us down the path of socialism. To the extent that these actions are tolerated by the public and endorsed by the law, they may distort our perception of fairness and degrade our moral standards.

Political correctness has been legally rejected when manifest in the form of numerical quotas per se. However, it has led to the concept of diversity in selection, a voluntary and arbitrary process justified by the presumed benefits accruing to all members of the selected group.

The protections sought are often in the general public interest, for instance in the case of product safety legislation, through which thoughtless design and/or production practices may be penalized. Their mere existence has encouraged a flood of lawsuits stemming from irresponsible product usage. Caution: improper use of these matches may cause serious fires or burns. Virtually every prescription drug preparation comes with a host of warnings such as "may cause headache, upset stomach, liver damage, or in some cases, cardiac arrest." They serve to protect producers from an ever more litigious public as well as qualify a drug for direct advertising to the public under FDA rules. The more rules that are written, the more loopholes that are found.

Claims of entitlement based on equality and discrimination spill over into group self-interest demands. In my memory, the country's leading athletes once were happy just to have the opportunity to play for a major league baseball team or in a national tennis tournament for almost any remuneration at all. Roosevelt Grier (recently deceased), a National Football League (NFL) standout, never earned more than $20,000 in his peak years. Now it is not uncommon for the best to command a million dollars or more a year, plus product endorsement contracts, complain about their treatment, and be indulging a drug habit at the same time.

By the last decades of the 1900s we were well on our way to living in pairs without the benefit of formal commitment, the less advantaged just moving on and leaving fatherless children to the care of working or even crack-smoking mothers. The illegitimacy rate soared, even with the bullet-proof birth control methods newly available to women. AFDC encouraged dead beat daddies to split, avoid the responsibility of fatherhood, sometimes even dropping by for an occasional dinner and whatever. This was an example of your tax dollars at work to promote equality, but resulting instead in the undermining of virtuous behavior.

In the spirit of "anything goes," the new morality has welcomed increasing doses of nudity, sex, and very earthy language in books, on film, tape, DVD, and especially on the Internet. Not even the sweetest and most proper of our old ladies bats an eye upon hearing that 500-year-old Anglo-Saxon word "fuck" tossed about. It is worked into almost every R-rated movie loudly and repeatedly. It too has been democratized. There are no more disrespectful expletives to lash out with to express frustration, anger, or disdain, with everyday discourse laced with "friggin" this or "freakin" that. "Awesome" and "cool" have been abandoned to grades one through four. Clearly we need a new bad word or two that some people are reluctant to use in public.

Both business and government leadership appear to be leading the way when it comes to financial irresponsibility. The captains of industry have installed sweetheart, interlocking boards of directors who approve truly huge salaries and lucrative incentive packages. Some even turn the other way when the CEO dips into the corporate treasury, even as a business might be suffering from fatal mismanagement practices. John Reh cited a Business Week article on the average CEO pay for America's major corporations. Salaries soared from 42 times the average worker's pay in 1980, to 85 in 1990, and on to 531 in 2000. Top executives are rewarded as owners, although they risk no capital, while the owners (you and I) stand by, uninformed and mute. Greed waxes when morality wanes.

Politicians elbow their way in front of the TV camera to announce new Medicare prescription drug benefits, much to the delight of the pharmaceutical firms that sell these drugs to you and me at twice the world price. While we are at it let's send a man to Mars, since we have already delivered on our promise to give you the moon. It won't cost much to get started and, like Scarlet, we can worry about the bills tomorrow.

These are just more "benefits" that your children and mine will have to pay for. President Clinton was noted for presenting a a host of smallish give-away programs in his annual State of the Union messages, but he was a comparative piker. In reality, politicians have nothing to give away since our national vault safeguards nothing but copies of IOUs. Over $7 trillion dollars worth. And our congressmen have signed them all with our names. The Republicans have now become the party of tax cuts *and* big spending.

Actual reality becomes always harder to distinguish as virtual reality invades our world. The mind of modern America is being shaped by Cyberspace, icons, websites, viruses, iPods, blogs, and all manner of symbols to save time and experience the world, all in the isolation of our own quiet corner. Our devotion to electronic gadgets, as an end unto themselves, results in students downloading a paper, on some school topic, off the Internet, and turning it in as a proxy for actually learning about the subject matter. "Executive Syndrome" is the term now applied to kids too busy or too uninspired to do the work of learning without a personal coach. There was a time when kids who didn't learn were called dumb, lazy, or just plain uninterested.

We might be living in the "Gen L" (Generation Lite) age or the "Cliff Notes Generation" where commitment to principle is a mile wide and an inch deep. David Brooks described us as *Bobos in Paradise* who want to identify with the idea of a thing but not be fully committed to its essence. A fashionable brand name that supersedes the actual value of the item. Instant gratification. Recognition without accomplishment. Maureen Dowd referred to the increasing tendency to put "...publicity over achievement, revelation over restraint, honesty over decency, victimhood over personal responsibility, confrontation over civility, psychology over morality." It would seem we are missing a good cause which might engage our passion, something other than personal gratification to which we might apply our energy and talents.

To be concerned about our personal well being is a necessary consequence of our built in survival imperative. There is a part of the brain called the limbic system. It is located at the base of the brain in the amygdala and is common to all mammals. This primitive part of the brain is the seat of smell, emotion, aggression, affection, motivation, and behavior. We *feel* as well as reason and calculate. Since our well being depends upon other people in our extended family, we come to value and trust others to the degree to which they are in close proximity, physically and psychologically. The higher animals exhibit this social attribute in the same way that men do toward family and friends.

To a somewhat lesser extent we may project these feelings of trust and even empathy beyond the boundary defined by our personal acquaintances. It may extend to others like us, persons of whom we have no firsthand knowledge. This feeling of empathy is an attribute fully developed only in man. It is characterized by the presence of a well-developed, prefrontal, cerebral cortex, capable of complex thought based on the abstract knowledge of others we have never had the pleasure of meeting face to face. Such knowledge may evoke the emotional response of compassion, perhaps our principal hope for avoiding continuing mortal conflict in a competitive and ever more crowded world. Fear of the unknown other or just disdain for others' freedom, opportunity, and dignity is at the root of much conflict and war.

It seems likely that we shall have organized armed conflict in this world until such time as we subscribe to the compassionate belief that each man has value in his own right, and not only for his contribution to our own well being. Since this high level emotion is easy enough to dismiss when it clashes with our drive for personal gain or survival, its group presence can be a measure of the degree to which any culture may be regarded as civilized. It would appear that global civilization rests on both morality and technology, with morality being the essential component.

The idea of morality takes hold when our emotional responses are tempered by the compassion evoked by our cerebral cortex. It is further influenced by the feedback our actions produce and the tutorial inputs received from authority figures. Without this gold standard against which we can measure our actions we are left to the indistinct ambiguities of situation ethics as we may choose to invoke and apply them. But without a power or spirit larger than our own life, there would be little wonder, promise of happiness, or joy of accomplishment.

Freedom allows you to do what you want but morality reminds you what the group believes you ought to do. The concepts of right and wrong, good and bad, are defined by morality and often associated with some external source or being. Can you perceive being moved to any action at all outside of the realm of survival, personal comfort, and self-gratification if there were no one else to share, recognize, applaud, or maybe even criticize your efforts? The need for recognition is a major motivation for terrorist activity, most often perpetrated by groups otherwise consigned to irrelevance. Put 'em on TV and they'll do it again.

Evidence of decay

Robert Putnam has conducted an extensive research survey dedicated to establishing the degree to which community social practices have changed in America and when these changes took place. He wanted to discover the relation between "social capital," the degree to which individuals are interconnected through civic organizations such as church, volunteer activities, parent-teacher associations, recreation, business, politics, and the many aspects of society representing our overall well being. He found that TV viewing time, violent crime, pugnacity, poor health, social isolation, death rate, tax evasion, income inequality, and minimum religious involvement, were all definitely correlated to a low level of social capital, that is, community involvement.

These social conditions were shown to have a high degree of correlation within each state. On the other hand, personal happiness was shown to be highly dependent on social capital up to about the level of 15 or 20 civic interactions each year. Moreover it was clearly the 1960s during which many elements of positive social action peaked and started to drop off–philanthropy, PTA membership, and participation in political campaigns. This was the decade in which the suburban population surpassed the rural population, state initiatives became popular, and the increase in the number of security personnel, as well as lawyers and judges, accelerated.

All decades in American history are marked by important events and changes, but the 1960s stand out for abrupt reversals in social practices and civic participation. The '60s started out with John F. Kennedy's exhortation to "...ask what you can do for your country" and ended with us asking what our country could do for us. It witnessed a sitting, first term president declining to run for a second term because he had lost the confidence of the American people and his leadership capital following his installation of The Great Society and prosecution of an unpopular, ill-fated war in Vietnam. Eleven days after Lyndon Baines Johnson took office, our military advisors in Vietnam were told to lock and load their M-16s and join the fight against Communism (C. Bloom, pers. comm.).

In 1963 Betty Friedan published her book, *The Feminine Mystique,* exhorting women to put on their shoes, leave the kitchen, and take the wonderful new pill discovered by Dr. Pincus. Soon women were burning their bras in the same fires that American boys had lit to burn their draft cards.

I remember the evening in 1970 that Lorrie and I went to the movies and saw Mash and Catch 22. When we came out, I knew our world had changed, and that I no longer understood it. I was a slow learner. The ghosts of Marilyn Monroe and John Wayne did not show up at in Haight-Asbury or at Woodstock They had been replaced by Joni Mitchell and Jimi Hendricks. Youth were not becoming interested in civic participation. They were interested in changing the world with public love and protest. They mistook being unbuttoned for being emancipated.

Putnam concluded that the loss in social capital and cultural happiness commencing in the '60s was due primarily to generational causes with a strong influence from television. The baby boomers brought different values to American culture. But he did not speculate as to why these sweeping social changes had taken place. Mark Kurlansky did, however. After 35 years of brooding over the meaning of the social upheavals of the 1960s, he outlined his conclusions in his book, *1968*. The cause was the starkly different world experienced by pre-World War II and post-World War II babies.

Kids in the 1950s were taught to "duck and cover" in case of nuclear attack. They were electronic witnesses to the marches, sit-ins, and riots leading up to civil rights legislation. They were treated to repeated scenes of emaciated corpses being unceremoniously dumped into mass graves at Auschwitz. Going into the 1960s they had a front row seat to a failed Bay of Pigs invasion, the terrifying Cuban Missile Crises, and a war in far off Vietnam, which they could not rationalize and which was never satisfactorily justified by Johnson or Nixon. In the meantime, John F. Kennedy and his killer, Lee Harvey Oswald, were shot dead on TV.

By the fateful year 1968, we saw the first pictures broadcast from the far side of the moon and a daily, graphic account of war in glorious color live on TV, thanks to the advent of geosynchronous satellites in stationary orbit in space some 22,000 miles overhead. Youth took note of hypocrisy and a deteriorating environment, and the ghettos in major American cities erupted. Black Power emerged and the 1968 Democratic Convention featured televised police brutality outside on the streets of Chicago. For a moment in time government had lost control and LBJ his political credibility as the result of the sharp differences of opinion in society and government over the war in Vietnam. As that war was still heating up in 1965, Secretary of Defense Robert McNamara, the Whiz Kid from Ford, designed the bombing raids that eventually caused several hundred thousand civilian deaths north of Saigon (Hedges). We may infer from this deed that technical brilliance is no substitute for social wisdom.

This generation was not interested in any process of implementing cultural change through peaceful negotiation. It took to the streets with sit-ins, protests, peace rallies, and public displays of affection and celebration; an unplanned outpouring of civic upheaval, leaving government and astonished old timers incredulous and even worried as social order threatened to implode in 1968, the year of two more assassinations–those of Robert Kennedy and Martin Luther King, Jr.

The fallout from the upheavals of the 1960s and the increasing emphasis on the quest for wealth became evident in the following decade. Until the early 1970s the Index of Social Health in the United States that measures such items as child poverty, health care coverage, and youth homicide, was improving roughly apace with the GDP. Then these indices diverged, the GDP doubling by 1996 while the Social Health Index fell off approximately 60 percent (Phillips). Clearly America had been undergoing a precipitous decay in its social infrastructure during the last quarter of the 20th century.

The decade in which our Index of Happiness plateaued saw the American Dream yield to dreams of entitlement as an accessory to the growing, middle class, money culture. A flight to the suburbs after World War II was fueled by Federal Housing Authority and GI home loans featuring easy credit, as well as cars and appliances bought and eventually paid for on the installment plan. Buy now and pay later. Plastic money was born and for the first time in history the nation's money supply and potential for inflation were partially entrusted to the public whim by the Federal Reserve Board. Eventually, instant credit inflated the money supply by over a trillion dollars.

This new prosperity marked the death of the Protestant Ethic (Bell), the coming of age of the money culture, and the idea that if you had a job, you could spend ahead and have it all now. By the 1960s the idea of "what's in it for me" was superseding "work and succeed" in our moral code.

Here it must be noted that the seeds of the money culture were planted in the 1890s and cultivated until the Great Depression starting in 1929. During this period a middle class was developing, and the idea of consumer capitalism was starting to challenge the church as the arbiter of value in society (Leach).

The American middle class was breaking away from the ancient "household" practice of domestic provisioning, wherein people for the most part worked to satisfy their everyday needs, if they could, then practiced life arts when they had time left over. In an agrarian economy any excess produce had been difficult to store and besides there wasn't a lot of "stuff" available to buy.

The excess wealth created in a prosperous, cash-money economy could be saved easily, however, and when augmented with easy credit, could be used to buy goods that were *wanted*, not just *needed*. This new opportunity gave rise to a new rationale for purchasing and changing acquisition patterns, as people now aspired to accumulate as much stuff as might appeal to their sense of vanity and desire for comfort, amusement, status, or conspicuous display. The effect was analogous to an experiment once performed with bananas and gorillas. As long as bananas were hard to find, they were eaten and shared as an occasional treat. But when the apes were turned loose on a large pile of bananas laid out for them, they went "bananas" so to speak, the most aggressive rushing in to steal as many as they could and fighting to make off with as many as they were able to carry.

The money culture flowered because basic needs had at last been satisfied for the common man. "'Consumer' is the modern label for the American individual in economic clothing" (Robertson). The consumer lifestyle values things more than relationships (Novak). But as Harountunian wrote, "The good is not in the goods. The good is in justice, mercy, and peace...it inheres in men and not in things."

Having attained unprecedented wealth as well as many new legal entitlements and protections, we are not now measurably happier than we were in 1960. The increase in standard of living we have experienced appears not to have made life that much more enjoyable. It is true that increasing happiness can accompany increasing incomes, but only to a point. During the 1990s, the Dutch sociologist Ruut

Veenhoven conducted a 54-country survey around the world on the dependence of happiness on income level. After reaching a per person income level of about $20,000, he found that additional income apparently brought little or no more enjoyment to life, signaling the onset of diminishing returns (Peck and Douthat).

At the time of Veenhoven's survey, our American income level was running close to $28,000 per person per annum. After a certain level the dependence of happiness on increasing wealth just disappears (Lane). In 1996 Richard Esterlin found that, "there has been no improvement [in happiness] in the United States over half a century–a period in which real GDP per capita more than doubled."

In retrospect it is clear that several important social attitudes and practices have changed radically since the 1960s. We have lost much of our social capital, our spirit of connectedness, by drawing away from community activities. We have become tolerant of, if not dedicated to, group entitlement claims for fairness, recognition, and sometimes just special privileges, using victimhood as a rationale. We have become addicted to consumption in a quest to satisfy a never ending list of wants, lured on by the Pied Pipers of Madison Avenue. These are all inward looking prescriptions. And you may have noticed: the incidence of diabetes is increasing steadily along with our average weight. So what?

Consider this. In the 1950s, boys were almost never asked to run more than a quarter of a mile in high school gym class. Girls were not physically active, only the Tom Boys. Yet obesity was not endemic. Today high school kids are sometimes challenged to run a mile or two in gym class. Since the advent of Title IX in 1972, girls have become competitors in almost all sports. Some schools even have a girl's, fourth grade, traveling basketball team. In spite of the brisk business in personal fitness equipment, we are heavier than ever before. Why is that?

When heart attacks were linked to cholesterol and saturated fats were prevalent in our diets, dietary experts started pushing carbohydrates, but people just got fatter (except for those on the protein-laden, carb-free Atkins diet). Meanwhile the best selling books in the bookstore are cook books and diet and fitness books. Why are we exercising more, eating less fat, and gaining more weight?

Have you ever noticed that if you stay home from work when you are just moderately ill, you feel worse than when you actually go to work? When you are alone and without external stimulation, your attention focuses on your favorite subject–you. Then you notice every physiological nuance signaled by your body. The great pacifier of these pangs, of course, is food. Food is also the great pacifier of mild anguish brought on by loneliness and fear; perhaps the gnawing fear that you are not fully making your mark in a society that is progressing faster than you are. Have another sandwich.

Is obesity just another symptom of withdrawal from group activities with a larger-than-self purpose? If so, how will we deal with the psychological effects of aloneness and extreme self-preoccupation when the new diet pills that kill appetite dead come on the market? You might draw the conclusion that obesity is just one more symptom of a society that has lost its group purpose and turned inward, just as Rome did when Stoicism died and Epicureanism became the fashion. Will war become the force that gives our lives meaning, as Chris Hedges suggested?

Economics is the science of production, distribution, and consumption of goods and services. Historically, it has been preoccupied with resolving the problem of scarcity. In the United States this problem was essentially solved by the mid 20th century, but we are still using the same economics today. We should be more than ready to pursue our happiness but we don't know where to look for it. Our new problem is coping with prosperity (D'Souza). Robert Theobald wrote in 1970 that the idea of scarcity was obsolete in the developed parts of the world and that we require a new socioeconomic science, based on the information age and a state of abundance. He felt even then that economic growth had become negatively correlated with societal and educational changes, and that we must not rely on government, but rather make our own socioeconomic decisions.

If happiness is facilitated by income level, at least to some point, what can we say about the relationship between income level and the degree of freedom in any given society? Mary O'Grady (Nov. 12, 2002) cited a survey ranking 156 nations according to an Index of Economic Freedom for 2003. As you might expect, it showed a definitive correlation between freedom and income; the 15 freest countries having per capita incomes almost 10 times the level of the 75 countries rated mostly unfree. But which was the cause and which the effect? Correlation does not prove causation.

All this is not to say most people are not honest and honorable, or that the country has not made some great social and technological strides since 1968.* Nor do I mean to pretend that there was not any skullduggery going on in business and government prior to World War I. Indeed such was the reason for adopting the Seventeenth Amendment, providing for the popular election of U.S. Senators in 1913. Nevertheless, I do mean to indicate that our social principles, our moral code, have been broadly tested and badly frayed even as our income level has grown steadily over time. Somewhere along the line a money culture invaded the pre-World War II emerging middle class and has infected the baby boomers too.

The arrival of the money culture, political correctness, and broad-based claims of entitlement have redefined the American agenda. For almost 200 years the liberal agenda had been for progress in the interest of all working Americans. By the end of the 1970s it had become anti-corporate, dedicated to near-equal outcomes, and adept at using social and government power to achieve the ends of minority interests.

Peterson (2004) spelled out the themes that accompany terminal social distress in a culture: growing institutional distress, mounting political dysfunction, weakening commitment to the future, strengthening cult of self, declining sense of social solidarity, grandiose ambitions alongside hopelessly polarized political factions, and vast future financial liabilities. The last two of these were cited by Edward Gibbon as factors leading to the fall of Rome. It cannot be denied that these elements, to a greater or lesser degree, increasingly describe American culture over the last 40 years.

---

* In fact, despite the litany of social degeneration presented in this work, there are definite indications that we may be headed for better times. The out-of-wedlock birth rate has been dropping. NGO membership is increasing, although participation may be limited to contributions and newsletters. The violent crime rate began dropping in the '90s, a phenomena attributed to the legalization of abortion in 1973, according to Levitt and Dubner. Moreover, there are early indications that the upcoming "Millennial" generation may exhibit a more positive, group-oriented, can-do ethos (Howe and Strauss).

Have the moral principles of pre-World War II America become just a set of hurdles to negotiate on the way to material success? Would greater attention to personal excellence, based on the ancient virtues, help restore America's basic freedoms? Or are we all just preoccupied with personal issues to the exclusion of the greater good?

Happiness

Perhaps as Kass (2003) put it in the most basic of terms, to be happy, all you need is someone to love, something to do, and a reason for both, greater than oneself.

I would venture that the requirement for happiness is some reasonable level of health and physical comfort, a sense of connectedness—to loved ones, extended family, community, and work. People are particularly pleased if they are appreciated for their good work, recognized by respected authority, and know they are part of an enterprise undertaken with the aim of doing good in the eyes of their fellow man. People want to know that their life has value and is significant. But all too often, many of us look at our balance sheet or paycheck and measure our value in dollars and cents. Counting your coin is a lonely process, one shared only with your accountant. You would secure greater happiness by doing a good deed unsolicited, taking the time to listen to someone's story, offering encouragement, celebrating accomplishment, and passing along something of social value to your own human creations.

In a clinical study, Michael Lerner and associates found that middle class people have been progressively withdrawing from social contacts beyond their own family and friends. They have been cowed by the extreme emphasis on meritocracy and the virtues of economic success. They hunger for a feeling of self-worth and dignity, the purpose and meaning of which may be found only in working for the community good, for some goal greater than one's own economic advancement. So they seek more money as confirmation that they have value in the eyes of society, but cannot capture the joy that comes only from serving some greater good.

Lerner quotes Rabbi Abraham Joshua Heschel as saying, "...life is not meaningful to us unless it is serving an end beyond itself, unless it is of value to someone else." If you want to cultivate happiness in the world, listen to, encourage, and recognize another human being, bearing in mind that you become what you do. So do something that gives you joy. As Joseph Campbell said, "Follow your Bliss."

While these changes have been playing out, we have been missing a truly historic opportunity to write another great American chapter in the history books. We have the wealth, the power, the talent, and the attention of nearly 200 nations focused on or at least cognizant of our attitudes and actions. We have the opportunity to influence billions of souls for good or for ill. If we think we subscribe to a better set of fundamental moral principles or have a superior operating system to that of most other countries, we should invite others to come and take a look for themselves, without proselytizing or propagandizing. They might have less sales resistance if we just stuck to the facts and showed them the goods, warts and all.

Likewise we should look a little more closely at the cultural imperatives and social systems of our global partners. Too often we have advanced our system of government on other parties without understanding the basis of their cultures. To forcibly impose our righteous vision of governance and social order on other nations might fail miserably as it has in Haiti and Vietnam. And it is certainly wrong by any reading of the moral code endorsed by our own Declaration of Independence, which was conceived in the interest of all men.

Unfortunately, the "striving and giving" aspects of our national myth, the American Dream, have yielded to an "expecting and taking" outlook now that our collective wealth exceeds the "happiness" zone. We can improve our sociopolitical system if we understand the significance of so doing, and go to work on our important problems under courageous leadership. The solution to our 40-year moral lapse lies in virtuous action and good works. The deed creates the pattern that begets the change in attitude, for better or for worse. That was the great teaching of Mother Teresa. It was the lesson to be learned from a nine year old girl in Bay Village, Ohio, when she made $900 for the relief of the tsunami victims in Asia–because an act of kindness and mercy made *her* feel good. The Golden Rule, reborn again and again in the bosom of men, is the sure basis for restoring exemplary moral standards when relations between persons or nations overlook the value of justice and equality.

Our ability to help others do what they can do and be what they can be starts with putting our own American house in order. This effort would not restore the American Dream, but it ought to burnish our moral values by infusing pride into some truly significant undertakings. In the same way that attitude adjustment can be effected by consciously doing good works, our morality will improve if we undertake constructive programs both large and small. You will know our American character has changed when you see it so portrayed in our culture: art, theatre, literature, law, and international policy.

The question is, What will our great grandchildren, not yet born, say of us as they review their heritage from the vantage point of the 22nd century? We are in a unique position to extend the blessings of our founding myth to other lands less fortunate. We would do well to share these blessings. We would do well to aspire to making the world a little better than it really is. It would not be a sign of weakness, but rather signify a strengthening of the American character, knowledge of which is revealed in our behavior. It would cost little and yield much. And it would accrue to our own happiness at the same time.

If happiness evades our search, it may be that it is not hiding somewhere among material things, or even to be found permanently in external pleasures, but rather that it accrues from doing. As Abe Lincoln once said, "Most people are about as happy as they want to be." It is through the exercise of our moral virtues and not through the acquisition of goods that we will make social progress and realize our happiness.

With freedom and virtue as our escorts into the future, where might this quest take us?

The 12th: North Carolina. November 21, 1789

CHAPTER 13

ASPIRATION, PURPOSE AND DESTINY

The Case For Action

The call for freedom voiced in 1776 was echoed by three British writers: in "Common Sense," by Thomas Paine; in *The Wealth of Nations,* by Adam Smith; in *The Rise and Fall of the Roman Empire,* by Edward Gibbon; and proclaimed for the first time in history in the Declaration of Independence. This last document ushered in the modern era of individual freedom, a Utopia-made-real by any standard of 18th century reality.

This freedom was put to work, exploiting the opportunities presented by the Industrial Revolution within the framework of free market economics. The result was analogous to watering good earth prepared with fertilizer and sown with good seed, that is, releasing the latent potential for growth and prosperity in America. This unparalleled economic achievement was so potent that in time the institutions put in place to support this economic progress became obsolescent and ripe for renovation. We have progressed beyond the point at which tinkering at the margins to shore up our current social structures can keep us humming along at a sustainable rate very far into the future. These systems were launched, developed, and matured while a number of significant social changes were taking place during the past century:

- Business, the engine of our prosperity, became so rich and powerful that the public had to be protected from its abuses.
- Success through virtue and personal effort gave way to success through knowledge of others.
- The imposition of a tax on income invited greatly increased spending and facilitated massive borrowing by government.
- Medical services evolved from their primitive beginning to the largest single commercial sector in the nation.
- As life expectancy increased from 47 to 77 years between 1900 and 2000, the population began to outlive its productive years and require supplemental resources to live with dignity.
- The basic economic problem of resource scarcity was solved.
- Formal education and training became essential stepping stones to personal success.
- Youth repudiated the drive for prosperity at the expense of the environment.
- The voting public became very effective in influencing elected officials to support its specialized social programs.
- Communication became unrestricted and instantaneous.
- The cost of political campaign financing ballooned.

Dynamic social change has rendered certain programs and institutions obsolescent in numerous important particulars. The shortcomings of health care, education, Social Security, the income tax code, and campaign financing have been discussed in some detail. Basic governance reform is necessary to protect our freedoms and nourish our prosperity. We must remodel a big brother government that increasingly micromanages the details of our lives and has become addicted to borrowing from the future. We must school ourselves, a public that is only faintly cognizant of the magnitude of the issues we face over the coming 50 years. Joseph Schumpeter pointed out we are becoming increasingly socialistic as the growth stimulation provided by entrepreneurs is overwhelmed by bureaucracy and government regulation. The growing backlash to this tendency is the increasing interest in fundamentalism and nationalism as reflected in our current foreign policy (Lukacs).

The principal threat to our individual freedom is the same one that operates, openly or clandestinely, in virtually every organized social system—the symbiotic relationship enjoyed by power and money. It is a relationship facilitated by public inertia and complacency. Public financing of election campaigns would help shift the attention of politicians away from corporate and other special interests to public interests. This one reform is probably the single most important structural change we might make in our national interest.

Although these changes are economically doable and would be immensely advantageous, they risk being labeled as utopian since the threat to those in possession of power and wealth is so obvious.

One purpose served by conjuring up utopias is to see how different reality is from what it might be in an ideal world. If our original utopian concept of America seems far different from our reality today, it is only an indication of how far we have strayed from our founding intentions. Is it possible that under the right circumstances, these original utopian ideals, updated and modernized, might be fully realized anew? The only fundamental question is whether these ideas are consistent with human nature in the context of our modern, technological society. We cannot change human nature (yet), but social change is always taking place. As Albert Einstein once said, "The problems that we have today were created at a particular level of thinking. We can not solve these problems at the same level of thinking." To this end, this work offers some new thinking. The old thinking will not protect us from straying off our original path of freedom. As we increase our means we seem to be losing sight of our better purposes.

Reluctance to address our problems soon, in a fundamental way, may result in loss of ability to do so later on. Some of America's leading economists believe we are headed for a financial meltdown sometime within the next decade unless significant reforms, not merely band aid patches, are put in place before then. Excessive deficit spending by government is a relatively new phenomenon. Except for war and depression years, Washington ran only 44 deficits, averaging 0.5 percent of our GDP each, over our first 171 years. Since 1960, we have run up deficits in 37 of the last 42 years, each averaging 2.5 percent of our GDP (Peterson 2004). Today's deficits are running about 4 percent of GDP, adding yearly to our $7.4 trillion national debt. America's founders were well aware that chronic deficits spell corrupt leadership, political decadence, and economic ruin.

The basic underlying problem worldwide among the industrialized countries is the burgeoning population of seniors relying upon the residual, productive public for care. In America, our $37.2 trillion unfunded medical and social security programs, our demand for more entitlements, our consumer mentality, our "guns, butter, *and* tax cuts" economics, and our neglect to educate our inner city youth, are factors converging on a meltdown event.

We know the tip off for pending disaster—a falling dollar, rising gold prices, weak treasury bond prices, and a cynical public, that all signal social distress. As has been shown, even our social capital has declined seriously over the past 40 years, along with our respect for government. At this late date, Social Security is the only significant issue on the political agenda.

It is imperative to understand that the path to adversity, if not ruin, is the same path traveled by many others before us: large budget and balance of trade deficits, an ever expanding national debt, dependency on foreign loans, a depreciating dollar, increasing subsidies to business, and ever more commitments to social programs, for which the only resolution is ever greater taxation. We have exceeded the level at which our immense ability to generate wealth can easily cover our spending habits and current financial obligations. Loss of financial control was a major factor in the downfall of Greece, Rome, Britain, the USSR, and numerous other smaller countries, such as Argentina. America has weathered two major crises in the 20th century and, out of ignorance and apathy, may be staring at its next crisis.

The mission to make this a better country and share our improved paradigm with our planetary neighbors is not only humane. This aspiration is a practical necessity in a shrinking world. Certainly we have no way of answering the metaphysical question of what might be our true purpose or why we are here in the first place, but we can point to several important ideas that hold the promise of enhancing the quality of life for everyman who is or will be here some day. Certainly, a worthy national purpose would be to advance the cause of freedom in the interest of prosperity, opportunity, and dignity, wherever in the world it might be welcome. We could realize true happiness and maybe even joy in the process.

Rationale For Progress

The primary intent and the anticipated result of considering proposals such as those outlined in this book, is that of accelerating our progress based on freedom's vector. The rationale for and the value of cranking up our rate of progress can be appreciated by citing a few beneficial or adverse outcomes:

1) Most of the changes proposed are designed to increase the efficacy of our collective efforts. The increased efficiency realizable from the overhaul of our systems of taxation, health care, Social Security, and campaign financing can be reckoned in the hundreds of billions of dollars annually.

2) Any dollars available in excess of the working needs of the nation can be put to the task of reducing the national debt and/or paying down our unfunded social commitments, thereby strengthening the nation's weak balance sheet.

3) There is a distinct tendency for the richest and most advanced nations to undergo a productivity lag (Boulding). Without a serious effort to enhance our productive efficiency we must prepare psychologically for a future with little or no prospect for growth. The ultimate price for maintaining the political status quo is socialism: equality of outcome at the expense of freedom and prosperity. We may face these dismal prospects unless we experience a financial meltdown first.

4) If we do not grow, we will stagnate. Stagnation does not mean maintaining the status quo indefinitely. Times and things change. People can lose the notion of progress and

improvement, as they did for 1,000 years in Europe. You thrive or you wither over time.

5) We are bound to make room for an additional 100 million souls in America alone by 2050, and 2.6 billion worldwide. Without sufficient growth our children will have to share our material prosperity with these newcomers as we encounter increasing difficulties in dealing with even our known problems.

6) Globalization and advancing educational attainment around the world increasingly are causing the loss of mid-level jobs in high wage countries, paving the way for even greater income differentials and social unrest. As an example, last year IBM proposed hiring computer programmers overseas for $12.50 an hour to do work that would cost $56 an hour domestically.

7) As the great majority of the world's people come to put technology to work in their quest for a better standard of living, the demand for energy will mushroom, intensifying competition and pollution. China's petroleum imports increased by 61 percent in 2004 alone, pushing up gas prices accordingly. This process, as well as the need for increasing crop yields, will make it essential that we develop a primary new energy source such as wind power to produce hydrogen to take the place of oil.

Any of the above prospects would be reason enough to pursue the beneficial proposals developed in this story. Over 3 billion souls will increasingly depend on the advanced, affluent nations to lead the way into a better future, lest they continue to live in poverty under tyranny. Should we realize any significant progress in maximizing individual freedom, opportunity, and dignity in America, we will be in a better position to extend these benefits to the least of us. Or the least of us will show their disappointment and resentment much to our regret. We now see resentment expressing itself as worldwide terrorism.

The most important international issue we have to contend with is energy. It threatens to escalate already serious international tensions to the point of overt hostility between an economically backward

Islam and a capitalist America. If not resolved, China and perhaps the EU will surely get into the act within a decade or two. The most important domestic problem facing America is the financial interdependence of politics and business. The most important long term threat to our political system and all of us is our huge national debt and the massive financial obligation looming just to cover our health care and Social Security commitments.

The unfunded $11.7 trillion liability attached to Social Security is the most recognized problem because its consequences can be expressed in terms of dollar-denominated premiums and benefits. However, the $25.5 trillion unfunded health care liability is by far the greatest financial problem emerging. If these important issues are allowed to fester by just ignoring them, these off-the-books commitments will destroy any residual trust between this nation and its citizens, producing social pain in a manner analogous to the disaster that overtook Enron, for the same reason, in the private sector.

The progressive assumption of more and more social and financial responsibilities by government over time has only promoted greater dissatisfaction with its meddling on one hand, and a demand for even more social programs on the other. Fifty years ago you might have heard someone say, "There outta be a law!" Today the cry is, "There outta be another government social program." Government micromanagement of the economy is bleeding off the head of economic steam we had worked up prior to the social deterioration experienced starting in the late 1960s. As Benjamin Friedman has written, "Economic growth is not merely the enabler of consumption: it is in many ways the wellspring from which democracy and civil society flow."

Failure of government to meet its financial promises can lead to a loss of confidence as the first step on the road to political turmoil. Charles Murray (1997) cited the findings of an annual survey taken by the American Enterprise Institute that posed the question, "How much do you think you can trust the government in Washington to do what is right?" The responses of "just about always" or "most of the time" scored over 70 percent in 1958, but had plummeted to 20 percent by 1997. Following the tragedy of 9/11, the President's rating soared, but at this writing has now sunk to a level consistent with his current difficulties in office.

Our American culture needs to find renewed purpose and a finer set of values with which we can lead the way to a world made safe for life, liberty and the pursuit of happiness. Fallows believes that, "The only chance for a new beginning is to make people believe there actually is a chance." Over the last four decades, a psychological divide has opened in this nation, separating the expectations of the public and the perceived practices of government. Too many Americans have the sense that our public officials are pursuing some agenda they can neither understand nor support. One consequence is the pronounced tendency of various public factions to lobby for exclusive protections and relative advantages on a group by group basis. As politics and the press become more polarized, the public interest becomes more fragmented (Baker). The grand mission to spread democracy and freedom to the ends of the earth has a noble appeal, but a scope too large to embrace, particularly in the absence of any discernable strategy for execution, short of war.

At this writing, I have just returned from a week's sojourn at Chautauqua, New York, where I was treated to a dozen lectures on different aspects of Land and Justice. The common idea, embedded in so very many questions from the thousands who thronged to these lectures, was not so much confined to the issues of land or justice, per se, but rather was centered on leadership. These questions seemed to be motivated by some deep yearning for a champion who might step forward and take up the cause of the common man against the interests of money and power–a leader who might unite people in some crusade of high merit through which we might all redeem our virtuous American character. This unarticulated undercurrent was almost Messianic it its feeling.

The reason that faith, trust, and confidence in government are important is that people will not follow leadership down a challenging pathway without them. A purpose, however laudable, cannot be achieved without the public dedication that arises from belief in both the mission and its leadership. The founders of our great nation gave us the charter by which we could undertake enterprises of great purpose. It was a charter to which they pledged their Lives, their Fortunes and their sacred Honor. A nation must have some purpose that transcends the private concerns of its individual citizens if it is to realize social progress, and especially if it is to fulfill the role of world leader.

Under tyranny, governments and the governed work at cross purposes and do not make much progress. Mao Tse-tung remained in power for over 25 years by repeatedly turning his people against each other, causing mass starvation and despair in the hearts of almost a billion Chinese people (Chang). Any government policy that causes sharp polarization or aggravated dissention in a society has the effect of suspending economic progress and sapping the moral strength of a society. People can no longer depend on realizing the implied promise of the Golden Rule and just stop working together for any common purpose. A disconnect between our people and our government delays and disrupts the task of finding the capstone for the unfinished pyramid on the back of our dollar bill, and Ronald Regan's "Shining City on the Hill."

It is not to achieve the perfection of a Utopia, but to realize the intention of our founders that we seek to restore our uniquely American freedoms and offer them to our fellow men and women—when they are ready to embrace them. As the founders did for us, we should do for our neighbors and must do for our progeny. In visualizing America's course over this century, it is difficult to see much farther over the horizon.

Better Life: Help Has Arrived

So far in our portrayal of America, we have offered answers to two of Immanuel Kant's three questions we set out to examine in this work. We have examined what we know about our democracy in the context of historical political practices and systems. This exercise was a simple matter of sifting out the pertinent historical facts and using them as a basis for assessing the strengths and weaknesses of our 21st century democratic system. We have also offered suggestions for what we might do with our freedom. This exercise required selecting key American institutions and applying a little imagination to invent better ways to organize and use them. This process required some elementary financial analysis to redesign and reassemble the pieces in such a way that they fit together in a coherent, economically feasible framework. Now we must proceed to address the last question, What can America aspire to?

This is an open-ended question with no obvious right answer; one only a visionary could begin to do justice to. But with no certified visionary immediately available for consultation, we will just have to do our best without one. The visionaries currently in control of America's aspirations are the neoconservatives. Their mission is the projection of American power in the Middle East. The American public is seriously divided in its support for this mission, whose first great adventure in Iraq is becoming very costly and whose goals are still very much in doubt after more than two years. It would be only rational to conclude that the neocons are getting the benefit of the doubt at this time simply because our sons (and daughters) are still in peril in the land of Islam. Can we amateurs do any worse in creating a plan worthy of the American imprimatur? Without pretending to offer any complete prescription for furthering America's greatness, we can develop a model program consistent with an America committed to freedom, opportunity, and dignity for all men.

Let's lay out some ground rules as guidelines to formulating a model program. We would want our grand aspiration to encompass some undertaking which would further America's greatness as judged by our descendants and others over time. We would want this to be a national project of enduring value domestically and/or internationally. It would be only prudent to formulate a plan that calls upon our strongest resources. It would be necessary that this venture be one that the American people would endorse wholeheartedly, based on their perception of value and perhaps because it might capture the spirit of compassion. And following the psychology of the PTO cookie bake sale, if many people were "hands-on" involved in some way, it would help to elicit a broad base of support.

Some preliminary suggestions have already been mentioned, for instance, four major areas of international concern in chapter 10, where America could or should develop a leadership strategy. A foreign student exchange study program with the mission of introducing or putting on display our version of democracy and freedom to those who live under less successful systems, was another suggestion. But these programs fall far short of tapping the dynamic energy of our society or the reservoir of good will residing in most

American hearts. So, based on our guidelines, what grand mission might some inspired visionary leadership put forth that we might lend our willing and enthusiastic support for?

Since Americans have become somewhat disenchanted with their government over the last four decades, you might be inclined to doubt that government would find a willing reception if it asked for any personal sacrifice (short of war), as JFK famously did almost 45 years ago. If so, consider that over the past 40 years, government has asked only two things of us. It has asked for our sons to fight in one disastrous war and another whose justification is in serious doubt. And even without asking, it has incurred a huge national debt and made outsize promises for services it can not deliver without requiring our children to live under socialism. On the other hand, for 25 years, until the mid '60s, American government was broadly supported in spite of the fact that many buckets of American blood were spilled by 14 million of its youth under arms in a war that never directly threatened our shores. Americans took such great pride in having sacrificed to meet and defeat the enemies of freedom, even the one in Europe that did not directly threaten us, that they spent another $13 billion to help pick up the pieces.

When the issue is noble enough, the spirit of Americans will rise to the occasion and they will make the necessary sacrifice, even as our forefathers did when they left their farms to fight the British during the revolutionary war. In fact, like the little girl in Bay Village with her $900 gift, it is just such an effort made to help our fellow man in distress, that calls forth our better virtues, makes us feel good about ourselves, and proud of our accomplishments—generating the feeling that our life had some laudable purpose. We just have to tap this social wellspring before the selfishness born of long term "me-ism" infects and sours our attitude. The American people are ripe for a crusade dedicated to acting on our better virtues. Our esteem for our federal government will rise when our potential for doing good deeds is called into service.

The two major resources we have in our arsenal are money and our idealistic youth, not yet committed to families or a career path. Better to capture their services in some noble mission then in camouflage fatigues with an M16 by their side. The working models we have for doing good deeds are the Peace Corp, Americorps, and the many hundreds of local charitable organizations that are at work every day in every city and town across the country. These are established volunteer activities that can be assisted and strengthened for the pursuit of some great common purpose. That common purpose could be a grass roots attack on poverty.

We have already considered the practical, psychological, and moral reasons for mounting a program to reduce poverty. Now we will attempt to structure a program to carry out such a mission proactively, without just throwing money at it. The idea would be to invest money in our youth, instead, who could transform it into a hands-on resource tailored to fulfilling real, everyday needs at the working level.

Since the long term solution to reducing poverty depends on steady employment at a fair wage, the mission to be accomplished would be to have virtually all children now growing up in poverty equipped to hold down a job or enter an occupation and be able to bring their talent, knowledge, and intellectual, as well as physical, abilities to bear on the position. The strategy to do this would be fourfold. First, assume the responsibility of expanding the current network of workshops aimed at teaching adults now to secure *and* hold a job. This activity would have to be staffed mainly by professionals paid out of program funds. Second, provide whatever hands-on, backup support might be necessary to help adults maintain some gainful employment. Third, help families to prepare preschool youngsters for a successful learning experience in school. Lastly, play the role of coach to teach and encourage school-age children to learn and succeed. Clearly this would be a generational program with the payoff at least 15 years down the road. Let's consider just how a program like this might be structured and executed.

Each year we have about 6 million young folks leaving high school or college to seek their place in the working world. Since these are the people most personally impacted by the ideals of equity, justice, fairness, and patriotism, these are the most likely and available candidates to participate in programs that might capture their imagination. They have proved this by volunteering to fight in two world wars and by signing up for service activities like the Peace Corp and Americorps. In fact, 25 to 30 percent of our young folks between 17 and 25 average 180 hours, or 10 percent of their time, in some form of volunteer activity (independentsector.org). Let us further assume that a mission lofty enough to capture the nation's imagination could induce 5 percent of these "availables" to volunteer their services for one year. How might they be put to work and financed?

The first key to success for such a program would be to get the public behind it. The proof of their approval would be their acceptance of a surcharge to their gross income to fund operations. If you could sell this, you would also have the psychological support required to spotlight and sustain the program and draw recruits. A 0.2 percent tax surcharge to income would produce $13 billion, or enough to provide $43,000 in funding for each of the anticipated 300,000 volunteers. This is the amount currently required to send one Peace Corp volunteer abroad for one year. About 10 percent of the more mature volunteers, or some 30,000, might serve in the Peace Corp, expanding its ranks about threefold. The balance could serve in the larger domestic counterpart to the Peace Corp.

This extensive domestic program, with over a quarter-million volunteers, would subsume part of the Americorps program and its community service activities. But it would not assume the Americorps grant making program, which is embroiled in politics because of its role in doling out money. Instead, the domestic volunteers would be available to work in high poverty area school systems as teaching assistants, playground monitors, and supplementary tutors for kids in and out of school. They could do child minding, read to preschoolers, supervise outings to the zoo, and run after-school community activities. They could work directly with poor families under the supervision of social case workers, do home visitations, minor home repairs, and provide emergency transportation services.

They could work in any tax exempt charitable organization serving the needy, in homeless shelters, soup kitchens, or city missions. They could work under the direction of professionals or adult volunteers in any of the many community charitable activities serving the disadvantaged. They could work in pairs or under the close supervision of senior volunteers. Before they leave the program, they could train new recruits right on the job.

The personal contact emphasis of this program would put a lot of responsibility on the shoulders of largely inexperienced young people. It is just this responsibility in the context of a "pure" program, free from outside political and monetary influence, which would be necessary to sustain the spirit of the program over the long term.

Coordination of these activities would take a good deal of planning and supervision. Training, living arrangements, transportation planning, work assignments, progress monitoring, and results appraising, would require some relatively mature and experienced supervision. Supervisors could be chosen from adult volunteers, second year program volunteers, or hired professionals as necessary.

These full time volunteers would be reimbursed for their living expenses, which might average around $10,000 a year, and be covered for health insurance. Many could live at home or as guests in private homes for the cost of room and board. It would be necessary to find public accommodations for small groups of volunteers and rehab abandoned warehouse space for many more. A city the size of Cleveland (~480,000), would require accommodations for about 1,000 volunteers, many of whom would live at home. After successfully completing a year of service, the volunteers could receive a credit of up to $10,000 toward advanced education and a lifelong exemption from the 0.2 percent program tax. Second year volunteers for supervisory positions could receive $5,000 in compensation and a second $10,000 credit. The availability of recruits could be managed, in part, by adjusting education or student loan repayment credits.

We could call this half-million-strong volunteer program *Better Life* in recognition of the program mission to facilitate overcoming the physical and psychological bonds of poverty. We could put this logo on the shirts of all volunteers.

Numerous overlapping programs already in effect across the nation do not all serve the problem of poverty well because the voiceless poor get nudged out of the way by other community interests with financial motives and vocal champions. This is the case for Americorps, with its more than 50,000 volunteers serving over 2,000 community organizations, where money and dependent clients are at stake and volunteers are recruited and supervised according to local standards, if any. Avoiding all involvement with other non poverty interests, no matter how important they may be, would be the second key to effectively servicing the needs of the poor, who otherwise have no spokesman for their plight. To insure the Better Life program would not be diluted and politicized, there would be no work for government agencies (other than those oriented toward poverty issues), political campaigns, faith-based organizations, or profit oriented ventures.

Many programs zeroing in on poverty issues feature studies, analyses, money, slogans, walks, soup kitchens, shelters, wristbands, etc., but almost none put live people on the streets in the community, in the schools, and in the homes. A helping hand featuring one on one contact where and when help is needed can do more to solve the poverty problem than all the well-intentioned people sitting around a conference table, discussing the terms of welfare, can hope to accomplish. That's the third key to success.

Better Life would be a massive attack on poverty, untainted by either political or money interests, and conducted by troops with no agenda other than helping wherever needed. A full year's program could cost about the same amount as a one month stay in Iraq, where we are not welcome guests. Under the motto, Help Has Arrived, it could accomplish much where others have repeatedly failed, and capture the spirit of the original American Dream buried somewhere inside of each of us.

The ultimate goal of this massive program would be to provide support aimed ar helping to get the youngest kids growing up in poverty, school-ready, and then work with and encourage them to stay the course through high school, accumulating as much academic training and socialization as they are able to absorb along the way. The execution of this program will not meet industrial efficiency standards and it would be abused from time to time. There would be virtually no money passed out in the course of operations, eliminating one common source of abuse. The results would have to speak for themselves over the long term. Certainly it can be no less effective than some of the welfare programs pursued in the past.

Clearly, this singular example of one mission cannot pretend to constitute a comprehensive national policy for a nation with far-reaching interests, ambitions, and responsibilities. Nevertheless, with the exception of winning the Cold War and adopting Civil Rights legislation, programs that were mandatory responses to urgent needs, I do not recall any other national mission undertaken by our country that better meets the challenge of realizing some great goal and shines any brighter. Our path into the future will be better lit if it is illuminated by worthy accomplishment.

Freedom's Vector

The story of America has been told from its rude beginnings through today's triumphs and tribulations. In the process, we have identified those practices that serve the interests of power and money, and those institutions that are simply tired and outdated. We have suggested specific remedies for these ills based on the cardinal belief that freedom is man's best friend. The mechanism by which freedom generates prosperity was identified as the symbiotic action of responsible behavior under a constitutional or liberal democracy. The metaphor for this process is a vector–freedom's vector.

Vector is the Latin word for a "bearer." In medical parlance, a vector is a carrier. For instance, a mosquito is the vector that carries the infectious parasitic agent that causes malaria. By analogy, freedom is the parasite that is carried by our twin vector–democracy and responsibility. When the parasite, freedom, infects a new host, the inevitable result, or "disease," is prosperity. Personal freedom is the natural consequence of having a strong democracy fortified by a package of broad individual rights in the hands of responsible people who respect each other's rights. It is these preconditions that allow people to voluntarily serve each other's needs, setting in play the Invisible Hand which leads to prosperity.

Tyrannical governments are not prosperous because they are afraid to cede any control to the public, who possess the power to create prosperity. When people do not trust their government to protect their rights under a just set of laws, they no longer trust each other either. They then abandon the wisdom of the Golden Rule and look out only for themselves. Without trust, prosperity just withers.

Nevertheless, there are other vectors that are not broadly democratic in nature, but do allow for the development of prosperity based narrowly on economic freedom alone. However, it is too early to know if the result in this case will be prosperity as we in the West know it, or some other variant as may be the case in China.

Our Western version of freedom and prosperity makes it possible for the infected nation to realize greater opportunity and dignity for all of its citizens, even though these ends are not achieved automatically for everyone. Neither does prosperity automatically confer greater wisdom, intelligence, creativity, or imagination. We know this because so many intellectual and creative breakthroughs have come from people in nations much less prosperous or even largely unfree.

What prosperity does facilitate, or make possible, is the translation of new ideas into practice. The automobile industry, electric lighting, telecommunications, and aviation were developed most fully in America, not because they were uniquely conceived of here, but because of the availability of capital to bankroll their development, and the economic incentive of commercialization in a free enterprise marketplace. And because government did not stand in the way out of some fear of encroachment on its power. As the most prosperous nation on earth, we Americans are judged by how we put this prosperity to use. As this work attempts to show, we are somewhat careless in husbanding our prosperity and have not been able to fully honor the founder's promise of equal opportunity and dignity for all.

As Westerners, we view history in our mind's eye as a series of events taking place along a timeline running horizontally from left to right, the same way you are reading this sentence. All of history ends today, with the last great earthquake in Pakistan. Today is the first day of the rest of the world. The question of where America or mankind will be in 50 or 100 years will be defined by events yet to take place on the blank timeline that fades farther in the mist of uncertainty.

What we are doing today and what we will do tomorrow will set the stage for the nature of events yet to follow. While doing *makes* the future, it is imagination that *shapes* the future. As Napoleon Hill preached, "What ever the mind of man can conceive and believe, it can achieve." The act must be preceded by the thought, or it is just another accident littering the pathway.

The prosperity made possible by freedom's vector has allowed America to lead the world technologically, and accelerate the pace of change along history's timeline. This is why the responsibility of world leadership rests on our shoulders. Just as we followed the lead of Great Britain in setting an example for democratic governments catering to the interests of free men, it is our responsibility to continue in that leadership role, achieving positive events along our timeline into the future. It is our responsibility to find the way to bring equal opportunity and human dignity to all Americans and let the world see this Shinning City Upon a Hill.

Unless you are curious about the future, this would be a good place to end the story of freedom's vector. We know absolutely zero about the future, except for certain near term events, such as the high statistical probability that the sun will show its face again tomorrow. At present, the future is filled only with hope, speculation, dire predictions, and fantasy. If you are not willing to take this imaginative journey, please skip along to the Afterword. Otherwise, follow me.

And the Future?

The power only we humans have to imagine and shape the future inevitably leads to speculation about purpose and destiny. While we may play a role in formulating our own purposes, our destiny, by definition, is fixed. It is our fate.

The question of perceiving our destiny seems to be in the same category as peering out past a gazillion stars ever farther, even beyond the time range of the Hubble telescope, in a vain attempt to sense the very edge of the universe. Except if we look farther away in the distance we are actually looking back in time. We are told the distant edge is in fact the beginning of time. Perhaps there is no edge, or edge and time cease to have a meaning "out there." Are our astrophysicists and particle physicists just modern day alchemists working opposite ends of the space/time continuum, armed with sophisticated telescopes and particle accelerators?

Perhaps there is no destiny and no meaning to the question, Where are we going? As Yogi Berra once said, "It's tough to make predictions, especially about the future." On the other hand, whenever we mortals have wanted to predict the future, we find the most reliable method is to extrapolate from the past. Confucius said, "Study the past, if you would divine the future" 2500 years ago. With the serious limitations of this method in mind, we may then look back upon the past of mankind and ask, what activity have men attended to that is dedicated to something more than just cutting the lawn or getting ready for another day at the office? Surely any such pursuit must have yielded benefits of some lasting value. What is the one endeavor that has produced continuous evolution, where what is so one day is the basis for finding that which is even more universally true tomorrow?

When I do this exercise, I see the evolution and progression of knowledge. I can almost hear Sir Isaac Newton saying, "If I have seen farther than others, it is because I was standing on the shoulders of giants." I see men who have worked through the ages to find the way to do something better or faster or with ever greater fidelity. I see knowledge, once gained, passed from mind to mind, generation after generation. And I see its companion, know-how, passed from hand to hand, and then improved upon, through those generations. Clearly some men want to know, and just as clearly some men want to know how to do. The pursuit of knowledge appears to be a drive built into the human psyche. Perhaps it is coded for in our DNA. The art of translating knowledge into a tangible result, technology, creates the basic material infrastructure of civilization. The art of just governance creates the institutional infrastructure by which we may thrive. If there is a purpose in life comprehensible to man, it must be expressed in his writing, his government, and his handiwork.

The American storehouse of knowledge is the Library of Congress, the home of over 100 million documents. One repository is the Madison Building, which bears this inscription to the left side of one entrance: "Knowledge Will Forever Govern Ignorance; And A People Who Mean To Be Their Own Governours Must Arm Themselves With The Power Which Knowledge Gives." To the right side of this same entrance is inscribed: "What Spectacle Can Be More

Edifying Or More Seasonable, Than That Of Liberty & Learning, Each Leaning On The Other For Their Mutual & Surest Support?" (Cole). American freedom is the gift of the founders' experience, study, and learning. Madison's reminders speak to my daughter each day when she reports for work at this same citadel of stories, ideas, and knowledge.

Even if we were convinced that knowledge is our destiny and the pursuit of knowledge is therefore man's proper interest, we must be careful of our perception of the idea of knowledge; what it truly is under all circumstances and for all people. Is it truth? Is there any such thing as immutable truth for all time and circumstance, or is the perception of the idea of knowledge or truth merely a product of our own limited perceptive and analytical ability? Comprehending the notion of truth is a little like the brain trying to understand the mind.

For instance, the most certain we can be of anything may be the truth and exactitude of mathematical relationships, derived by pure logic without reference to any worldly influence or prejudice. Surely $2 + 2$ *does* $= 4$! But does it always? At the speed of light, at the edge of the universe, or for the 16-dimensional "strings" currently hypothesized to be the building blocks of *everything* (Greene)? While most elementary math meets the test of logic, it is not real in a tangible sense. It is nothing more than a logical construct, defining the relationship of certain of the forces operating in our universe, but endowed with no tangible reality of its own.

I never saw a quadratic equation walking in the woods. I never heard a prime number step up and order a latte at Starbucks. We experience the world not by algebra, but by the emotions produced by the stimulation of our senses, the deprivation of which leads to madness. We explain how the elements of the universe fit together through the use of mathematics—symbolic metaphors for reality.

Knowledge is a related set of scientifically plausible and self-consistent facts, relationships, and descriptions thought to embody the property of truth. The underlying validity of science is not that it is in possession of the ultimate or only truth, but that it continues seeking and correcting its own misperceptions.

Robert Persig, a one time rhetoric teacher and motorcycle rider, once set out on a cross-country trip to discover his own identity, using his bike as a metaphor for life. He wondered about the purpose of rhetoric according to its archaic sense as a branch of philosophy. He decided the purpose of rhetoric was to find Truth, and that the way to teach modern day rhetoric was to let students discover for themselves the elements of Quality in writing. However, the root problem was to know if Quality was objective, a property of the object and therefore measurable, or subjective, a property of viewership. In Plato's dialogue between Phaedrus and Socrates, Beauty *was* Truth.

Each night after miles of riding, Persig assumed the role of Phaedrus the wolf, reasoning with Socrates, in his search for an answer. But since everyone's perception of Quality, Truth, and Beauty is different one from the other, these perceptions could not be a standard property of universal viewership. The default conclusion was that Quality, as well as Truth and Beauty, were in the eye of each beholder.

So, can the truth of a thing be judged by its beauty? Is beauty an intrinsic property or does it depend on the prior conditioning, emotional state, and viewing angle of the beholder? At the end of his journey, Robert Persig stopped his bike along Rt. 101 overlooking the Pacific Ocean, after many days of riding since leaving Minneapolis. After remarking on the beauty of the scenery witnessed during the trip he turned to his 12 year old son Chris and said, "What's the matter?" Chris said, "Everything. I never could see over your shoulders before." Perhaps the truth of a thing or idea is different depending on whether we are riding on the front or the back of our bike. For as written in the Talmud, "We do not see things as they are; we see them as we are."

If the pursuit of knowledge is man's destined purpose in life, artistic expression, an equally ubiquitous quest, must be its handmaiden. The meaning of man's exploration of the reality of the tangible world must be translated into sensory impressions that reach beyond cerebral intellect and stir the discharge of our neurotransmitters and the production and flow of our hormones. By this process, perhaps we may come closer to the Truth, the Beauty, the Quality of the idea conceived or object created.

While nonfiction teaches and describes, fiction and theater reenact the ancient myths and stories of relationships and human behavior. Only, as with Jewish Midrash, these ancient stories are presented in today's moral context, updated with a modern cultural perspective, and subject to both the current offerings of our contemporary technology and deceptions.

Charles Murray (2003) did a statistical study of human accomplishment from 800 BC through 1950. His principal conclusion was that the major breakthroughs in science and art were made by people who had a sense of individual purpose and belief in their own capability. Their goal was to achieve the transcendental goods: *truth* in the case of science, *beauty* in the case of art or abstract concepts, and *good* itself, which might be spelled with a capital G if the overall good was perceived of as God secularized with an extra "o."

Is knowledge our destiny? Jacob Bronowski said it was and Carl Sagan acknowledged the veracity of this proclamation by concurring in the concluding statement of his work on the evolution of human intelligence. But it was Immanuel Kant who first concluded that our duty and our destiny can only be addressed by first answering the question: What can I know (Cath. Encyc., newadvent.org)?

Drusilla Scott, in her book interpreting the social philosophy of the scientist Michael Polanyi, illustrated the relation she saw between science and beauty. A graciously adorned woman stands looking at a Scientist clothed in his white lab coat. She is holding his glasses extended outward between the two figures.

"Take off your spectacles sometimes!" says Beauty to Science. "There are other ways of seeing the world."

"But how will Everyman know if he is seeing true if I do not tell Him?" asks Science.

"No-one can tell for sure, but together we can help him find the way."

Science and law must be explicit to function. Art and religion never will be. They teach and inform us of ideas, through emotion, that transcend the scope of science and law. If we are able to reconcile science (objective reality) with beauty (perception of value) we may approach a fuller understanding of Truth. Indeed, the reconciliation of what a thing is and what it means has been the quest of philosophers since the first great Western one, Plato, proposed his Theory of Forms.

No man knows all and no man will ever know all. By definition, only God is omnipotent. Whenever man has questioned the nature of things or the mysterious forces that inhabit them, the wind, the rain, lightning, thunder, earth tremors, cold, sickness, death, the inevitable passion of love, and the inexorable cyclic rhyme of the seasons, he assigned the causation and comprehension of these things to a province outside of himself. He called this province God. Many men find it difficult to live with uncertainty. Since there had to be a cause behind each effect, the role of first cause and all that followed certainly had to be the doing of some God. So say the Deists. Today, the followers of Chaos Theory might suggest that all relative motion could be the result of the mere flutter of a butterfly's wings.

Just in our own time, we have staked out a new claim in God's territory. Twenty-seven years ago Louise Brown was born, the first virgin birth of our species, at least for 2,000 years, as some may believe. We can now determine the sex of our child to be, still in the petri dish. We have cloned a number of animal species working up the evolutionary chain to cats and sheep. You know who's next. We can splice genes by inserting snippets of DNA from one species into the cells of another. Many of us will witness the creation of many strange, new, transgenic animals in our lifetime. To what purposes will these creatures be put? Who will decide? What manner of grotesque beings might be created in the process? How will we deal with the moral, social, and political fallout of this work? Each new advance in understanding comes packaged with dangers to be surmounted. It is Shelly's literary creation become incarnate and more—much, much more. Is not Truth indeed stranger than fiction?

But we do want to know. And bit by bit we learn today, that which we did not know yesterday. By any traditional interpretation of spiritual mystery we are now invading God's workshop and even preparing to improve on his handiwork. As we acquire more knowledge and skill—and we will—we enlarge our human domain and diminish God's sacred territorial boundaries. The cutting edge of science defines the intersection of human knowledge with God's territory.

Norman Podhoretz has studied the Biblical prophets of the Old Testament who warned repeatedly of the perils of worshiping graven images and practicing idolatry. He concluded that the hazard of this practice is not just that God is diminished in the process, but that men promote themselves to *be* God by worshiping their own creations. As we learn more and reduce this new learning to practice, it follows that we view ourselves to be more and more God-like. M. Scott Peck understands our collective unconscious to be God. As our consciousness matures along with our spiritual growth we draw always closer to becoming as one with God. Perhaps a God is in our genes.

Will we someday marginalize God and consign him to the scrap heap of history as Nietzsche suggested much of Western Europe was doing in 1882 when he wrote "God is dead"? Will we unmask him like Dorothy did the Wizard of Oz? Or is it our destiny to become God?

If so, whom shall we call upon to guide us when we lose our way? Until we know and can do everything, surely there will be a place for God and a place for religion. Think of the many attributes of religion:

✓ rationalization of the unexplainable
✓ the wonder of something greater than self (an antidote for hubris)
✓ assurance that something of your spirit survives your earthly sojourn
✓ culturally collective social ideas
✓ rules for social stability
✓ conformation of values (a reason for being–not being in vain)
✓ the security of ritual
✓ comfort of commitment to something that cannot be taken away
✓ the grace of forgiveness
✓ and hope–always hope

Since God belongs to everyone, at least in the Western tradition, he is the symbolic repository of virtue as may be believed by well over two billion souls. Because it is so powerful, this source of ancient community wisdom has often been expropriated in the interest of governments and hijacked to serve the purposes of extremists. It is interpreted by high priests to serve the cultural needs of different peoples, but in the end is the source of a guidance no authority or rogue movement can control. It is yours to draw upon or dispute as a matter of individual freedom. As Lane pointed out, all men are free to believe or deny as they may choose.

The intersection of knowledge and belief is a contested battleground. On one side, belief is the powerful force that drives men's actions; actions that seem to be limited only by the imperative of survival and the even stronger attractions of economic advantage and political power. When belief prevails over reality and presumes the cloak of certainty, it leads to trouble, and men then no longer live in harmony with nature or each other.

During the first two millennia of the common era, belief was enlisted intermittently to justify the repression of Jews, and continuously in the interest of slavery. It took the discoveries of Copernicus and Galileo Galilei to break the belief tenets of a distorted version of Christ's message, a version featuring Western man at the center of the universe. Along with Columbus' demonstration that the world was round, these contributions to our knowledge base played a major role in freeing men from the shackles of superstition and expanding his innate capacities. The rollback of superstition by new knowledge only renders belief, thus reformed, a more reliable guide to successful living. This is what Socrates meant when he asserted that the value of a life can only be established by an honest examination of one's own life experiences. This is what the Bible implied when it asserted, "...the truth shall make you free."

Today it is the scientific examination of our biological makeup that is the harbinger of continuing alteration of our belief patterns and revolutionary expansion of our capacities. This is an inquiry set in motion by Wallace and Darwin, based on their observations of natural selection in the animal kingdom. The end result of these discoveries, the Theory of Evolution, is now considered fact, but is at odds with the belief principles of some religious fundamentalist groups. The science of molecular biology features ongoing and expanding investigations that will proceed and overwhelm old belief systems and values, and open new avenues of both peril and possibility for mankind. It may come to pass that our accumulating knowledge of self will inspire us to even greater respect for the mysteries of life as yet unrevealed.

The bottom line, the glue of civilization, is the Golden Rule, rediscovered and taught many times over again. You may have discovered it yourself if you have ever pondered the question "How shall I behave and conduct my social relationships?" It is the idea that evokes the cerebral emotion of compassion and bestows the quality of value on all men. It is the self-evident, a priori standard of behavior to which we must repair if there is ever to be peace on earth.

It was Galileo who said, "I do not feel obliged to believe that the same god who has endowed us with sense, reason and intellect has intended us to forgo their use." Following his perceptive reconciliation of God with his handiwork, we may proceed with all hope and confidence to roll back the boundaries of superstition and fill the void with our best understanding of Truth, based on knowledge illuminated by Beauty. Certainly it is not our obligation to solve all our earthly problems, even though most of these are just of our own making. But certainly we would like to offer our descendents a greater measure of place and space, psychological as well as intellectual, in which to apply their talents to problem solving, creative accomplishment, celebration, and learning. Then perhaps, when man's stewardship of this planet ever ends, it will not have ended before we have mastered this great experiment embedded in our DNA, an experiment that could transcend the human condition and morph into a more advanced life form which we, in partnership with God, might play a role in creating. Or maybe, as seekers of Truth and Beauty, we shall be content just to find out and know who we are, and understand what it means to be. For now, we are fortunate to be able to fly into the future on the wings of freedom's vector, with optimism, determination, and hope—each to realize our own destiny.

The 13th: Rhode Island. May 29, 1790

AFTERWORD

It is clear that over time our government has not been able to meet the lofty standards set down in our founding documents.

Government has abused its power to impose a direct tax on labor granted under the Sixteenth Amendment in 1913. This amendment was designed to be the American solution to the ancient problem of extreme wealth difference between rich and poor. While the rich do in fact pay more than the poor, America still has the highest income inequality and level of social unrest of any developed nation except Russia.

Government has used the tax code as the principal vehicle with which to control the social and economic behavior of Americans. Unlimited powers of taxation have made it possible for the government to grant special tax concessions to targeted groups in the interest of currying political and/or financial support. Our convoluted tax code serves no useful purpose other than that of providing revenue for government programs and redistributing income. The remaining 99.9 percent of the tax code is only the fallout from political battles serving to complicate life and confuse the public.

Government has demonstrated over and over again that it is not a responsible steward of the public purse. America's citizens are in debt to the level of 70 percent of their annual productive power. These bills will not be forgiven—they must be paid from future tax revenues.

Government is deeply involved in managing American business, the engine of our prosperity. The net result is misallocation of capital investment, business inefficiency, and a negation of the risk inherent in successful capitalism. The power to tax business has facilitated government's capacity to legislate operating privileges according to political interest.

Government abused the intent of Social Security legislation by not funding a trust, even as it authorized increasing levels of support for seniors. The implied future funding liability is equal to one entire year's national productive power. These promises were expanded even when the ratio of payers to beneficiaries was known to be becoming dangerously unbalanced.

Government is the primary factor in a medical delivery system that is the largest interdisciplinary business system in the country. Our health care system may not be the best in the world, but it is by far the most expensive. The unfunded service commitments to the American people exceed our annual national productive power by 150 percent. In 2003, congress increased significantly the promised level of medical services without a thought for the cost.

Government has not been able to honor the implied promise of our founders to provide equal opportunity for all and universal respect for human dignity, in spite of our material wealth.

Government has allowed the power of democracy to be frustrated in its role as a tool of the demos, by the process of gerrymandering.

Congress has abrogated its constitutional responsibility to declare war by abandoning that right to the president.

Political candidates solicit and accept billions from special interest groups, representing business and nonprofit organizations, for election campaigns. The result is legislation by the victors favoring the donors, with insufficient concern for the interests of all American citizens. We may vote for our congressmen and pay for their upkeep, but we do not control them–special interests do.

After a year and a half of vigorous campaigning leading up to the 2004 general election, the tax system was not voluntarily mentioned. The social security system was mentioned only in passing. The medical delivery system was mentioned only as the beneficiary of another expensive program. The national debt was mentioned, but as if it were only an accounting fiction of no consequence. The deficit was mentioned only in the context of a promise to cut it in half over the next five years. Campaign financing was not mentioned. Outsourcing was mentioned, but not our massive trade deficit. Government has no plan or strategy for addressing these issues.

Neither has it a plan for dealing with our dependence on foreign oil, or the potential for global warming, or the social implications of biotechnical development. In our personal affairs, failure is the inevitable consequence of maxing out our credit cards, watching our vital systems fall into disrepair, and selling our birthright, while telling our family that we are doing just great–that we are lucky to be living in this cool neighborhood at the intersection of Democracy Avenue and Freedom Street. The same is true for our Uncle Sam.

The baby boomers will start to retire en masse during the 2012 election year. That is when these old chickens will come home to roost and you will hear then of the necessity for increasing payroll taxes and/or cutting benefits.

The root problem we must confront in the interest of continued American greatness is the virtual lack of accountability by a government and its elected officials who have secured for themselves a 98 percent certainty of reelection based on private campaign contributions and the practice of gerrymandering. By these means, democracy, the first line of defense against tyranny, has been undermined, paving the way for moneyed interests to gain an unhealthy leverage over government–that same government we are told is of, by and for us people.

Were our elected leaders personally and collectively responsible for these failings out of neglect or intent, or were they just lesser men than were the founders? We may not lay these failings exclusively at the feet of our politicians. Our forefathers rebelled against taxation without representation; however, we have been content to accept taxation with insufficient information or justification. Government officials are incapable of overhauling our major institutional systems gone awry, working within the present rules. They are playing by the rules in a system that falls short of allowing for effectively governing a modern, technological, credit society unknown to Jefferson or Madison.

Were they here now, they would remind us that they gave us a government of, by and for the people, and it is our responsibility to amend it that it might continue to light the way for freedom's vector. If our America is falling short of realizing its full potential, it may just be an indication that we Americans have not risen to the level of personal responsibility required as our last line of defense against tyranny–that we are asking for security when we should be demanding accountability. We must take advantage of our constitutional democracy to strengthen our freedom in the interest of prosperity, opportunity, and dignity.

The 14th: Vermont. March 4, 1791–the last to sign on

AUTHOR'S NOTE

When our children reach our ripe old age, certainly the world will have changed. But will it be better? The agents of change will be individuals just like us. Should you believe there is no hope of changing the world to your liking, others surely will change it to their liking. The first step is to envision a better world in concrete terms. It is not important that you agree with the ideas in this story. It is important that you reflect on your own story for America. If you think not, both you and it may vanish, as we may infer from Descartes' metaphysical conjecture.

Looking back at the ideas expressed in Jefferson's founding document, it is apparent that the intent he honored with his unalienable rights was that of a people who would be free and equal in opportunity in the name of human dignity. When James Madison came to Philadelphia in 1787, he had the first draft of our constitution in his back pocket, a plan designed to secure these rights. We still live by his brilliant design.

What is your idea of a better world? What do you think Antigone, Thoreau, Gandhi, King, or Honest Abe might do today to point freedom's vector in a right direction? What will you do?

ACRONYMS

AARP	American Association of Retired Persons
ACE	Association for Continuing Education
ACGA	American Corn Growers Association
ACLU	American Civil Liberties Union
AFDC	Aid to Families with Dependent Children
AMT	Alternative Minimum Tax
ARAMCO	Arabian American Oil Company
ASBJ	American School Board Journal
BEA	Bureau of Economic Analysis
CAFTA	Central American Free Trade Agreement
CBO	Congressional Budget Office
CEO	Chief Executive Officer
CCC	Civilian Conservation Corp
CCF	Cleveland Clinic Foundation
COBRA	Consolidated Omnibus Budget Reconciliation Act
EITC	Earned Income Tax Credit
EU	European Union
FASB	Federal Accounting Standards Board
FCC	Federal Communications Commission
FDA	Food and Drug Administration
FEC	Federal Elections Commission
FERC	Federal Energy Regulation Agency
FSSP	Foreign Students Studies Program
FTAA	Free Trade Area of the Americas
FTC	Federal Trade Commission
GATT	General Agreement on Tariffs and Trade
GDP	Gross Domestic Product
GMO	Genetically Modified Organism
HHS	Health and Human Services
HMO	Health Maintenance Organization
IMF	International Monetary Fund
IRA	Individual Retirement Account
IRS	Internal Revenue Service
MRI	Magnetic Resonance Imaging

MTBE	Methyl Tertiary Butyl Ether
NAFTA	North American Free Trade Association
NATO	North Atlantic Treaty Organization
NCES	National Center for Education Statistics
NGO	Non-Government Organization
NIDC	National Identification Debit Card
NIPA	National Income and Product Accounts
NRA	National Rifle Association
OECD	Organization for Economic Co-operation and Development
OHP	Oregon Health Plan
PAC	Political Action Committee
PIN	Personal Identification Number
PPO	Preferred Provider Organization
REIT	Real Estate Investment Trust
SAT	Student Aptitude Test
SCHIP	State Children's Health Insurance Program
SEC	Securities and Exchange Commission
TANF	Temporary Assistance for Needy Families
UHIP	Universal Health Insurance Plan
UK	United Kingdom
UN	United Nations
VOA	Voice of America
WHO	World Health Organization
WMD	Weapons of Mass Destruction
WPA	Work Projects Administration
WSJ	Wall Street Journal
WTC	Wealth Tax Credit
WTO	World Trade Organization

APPENDICES

TAX AND PROGRAM COST CALCULATIONS *

There are some benchmark financial numbers we need to know from the year 2001 in order to see how our two tax systems fit together.

Gross Domestic Product (GDP): **$10.082** trillion

Government Tax Revenues: **$2.952** trillion, **29.3%** of GDP
  Federal: $1.936 trillion
  State and Local: $0.984 trillion

Government Expenditures: **$2.920** trillion
  Federal: $1.627 trillion (net of transfers)
  State and Local: $1.293 trillion
  Grant-in-Aid transfers from Federal Government: $309 billion

Public school enrollment, K-12: 62 million
  Average annual operating cost per student: **$7,100**
    (Nat. Ctr. For Edu. Stats. 2002)
  Capital cost per student at 10% of operating: **$710**
    (S. Osborne, pers. comm.)
  Total cost per student: **$7,810**
  Private school enrollment, K-12: 8 million
    (Univ. of Oregon CEPM)

One half of total education cost assuming 70 million children in a
  public/private school system: **$273** billion   (70x7,810/2)

Total Personal Income: **$8.685** trillion**

345

TAX AND PROGRAM COST CALCULATIONS
(cont.)

Contributions to Tax-Exempt Organizations: **$250** billion
    Public Charity and Foundations: $174 billion
    Private Foundations : $38 billion
    Religious Organizations: $30 billion
    Miscellaneous: $8 billion
       (IRS, The Found. Ctr., and Nat. Coun. of Churches)

Investment Income: **$1.651** trillion
    Interest: $1,091 billion
    Dividends: $409 billion
    Capital Gain: $151 billion (0.5x0.03x10.082 trillion) (assumes a
       50% tax preference on capital gains, which have averaged 3%
       of GDP from 1974 to 1994) (Gwartney and Holcombe)

---

* All data are from the Bureau of Economic Analysis (BEA), National Income and Product Account (NIPA) tables for the year 2001, except as otherwise noted.

** Total Personal Income includes compensation for labor, profit, investment returns, and transfer payments. All transfer payments were financed by the government from taxes on the economy or by government borrowing, i.e., future taxes. Since the total net compensation for labor should remain about the same under the proposed tax system, and there was a slight budget surplus in 2001, we need only subtract that income derived from investment in order to determine a revised taxable income base.

APPENDIX A

PROPOSED GOVERNMENT FUNDING

Table 1. Sources of Government Income:

2001 TAX REVENUE SOURCES IN $ BILLIONS

	FEDERAL	STATE/LOCAL
INCOME	1000	211
CORPORATE	170	36
ESTATE	28	7
EXCISE	66	0
SSA	716	0
SALES	0	309
PROPERTY	0	248
VIHICLE	0	16
OTHER	28	467
TOTAL	2008	1294

Grand total: **$2.992** trillion (excluding $309 billion in transfers to the states)

APPENDIX A (cont.)

Table 2. Dispersal of Government Funds:

2001 EXPENDITURES IN $ BILLIONS

	FEDERAL	STATE/LOCAL
GENERAL PUBLIC SERVICE	278	124
NATIONAL DEFENSE	347	0
PUBLIC ORDER & SAFETY	28	182
ECONOMIC AFFAIRS	109	108
HOUSING/COMM. SERVICES	32	7
HEALTH	447	268
EDUCATION	48	475
RECREATION & CULTURE	3	17
INCOME SECURITY	644	112
TOTAL	1936	1293

Grand total: **$2.920** trillion (excluding $309 billion in transfers to the states)

APPENDIX A (cont.)

Proposed changes to expenditures:
> Federal government to pay all UHIP expense @11.9% of GDP, or
> **$1,195** billion (from appendix F)
> Federal government to pay 1/2 of present public school costs: **$273**
> billion (0.5x70 million students @ $7,810 ea)
> (includes 8 million private school students)
> Social Security Trust Fund collections will not be included in
> government budget or expense accounting
> State and local government will not directly collect or disburse
> funds for health, education, or income security purposes

Proposed government expenditures would now look like this:

Table 3. Proposed dispersal of government funds:

PROPOSED 2001 EXPENDITURES IN $ BILLIONS

	FEDERAL	STATE/LOCAL
GENERAL PUBLIC SERVICE	278	124
NATIONAL DEFENSE	347	0
PUBLIC ORDER & SAFETY	28	182
ECONOMIC AFFAIRS	109	108
HOUSING/COMM. SERVICES	32	7
HEALTH	1195	0
EDUCATION	273	0
RECREATION & CULTURE	3	17
INCOME SECURITY	0	0
TOTAL	2265	438

Grand total: **$2.703** trillion, reducing total government
expenditures by $217 billion.

APPENDIX B

PROPOSED INCOME TAX RATE

Now let us examine how we propose to fund the remaining combined government expense total of $2.703 trillion. This will be done with a flat tax on virtually all earned income over $10,000, with the exceptions noted in chapter 7. In order to arrive at a flat tax percentage we will have to account for these exceptions to taxable income as follows.

Over time, realized capital gains that are reported as income vary considerably as tax law changes and equity market values fluctuate. This makes any estimate of contribution to taxable income impossible to quantify with any certitude. Over several decades, reported realized capital gains have averaged about 3% of GDP. For 2001, at 3%, this reported income would come to $302 billion (0.03x10082). Since capital gain is a tax preference item, I would estimate the impact on loss of taxable income might be about half that amount, or **$151** billion, based on a capital gains tax rate of 50% of normal.

PROPOSED TAXABLE INCOME BASE:

original 2001 income total	8685
charitable contributions	-250
interest	-1091
dividends	-409
capital gains	-151
income exemption*	-1300
proposed taxable income base	5484

To finance our new federal government at $2.265 trillion, it will take a flat tax rate of **41.3%** (100x2265/5484) of our taxable income.

State and local government would require **8.0%** (100x438/5484), for a combined income tax rate of **49.3%**.

---

*130 million returns x $10,000 exemption.

APPENDIX C

SOCIAL SECURITY BENEFITS

Social security tax rate: 5% of payroll up to $60,000 ($3,000 max)

Retirement benefits
Population: 284 million
Population between age 20 and 65: 164 million (57.8% of 284
   million) (U.S. Census, factfinder.census.gov)
Assumed average annual Social Security collection rate for 164
   million people: $1,500 (1/2 of the maximum)
Average *real* rate of return anticipated for social security account
   funds: 4.5% (40% equities @ 6.7%+60% bonds @ 3%)
   (see Appendix E)
Individual account value after 40 years: $168,000
Annual benefit for life starting at age 65: **$10,600**, or about 80% of
   2001 maximum benefit (based on a 4% annuity payout rate
   inflating at 3% per year) (Annuity Calculator)

Social security tax required for full current benefit = $1,875
   (1,500/0.8)

Projected return on private social security accounts = 4.5%
Return relative to interest free savings = 2.75 times after 40 years or
   3.25 times after 45 years

*** Total wealth, or capital, is the net sum of the nation's tangible assets, such
as real estate, plus financial assets including savings, equities, pension fund
reserves, and equity in non public business.

APPENDIX D

WEALTH TAX CREDIT

Now we must calculate an adjusted national taxable net worth or wealth figure to determine how much revenue a 2% tax on wealth would yield. Recall that assets tied up in tax exempt organizations and individual social security accounts would not be subject to the wealth tax.

Total Net Wealth (in private hands): **$53.0** trillion***
   (Fed. Res. Brd., federal reserve.gov)

Average social security account balance: $57,400 (from benefits
   calculation above)
Total social security account holdings: $9.4 trillion exempt from
   wealth tax (164 millionx$57,400, neglecting early deaths)

Tax-Exempt funds held by private and public charitable
   foundations: ~$500 billion (The Found. Ctr.)

Taxable wealth: $43.1 trillion (53 trillion-9.4 trillion-0.5 trillion)

Wealth tax credit total: $862 billion (.02x43.1 trillion)
   (assumes a 2% wealth tax rate)

Wealth tax credit per person: **$3,035** (862 billion/284 million)

*** Total wealth, or capital, is the net sum of the nation's tangible assets, such as real estate, plus financial assets including savings, equities, pension fund reserves, and equity in non public business.

APPENDIX E

TAXATION COMPARISON
CURRENT VS. PROPOSED

Comparison of 2001 with proposed investment returns for the <u>highest</u> earners (**federal only**, lesser payers pay at lower rates)

The following numbers will be used for analysis:
    2001 net income tax rate: 33% of adjusted gross income (AGI) for
      top earners (27.5% federal+5.5% state and local)
    2001 net capital gain tax rate: 16.5% (0.5x33%)
      (Tax Bites)
    Proposed wealth tax rate: 2% annually (marked to market)
    Real level of yield on investment grade bonds as in Dow Jones
      Bond Index (DJB): Average real return for DJB (after inflation)
      from 1920 to 2000: 3.0%
    Actual level of capital appreciation for Dow Jones Industrial
      Average (DJIA) from 1920 to 2000: 6.0%
    Actual level of dividend yield from DJIA from 1920 to 2000: 3.5%
    Average level of inflation from 1920 to 2000: 2.8% as measured
      by the Consumer Price Index (CPI)
    Real total appreciation rate for investment grade equities as in Dow
      Jones Industrial Index (DJIA): 6.7% *real* return (after inflation)
      (6.0% equities+3.5% dividends-2.8% inflation)

Notes: (1) unrealized capital gain on assets do not apply to inherited assets and (2) potential estate tax liabilities are not taken into account

APPENDIX E (cont.)

Comparison of present with proposed system investment yields:

For bonds - 2001 net income tax rates

Actual yield	5.80%	(3.0+2.8)
Yield after income tax	3.89%	(0.67x5.8)
Net yield after inflation	1.09%	(3.89-2.8)

For bonds - proposed wealth tax rate

Actual yield	5.80%	(3.0+2.8)
Yield after wealth tax	3.80%	(5.8-2.0)
Net yield after inflation	1.00%	(3.8-2.8)

For equities - 2001 net tax rates, if sold annually

Actual return	9.50%	(3.5 dividendss+6.0 capital gain)
Return after income tax	7.35%	(0.67x3.5+0.835x6.0)
Net return after inflation	4.55%	(7.35-2.8)

For equities - 2001 net tax rates, if never sold

Actual return	9.50%	(3.5 dividendss+6.0 capital gain)
Return after income tax	8.74%	(0.67x3.5+6)
Net return after inflation	5.94%	(8.74-2.8)

For equities - proposed wealth tax rate

Actual return	9.50%	(3.5 dividendss+6.0 capital gain)
Return after wealth tax	7.50%	(9.5-2.0)
Net return after inflation	4.70%	(7.54-2.8)

Conclusion: The tax consequences of investing are roughly comparable for the current and proposed taxation systems.

APPENDIX F

PROPOSED HEALTH CARE FINANCING
(see Terhune, and Woolhandler and Himmelstein)

For 2001, total health care costs = $1,440 billion or 14.3% of GDP
    (0.143x10.08 trillion)

Federal Medicaid cost = $129 billion or 60% of total cost
Total Medicaid cost = $215 billion
    (129/0.6)

People on Medicaid = 15% or 42.6 million
    (0.15x284) (assumes all to be uninsured)
Cost per Medicaid recipient = $5,050 ea
    (215/42.6)
Cost per non-Medicaid recipient = $4,075 ea
    ((1440-215)/(284-42.6))
Therefore, all recipients can be treated equally in a prepaid health care
system

Current administrative cost = $446 billion or 31% of total cost
    (0.31x1440 billion)
Administrative cost rate for single payer Canadian system = 16.7%
Potential savings at Canadian administrative rate = $206 billion
    ((0.31-0.167)x1.440)

Current profits of private health insurance companies
    Premiums paid in: $477 billion
    Claims paid out: $382 billion
    Overhead at 11.7%: $56 billion
    Gross profit = $39 billion
        (477-382-56)

APPENDIX F (cont.)

Total potential cost savings = **$245** billion   (206+39)
For 2001, revised health care cost would be = $1,195 billion or
   11.9% of GDP
      (100x1.195/10.08)

APPENDIX G

OVERALL PROGRAM FINANCIAL IMPACT

Total revenues required:
Income: $2.703 trillion for proposed program
Social security: $716 billion
Education: $273 billion for optional education program from WTC
Total: $3.639 trillion to cover all programs

Current (2001) government revenues: $2.992 trillion
Difference: $647 billion additional program cost
(3.639-2.992)

Financial benefits: lower retail prices (and higher wages?)
Private insurance business cost: $477 billion
Business profit tax elimination: $206 billion
State sales tax elimination: $309 billion
SSA tax elimination: $358 billion
Total: $1,350 billion in business/organizational costs eliminated
Average per capita benefit: $4,750
(1350/284)

Difference: $703 billion lower net program and market cost
(1350-647)

Note: after 45 years when Social Security is fully converted to a private plan, the personal costs for social security will decrease by $326 billion, the 6% surcharge on labor appended to social security
(.06x$5,434 taxable income = $326 billion)

BIBLIOGRAPHY

Aaron, Henry J., and William B. Schwartz, with Melissa Cox. *Can We Say No?: The Challenge of Rationing Health Care.* Washington, DC: Brookings Institution Press,2005. Lord Acton. In a letter to Bishop Mandell Creighton, 1887.

Adams, James Truslow. *The Epic of America.* Reprint. Simon, 2001.

Adams, Mike S. *Welcome to the Ivory Tower of Babel: Confession of a Conservative College Professor.* Augusta, GA: Harbor House, 2004.

Adler, Mortimer J. *Six Great Ideas.* Collier Books, 1981.

Alger, Horatio, Jr. *Ragged Dick, or Street Life in New York With the Bootblacks.* 1854. Reprint. New York: Signet, 1990.

American Association of Fundraising Counsel. "Charity Holds its Own in Tough Times." AAFRC Trust Press Releases, Giving USA, 2003, http://www.aafrc.org/press_releases/trustreleases/charityholds.html.

American Bar Association. "Letter to the U.S. Secretary of the Treasury." American Institute of CPA's and Tax Executives. *Wall Street Journal,* April 2001.

American School Board Journal. "Education Vital Signs." February 2003, http://www.asbj.com/evs/03/2003pdf/EVS03_southwest pdf.

Amistad Academy. "A College Preparatory Middle School for Urban Students," http://www.amistadacademy.org./.

Angell, Marcia. *The Truth About the Drug Companies: How They Deceive Us and What We Can Do About It.* New York: Random House, 2004.

Annas, Julia. *The Morality of Happiness.* New York: Oxford Univ. Press, 1993.

Annuity Calculator, http://calc.tsp.gov/annuityCalculators/annuity.cfm.

Anon. *Harper's,* March 2004.

Anon [Scheuer, Michael]. *Imperial Hubris: Why the West is Losing the War on Terror.* Dulles, VA: Brassey's, 2004.

Armington, R. Q., and William D. Ellis. *More: The Rediscovery of American Common Sense.* Washington, DC: Regnery Gateway, 1984.

Bacevich, Andrew J. *American Empire: The Realities and Consequences of U.S. Diplomacy.* Cambridge, MA: Harvard Univ. Press, 2002.

Bacevich, Andrew J. *The New American Militarism: How Americans are Seduced by War.* New York: Oxford Univ. Press, 2005.

Baer, Robert. "The Fall of the House of Saud." *Atlantic Monthly,* May 2003.

Bailey, Dennis. *The Open Society Paradox.* Herndon, VA: Potomac Books, 2004.

Baker, Wayne E. *America's Crisis of Values: Reality and Perception.* Princeton, NJ: Princeton Univ. Press, 2004.

Ball, Jeffrey. "Hydrogen Fuel May Be Clean but Getting It Here Looks Messy." *Wall Street Journal,* March 7, 2003.

Barlett, Donald, and James Steele. *Critical Condition: How Health Care in America Became Big Business-and Bad Medicine.* New York: Doubleday, 2004.

Bauer, Peter. "Development Aid." Institute for Contemporary Studies, Paper No. 43, 1993.

Beck, Robert N., Ed. *Perspectives in Social Philosophy.* Austin, TX: Holt, Rinehart & Winston, 1967.

Beard, Charles Austin, and Mary Ritter Beard. *A Basic History of the United States.* Garden City, 1944.

Beever, Charles, Heather Burns, and Melanie Karbe. "U.S. Health Care's Technology Cost Crisis," http://www.strategy-business.com/enewsarticle/enews033104?Tid=230&pg=all.

Bellamy, Edward. *Looking Backward.* 1897. 4th Printing. New York: Signet, 1964.

Bell, Daniel. *The Cultural Contradictions of Capitalism.* New York: Basic Books, 1976.

Bennett, William J. *Book of Virtues.* New York: Simon & Schuster, 1993.

Biden, Joseph. Remarks on Meet the Press. Televised August 24, 2003.

Bildt, Carl. "Fight Poverty, Not Patents." *Wall Street Journal,* January 7, 2002.

Blackman, Irving L. "Your Business —- America's Best Tax Shelter." Chicago: Blackman Kallick, 1987.

Blustein, Paul. *The Chastening: Inside the Crisis that Rocked the Global Financial System and Humbled the IMF.* New York: Public Affairs, 2002.

Blustein, Paul. *And the Money Kept Rolling In (and out): Wall Street, the IMF, and the Bankrupting of Argentina.* New York: Public Affairs, 2005.

Bonhoeffer, Dietrich. Brainy Quotes, www.brainyquote.com/ quotes/ authors/d/dietrich_bonhoeffer.

Boo, Katherine. "The Factory." *New Yorker,* October 18, 2004.

Boulding, Kenneth E. *Economics as a Science.* New York: McGraw Hill, 1970.

Bowen, Catherine Drinker. *Miracle at Philadelphia: The Story of the Constitutional Convention May to September 1787.* Boston: Atlantic Monthly Press, 1966.

Bradbury, Ray. *Fahrenheit 451.* Reissue ed. New York: Del Rey, 1987.

Bronowski, Jacob. *The Ascent of Man.* 7th printing. Boston: Little, Brown, 1973.

Brooks, David. *Bobos in Paradise: The New Upper Class and How They Got There.* New York: Simon & Schuster, 2001.

Brownlee, Shannon. "Major Flaws in U.S. Health System." 2nd Annual Atlantic Monthly Conference on Book TV television. C-SPAN 2, January 13, 2004.

Budget Documentation, http://www.fda.gov/oc/oms/ofm/budget/ documentation.htm.

Bureau of Economic Analysis, "National Income and Product Account tables." 2001, http://www.bea.gov/bea/dn/nipaweb/ SelectTable .asp?Selected=N.

Butler, Stuart M. *Privatizing Federal Spending: A Strategy to Eliminate the Deficit.* New York: Universe Books, 1985.

California Secretary of State. "Vote 2002 United States Congress," http://vote2002.ss.ca.gov/Returns/usrep/00.htm.

Campbell, Joseph. *The Hero With a Thousand Faces.* 2nd ed. Princeton, NJ: Princeton Univ. Press 3rd printing, 1973.

Campbell, Joseph. *The Power of Myth.* Reprint. Virginia Beach: Anchor, 1991.

Carnegie, Dale. *How to Win Friends and Influence People. 1937.* Reissue ed. Pocket, 1990.

Carter, Stephen L. *Integrity.* New York: Basic Books, 1996.

Cashill, Jack. *Hoodwinked: How Intellectual Hucksters Have Hijacked American Culture.* Nelson Current, 2005.

Cassingham, Randy. "The True 2002 Stella Awards Winners," http:// www.StellaAwards.com/2002.html.

Cassingham, Randy. "The True 2003 Stella Awards Winners," http:// www.StellaAwards.com/2003.html.

Cassingham, Randy. "The True 2004 Stella Awards Winners," http:// www.StellaAwards.com/2004.html.

Cassirer, Ernst. *Myth of the State.* New Haven, CT: Yale Univ. Press, 1946.

Catholic Encyclopedia. "The Philosophy of Immanuel Kant," http:// www.newadvent.org/cathen/08603a.htm.

Chang, Jung. *Wild Swans : Three Daughters of China,* Touchstone, 2003.

Chatterjee, Pranab. *Approaches to the Welfare State.* Washington, DC: Natl. Assn. Of Social Workers Press, 1996.

The Civil War Center. "Statistical Summary of America's Major Wars," http://www.cwc.lsu.edu/cwc/other/stats/ warcost.htm.

Clinton, William. *My Life.* New York: Knopf, 2004.

Coburn, Tom A., and John Hart. *Breach of Trust: How Washington Turns Outsiders Into Insiders.* WND Books, 2003.

Cole, John Young. *On These Walls: Inscription and Quotations in the Buildings of the Library of Congress.* Washington, DC: Library, 1994.

Collins (Sen.). "Statement of Investigation into Former Iraqui Abuse of U.N. Oil for Food Program." Homeland Security and Government Affairs. November 15, 2004, http:// hsgac.senate .gov/index.cfm?FuseAction=PressReleases. Detail&PressRelease _id=848&Affiliation=C.

Congressional Budget Office. "A Detailed Description of CBO's Cost Estimate for the Medicare Prescription Drug Benefit." Section 2. July 2004, http://cbo.gov/showdoc.cfm?index=5668& sequence=1&from=0.

Congressional Budget Office. "What Accounts for the Decline in Manufacturing Employment?" ECONOMIC AND BUDGET ISSUE BRIEF, February 18, 2004, http://cbo.gov/showdoc .cfm?Index=5078& sequence=0.

Connolly, Ceci, and Mike Allen. "Medicare Drug Benefit May Cost $1.2 Trillion." *Washington Post*, February 9, 2005.

Cornwell, Susan. "Asbestos Costs US companies $70 bln So Far." RAND Institute for Civil Justice study. *Reuters,* February 6, 2004.

CorpWatch. "Corporate Globalization Fact Sheet." March 22, 2001.

Cox, Jacob Dolson, Jr. *Material Human Progress.* Cleveland: Stratford Press, 1954.

Crile, George. *Charlie Wilson's War: The Extraordinary Story of the Largest Covert Operation in History.* Atlantic Monthly Press, 2003.

Damon, William. *Greater Expectations: Overcoming the Culture of Indulgence in America's Homes and Schools.* New York: Free Press, 1995.

Daschle, Tom. "Breakthrough Achieved on Important Ethanol Legislation." February 24, 2004, http://www.daschle.senate .com (withdrawn).

Dawson, Christopher, John J. Mulloy, and Dermot Quinn. *Dynamics of World History.* Introduction by Quinn. Intercollegiate Studies Inst., 2002.

DeParle, Jason. *American Dream: Three Women, Ten Kids, and a Nation's Drive to End Welfare.* New York: Viking Press, 2004.

De Soto, Hernando. *The Mystery of Capital: Why Capitalism Triumphs in the West and Fails Everywhere Else.* New York: Basic Books, 2000.

De Tocqueville, Alexis. *Democracy in America.* 1831. Reprint. Chicago: Univ. of Chicago Press, 2000.

Diamond, Jared. *Guns, Germs and Steel.* New York: Norton, 1999.

Dictionary.com. "Alphabet of Most Looked-Up Words in 2004," http://dictionary.reference.com/features/dictionaryalphabet2004 .html.

Dostoyevsky, Fyodor. *Crime and Punishment.* Reprint. New York: Bantam, 1984.

Dowd, Maureen. 1995. Quoted in Jaques Barzun, *From Dawn to Decadence: 500 Years of Western Cultural Life: 1500 to the Present.* New York: Harper Collins, 2000.

D'Souza, Dinesh. *The Virtue of Prosperity: Finding Values in an Age of Techno-Affluence.* New York: Free Press, 2000.

Du Pont, Pete. "Called to Account." National Center for Policy Analysis. *Wall Street Journal,* June 6, 2001.

Durant, Will, and Ariel Durant. *The Story of Civilization.* 11 vols., 12th printing. New York: Simon & Schuster, 1954-68.

Eban, Katherine. *Dangerous Doses: How Counterfeiters Are Contaminating America's Drug Supply.* New York: Harcourt, 2005.

Editorial. *Wall Street Journal,* April 15, 2002.

Editorial. *Wall Street Journal,* May 1, 2002.

Ellwood, David T. *Poor Support: Poverty in the American Family.* New York: Basic Books, 1988.

Erdman, Paul Emil. *The Last Days of America.* New York: Simon & Schuster, 1983.

Esterlin, Richard. *Growth Triumphant: The Twenty-First Century in Historical Perspective (Economics, Cognition, and Society).* Ann Arbor: Univ. of Michigan Press, 1996.

Evers-Williams, Myrlie, and Minning Marable, Eds. *The Autobiography of Medgar Evers: A Hero's Life and Legacy Revealed Through His Writings, Letters, and Speeches.* Basic Civitas Books, 2005.

Falconer, Bruce. "U.S. Military Statistics." *Atlantic Monthly,* May 2003.

Fallows, James. "Countdown to a Meltdown." *Atlantic Monthly,* July/August 2005.

Fears, Rufus. "History of Freedom." The Teaching Company Course Tape No. 480.

Federal Reserve Board. "Balance Sheets for Households, Organizations, and Business, B.100, 102 and 103." Flow of Funds Accounts of the United States. September 16, 2004, http://www.federalreserve.gov/releases/Z1/Current/annuals/a1995-2003.pdf.

The Federated Church of Chagrin Falls, Ohio. Members Communication. March 15, 2005.

Feiler, Bruce. *Abraham: A Journey to the Heart of Three Faiths.* New York: William Morrow, 2002.

Ferguson, Niall. "The 'E' Word." *Wall Street Journal,* June 6, 2003.

Ferguson, Niall. *Colossus: The Price of America's Empire.* New York: Penguin Press, 2004.

Ferguson, Niall. *Empire: The Rise and Demise of the British World Order and the Lessons for Global Power.* New York: Basic Books, 2004.

Ferrara, Peter. "John Dow's Retirement." *Wall Street Journal,* August 27, 2002.

Fialka, John J. "After a Long Debate, Corn May Soon Be In More Gas Tanks." *Wall Street Journal,* August 23, 2002.

Fialka, John J. "Panel to Tackle U.S. Energy Policy." *Wall Street Journal,* November 26, 2002.

Fialka, John J. "Mercury Threat to Children Rising." *Wall Street Journal,* February 20, 2003.

Figgie, Harry E., and Gerald J. Swanson. *Bankruptcy 1995: The Coming Collapse of America and How to Stop It.* Boston: Little, Brown, 1992.

Finnegan, William. "The Economics of Empire." *Harper's,* May 2003.

Fonda, Jane. *My Life So Far.* New York: Random House, 2005.

Foner, Eric. *The Story of American Freedom.* New York: Norton, 1999.

The Foundation Center. "Foundation Growth and Giving Centers." 2002, http://fdncenter.org/media/stats.html.

Frangos, Alex. "Model vs. Model." *Wall Street Journal,* February 21, 2001.

Franklin, Benjamin. Brainy Quotes, http://www.brainyquote.com/quotes/authors/b/benjamin_franklin.html.

Friedan, Betty. *The Feminine Mystique.* 1963. Reprint. New York: Norton, 1997.

Friedman, Benjamin M. "Meltdown: A Case Study." *Atlantic Monthly,* July/August 2005.

Friedman, Milton, and Rose Friedman. *Free to Choose: A Personal Statement.* New York: Harcourt Brace Jovanovich, 1980.

Friedman. Thomas L. *From Beirut to Jerusalem.* Virginia Beach: Anchor Books, 1989.

Friedman, Thomas L. *The and the Olive Tree.* 3rd reprint. New York: Farrar, Straus and Giroux, 1999.

Friedman, Thomas L. *The World Is Flat: A Brief History of the Twenty-First Century.* New York: Farrar, Straus and Giroux, 2005,

PBS Frontline. "The War Behind Closed Doors." February 20, 2003, http://www.pbs.org/wgbh/pages/frontline/shows/iraq/view/.

PBS Frontline. "The Other Drug War." June 19, 2003, http://www. pbs .org/wgbh/pages/frontline/shows/other/themes/.

PBS Frontline. "Tax Me If You Can." February 19, 2004, http:// www .pbs.org/wgbh/pages/frontline/shows/tax/shelter/oped. html.

PBS Frontline. "The Jesus Factor." April 29, 2004, http://www.pbs .org/wgbh/pages/frontline/shows/jesus/.

PBS Frontline. "The New Asylums." May 10, 2005, http://www.pbs .org/wgbh/pages/frontline/shows/asylums/.

Fusfeld, Daniel R. *The Age of the Economist.* New York: William Morrow, 1968.

Fukuyama, Francis. *State Building: Governance and World Order in the 21st Century.* Ithaca, NY: Cornell Univ. Press, 2004.

Garment, Suzanne. *Scandal: The Culture of Mistrust in American Politics.* Virginia Beach: Anchor Books, 1992.

Gates, William H., Sr., and Chuck Collins. *Wealth and Commonwealth: Why America Should Tax Accumulated Fortunes.* Boston: Beacon Press, 2003.

Gatto, John Taylor. "Against School." *Harper's,* September 2003.

Gibbon, Edward. *The Decline and Fall of the Roman Empire: Volumes 1,2,3.* Everynam's Library, 1993.

Giombetti, Rick. "'Progressives for Enron?" January 22, 2002, http:// www.counterpunch.org/giombettienron.html.

Goodman, John C., and Gerald L. Musgrave. "Controlling Health Care Costs With Medical Savings Accounts." National Center for Policy Analysis Study #168, January 1992, http://www.ncpa .org/studies/s168/s168.html.

Graig, Laurene A. *Health of Nations: An International Perspective on U.S. Health Reform.* Wyatt, 1991.

Greene, Brian. *The Elegant Universe: Superstrings, Hidden Dimensions, and the Quest for the Ultimate Theory.* New York: Vintage, 2000.

Greenspan, Alan. Testimony before the House Financial Services Committee. July 2003.

Greenspan, Alan. Testimony before the Joint Economic Committee, U.S. Congress. June 9, 2005.

Grillo, Jerry. "Much More Than Golf." *Georgia Trend,* February 2005, http://www.georgiatrend.com/site/page7350.html.

Griswold v. Connecticut, 381 U.S. 479 (1965).

Gwartney, James D., and Randall G. Holcombe. "Optimal Capital Gains Tax Policy." Joint Economic Committee Study, June 1997, http://www.house.gov/jec/fiscal/txgrwth/gwartney/ optimal/opmal.pdf.

Halperin, Morton H., Joseph T. Siegle, and Michael M. Weinstein. *The Democracy Advantage: How Democracies Promote Prosperity and Peace.* New York: Routledge, 2004.

Halper, Stefan, and Jonathan Clarke. *America Alone: The Neo-Conservatives and the Global Order.* New York: Cambridge Univ. Press, 2004.

Hamilton, Lee. *How Congress Works and Why You Should Care.* Bloomington, IN: Indiana Univ. Press, 2004.

Harountunian, Joseph. *Lust for Power.* New York: 1949.

Hart, Gary. *The Fourth Power: A Grand Strategy for the United States in the Twenty-First Century.* New York: Oxford Univ. Press, 2004.

Harvard Gazette Archives. "Melton Derives New Stem Cell Lines." March 4, 2004, http://www.news.harvard.edu/gazette/2004/03 .04/01-stemcells.html.

Hawthorne, Fran. *Inside the FDA: The Business and Politics Behind the Drugs We Take and the Food We Eat.* Hoboken, NJ: John Wiley & Sons, 2005.

Hawthorne, Nathaniel. *The Scarlet Letter.* Reissue ed. New York: Bantam Classics, 1981.

Hedges, Chris. *War is a Force that Gives Us Meaning.* New York: Public Affairs, 2002.

Heil, Alan L. *Voice of America.* New York: Columbia Univ. Press, 2003.

Heilbroner, Robert L., and Lester C. Thurow. *Economics Explained.* Update ed. New York: Simon & Schuster, 1987.

Henninger, Daniel. "Marcus Welby Doesn't Live Here Anymore." *Wall Street Journal,* January 10, 2003.

Hess, Frederick M. *Common Sense School Reform.* New York: Palgrave Macmillan, 2004.

Hill, Napoleon. *Think and Grow Rich.* 1937. Ballantine Books, Reissue ed. 1987.

Hoffer, Eric. *The True Believer: Thoughts on the Nature of Mass Movements.* Harper & Row, 1951.

Holtz-Eakin, Douglas. "Prescription Drug Coverage and Medicare's Fiscal Challenges." April 9, 2003, http://www.cbo.gov./ showdoc.cfm?index=4159&sequence=0:html.

Homer. *The Iliad.* Reissue ed. New York: Penguin Books, 1998.

Hoover, Randy L. "Forces and Factors Affecting Ohio Proficiency Test Performance," Youngstown State Univ. Youngstown, OH: February 27, 2000.

Howe, Neil, and William Strauss. *The Next Great Generation.* New York: Random House, 2005.

Huber, Peter, and Mark Mills. *The Bottomless Well: The Twilight of Fuel, the Nirtue of Waste, and Why We Will Never Run Out of Energy.* New York: Basic Books, 2005.

Hymowitz, Kay S. *Liberation's Children: Parents and Kids in a Postmodern Age.* Chicago: Ivan R Dee, 2003.

Imelt, Jeff. Quoted in "Solar Opposites." *Wired,* January 2004.

Independent Sector. "Value of Volunteer Time." 2004, http://www.independentsector.org/programs/research/volunteer_time.html.

International Monetary Fund. "The Poverty Reduction and Growth Facility (PRGF)," http://www.imf.org/external/np/exr/facts/prgf.htm.

IRS Historical Tables. "Private Foundation Information Returns, and Tax-Exempt Organization Business Income Tax Returns: Selected Financial Data, "http://www.irs.gov/taxstats/charitablestats/ article/0,,id=123185,00.html.

Jacoby, Jeff. "Why Free Speech is so Expensive." *The Boston Globe,* January 23, 2004.

Jaffe, Greg. "Pentagon Prepares to Scatter Soldiers in Remote Corners." *Wall Street Journal,* May 27, 2003.

Johnson, Chalmers. "The War Business." *Harper's,* November 2003.

Jones, Ruth S. (Chair). *Citizens Clean Elections User's Handbook.* [Arizona] Citizens Clean Elections Commission, 2003.

Judis, John B. *Folly of Empire.* New York: Scribner, 2004.

Kaplan, Robert D. "Supremacy By Stealth." *Atlantic Monthly,* July/August, 2003.

Karatnycky, Adrain. "Gains for Freedom Amid Terror and Uncertainty." Freedom House, November 30, 2003, http://www.freedomhouse.org/research/freeworld/2004/essay2004.pdf.

Kass, Leon R. *Life, Liberty and the Defense of Dignity: The Challenge for Bioethics.* San Francisco: Encounter Books, 2002.

Kass, Leon. *The Beginning of Wisdom: Reading Genesis.* The Free Press, 2003.

Kennedy, Paul. *Preparing for the Twenty-First Century.* New York: Random House, 1993.

Kennedy, Robert F, Jr. *Crimes Against Nature: How George W. Bush and His Corporate Pals Are Plundering the Country and Hijacking Our Democracy.* New York: Harper Collins, 2004.

Kinzer, Stephen. *All the Shah's Men: An American Coup and the Roots of Middle East Terror.* Hoboken, NJ: Wiley, 2003.

Koh, Harold Hongju. "Preserving American Values: The Challenge at Home and Abroad." *The Age of Terror.* Strobe Talbott and Nayan Chanda, Eds. New York: Basic Books, 2002.

Kotlikoff, Laurence J., and Scott Burns. *The Coming Generational Storm: What You Need to Know about America's Economic Future.* Cambridge, MA: MIT Press, 2004.

Kozol, Johnathan. *The Shame of the Nation : The Restoration of Apartheid Schooling in America.* New York: Crown, 2005.

Kristol, Irving. *On the Democratic Idea in America.* Harper & Row, 1972.

Kristol, Irving. *Two Cheers for Capitalism.* New York: Basic Books, 1978.

Kurlansky, Mark. *1968: The Year That Rocked the World.* Ballantine Books, 2003.

Lamm, Richard D. *The Brave New World of Health Care.* Golden, CO: Fulcrum Publishing, 2004.

Lane, Rose Wilder. *The Discovery of Freedom: Man's Struggle Against Authority.* 1943. Reprint. San Francisco: Fox & Wilkes, 1993.

J.K. Lasser Institute. *Your Income Tax.* IDG Book Worldwide, 1999.

Leach, William. *Land of Desire: Merchants, Power, and the Rise of a New American Culture.* New York: Pantheon Books, 1993.

Leone, Robert A. *Who Profits: Winners, Losers, and Government Regulation.* New York: Basic Books, 1986.

Lerner, Michael. *The Politics of Meaning: Restoring Hope and Possibility in an Age of Cynicism.* New York: Addison-Wesley, 1996.

LeRoy, Greg. *The Great American Jobs Scam: Corporate Tax Dodging and the Myth of Job Creation.* San Francisco: Barrett-Koehler Publishers, 2005.

Lessig, Lawrence. "Stop Making Pills Political Prisoners." *Wired,* February 2004.

Letters to the Ed. *Wall Street Journal,* April 2001.

Levin, Ira. *Boys From Brazil.* Reprint. New York: Dell, 1977.

Levitt, Steven D., and Stephen J. Dubner. *Freakonomics: A Rogue Economist Explores the Hidden Side of Everything.* New York: William Morrow, 2005.

Lewis, Bernard. *What Went Wrong?: The Clash Between Islam and Modernity in the Middle East.* Perennial, 2003.

Libertariaism.com. "Catch the wave! Welcome to your one-stop, quick and clear introduction to the ideas of liberty and the libertarian movement," http://www.libertarianism.com/.

Lim, Linda Y. C. "The Globalization Debate." International Labor Office in Geneva, 2001, http://www.ucd.ie/economic/workingpapers/WP03.23. (withdrawn).

Llosa, Alvaro Vargas. *Liberty for Latin America: How to Undo 500 Years of State Oppression.* New York: Farrar, Straus and Giroux, 2005.

Locke, John. *The Second Treatise on Civil Government.* 1690. Great Books in Philosophy reprint. Amherst, NY: Prometheus Books, 1986.

Lognado, Lucette. "Last Hope for Lymphoma, $28,000 a Dose." *Wall Street Journal,* June 18, 2003.

Lukacs, John. *Democracy and Populism: Fear and Hatred.* New Haven, CT: Yale Univ. Press.2005.

"Lysenkoism," http://www.nationmaster.com/encyclopedia/Lysenkoism.

MacGuineas, Maya. "Radical Tax Reform." *Atlantic Monthly,* January/February 2004.

MacIntyre, Alasdair. *After Virtue: A Study in Moral Theory.* Reprint. Notre Dame, IN: Univ. of Notre Dame Press, 1984.

Madison, James. "The Union as a Safeguard Against Domestic Faction and Insurrection." The Federalist Papers. Federalist No. 10, 1787.

Malkiel, Burton G. *A Random Walk Down Wall Street.* New York: Norton, 1973.

Mandela, Nelson. *Long Walk to Freedom.* Boston: Little, Brown, 1994.

Mann, Charles C. *1491 : New Revelations of the Americas Before Columbus.* New York: Knopf 2005.

Manning, Richard. "The Oil We Eat." *Harper's,* February 2004.

Manning, Richard. "Super Organics." *Wired,* May, 2004.

Marbury v. Madison, 5 U.S. 137 (1803).

Marcus, Amy Dockser. "Sorry, Only Half of That Surgery Is Covered." *Wall Street Journal,* March 12, 2003.

Martinez, Barbara. "Behind the Curtain." *Wall Street Journal*, February 21, 2001.

Marx, Karl, and Friedrich Engels. *The Communist Manifesto*. 1848. Signet Classic reprint. New York: Mass Market Paperback, 1998.

Mathematically Correct. "Glossary of Terms," http://www.mathematicallycorrect.com./.

McGowan, William. *Coloring the News: How Political Correctness Has Corrupted American Journalism*. San Francisco: Encounter Books, 2001.

McInerney, Jeremy. "Ancient Greek Civilization." The Teaching Company Course Tape No. 323.

Meade, Walter Russell. *Special Providence: American Foreign Policy and How It Changed the World*. New York: Knopf, 2001.

Meltzer, Milton. *Slavery: From the Rise of Western Civilization to Today*. 1st Laurel-Leaf ed. New York: Dell, 1977.

Merrow, John. "California's Public Schools: From First to Worst." American Youth Policy Forum, January 8, 2004, http://www.aypf.org/forumbriefs/2004/fb010804.htm.

Merry, Robert W. *Sands of Empire: Missionary Zeal, American Foreign Policy, and the Hazards of Global Ambition*. New York: Simon & Schuster, 2005.

Mill, John Stuart, and John Gray. *On Liberty and Other Essays*. Oxford World Classics, New ed. New York: Oxford Univ. Press, April 1998.

Mittal, Anuradha. "Giving Away the Farm: The 2002 Farm Bill." Institute for Food and Development, Policy Backgrounder, vol. 8, no.3, Summer 2002, http://www.foodfirst.org/pubs/backgrdrs/2002/s02v8n3html.

Montesquieu, Barron de (Charles de Secondat). *The Spirit of the Laws*. 1748. Great Books in Philosophy reprint. Amherst, NY: Prometheus Books, 2002.

Moore, James H., Jr. "Hospital Room and Board Benefits," http://64.233.167.104/search?q=cache:mmVAoKc2PsoJ:www.bls.govopub/cwc/archive/summer1998art4.pdf+&hl=en.

Morone, James A. *Hellfire Nation: The Politics of Sin in American History*. New Haven, CT: Yale Univ. Press, 2003.

Moscoso, Eunice. "NRA, Gun Control Groups Gearing Up for Elections." *News-Journal,* June 24, 2004, http://www .news-journal.com/news/content/shared/news/stories/GUNS _POLITICS24_2NDLD_COX.html;COXnetJSessionID =AbjTdX6LRQQA3Lt3W7rSxE9TGU929UedROccXjlQwCO UG6kFkZRT!2108111922?urac=n&urvf=10881196350520 .22787326702579613.

Moynihan, Daniel Patrick. Quoted in the *Wall Street Journal,* December 30, 1999.

Murray, Alan. "Both Parties Vie to Buy Your Vote - With Your Money." *Wall Street Journal,* May 21, 2002.

Murray, Charles. "Americans Remain Wary of Washington." *Wall Street Journal,* December 23, 1997.

Murray, Charles. *Human Accomplishment: The Pursuit of Excellence in the Arts and Sciences, 800 B.C. to 1950.* New York: Harper Collins, 2003.

National Center for Education Statistics. "Projections in Education Statistics to 2011." Table 34, http://nces.ed.gov/pubs2001/ proj01/tables/table34.asp.

National Center for Education Statistics. Digest of Education Statistics Tables and Figures 2002, Table 166, http://nces. ed.gov/ programs/digest/d02/dt166.asp.

National Council of Churches. "2001 Yearbook Reports," http:// www .ncccusa.org/news/01news15.html.

Nicolson, Adam. *God's Secretaries: The Making of the King James Bible.* Perennial, 2004.

Novak, Michael. *The Spirit of Democratic Capitalism.* Madison Books, 1991.

O'Grady, Mary Anastasia. "Liberty = Prosperity." *Wall Street Journal,* November 12, 2002.

O'Grady, Mary Anastasia. "Clinton's Sugar Daddy Games Now Threaten Nafta's Future." *Wall Street Journal,* December 20, 2002.

O'Grady, Mary Anastasia. "Setting the Record Straight on Allende, once More." *Wall Street Journal,* April 25, 2003.

O'Grady, Mary Anastasia. "Giving 'Little Guys' a Better Deal in Debt Workouts." *Wall Street Journal,* May 9, 2003.

Olson, Walter. "Delivering Justice." *Wall Street Journal,* February 27, 2003.

Palmer, Mark. *Breaking the Real Axis of Evil: How to Oust the World's Last Dictators by 2025.* Lanham, MD: Rowman and Littlefield, 2003.

Pape, Robert. *Dying to Win: The Strategic Logic of Suicide Terrorism.* New York: Random House, 2005.

Parker, Star. *Uncle Sam's Plantation: How Big Government Enslaves America's Poor and What We Can Do About It.* WMD Books, 2003.

Parsons, Dick. "Diversity and the Media." UNITY: Journalists of Color Conference on television. C-SPAN 1, August 6, 2004.

Peck, Don, and Ross Douthat. "Does Money Buy Happiness." *Atlantic Monthly,* January/February 2003.

Peck, Don. "Putting a Value on Health." *Atlantic Monthly,* January/ February 2004.

Peck, M. Scott. *The Road Less Traveled: A New Psychology of Love, Traditional Values and Spiritual Growth.* New York: Simon & Schuster, 1978.

Perkins, John. *Confessions of an Economic Hit Man.* San Francisco: Berrett-Koehler, 2004.

Persig, Robert M. *Zen and the Art of Motorcycle Maintenance: An Inquiry Into Values.* Bantam Ed. New York: William Morrow, April 1975.

Peterson, Peter G. *Gray Dawn: How the Coming Age Wave Will Transform America—and the World.* New York: Times Books, 1999.

Peterson, Peter G. *Wall Street Journal,* June 23, 2003.

Peterson, Peter G. *Running on Empty: How the Democratic and Republican Parties Are Bankrupting Our Future and What Americans Can Do About It.* New York: Farrar, Straus and Giroux, 2004.

Phillips, Kevin. *Wealth and Democracy: A Political History of the American Rich.* New York: Broadway Books, 2003.

Podhoretz, Norman. *The Prophets: Who They Were, What They Are.* Free Press, 2003.

Public Citizen. "Drug Industry Employs 675 Washington Lobbyists, Many with Revolving-Door Connections, New Report Finds." June 23, 2003, http://www.citizen.org/pressroom/release.cfm?ID=1469.

Putnam, Robert D. *Bowling Alone: The Collapse and Revival of American Community*. New York: Simon & Schuster, 2000.

Radvitch, Diane. *The Language Police: How Pressure Groups Restrict What Students Learn*. New York: Knopf, 2003.

Rand, Ayn. *Atlas Shrugged*. New York: Random House, 1957.

Raphael, Ray. *A People's History of the American Revolution: How Common People Shaped the Fight for Independence*. Perennial, 2002.

Rauch, Jonathan. "Will Frankenfood Save the Planet?" *Atlantic Monthly*, October, 2003.

Rector, Robert. "Combating Family Disintegration, Crime and Dependence." Heritage Backgrounder No. 983, April 8, 1994.

Reh, John. "CEOs Are Overpaid," http://management.about.com/cs/ generalmanagement/a/CEOsOverpaid.htm.

Riesman, David, Nathan Glazer, and Reuel Denny. *The Lonely Crowd*. 1950. Revised ed. New Haven, CT: Yale Univ. Press, 2001.

Reiss, Spencer. "Size Matters." *Wired*, February 2004.

Robertson, James Oliver. *American Myth, American Reality*. New York: Hill & Wang, 1980.

Roche, George Charles, III. *Legacy of Freedom*. 1st pbk. printing. Hillsdale, MI: Hillsdale College Press, 1973.

Rohm, Wendy Goldman. "Seven Days of Creation." *Wired*, January 2004.

Roodman, David Malin. "Paying the Piper: Subsidies, Politics, and the Environment." Worldwatch Institute Paper 133, December 1996.

Rossiter, Clinton. *The Grand Convention: The Year That Made a Nation*. New York: Macmillan, 1966.

Sagan, Carl. *The Dragons of Eden: Speculation on the Evolution of Human Intelligence*. New York: Random House, 1977.

Salinger, J. D. *The Catcher in the Rye*. Boston: Little, Brown, 1951.

Samuels, David. "In a Ruined Country." *Atlantic Monthly,*
September 2005.
Sandel, Michael J. "The Case Against Perfection." *Atlantic
Monthly,* April 2004.
Sanger, David E. "Steel reversal establishes WTO authority."
New York Times. Reprinted in The Cleveland Plain Dealer,
December 5, 2003.
Schumpeter, Joseph R. *Capitalism, Socialism and Democracy.*
1943. 3rd ed. Harper & Row, 1950.
Scott, Drusilla. *Everyman Revived: The Common Sense of Michael
Polanyi.* 1985. Reprint. Sussex, UK: Book Guild Limited, 1987.
Sen, Amartya. *Development as Freedom.* New York: Knopf, 1999.
Sennett, Richard. *Respect in a World of Inequality.* New York:
Norton, 2004.
Shah, Anup. "The US and Foreign Aid Assistance." July 11, 2004,
http://www.globalissues.org/TradeRelated/Debt/USAid.asp#.
Shane, Mathew. "World Bank Development Indictors (for 2000)."
International macroeconomic data set, http://www.ers .usda.
gov/data/macroeconomics/.
Shelly, Mary Wollstonecraft. *Frankenstein.* 1818. Reprint. New
York: Norton, 1996.
Sifry, Micah, and Nancy Watzman. *Is That a Politician in Your
Pocket?: Washington on $2 Million a Day.* Hoboken, NJ:
Wiley, 2004.
Silko, Leslie Marmon. *Ceremony.* New York: Penguin Books,
1986.
Skousen, Mark. Presentation of "Bestselling Books of 1776."
Freedom Fest convention on Book TV television. C-SPAN 2,
July 17, 2004.
Slemrod, Joel, and Jon Bakija. *Taxing Ourselves: A citizen's Guide
to the Great Debate Over Tax Reform.* Cambridge, MA: MIT
Press, 1996.
Smith, Adam. *An Inquiry into the Nature and Causes of the Wealth
of Nations.* 1776. Edited by Edwin Cannan. The Modern
Library reprint. New York: Random House, 1937.
Sophocles, E. A. *Antigone.* Thrift Eds. Reprint. Mineola, NY:
Dover 1993.

Storey, Robert Gerald. *Our Unalienable Rights*. Charles C. Thomas, 1965.

Soros, George. "The Bubble of American Supremacy." *Atlantic Monthly,* December 2003.

Sourcebook for Journalists 2003: Health Care Costs. "U.S. Health Spending vs. that of Other Nations." October 2002, http://www .allhealth.org./sourcebook2002/ch8_8.html.

Spartacus: Historical Background, http://www.vroma.org/ ~bmcmanus/ spartacus.html.

Stein, Ben. *Can America Survive?: The Rage of the Left, the Truth, and What to Do About It*. Carlsbad, CA: New Beginnings, 2004.

Stern, Jessica. *Terror in the Name of God: Why Religious Militants Kill*. New York: Harper Collins, 2003.

Stiglitz, Joseph E. *Globalization And Its Discontents*. New York: Norton, 2003.

Suskind, Ron. *The Price of Loyalty: George W. Bush, the White House, and the Education of Paul O'Neill*. New York: Simon & Schuster, 2004.

Sykes, Charles J. *A Nation of Victims: The Decay of the American Character*. New York: St. Martin's Press, 1992.

Tax Foundation Publications. "Summary of Federal Individual Income Tax Data, 2002," http://www.taxfoundation.org/ prtopincometable.html.

Taylor, Timothy. "A History of the U.S. Economy in the 20th Century." The Teaching Company Course Tape No. 529.

Teresi, Dick. *Lost Discoveries: The Ancient Roots of Modern Science—from the Babylonians to the Maya*. New York: Simon & Schuster, 2002.

Terhune, Ichad. "Insurers Tactic: If You Get Sick, The Premium Rises." *Wall Street Journal,* April 9, 2002.

Terrill, Ross. *The New Chinese Empire: And What It Means for the United States*. New York: Basic Books; 2003.

Thayer, George. *Who Shakes the Money Tree?* New York: Simon & Schuster, 1973.

Theobald, Robert. *The Economics of Abundance: A Non-Inflationary Future*. New York: Pitman, 1970.

Thernstrom, Abigail, and Stephan Thernstrom. *No Excuses: Closing the Racial Gap in Learning.* New York: Simon & Schuster, 2003.

Thoreau, Henry David. *Civil Disobedience and Other Essays.* 1849. Reprint. Mineola, New York: Dover, 1993.

Trueblood, Elton. *Declaration of Freedom.* 5th ed. New York: Harper & Brothers, 1955.

Thurow, Lester. *Head to Head: The Coming Economic Battle Among Japan, Europe and America.* New York: Warner Books, 1993.

Tuchman, Barbara W. *The March of Folly: From Troy to Vietnam.* New York: Knopf, 1984.

Turkish Press. "Saudi Arabia Set To Exceed Record Budget Surplus Projections." Agence France Presse, August 21, 2004, http://www.turkishpress.com/news.asp?id=25040.

United Nations. "World Population Prospects." United Nations Division on Population, 2002, http://www.un.org/esa/population/publications/wpp2002/WPP2002HIGHLIGHTSrev1. PDF.

U.S. Census Bureau. DP-1. Profile of General Demographic Characteristics: 2000, http://factfinder.census.gov/servlet/QTTable?_bm=y&-geo_id=D&-qr_name=DEC_2000_SF1_U_DP1&-ds_name= D&-_lang=en&-redoLog=false.

U.S.Census Bureau. "Number in Poverty and Poverty Rate: 1959 to 2003, "http://www.census.gov/hhes/poverty/poverty03/pov03fig03 .pdf.

Univ. of California Regents v. Bakke, 438 U.S. 265 (1978).

Univ. of Oregon Clearinghouse on Educational Policy and Management. "Trends and Issues: School Choice." College of Education, Univ. of Oregon, http://eric.uoregon.edu/trends_issues/choice/#prevalence.

U.S. Department of Health and Human Services. "FY 2004 Budget in Brief," http://www.firstgov.gov/fgsearch/index.jsp?mw0=FY+2004+Budget+in+Brief&ctx=1&in0=domain&dom0=&parsed =tru&Fqlplus=spc&rn=315&Submit.x=15&Submit.y=9.

U.S. Department of Health and Human Services. National Center for Health Statistics, .http://www.cdc.gov/nchs/fastats/disable. htm.

U.S. Deptartment of Health and Human Services. "The Evolution of the Oregon Health Plan." Many authors. December 12, 1997, http://www.cms.hhs.gov/researchers/reports/OregonState/1.01 _FIRST %20INTERIM%20REPORT%20RTI.PDF.

Veenhoven, Ruut. "Conditions of Happiness." Netherlands: Kluwer Academic, 1984.

Wallach, Lori, and Michelle Sforza. *Whose Trade Organization?: Corporate Globalization and the Erosion of Democracy.* New York: Public Citizen, 1999.

Weiss, Ann E. *Welfare: Helping Hand or Trap?* Hillside, NJ: Enslow, 1990.

Weiss, Steven. "The Fall of a Giant." *Money in Politics Alert,* November 9, 2001.

Wessel, David. "Why the Bad Guys Of the Boardroom Emerged en Masse." *Wall Street Journal,* June 20, 2002.

Wheelock, Divid C. "Conducting Monetary Policy Without Government Debt: The Fed's Early Years," http://research .stlouisfed.org/publications/review/02/05/0205dwd.txt.

Wang, Frank. Panel on Textbooks on Book TV television. C-SPAN 2, January 12, 2004.

Williams, Walter E. "The Legitimate Role of Government in a Free Economy." The Frank M. Engle Lecture. Bryn Mawr, PA: American College, May 24, 1993.

Wired. "How a Peble-Bed Reactor Works." September 2004.

Wood, Gordon S. *The Radicalism of the American Revolution.* New York: Vintage Books, 1993.

Wood, Peter. *Diversity: The Invention of a Concept.* San Francisco: Encounter Books, 2003.

Woodruff, Paul. *First Democracy: The Challenge of an Ancient Idea.* New York: Oxford Univ. Press, 2004.

Woolhandler, Steffie and David U. Himmelstein. "Study: $286 Billion on Health Care Paperwork, Medicare Drug Bill Will Increase Bureaucratic Costs, Reward Insurers and the AARP."

February 2004, http://www.thirdworldtraveler.com/Health/
HealthCosts _MedicareDrugs.html.

Woolhandler, Steffie and David U. Himmelstein. "Study Shows
U.S. Health Care Paperwork Cost $294.3 Billion in 1999-More
than $1,000 per person; far more than in Canada." August
20, 2003, http://www.researchmatters.harvard.edu/story.
php?article_id =677.

World Health Organization. "World Health Report 2000," http://
www .who.int/whr2001/2001/archives/2000/en/index.htm.

Wormser, Rene A. *The Law.* New York: Simon & Schuster, 1949.

Yergin, Daniel. Remarks on Book TV television. C-SPAN 2, May
18, 2003.

Zakaria, Fareed. *The Future of Freedom: Illiberal Democracy at
Home and Abroad.* New York: Norton, 2002.

Zogby, James, and Shibley Telhami. "Poll Shows Growing Arab
Rancor at U.S." American Muslim News Briefs, July 23, 2004,
http:// www.cair-net.org/asp/article.asp?id=34084&page=NB.

ABOUT THE AUTHOR

Dick Anderson is a retired research scientist, investment advisor, and veteran U.S. citizen. He and Lorraine, his wife of 50 years, have made their home in South Russell, Ohio, since 1970.

Freedom's Vector started out as an exercise in learning and self-discovery. It ended up as this book, which Dick is pleased to share with you.

Printed in the United States
74124LV00003B/67